THE POLICE & SOCIETY
TOUCHSTONE
READINGS

Victor E. Kappeler
Eastern Kentucky University

WAVELAND
PRESS, INC.

Prospect Heights, Illinois

For information about this book, write or call:

    Waveland Press, Inc.
    P.O. Box 400
    Prospect Heights, Illinois 60070
    (847) 634-0081

Contents

iii

Preface

At some point in a student's education, empirical knowledge must be linked with the social context engulfing a specialization. Whether a student begins with a course of study that accentuates the social context or one that emphasizes the particularities of a specialization matters little if the two are eventually integrated. This collection attempts to make a contribution to the integration of policing into the broader social context, whether used at the beginning of a student's course of study or in a capstone course. The anthology strives to facilitate systematic inquiry—to help students identify and dissect underlying assumptions, to understand how values influence questions, to discover connections, mutual influence, and divergences of opinion. Examining both the macro (the context within which social action takes place) and the micro (the specific actions) is the most productive route to reaching understanding. If the recurring, central themes in policing are analyzed by informed participants, perhaps the exploration will provide a better grasp of the many issues facing the police and society.

This anthology is divided into five windows of inquiry: "A History of Police and Society," "The Role of the Police in Society," "The Society of Police," "Policing Society," and "The Police in Post-Modern Society." Each window is framed by a particular way of viewing policing; each is devoted to a critical aspect of the interrelationship between police and society; and each opens with an article that presents a unique contribution to our awareness of this complex relationship. The essays that follow then either build on predecessors' foundations or fill intellectual voids. These articles often take issue with previous conceptions or with the very assumptions on which those conceptions were built. In this fashion, the articles that comprise this collection serve as touchstones for one another—measuring and questioning the value of each contribution to our understanding of the dynamic interrelationships between the police and society.

The articles that comprise this anthology, however, are more than informative. They are as much about questions as they are about answers. They are as much about conflict as they are about agreement. And, they are as much about issues as they are about solutions. Some of the many questions, conflicts, and issues raised in this collection include: How many "publics" are there? What does "the public" expect of the police institution? What is the nature of the police role and function? Who benefits from police service; who is harmed? How does society reconcile its desire for law enforcement with its disdain for governmental restriction? How are public safety and social order secured while maintaining individual rights and freedoms? To what extent are our assumptions about the police and society reflective of our values, expectations, and demands? Are values, expectations, and demands timeless and universal or confined to a particular audience in a specific time and place? To what extent do the police generate values, expectations, and demands? Are the police free of the social influences that shape citizens' values and expectations? Are the police a society unto themselves? Is policing at a critical crossroads? Is the nature of the police role and function likely to change in the near future? These are but a few of the questions, conflicts, and issues that students should be mindful of as they work their way through this anthology.

The articles in this collection were selected for both their complementary and competing natures; the reader will note some disjuncture and a few sharp contrasts in thought. This is, however, as it should be because the growth of knowledge in any field of study seldom reflects a deliberate and linear progression. Therefore, no attempt was made to force the essays into an unnatural chronological sequence. Nor is the position of any single article intended to indicate that it is the first or last word on any particular policing discourse. While many of the articles build directly upon their predecessors' ideas, others briefly detour only to return at a later point to the many interrelated issues under consideration. Because of this, the reader may not feel an immediate sense of continuity until after considering each of the articles in a particular window, only to find that sense of resolution washed away by another challenging view of policing in a subsequent section of the anthology.

Most of the articles selected for inclusion in this collection were chosen because of the timeless nature of their contribution to our understanding of policing. Several were created when gender neutrality and racial sensitivity were not integrated into either popular or scholarly writing; most reflect a style not only unique to the author but also to the audience for which they were originally written. Some of the articles have been updated by the authors to reflect not only current sensitivities but the different audiences this collection addresses.

These admissions, however, play into a larger theme of the anthology. A careful reading of the works reveals a critique and inquiry into the growth of knowledge on the police and society. Many of the articles not only challenge the information within the pages of this book but inquire as to whether the information presented was an artifact of a unique time, the manner in which the information was acquired, the way the presentation was constructed, or the background assumptions that drove their creation. Despite a few scars of time, these articles collectively represent some of the best scholarship and thought on the relationship between the police and society. They provide multiple foundations for understanding some of the most compelling issues confronting both the police and society. Together they make a statement not only on the interrelationship between the police and society but on our construction and perception of that relationship and its efficacy for the future.

Victor E. Kappeler
Eastern Kentucky University

Part I

A History of Police and Society

1

The Evolving Strategy of Policing

George L. Kelling and Mark H. Moore

Policing, like all professions, learns from experience. It follows, then, that as modern police executives search for more effective strategies of policing, they will be guided by the lessons of police history. The difficulty is that police history is incoherent, its lessons hard to read. After all, that history was produced by thousands of local departments pursuing their own visions and responding to local conditions. Although that varied experience is potentially a rich source of lessons, departments have left few records that reveal the trends shaping modern policing. Interpretation is necessary.

This article presents an interpretation of police history that may help police executives considering alternative future strategies of policing. Our reading of police history has led us to adopt a particular point of view. We find that a dominant trend guiding today's police executives—a trend that encourages the pursuit of independent, professional autonomy for police departments—is carrying the police away from achieving their maximum potential, especially in effective crime fighting. We are also convinced that this trend in policing is weakening *public* policing relative to *private* security as the primary institution providing security to society. We believe that this has dangerous long-term implications not only for police departments but also for society. We think that this trend is shrinking rather than enlarging police capacity to help create civil communities. Our judgment is that this trend can be reversed only by refocusing police

National Institute of Justice, *Perspectives on Policing*, 4 (November 1988).

attention from the pursuit of professional autonomy to the establishment of effective problem-solving partnerships with the communities they police.

Delving into police history made it apparent that some assumptions that now operate as axioms in the field of policing (for example that effectiveness in policing depends on distancing police departments from politics; or that the highest priority of police departments is to deal with serious street crime; or that the best way to deal with street crime is through directed patrol, rapid response to calls for service, and skilled retrospective investigations) are not timeless truths, but rather choices made by former police leaders and strategists. To be sure, the choices were often wise and far-seeing as well as appropriate to their times. But the historical perspective shows them to be choices nonetheless, and therefore open to reconsideration in the light of later professional experience and changing environmental circumstances.

We are interpreting the results of our historical study through a framework based on the concept of "corporate strategy."[1] Using this framework, we can describe police organizations in terms of seven interrelated categories:

- The sources from which the police construct the legitimacy and continuing power to act on society.

- The definition of the police function or role in society.
- The organizational design of police departments.
- The relationships the police create with the external environment.
- The nature of police efforts to market or manage the demand for their services.
- The principal activities, programs, and tactics on which police agencies rely to fulfill their mission or achieve operational success.
- The concrete measures the police use to define operational success or failure.

Using this analytic framework, we have found it useful to divide the history of policing into three different eras. These eras are distinguished from one another by the apparent dominance of a particular strategy of policing. The political era, so named because of the close ties between police and politics, dated from the introduction of police into municipalities during the 1840s, continued through the Progressive period, and ended during the early 1900s. The reform era developed in reaction to the political. It took hold during the 1930s, thrived during the 1950s and 1960s, began to erode during the late 1970s. The reform era now seems to be giving way to an era emphasizing community problem solving.

By dividing policing into these three eras dominated by a particular strategy of policing, we do not mean to imply that there were clear boundaries between the eras. Nor do we mean that in those eras everyone policed in the same way. Obviously, the real history is far more complex than that. Nonetheless, we believe that there is a certain professional ethos that defines standards of competence, professionalism, and excellence in policing; that at any given time, one set of concepts is more powerful, more widely shared, and better understood than others; and that this ethos changes over time. Sometimes, this professional ethos has been explicitly articulated, and those who have articulated the concepts have been recognized as the leaders of their profession. O. W. Wilson, for example, was a brilliant expositor of the central elements of the reform strategy of policing. Other times, the ethos is implicit—accepted by all as the tacit assumptions that define the business of policing and the proper form for a police department to take. Our task is to help the profession look to the future by representing its past in these terms and trying to understand what the past portends for the future.

❖ THE POLITICAL ERA ❖

Historians have described the characteristics of early policing in the United States, especially the struggles between various interest groups to govern the police.[2] Elsewhere, the authors of this article analyzed a portion of American police history in terms of its organizational strategy.[3] The following discussion of elements of the police organizational strategy during the political era expands on that effort.

Legitimacy and Authorization

Early American police were authorized by local municipalities. Unlike their English counterparts, American police departments lacked the powerful, central authority of the crown to establish a legitimate, unifying mandate for their enterprise. Instead, American police derived both their authorization and resources from local political leaders, often ward politicians. They were, of course, guided by the law as to what tasks to undertake and what powers to utilize. But their link to neighborhoods and local politicians was so tight that both Jordan[4] and Fogelson[5] refer to the early police as adjuncts to local political machines. The relationship was often reciprocal: political machines recruited and maintained police in office and on the beat, while police helped ward political leaders maintain their political offices by encouraging citizens to vote for certain candidates, discouraging them from voting for others, and, at times, by assisting in rigging elections.

The Police Function

Partly because of their close connection to politicians, police during the political era provided a wide array of services to citizens. Inevitably police departments were involved in crime prevention and control and order maintenance, but they also provided a wide variety of social services. In the late 19th century, municipal police departments ran soup lines; provided temporary lodging for newly arrived immigrant workers in station houses;[6] and assisted ward leaders in finding work for immigrants, both in police and other forms of work.

Organizational Design

Although ostensibly organized as a centralized, quasi-military organization with a unified chain of command, police departments of the political era were nevertheless decentralized. Cities were divided into precincts, and precinct-level managers often, in concert with the ward leaders, ran precincts as small-scale departments—hiring, firing, managing, and assigning personnel as they deemed appropriate. In addition, decentralization combined with primitive communications and transportation to give police officers substantial discretion in handling their individual beats. At best, officer contact with central command was maintained through the call box.

External Relationships

During the political era, police departments were intimately connected to the social and political world of the ward. Police officers often were recruited from the same ethnic stock as the dominant political groups in the localities, and continued to live in the neighborhoods they patrolled. Precinct commanders consulted often with local political representatives about police priorities and progress.

Demand Management

Demand for police services came primarily from two sources: ward politicians making demands on the organization and citizens making demands directly on beat officers. Decentralization and political authorization encouraged the first; foot patrol, lack of other means of transportation, and poor communications produced the latter. Basically, the demand for police services was received, interpreted, and responded to at the precinct and street levels.

Principal Programs and Technologies

The primary tactic of police during the political era was foot patrol. Most police officers walked beats and dealt with crime, disorder, and other problems as they arose, or as they were guided by citizens and precinct superiors. The technological tools available to police were limited. However, when call boxes became available, police administrators used them for supervisory and managerial purposes; and, when early automobiles became available, police used them to transport officers from one beat to another.[7] The new technology thereby increased the range, but did not change the mode, of patrol officers.

Detective divisions existed but without their current prestige. Operating from a caseload of "persons" rather than offenses, detectives relied on their caseload to inform on other criminals.[8] The "third degree" was a common means of interviewing criminals to solve crimes. Detectives were often especially valuable to local politicians for gathering information on individuals for political or personal, rather than offense-related, purposes.

Measured Outcomes

The expected outcomes of police work included crime and riot control, maintenance of order, and relief from many of the other problems of an industrializing society (hunger and temporary homelessness, for example). Consistent with their political mandate, police emphasized maintaining citizen and political satisfaction with police services as an important goal of police departments.

In sum, the organizational strategy of the political era of policing included the following elements:

- Authorization—primarily political.
- Function—crime control, order maintenance, broad social services.
- Organizational design—decentralized and geographical.
- Relationship to environment—close and personal.
- Demand—managed through links between politicians and precinct commanders, and face-to-face contacts between citizens and foot patrol officers.

- Tactics and technology—foot patrol and rudimentary investigations.
- Outcome—political and citizen satisfaction with social order.

The political strategy of early American policing had strengths. First, police were integrated into neighborhoods and enjoyed the support of citizens—at least the support of the dominant and political interests of an area. Second, and probably as a result of the first, the strategy provided useful services to communities. There is evidence that it helped contain riots. Many citizens believed that police prevented crimes or solved crimes when they occurred.[9] And the police assisted immigrants in establishing themselves in communities and finding jobs.

The political strategy also had weaknesses. First, intimacy with community, closeness to political leaders, and a decentralized organizational structure, with its inability to provide supervision of officers, gave rise to police corruption. Officers were often required to enforce unpopular laws foisted on immigrant ethnic neighborhoods by crusading reformers (primarily of English and Dutch background) who objected to ethnic values.[10] Because of their intimacy with the community, the officers were vulnerable to being bribed in return for nonenforcement or lax enforcement of laws. Moreover, police closeness to politicians created such forms of political corruption as patronage and police interference in elections.[11] Even those few departments that managed to avoid serious financial or political corruption during the late 19th and early 20th centuries, Boston for example, succumbed to large-scale corruption during and after Prohibition.[12]

Second, close identification of police with neighborhoods and neighborhood norms often resulted in discrimination against strangers and others who violated those norms, especially minority ethnic and racial groups. Often ruling their beats with the "ends of their nightsticks," police regularly targeted outsiders and strangers for rousting and "curbstone justice."[13]

Finally, the lack of organizational control over officers resulting from both decentralization and the political nature of many appointments to police positions caused inefficiencies and disorganization. The image of Keystone Cops—police as clumsy bunglers—was widespread and often descriptive of realities in American policing.

❖ THE REFORM ERA ❖

Control over police by local politicians, conflict between urban reformers and local ward leaders over the enforcement of laws regulating the morality of urban migrants, and abuses (corruption, for example) that resulted from the intimacy between police and political leaders and citizens produced a continuous struggle for control over police during the late 19th and early 20th centuries.[14] Nineteenth-century attempts by civilians to reform police organizations by applying external pressures largely failed; 20th-century attempts at reform, originating from both internal and external forces, shaped contemporary policing as we knew it through the 1970s.[15]

Berkeley's police chief, August Vollmer, first rallied police executives around the idea of reform during the 1920s and early 1930s. Vollmer's vision of policing was the trumpet call: police in the post-flapper generation were to remind American citizens and institutions of the moral vision that had made America great and of their responsibilities to maintain that vision.[16] It was Vollmer's protege, O. W. Wilson, however, who taking guidance from J. Edgar Hoover's shrewd transformation of the corrupt and discredited Bureau of Investigation into the honest and prestigious Federal Bureau of Investigation (FBI), became the principal administrative architect of the police reform organizational strategy.[17]

Hoover wanted the FBI to represent a new force for law and order, and saw that such an organization could capture a permanent constituency that wanted an agency to take a stand against lawlessness, immorality, and crime. By raising eligibility standards and changing patterns of recruitment and training, Hoover gave the FBI agents stature as upstanding moral crusaders. By committing the organization to attacks on crimes such as kidnapping, bank robbery, and espionage—crimes that attracted wide publicity and required technical sophistication, doggedness, and a national jurisdiction to solve—Hoover established the organization's reputation for professional competence and power. By establishing tight central control over his agents, limiting their use of controversial investigation procedures (such as undercover operations), and keeping them out of narcotics enforcement, Hoover was also able to maintain an unparalleled record of integrity. That, too, fitted the image of a dogged, incorruptible crime-fighting organization. Finally, lest anyone fail to notice the important developments within the Bureau, Hoover developed impressive public relations programs that presented the FBI and its agents in the most favorable light. (For those of us who remember the 1940s, for example, one of the most popular radio phrases was, "The FBI in peace and war"—the introductory line in a radio program that portrayed a vigilant FBI protecting us from foreign enemies as well as villains on the "10 Most Wanted" list, another Hoover/FBI invention.)

Struggling as they were with reputations for corruption, brutality, unfairness, and downright incompetence, municipal police reformers found Hoover's path a compelling one. Instructed by O. W. Wilson's texts on police administration, they began to shape an organizational strategy for urban police analogous to the one pursued by the FBI.

Legitimacy and Authorization

Reformers rejected politics as the basis of police legitimacy. In their view, politics and political involvement was the *problem* in American policing. Police reformers therefore allied themselves with Progressives. They moved to end the close ties between local political leaders and police. In some states, control over police was usurped by state government. Civil service eliminated patronage and ward influences in hiring and firing police officers. In some cities (Los Angeles and Cincinnati, for example), even the position of chief of police became a civil service position to be attained through examination. In others (such as Milwaukee), chiefs were given lifetime tenure by a police commission, to be removed from office only for cause. In yet others (Boston, for example), contracts for chiefs were staggered so as not to coincide with the mayor's tenure. Concern for separation of police from politics did not focus only on chiefs, however. In some cities, such as Philadelphia, it became illegal for patrol officers to live in the beats they patrolled. The purpose of all these changes was to isolate police as completely as possible from political influences.

Law, especially criminal law, and police professionalism were established as the principal bases of police legitimacy. When police were asked why they performed as they did, the most common answer was that they enforced the law. When they chose not to enforce the law—for instance, in a riot when police isolated an area rather than arrested looters—police justification for such action was found in their claim to professional knowledge, skills, and values which uniquely qualified them to make such tactical decisions. Even in riot situations, police rejected the idea that political leaders should make tactical decisions; that was a police responsibility.[18]

So persuasive was the argument of reformers to remove political influences from policing, that police departments became one of the most autonomous public organizations in urban government.[19] Under such circumstances, policing a city became a legal and technical matter left to the discretion of professional police executives under the guidance of law. Political influence of any kind on a police department came to be seen as not merely a failure of police leadership but as corruption in policing.

The Police Function

Using the focus on criminal law as a basic source of police legitimacy, police in the reform era moved to narrow their functioning to crime control and criminal apprehension. Police agencies became *law enforcement* agencies. Their goal was to control crime. Their principal means was the use of criminal law to apprehend and deter offenders. Activities that drew the police into solving other kinds of community problems and relied on other kinds of responses were identified as "social work," and became the object of derision. A common line in police circles during the 1950s and 1960s was, "If only we didn't have to do social work, we could really do something about crime." Police retreated from providing emergency medical services as well—ambulance and emergency medical services were transferred to medical, private, or firefighting organizations.[20] The 1967 President's Commission on Law Enforcement and Administration of Justice ratified this orientation: heretofore, police had been conceptualized as an agency of urban government; the President's Commission reconceptualized them as part of the criminal justice system.

Organizational Design

The organizational form adopted by police reformers generally reflected the *scientific* or *classical* theory of administration advocated by Frederick W. Taylor during the early 20th century. At least two assumptions attended classical theory. First, workers are inherently uninterested in work and, if left to their own devices, are prone to avoid it. Second, since workers have little or no interest in the substance of their work, the sole common interest between workers and management is found in economic incentives for workers. Thus, both workers and management benefit economically when management arranges work in ways that increase workers' productivity and link productivity to economic rewards.

Two central principles followed from these assumptions: division of labor and unity of control. The former posited that if tasks can be broken into components, workers can become highly skilled in particular components and thus more efficient in carrying out their tasks. The latter posited that the workers' activities are best managed by a *pyramid of control*, with all authority finally resting in one central office.

Using this classical theory, police leaders moved to routinize and standardize police work, especially patrol work. Police work became a form of crimefighting in which police enforced the law and arrested criminals if the opportunity presented itself. Attempts were made to limit discretion in patrol work: a generation of police officers was raised with the idea that they merely enforced the law.

If special problems arose, the typical response was to create special units (e.g., vice, juvenile, drugs, tactical) rather than to assign them to patrol. The creation of these special units, under central rather than precinct command, served to further centralize command and control and weaken precinct commanders.[21]

Moreover, police organizations emphasized control over workers through bureaucratic means of control: supervision, limited span of control, flow of instructions downward and information upward in the organization, establishment of elaborate record-keeping systems requiring additional layers of middle managers, and coordination of activities between various production units (e.g., patrol and detectives), which also required additional middle managers.

External Relationships

Police leaders in the reform era redefined the nature of a proper relationship between police officers and citizens. Heretofore, police had been intimately linked to citizens. During the era of reform policing, the new model demanded an impartial law enforcer who related to citizens in professionally neutral and distant terms. No better characterization of this model can be found than television's Sergeant Friday, whose response, "Just the facts, ma'am," typified the idea: impersonal and oriented toward crime solving rather than responsive to the emotional crisis of a victim.

The professional model also shaped the police view of the role of citizens in crime control. Police redefined the citizen role during an era when there was heady confidence about the ability of professionals to manage physical and social problems. Physicians would care for health problems, dentists for dental problems, teachers for educational problems, social workers for social adjustment problems, and police for crime problems. The proper role of citizens in crime control was to be relatively passive recipients of professional crime control services. Citizens' actions on their own behalf to defend themselves or their communities came to be seen as inappropriate, smacking of vigilantism. Citizens met their responsibilities when a crime occurred by calling police, deferring to police actions, and being good witnesses if called upon to give evidence. The metaphor that expressed this orientation to the community was that of the police as the "thin blue line." It connotes the existence of dangerous external threats to communities, portrays police as standing between that danger and good citizens, and implies both police heroism and loneliness.

Demand Management

Learning from Hoover, police reformers vigorously set out to sell their brand of urban policing.[22] They, too, performed on radio talk shows, consulted with media representatives about how to present police, engaged in public relations campaigns, and in other ways presented this image of police as crime fighters. In a sense, they began with an organizational capacity—anticrime police tactics—and intensively promoted it. This approach was more like selling than marketing. Marketing refers to the process of carefully identifying consumer needs and then developing goods and services that meet those needs. Selling refers to having a stock of products or goods on hand irrespective of need and selling them. The reform strategy had as its starting point a set of police tactics (services) that police promulgated as much for the purpose of establishing internal control of police officers and enhancing the status of urban police as for responding to community needs or market demands.[23] The community "need" for rapid response to calls for service, for instance, was largely the consequence of police selling the service as efficacious in crime control rather than a direct demand from citizens.

Consistent with this attempt to sell particular tactics, police worked to shape and control demand for police services. Foot patrol, when demanded by citizens, was rejected as an outmoded, expensive frill. Social and emergency services were terminated or given to other agencies. Receipt of demand for police services was centralized. No longer were citizens encouraged to go to "their" neighborhood police officers or districts; all calls went to a central communications facility. When 911 systems were installed, police aggressively sold 911 and rapid response to calls for service as effective police service. If citizens continued to use district, or precinct, telephone numbers, some police departments disconnected those telephones or got new telephone numbers.[24]

Principal Programs and Technologies

The principal programs and tactics of the reform strategy were preventive patrol by automobile and rapid response to calls for service. Foot patrol, characterized as outmoded and inefficient, was abandoned as rapidly as police administrators could obtain cars.[25] The initial tactical reasons for putting police in cars had been to increase the size of the areas police officers could patrol and to take the advantage away from criminals who began to use automobiles. Under reform policing, a new theory about how to make the best tactical use of automobiles appeared.

O. W. Wilson developed the theory of preventive patrol by automobile as an anticrime tactic.[26] He theorized that if police drove conspicuously marked cars randomly through city streets and gave special attention to certain "hazards" (bars and schools, for example), a feeling of police omnipresence would be developed. In turn, that sense of omnipresence would both deter criminals and reassure good citizens. Moreover, it was hypothesized that vigilant patrol officers moving rapidly through city streets would happen upon criminals in action and be able to apprehend them.

As telephones and radios became ubiquitous, the availability of cruising police came to be seen as even more valuable: if citizens could be encouraged to call the police via telephone as soon as problems developed, police could respond rapidly to calls and establish control over situations, identify wrong-doers, and make arrests. To this end, 911 systems and computer-aided dispatch were developed throughout the country. Detective units continued, although with some modifications. The "person" approach ended and was replaced by the case approach. In addition, forensic techniques were upgraded and began to replace the old "third degree" or reliance on informants for the solution of crimes. Like other special units, most investigative units were controlled by central headquarters.

Measured Outcomes

The primary desired outcomes of the reform strategy were crime control and criminal apprehension.[27] To measure achievement of these outcomes, August Vollmer, working through the newly vitalized International Association of Chiefs of Police, developed and implemented a uniform system of crime classification and reporting. Later, the system was taken over and administered by the FBI and the *Uniform Crime Reports* became the primary standard by which police organizations measured their effectiveness. Additionally, individual officers' effectiveness in dealing with crime was judged by the number of arrests they made; other measures of police effectiveness included response time (the time it takes for a police car to arrive at the location of a call for service) and "number of passings" (the number of times a police car passes a given point on a city street). Regardless of all other indicators, however, the primary measure of police effectiveness was the crime rate as measured by the *Uniform Crime Reports*.

In sum, the reform organizational strategy contained the following elements:

- Authorization—law and professionalism.
- Function—crime control.
- Organizational design—centralized, classical.
- Relationship to environment—professionally remote.
- Demand—channeled through central dispatching activities.
- Tactics and technology—preventive patrol and rapid response to calls for service.
- Outcome—crime control.

In retrospect, the reform strategy was impressive. It successfully integrated its strategic elements into a coherent paradigm that was internally consistent and logically appealing. Narrowing police functions to crime fighting made sense. If police could concentrate their efforts on prevention of crime and apprehension of criminals, it followed that they could be more effective than if they dissipated their efforts on other problems. The model of police as impartial, professional law enforcers was attractive because it minimized the discretionary excesses which developed during the political era. Preventive patrol and rapid response to calls for service were intuitively appealing tactics, as well as means to control officers and shape and control citizen demands for service. Further, the strategy provided a comprehensive, yet simple, vision of policing around which police leaders could rally.

The metaphor of the thin blue line reinforced their need to create isolated independence and autonomy in terms that were acceptable to the public. The patrol car became the symbol of policing during the 1930s and 1940s; when equipped with a radio, it was at the limits of technology. It represented mobility, power, conspicuous presence, control of officers, and professional distance from citizens.

During the late 1960s and 1970s, however, the reform strategy ran into difficulty. First, regardless of how police effectiveness in dealing with crime was measured, police failed to substantially improve their record. During the 1960s, crime began to rise. Despite large increases in the size of police departments and in expenditures for new forms of equipment (911 systems, computer-aided dispatch, etc.), police failed to meet their own or public expectations about their capacity to control crime or prevent its increase. Moreover, research conducted during the 1970s on preventive patrol and rapid response to calls for service suggested that neither was an effective crime control or apprehension tactic.[28]

Second, fear rose rapidly during this era. The consequences of this fear were dramatic for cities. Citizens abandoned parks, public transportation, neighborhood shopping centers, churches, as well as entire neighborhoods. What puzzled police and researchers was that levels of fear and crime did not always correspond: crime levels were low in some areas, but fear high. Conversely, in other areas levels of crime were high, but fear low. Not until the early 1980s did researchers discover that fear is more closely correlated with disorder than with crime.[29] Ironically, order maintenance was one of those functions that police had been downplaying over the years. They collected no data on it, provided no training to officers in order maintenance activities, and did not reward officers for successfully conducting order maintenance tasks.

Third, despite attempts by police departments to create equitable police allocation systems and to provide impartial policing to all citizens, many minority citizens, especially blacks during the 1960s and 1970s, did not perceive their treatment as equitable or adequate. They protested not only police mistreatment, but lack of treatment—inadequate or insufficient services—as well.

Fourth, the civil rights and antiwar movements challenged police. This challenge took several forms. The legitimacy of police was questioned: students resisted police, minorities rioted against them, and the public, observing police via live television for the first time, questioned their tactics. Moreover, despite police attempts to upgrade personnel through improved recruitment, training, and supervision, minorities and then women insisted that they had to be adequately represented in policing if police were to be legitimate.

Fifth, some of the myths that undergirded the reform strategy—police officers use little or no discretion and the primary activity of police is law enforcement—simply proved to be too far from reality to be sustained. Over and over again research showed that use of discretion characterized policing at all levels and that law enforcement comprised but a small portion of police officers' activities.[30]

Sixth, although the reform ideology could rally police chiefs and executives, it failed to rally line police officers. During the reform era, police executives had moved to professionalize their ranks. Line officers, however, were managed in ways that were antithetical to professionalization. Despite pious testimony from police executives that "patrol is the backbone of policing," police executives behaved in ways that were consistent with classical organizational theory—patrol officers continued to have low status; their work was treated as if it were routinized and standardized; and petty rules governed issues such as hair length and off-duty behavior. Meanwhile, line officers received little guidance in use of discretion and were given few, if any, opportunities to make suggestions about their work. Under such circumstances, the increasing "grumpiness" of officers in many cities is not surprising, nor is the rise of militant unionism.

Seventh, police lost a significant portion of their financial support, which had been increasing or at least constant over the years, as cities found themselves in fiscal difficulties. In city after city, police departments were reduced in size. In some cities, New York for example, financial cutbacks resulted in losses of up to one-third of departmental personnel. Some, noting that crime did not increase more rapidly or arrests decrease during the cutbacks, suggested that New York City had been overpoliced when at maximum strength. For those concerned about levels of disorder and fear in New York City, not to mention other problems, that came as a dismaying conclusion. Yet it emphasizes the erosion of confidence that citizens, politicians, and academicians had in urban police—an erosion that was translated into lack of political and financial support.

Finally, urban police departments began to acquire competition: private security and the community crime control movement. Despite the inherent value of these developments, the fact that businesses, industries, and private citizens began to search for alternative means of protecting their property and persons suggests a decreasing confidence in either the capability or the intent of the police to provide the services that citizens want.

In retrospect, the police reform strategy has characteristics similar to those that Miles and Snow[31] ascribe to a defensive strategy in the private sector. Some of the characteristics of an organization with a defensive strategy are (with specific characteristics of reform policing added in parentheses):

- Its market is stable and narrow (crime victims).
- Its success is dependent on maintaining dominance in a narrow, chosen market (crime control).
- It tends to ignore developments outside its domain (isolation).
- It tends to establish a single core technology (patrol).
- New technology is used to improve its current product or service rather than to expand its product or service line (use of computers to enhance patrol).
- Its management is centralized (command and control).
- Promotions generally are from within (with the exception of chiefs, virtually all promotions are from within).
- There is a tendency toward a functional structure with high degrees of specialization and formalization.

A defensive strategy is successful for an organization when market conditions remain stable and few competitors enter the field. Such strategies are vulnerable, however, in unstable market conditions and when competitors are aggressive.

The reform strategy was a successful strategy for police during the relatively stable period of the 1940s and 1950s. Police were able to sell a relatively narrow service line and maintain dominance in the crime control market. The social changes of the 1960s and 1970s, however, created unstable conditions. Some of the more significant changes included: the civil rights movement; migration of minorities into cities; the changing age of the population (more youths and teenagers); increases in crime and fear; increased oversight of police actions by courts; and the decriminalization and deinstitutionalization movements. Whether or not the private sector defensive strategy properly applies to police, it is clear that the reform strategy was unable to adjust to the changing social circumstances of the 1960s and 1970s.

❖ THE COMMUNITY PROBLEM-SOLVING ERA ❖

All was not negative for police during the late 1970s and early 1980s, however. Police began to score victories which they barely noticed. Foot patrol remained popular, and in many cities citizen and political demands for it intensified. In New Jersey, the state funded the Safe and Clean Neighborhoods Program, which funded foot patrol in cities, often over the opposition of local chiefs of police.[32] In Boston, foot patrol was so popular with citizens that when neighborhoods were selected for foot patrol, politicians often made the announcements, especially during election years. Flint, Michigan, became the first city in memory to return to foot patrol on a citywide basis. It proved so popular there that citizens twice voted to increase their taxes to fund foot patrol—most recently by a two-thirds majority. Political and citizen demands for foot patrol continued to expand in cities throughout the United States. Research into foot patrol suggested it was more than just politically popular, it contributed to city life: it reduced fear, increased citizen satisfaction with police, improved police attitudes toward citizens, and increased the morale and job satisfaction of police.[33]

Additionally, research conducted during the 1970s suggested that one factor could help police improve their record in dealing with crime: information. If information about crimes and criminals could be obtained from citizens by police, primarily patrol officers, and could be properly managed by police departments, investigative and other units could significantly increase their effect on crime.[34]

Moreover, research into foot patrol suggested that at least part of the fear reduction potential was linked to the order maintenance activities of foot patrol officers.[35] Subsequent work in Houston and Newark indicated that tactics other than foot patrol that, like foot patrol, emphasized increasing the quantity and improving the quality of police-citizen interactions had outcomes similar to those of foot patrol (fear reduction, etc.).[36] Meanwhile, many other cities were developing programs, though not evaluated, similar to those in the foot patrol, Flint, and fear reduction experiments.[37]

The findings of foot patrol and fear reduction experiments, when coupled with the research on the relationship between fear and disorder, created new opportunities for police to understand the increasing concerns of citizens' groups about disorder (gangs, prostitutes, etc.) and to work with citizens to do something about it. Police discovered that when they asked citizens about their priorities, citizens appreciated the inquiry and also provided useful information often about problems that beat officers might have been aware of, but about which departments had little or no official data (e.g., disorder). Moreover, given the ambiguities that surround both the definitions of disorder and the authority of police to do something about it, police learned that they had to seek authorization from local citizens to intervene in disorderly situations.[38]

Simultaneously, Goldstein's problem-oriented approach to policing[39] was being tested in several communities: Madison, Wisconsin; Baltimore County, Maryland; and Newport News, Virginia. Problem-oriented policing rejects the fragmented approach in which police deal with each incident, whether citizen- or police-initiated, as an isolated event with neither history nor future. Pierce's findings about calls for service illustrate Goldstein's point: 60 percent of the calls for service in any given year in Boston originated from 10 percent of the households calling the police.[40] Furthermore, Goldstein and his colleagues in Madison, Newport News, and Baltimore County discovered the following: police officers enjoy operating with a holistic approach to their work; they have the capacity to do it successfully; they can work with citizens and other agencies to solve problems; and citizens seem to appreciate working with police— findings similar to those of the foot patrol experiments (Newark and Flint)[41] and the fear reduction experiments (Houston and Newark).[42]

The problem confronting police, policymakers, and academicians is that these trends and findings seem to contradict many of the tenets that dominated police thinking for a generation. Foot patrol creates new intimacy between citizens and police. Problem solving is hardly the routinized and standardized patrol modality that reformers thought was necessary to maintain control of police and limit their discretion. Indeed, use of discretion is the *sine qua non* of problem-solving policing. Relying on citizen endorsement of order maintenance activities to justify police action acknowledges a continued or new reliance on political authorization for police work in general. And, accepting the quality of urban life as an outcome of good police service emphasizes a wider definition of the police function and the desired effects of police work.

These changes in policing are not merely new police tactics, however. Rather, they represent a new organizational approach, properly called a community strategy. The elements of that strategy are:

Legitimacy and Authorization

There is renewed emphasis on community, or political, authorization for many police tasks, along with law and professionalism. Law continues to be the major legitimating basis of the police function. It defines basic police powers, but it does not fully direct police activities in efforts to maintain order, negotiate conflicts, or solve community problems. It becomes one tool among many others. Neighborhood, or community, support and involvement are required to accomplish those tasks. Professional and bureaucratic authority, especially that which tends to isolate police and insulate them from neighborhood influences, is lessened as citizens contribute more to definitions of problems and identification of solutions. Although in some respects similar to the authorization of policing's political era, community authorization exists in a different political context. The civil service movement, the political centralization that grew out of the Progressive era, and the bureaucratization, professionalization, and unionization of police stand as counterbalances to the possible recurrence of the corrupting influences of ward politics that existed prior to the reform movement.

The Police Function

As indicated above, the definition of police function broadens in the community strategy. It includes order maintenance, conflict resolution, problem solving through the organization, and provision of services, as well as other activities. Crime control remains an important function, with an important difference, however. The reform strategy attempts to control crime directly through preventive patrol and rapid response to calls for service. The community strategy emphasizes crime control *and prevention* as an indirect result of, or an equal partner to, the other activities.

Organizational Design

Community policing operates from organizational assumptions different from those of reform policing. The idea that workers have no legitimate, substantive interest in their work is untenable when programs such as those in Flint, Houston, Los Angeles, New York City, Baltimore County, Newport News, and others are examined. Consulting with community groups, problem solving, maintaining order, and other such activities are antithetical to the reform ideal of eliminating officer discretion through routinization and standardization of police activities. Moreover, organizational decentralization is inherent in community policing: the involvement of police officers in diagnosing and responding to neighborhood and community problems necessarily pushes operational and tactical decision making to the lower levels of the organization. The creation of neighborhood police stations (storefronts, for example), reopening of precinct stations, and establishment of beat offices (in schools, churches, etc.) are concrete examples of such decentralization.

Decentralization of tactical decision making to precinct or beat level does not imply abdication of executive obligations and functions, however. Developing, articulating, and monitoring organizational strategy remain the responsibility of management. Within this strategy, operational and tactical decision making is decentralized. This implies what may at first appear to be a paradox: while the number of managerial levels may decrease, the number of managers may increase. Sergeants in a decentralized regime, for example, have managerial responsibilities that exceed those they would have in a centralized organization.

At least two other elements attend this decentralization: increased participative management and increased involvement of top police executives in planning and implementation. Chiefs have discovered that programs are easier to conceive and implement if officers themselves are involved in their development through task forces, temporary matrix-like organizational units, and other organizational innovations that tap the wisdom and experience of sergeants and patrol officers. Additionally, police executives have learned that good ideas do not translate themselves into successful programs without extensive involvement of the chief executive and his close agents in every stage of planning and implementation, a lesson learned in the private sector as well.[43]

One consequence of decentralized decision making, participative planning and management, and executive involvement in planning is that fewer levels of authority are required to administer police organizations. Some police organizations, including the London Metropolitan Police (Scotland Yard), have begun to reduce the number of middle-management layers, while others are contemplating doing so. Moreover, as in the private sector, as computerized information gathering systems reach their potential in police departments, the need for middle managers whose primary function is data collection will be further reduced.

External Relationships

Community policing relies on an intimate relationship between police and citizens. This is accomplished in a variety of ways: relatively long-term assignment of officers to beats, programs that emphasize familiarity between citizens and police (police knocking on doors, consultations, crime control meetings for police and citizens, assignment to officers of "caseloads" of households with ongoing problems, problem solving, etc.), revitalization or development of Police Athletic League programs, educational programs in grade and high schools, and other programs. Moreover, police are encouraged to respond to the feelings and fears of citizens that result from a variety of social problems or from victimization.

Further, the police are restructuring their relationship with neighborhood groups and institutions. Earlier, during the reform era, police had claimed a monopolistic responsibility for crime control in cities, communities, and neighborhoods; now they recognize serious competitors in the ''industry'' of crime control, especially private security and the community crime control movement. Whereas in the past police had dismissed these sources of competition or, as in the case of community crime control, had attempted to co-opt the movement for their own purposes,[44] now police in many cities (Boston, New York, Houston, and Los Angeles, to name a few) are moving to structure working relationships or strategic alliances with neighborhood and community crime control groups. Although there is less evidence of attempts to develop alliances with the private security industry, a recent proposal to the National Institute of Justice envisioned an experimental alliance between the Fort Lauderdale, Florida, Police Department and the Wackenhut Corporation in which the two organizations would share responses to calls for service.

Demand Management

In the community problem-solving strategy, a major portion of demand is decentralized, with citizens encouraged to bring problems directly to beat officers or precinct offices. Use of 911 is discouraged, except for dire emergencies. Whether tactics include aggressive foot patrol as in Flint or problem solving as in Newport News, the emphasis is on police officers' interacting with citizens to determine the types of problems they are confronting and to devise solutions to those problems. In contrast to reform policing with its selling orientation, this approach is more like marketing: customer preferences are sought, and satisfying customer needs and wants, rather than selling a previously packaged product or service, is emphasized. In the case of police, they gather information about citizens' wants, diagnose the nature of the problem, devise possible solutions, and then determine which segments of the community they can best serve and which can be best served by other agencies and institutions that provide services, including crime control.

Additionally, many cities are involved in the development of demarketing programs.[45] The most noteworthy example of demarketing is in the area of rapid response to calls for service. Whether through the development of alternatives to calls for service, educational programs designed to discourage citizens from using the 911 system, or, as in a few cities, simply not responding to many calls for service, police actively attempt to demarket a program that had been actively sold earlier. Often demarketing 911 is thought of as a negative process. It need not be so, however. It is an attempt by police to change social, political, and fiscal circumstances to bring consumers' wants in line with police resources and to accumulate evidence about the value of particular police tactics.

Tactics and Technology

Community policing tactics include foot patrol, problem solving, information gathering, victim counseling and services, community organizing and consultation, education, walk-and-ride and knock-on-door programs, as well as regular patrol, specialized forms of patrol, and rapid response to emergency calls for service. Emphasis is placed on information sharing between patrol and detectives to increase the possibility of crime solution and clearance.

Measured Outcomes

The measures of success in the community strategy are broad: quality of life in neighborhoods, problem solution, reduction of fear, increased order, citizen satisfaction with police services, as well as crime control. In sum, the elements of the community strategy include:

- Authorization—community support (political), law, professionalism.
- Function—crime control, crime prevention, problem solving.
- Organizational design—decentralized, task forces, matrices.
- Relationship to environment—consultative, police defend values of law and professionalism, but listen to community concerns.
- Demand—channelled through analysis of underlying problems.
- Tactics and technology—foot patrol, problem solving, etc.
- Outcomes—quality of life and citizen satisfaction.

❖ CONCLUSION ❖

We have argued that there were two stages of policing in the past, political and reform, and that we are now moving into a third, the community era. To carefully examine the dimensions of policing during each of these eras, we have used the concept of organizational strategy. We believe that this concept can be used not only to describe the different styles of policing in the past and the present, but also to sharpen the understanding of police policymakers of the future.

For example, the concept helps explain policing's perplexing experience with team policing during the 1960s and 1970s. Despite the popularity of team policing with officers involved in it and with citizens, it generally did not remain in police departments for very long. It was usually planned and implemented with enthusiasm and maintained for several years. Then, with little fanfare, it would vanish—with everyone associated with it saying regretfully that for some reason it just did not work as a police tactic. However, a close examination of team policing reveals that it was a strategy that innovators mistakenly approached as a tactic. It had implications for authorization (police turned to neighborhoods for support), organizational design (tactical decisions were made at lower levels of the organization), definition of function (police broadened their service role), relationship to environment (permanent team members responded to the needs of small geographical areas), demand (wants and needs came to team members directly from citizens), tactics (consultation with citizens, etc.), and outcomes (citizen satisfaction, etc.). What becomes clear, though, is that team policing was a competing strategy with different assumptions about every element of police business. It was no wonder that it expired under such circumstances. Team and reform policing were strategically incompatible—one did not fit into the other. A police department could have a small team policing unit or conduct a team policing experiment, but business as usual was reform policing.

Likewise, although foot patrol symbolizes the new strategy for many citizens, it is a mistake to equate the two. Foot patrol is a tactic, a way of delivering police services. In Flint, its inauguration has been accompanied by implementation of most of the elements of a community strategy, which has become business as usual. In most places, foot patrol is not accompanied by the other elements. It is outside the mainstream of "real" policing and often provided only as a sop to citizens and politicians who are demanding the development of different policing styles. This certainly was the case in New Jersey when foot patrol was evaluated by the Police Foundation.[46] Another example is in Milwaukee, where two police budgets are passed: the first is the police budget; the second, a supplementary budget for modest levels of foot patrol. In both cases, foot patrol is outside the mainstream of police activities and conducted primarily as a result of external pressures placed on departments.

It is also a mistake to equate problem solving or increased order maintenance activities with the new strategy. Both are tactics. They can be implemented either as part of a new organizational strategy, as foot patrol was in Flint, or as an "add-on," as foot patrol was in most of the cities in New Jersey. Drawing a distinction between organizational add-ons and a change in strategy is not an academic quibble; it gets to the heart of the current situation in policing. We are arguing that policing is in a period of transition from a reform strategy to what we call a community strategy. The change involves more than making tactical or organizational adjustments and accommodations. Just as policing went through a basic change when it moved from the political to the reform strategy, it is going through a similar change now. If elements of the emerging organizational strategy are identified and the policing institution is guided through the change rather than left blindly thrashing about, we expect that the public will be better served, policymakers and police administrators more effective, and the profession of policing revitalized.

A final point: the classical theory of organization that continues to dominate police administration in most American cities is alien to most of the elements of the new strategy. The new strategy will not accommodate to the classical theory: the latter denies too much of the real nature of police work, promulgates unsustainable myths about the nature and quality of police supervision, and creates too much cynicism in officers attempting to do creative problem solving. Its assumptions about workers are simply wrong.

Organizational theory has developed well beyond the stage it was at during the early 1900s, and policing does have organizational options that are consistent with the newly developing organizational strategy. Arguably, policing, which was moribund during the 1970s, is beginning a resurgence. It is overthrowing a strategy that was remarkable in its time, but which could not adjust to the changes of recent decades. Risks attend the new strategy and its implementation. The risks, however, for the community and the profession of policing, are not as great as attempting to maintain a strategy that faltered on its own terms during the 1960s and 1970s.

Notes

[1] Kenneth R. Andrews, *The Concept of Corporate Strategy* (Homewood, Illinois: Richard D. Irwin, Inc., 1980).

[2] Robert M. Fogelson, *Big-City Police* (Cambridge: Harvard University Press, 1977); Samuel Walker, *A Critical History of Police Reform: The Emergence of Professionalism* (Lexington: Massachusetts, Lexington Books, 1977).

[3] Mark H. Moore and George L. Kelling, "To Serve and Protect: Learning From Police History," *The Public Interest*, 7 (Winter 1983).

4 K. E. Jordan, *Ideology and the Coming of Professionalism: American Urban Police in the 1920s and 1930s*, Dissertation, Rutgers University (1972).

5 Fogelson, *Big-City Police*.

6 Eric H. Monkkonen, *Police in Urban America, 1860–1920* (Cambridge: Cambridge University Press, 1981).

7 *The Newark Foot Patrol Experiment* (Washington, D.C.: Police Foundation, 1981).

8 John Eck, *Solving Crimes: The Investigation of Burglary and Robbery* (Washington, D.C.: Police Executive Research Forum, 1984).

9 Thomas A. Reppetto, *The Blue Parade* (New York: The Free Press, 1978).

10 Fogelson, *Big-City Police*.

11 *Ibid.*

12 George L. Kelling, "Reforming the Reforms: The Boston Police Department," Occasional Paper, Joint Center for Urban Studies of M.I.T. and Harvard, Cambridge (1983).

13 George L. Kelling, "Juveniles and Police: The End of the Nightstick," in *From Children to Citizens, Vol. II: The Role of the Juvenile Court*, ed. Francis X. Hartmann (New York: Springer-Verlag, 1987).

14 Walker, *A Critical History of Police Reform: The Emergence of Professionalism*.

15 Fogelson, *Big-City Police*.

16 Kelling, "Juveniles and Police: The End of the Nightstick."

17 Orlando W. Wilson, *Police Administration* (New York: McGraw-Hill, 1950).

18 "Police Guidelines," John F. Kennedy School of Government Program #C14-75-24 (1975).

19 Herman Goldstein, *Policing a Free Society* (Cambridge, Massachusetts: Ballinger, 1977).

20 Kelling, "Reforming The Reforms: The Boston Police Department."

21 Fogelson, *Big-City Police*.

22 William H. Parker, "The Police Challenge in Our Great Cities," *The Annals*, 29 (January 1954): 5–13.

23 For a detailed discussion of the differences between selling and marketing, see John L. Crompton and Charles W. Lamb, *Marketing Government and Social Services* (New York: John Wiley and Sons, 1986).

24 Commissioner Francis "Mickey" Roache of Boston has said that when the 911 system was instituted there, citizens persisted in calling "their" police—the district station. To circumvent this preference, district telephone numbers were changed so that citizens would be inconvenienced if they dialed the old number.

25 *The Newark Foot Patrol Experiment*.

26 O. W. Wilson, *Police Administration*.

27 A. E. Leonard, "Crime Reporting as a Police Management Tool," *The Annals*, 29 (January 1954).

28 George L. Kelling, et al., *The Kansas City Preventive Patrol Experiment: A Summary Report* (Washington, D.C.: Police Foundation, 1974); William Spelman and Dale K. Brown, *Calling the Police* (Washington, D.C.: Police Executive Research Forum, 1982).

29 *The Newark Foot Patrol Experiment*; Wesley G. Skogan and Michael G. Maxfield, *Coping With Crime* (Beverly Hills, California: Sage, 1981); Robert Trojanowicz, *An Evaluation of the Neighborhood Foot Patrol Program in Flint, Michigan* (East Lansing: Michigan State University, 1982).

[30] Mary Ann Wycoff, *The Role of Municipal Police Research as a Prelude to Changing It* (Washington, D.C.: Police Foundation, 1982); Goldstein, *Policing a Free Society*.

[31] Raymond E. Miles and Charles C. Snow, *Organizational Strategy, Structure and Process* (New York: McGraw-Hill, 1978).

[32] *The Newark Foot Patrol Experiment.*

[33] *The Newark Foot Patrol Experiment*; Trojanowicz, *An Evaluation of the Neighborhood Foot Patrol Program in Flint, Michigan.*

[34] Tony Pate et al., *Three Approaches to Criminal Apprehension in Kansas City: An Evaluation Report*, Washington, D.C., Police Foundation, 1976; Eck, *Solving Crimes: The Investigation of Burglary and Robbery.*

[35] James Q. Wilson and George L. Kelling, "Police and Neighborhood Safety: Broken Windows," *Atlantic Monthly*, March, 1982: 29–38.

[36] Tony Pate et al., *Reducing Fear of Crime in Houston and Newark: A Summary Report* (Washington, D.C.: Police Foundation, 1986).

[37] Jerome H. Skolnick and David H. Bayley, *The New Blue Line: Police Innovation in Six American Cities* (New York: The Free Press, 1986); Albert J. Reiss, Jr., *Policing a City's Central District: The Oakland Story* (Washington, D.C.: National Institute of Justice, March 1985).

[38] Wilson and Kelling, "Police and Neighborhood Safety: Broken Windows."

[39] Herman Goldstein, "Improving Policing: A Problem-Oriented Approach," *Crime and Delinquency* (April 1979), 236–258.

[40] Glenn Pierce et al., "Evaluation of an Experiment in Proactive Police Intervention in the Field of Domestic Violence Using Repeat Call Analysis," Boston, Massachusetts, The Boston Fenway Project, Inc. (May 13, 1987).

[41] *The Newark Foot Patrol Experiment*; Trojanowicz, *An Evaluation of the Neighborhood Foot Patrol Program in Flint, Michigan.*

[42] Pate et al., *Reducing Fear of Crime in Houston and Newark: A Summary Report.*

[43] James R. Gardner, Robert Rachlin, and H. W. Allen Sweeny, eds., *Handbook of Strategic Planning* (New York: John Wiley and Sons, 1986).

[44] Kelling, "Juveniles and Police: The End of the Nightstick."

[45] Crompton and Lamb, *Marketing Government and Social Services.*

[46] *The Newark Foot Patrol Experiment.*

2

The Evolving Strategy of Police
A Minority View

Hubert Williams and Patrick V. Murphy

> *. . . there is an underside to every age about which history does not often speak, because history is written from records left by the privileged. We learn about politics from the political leaders, about economics from the entrepreneurs, about slavery from the plantation owners, about the thinking of an age from its intellectual elite.*

> Howard Zinn[1]

Kelling and Moore, in their recent interpretation of the strategic history of American policing, succinctly summarize that history as falling generally into three eras: (1) political, (2) reform, and (3) community.[2] This attempt to create paradigms, as with all such attempts, should be seen metaphorically, providing us with ways to crystallize the complexities of history in simplified terms. Seen in this way, their analysis provides useful insights and a clearer interpretation of the changing role of police in American society—at least with respect to the majority in that society. Despite its utility, we find their analysis disturbingly incomplete. It fails to take account of how slavery, segregation, discrimination, and racism have affected the development of American police departments—and how

National Institute of Justice, *Perspectives on Policing*, 13 (January 1990).

these factors have affected the quality of policing in the nation's minority communities. Furthermore, we find Kelling and Moore to be silent on the important role that minorities have played in the past, and will play in the future, in affecting and improving the quality of policing in America. These omissions seriously diminish the accuracy and objectivity of their analysis and make it less useful than it otherwise could be in understanding the past and predicting the future of American policing.

This article addresses these omissions by adding a "minority perspective." Ours represents a "minority perspective" in two different senses. First, our understanding of what factors have shaped the evolution of policing was shared by only a minority of those participating in the discussions of the Harvard Executive Session on Community Policing. Whereas Kelling and Moore (and many others) attempted to explain the evolution of policing in terms of strategic choices made by police executives who were developing a professional ideology, we see policing as powerfully conditioned by broad social forces and attitudes—including a long history of racism. They see police departments as largely autonomous; we see them as barometers of the society in which they operate.

Second, our view is particularly attuned to how institutions, norms, and attitudes have dealt with racial minorities and how those dealings affected the role of police during each of the eras described by Kelling and Moore. More optimistically, we believe that improvements have occurred in the last several years and that further improvements are possible, although not assured, in the future. We are particularly aware of the implications for African-American minorities, but we believe that the patterns set in these relations have importantly affected relations with other racially distinctive minorities such as Hispanics, Asians, Native Americans, and other people of color.

In this article, we contend that the strategies of police in dealing with minorities have been different from those in dealing with others, that the changes in police strategies in minority communities have been more problematic, and that, therefore, the beneficial consequences of those changes for minorities have been less noticeable. Specifically, we argue that:

- The fact that the legal order not only countenanced but sustained slavery, segregation, and discrimination for most of our nation's history—and the fact that the police were bound to uphold that order—set a pattern for police behavior and attitudes toward minority communities that has persisted until the present day. That pattern includes the idea that minorities have fewer civil rights, that the task of the police is to keep them under control, and that the police have little responsibility for protecting them from crime within their communities.

- The existence of this pattern of police behavior and attitudes toward minority communities meant that, while important changes were occurring in policing during our nation's history, members of minority groups benefited less than others from these changes—certainly less than it might have seemed from the vantage point of the white community and the police executives who were bringing about those changes.

- The Kelling and Moore discussion of the "political era" of policing, a period generally defined by them as extending from after Reconstruction through the first decade of the twentieth century, neglects the early role of the first varieties and functions of police in this country—as well as the legal and political powerlessness of minority communities in both the North and the South. This omission means that their analysis fails to recognize that members of those minority communities received virtually none of the benefits of policing that were directed to those with more political clout.

- Many of the most notable advances in policing brought about by the advent of the "reform era" proved to be elusive, if not counterproductive, for minorities. Several of the hiring and promotional standards, although implemented as antidotes to the rampant nepotism and political favoritism that had characterized policing during the "political era" proved to be detrimental to blacks—just at the time when, to a limited extent, because of their increasing political power, they were beginning to acquire the credentials that would have allowed them to qualify by the old standards.

- The potential of "professional policing" during the reform era was not fully realized either for minorities or for whites—until the civil rights revolution of the late 1960s and the coming to power of progressive mayors, both black and white, and the police executives appointed by them who were capable of bringing about changes relevant to blacks and other minorities. It was that movement, led primarily by black Americans, and that political empowerment that finally began to produce the putative benefits of professional policing: a fairer distribution of police services, less use of deadly force, greater respect for individual rights, and equal opportunity for minorities within the nation's police departments. Without that movement, the promise of professional policing would have remained hollow.

- The minority community also played a key role in initiating the era of community policing. It was the riots of the late 1960s—and the election of many black and white progressive mayors, who appointed likeminded police chiefs—that stimulated broad social investments in police agencies, therefore putting the issue of police-community relations inescapably on the minds of police executives and the mayors who appointed them. The fact that police actions triggered many of the riots and then could not control them revealed to everyone the price of having a police department backed only by the power of the law, but not by the consent, much less active support, of those being policed.

- The era of community policing holds potential benefits and hazards for the quality of American policing. The potential benefits lie in the fundamental tenet of community policing: the empowerment of communities to participate in problem solving and decisions about delivery of services based on the needs of individual neighborhoods. The hazards lie in the possibility of excluding those communities that have been the least powerful and least well organized and thus repeating the historical patterns of race relations in the United States. If, however, the more recent trends towards inclusion of African-Americans and other minorities in policing and in the broader society are continued, then community policing might finally realize a vision of police departments as organizations that protect the lives, property, and rights of all citizens in a fair and effective way.

❖ THE POLITICAL ERA ❖
POLICING THE POWERLESS

Kelling and Moore argue that during the political era, from the introduction of the "new police" in the 1840s until the early 1900s, American police derived both their authority and resources from local political leaders. We maintain that their account is based largely on an analysis of policing in the cities of the northeastern United States, mostly following the Civil War and Reconstruction, and omitting the importance of racial and social conflicts in the origination of American police departments. As such, their analysis omits several crucial parts of the story of policing in America: the role of "slave patrols" and other police instruments of racial oppression; the role of the police in imposing racially biased laws; and the importance of racial and social turmoil in the creation of the first versions of America's "new police."

Most analyses of early American history reflect an understandable, white, twentieth-century bias toward northern, urban, white conditions. While the literature is replete with studies of the growth of law enforcement in northern urban areas in general[3] and northern cities such as Boston,[4] Chicago,[5] Detroit,[6] and New York City,[7] in particular, little attention has been paid to police development outside the urban North. Kelling and Moore reflect a similar bias. Since the vast majority of blacks in the early years of America lived in the South, and about 80 percent of those lived outside of cities, this perspective creates a significant distortion.

Prominent police historian Samuel Walker has noted the difficulty of establishing dates marking the origins of American modern-style policing, that is, a system of law enforcement involving a permanent agency employing full-time officers who engage in continuous patrol of fixed beats to prevent crime. The traditional analyses, based on urban evidence, have suggested that such policing evolved from older systems of militias, sheriffs, constables, and night watches, and culminated in the "new police" of Boston in 1838, New York City in 1845, Chicago in 1851, New Orleans and Cincinnati in 1852, Philadelphia in 1854, St. Louis in 1855, Newark and Baltimore in 1857, and Detroit in 1865.[8]

As Richardson points out, however, these analyses neglect that:

> [many other cities with] elaborate police arrangements were those with large slave populations where white masters lived in dread of possible black uprisings. Charleston, Savannah, and Richmond provided for combined foot and mounted patrols to prevent slaves from congregating and to repress any attacks upon the racial and social status quo. In Charleston, for example, police costs constituted the largest item in the municipal budget.[9]

Indeed, as both Walker[10] and Reichel[11] contend, there is a strong argument to be made that the first American modern-style policing occurred in the "slave patrols," developed by the white slave owners as a means of dealing with runaways. Believing that their militia was not capable of dealing with the perceived threat, the colonial state governments of the South enacted slave patrol legislation during the 1740s, e.g., in South Carolina:

> Foreasmuch [sic] as many late horrible and barbarous massacres have been actually committed and many more designed, on the white inhabitants of this Province, by negro slaves, who are generally prone to such cruel practices, which makes it highly necessary that constant patrols should be established.[12]

Neighboring Georgians were also concerned with maintaining order among their slaves. The preamble to their 1757 law establishing and regulating slave patrols contends:

> . . . it is absolutely necessary for the Security of his Majesty's Subjects in this Province, that Patrols should be established under proper Regulations in the settled parts thereof, for the better keeping of Negroes and other Slaves in Order and prevention of any Cabals, Insurrections or other Irregularities amongst them.[13]

Such statutes were eventually enacted in all southern states. Although specific provisions differed from state to state,[14] most of these laws responded to complaints that militia duty was being shirked and demands that a more regular system of surveillance be established.

In Georgia, all urban white men aged sixteen to sixty, with the exception of ministers of religion, were to conduct such patrol "on every night throughout the year." In the countryside, such patrols were to "visit every Plantation within their respective Districts once in every Month" and whenever they thought it necessary, "to search and examine all Negro-Houses for offensive weapons and Ammunition." They were also authorized to enter any "disorderly tipling-House, or other Houses suspected of harbouring, trafficking or dealing with Negroes" and could inflict corporal punishment on any slave found to have left his owner's property without permission.[15]

Foner points out that "slave patrols" had full power and authority to enter any plantation and break open Negro houses or other places when slaves were suspected of keeping arms; to punish runaways or slaves found outside their plantations without a pass; to whip any slave who should affront or abuse them in the execution of their duties; and to apprehend and take any slave suspected of stealing or other criminal offense, and bring him to the nearest magistrate.[16] Understandably, the actions of such patrols established an indelible impression on both the whites who implemented this system and the blacks who were the brunt of it.

Reflecting the northern, urban perspective, Kelling and Moore begin their consideration of American policing only after the earliest "new police" were established in the 1840s and 1850s. Even so, their analysis neglects to point out the importance of the role played by social discord in general, and the minority community in particular, in the creation of these departments. Phenomenal increases in immigration, rapid population growth, and major changes in industrialization led to more and more people, many of whom were from an impoverished, rural background, settling in an alien urban environment. Conflicts between black freedmen and members of the white urban working class significantly contributed to social unrest.

In 1830 Alexis de Tocqueville toured the United States to study prison reform. Unfamiliar with American norms, he was surprised to discover that there was more overt hostility and hatred toward blacks in the North, where slavery did not exist, than in the South, where it did. Those who challenged the status quo by demanding the abolition of slavery suffered verbal and physical abuse in northern cities.[17] This tension was reflected in a number of race riots in the mid-1830s in America's major cities. New York City had so many racial disorders in 1834 that it was long remembered as the "year of the riots." Boston suffered three major riots in the years 1834 to 1837, all of which focused on the issues of anti-abolitionism or anti-Catholicism. Philadelphia, the "City of Brotherly Love," experienced severe anti-Negro riots in 1838 and 1842; overall, the city had eleven major riots between 1834 and 1849. Baltimore experienced a total of nine riots, largely race-related, between 1834 and the creation of its new police in 1857. In a desperate attempt to cope with the social disorder brought about by this conflict, America's major cities resorted to the creation of police departments. Clearly, this was a case of the political system responding to incendiary conflict within the society at large by demanding that the police be reorganized to deal with those conflicts.

In their discussion of the political era, Kelling and Moore observe that the police found their legitimacy either in politics or in law. For blacks, both before and several generations after the Civil War, neither of these bases of legitimacy provided much, if any, opportunity to shape policing to their benefit. As the authors point out, local political machines often recruited and maintained police in their positions, from foot officer to police chief. In return, the police encouraged voters to support certain candidates and provided services designed to enhance that support. Departments were organized in a decentralized manner, giving officers a great deal of discretion in carrying out their responsibilities. Police officers were closely linked to the neighborhoods in which they patrolled, often living there and usually of the same ethnic stock as the residents.

For those with political influence, this era provided close proximity to power. Good jobs could be had. Special favors could be obtained. The police could be expected to be extremely sensitive to community concerns—or lose their jobs if they were not.

For those with no access to political power, however, the situation was very different. Before slavery was abolished, the issue of black political power in the South was moot. The Constitution itself provides a sardonic reflection on the state of political power assigned to slaves. The group of white delegates assembled in Philadelphia never even considered slave representation, slave votes, or slave power. The only issue was whether a slave owner would enjoy a three-fifths increment of presentation for every slave he owned.

During the debate, William Paterson stated bluntly that slaves were "no free agents, have no personal liberty, no faculty of acquiring property, but on the contrary, are themselves property" and hence like other property "entirely at the will of the master." To make certain there was no mistake, the Constitution explicitly prohibited Congress from abolishing the international slave trade to the United States before 1808.

Early American law enforcement officials in slave states were empowered—and expected—to enforce statutes carrying out the most extreme forms of racism, not restricted solely to enforcing slavery. In 1822, for example, Charleston, South Carolina, experienced a slave insurrection panic, caused by a supposed plot of slaves and free blacks to seize the city. In response, the state legislature passed the Negro Seamen's Act, requiring free black seamen to remain on board their vessels while in Carolina harbors. If they dared to leave their ships, the police were instructed to arrest them and sell them into slavery unless they were redeemed by the ship's master. The other coastal slave states soon enacted similar legislation.

Berlin presents this brief synopsis of Southern justice:

> Southern law presumed all Negroes to be slaves, and whites systematically barred free Negroes from any of the rights and symbols they equated with freedom. Whites legally prohibited Negro freemen from moving freely, participating in politics, testifying against whites, keeping guns, or lifting a hand to strike a white person . . . In addition they burdened free Negroes with special imposts, barred them from certain trades, and often tried and punished them like slaves. To enforce their proscriptive codes and constantly remind free Negroes of their lowly status, almost every state forced free Negroes to register and carry freedom papers, which had to be renewed periodically and might be inspected by any suspicious white.[18]

Police supervision further strengthened the registration system. City officials periodically ordered police to check the papers of all newly arrived free Negroes or investigate freedmen who failed to register or lacked visible means of support.[19]

Outside the slave states, the rights of blacks were only somewhat less restricted. Although Henry David Thoreau and William Lloyd Garrison exaggerated when they called Massachusetts a slave state, their harsh denunciation is a reminder that a black person could be a slave there or in any of the other "free" states because of the protection afforded by the federal and state constitutions for masters' rights in fugitive and sojourning slaves. It fell to agents of law enforcement, constables and members of the day and night watches, to carry out these laws. By 1800, some 36,505 northern Negroes still remained in bondage, most of them in New York and New Jersey.[20]

Several northern states enacted gradual emancipation statutes after the Revolution. Because such statutes freed only children born after a specified date, however, many slaves remained unaffected, and the freed children were held in apprenticeship until some time in their adult years. The state of New Jersey was typical. In 1804, the legislature freed the children born to slave mothers after July 4 of that year; the child so freed would be "apprenticed" to its mother's owner, men until age 25, women until 21. Only in 1844 did it remove all barriers to the freeing of slaves. Again, these laws were also enforced by the local constable.

Even after the northern states took action to free slaves—ranging from constitutional provisions in Vermont in 1777 to gradual-abolition acts in New Jersey in 1804 and New York in 1817, the legal and political rights of blacks were quite circumscribed. Every new state admitted to the Union after 1819 restricted voting to whites. Only five states—Massachusetts, Rhode Island, Maine, New Hampshire, and Vermont—provided equal voting rights for black and white males. Illinois, Ohio, Indiana, Iowa, and California prohibited black testimony in court if whites were a party to the proceeding, and Oregon forbade Negroes to hold real estate, make contracts, or maintain lawsuits. Massachusetts banned intermarriage of whites with blacks and enforced segregation in hotels, restaurants, theaters, and transportation. Berlin describes a raid in 1853 in which St. Louis police raided well-known hangouts of freedmen, whipped those who were unregistered, and shipped them out of town. Such raids continued for almost a year.[21]

Litwack describes the situation of northern blacks this way:

> In virtually every phase of existence, Negroes found themselves systematically separated from whites. They were either excluded from railway cars, omnibuses, stagecoaches, and steamboats or assigned to special "Jim Crow" sections; they sat, when permitted, in secluded and remote corners of theaters and lecture halls; they could not enter most hotels, restaurants, and resorts, except as servants; they prayed in "Negro pews" in the white churches, and if partaking of the sacrament of the Lord's Supper, they waited until the whites had been served the bread and wine. Moreover, they were often educated in segregated schools, punished in segregated prisons, nursed in segregated hospitals, and buried in segregated cemeteries.[22]

Indeed, as pointed out by C. Vann Woodward, an eminent historian of the South, "One of the strangest things about Jim Crow [the laws and practices separating the races] was that the system was born in the North and reached an advanced age before moving South in force."[23]

With neither political power nor legal standing, blacks could hardly be expected to share in the spoils of the political era of policing. There were virtually no black police officers until well into the twentieth century. Thus, police attention to, and protection for, areas populated primarily by racial minorities was rare during this era.

❖ THE REFORM ERA ❖
POLICING BY THE LAW FOR THOSE UNPROTECTED BY IT

According to Kelling and Moore's interpretation, the basic police strategy began to change during the early 1900s. By the 1930s, they argue, the reform era of policing was in full sway. Strikingly, their discussion completely overlooks the momentous events of the Civil War and Reconstruction, a time of great change in the legal and political status of minorities.

In the earliest days of the Civil War, President Lincoln and other northern politicians insisted that the issue of slavery had little to do with the conflict. In fact, in July 1861, when Congress assembled in special session, one of its first acts was to pass, almost unanimously, the Crittenden Resolution, affirming that the "established institutions" of the seceding states were not to be a military target. To a large extent, this position was dictated by political forces—to keep the border states in the Union, generate support among the broadest constituency in the North, and weaken the Confederacy by holding out the possibility that they could return to the Union with their property, including their slaves, intact.[24]

Eventually, however, as the Confederacy put slaves to work as military laborers and the presence of Union troops precipitated large-scale desertion of plantation slaves, this policy was overcome by events. On January 1, 1863, Lincoln signed the Emancipation Proclamation. Bowing to political reality, however, he excluded from its purview the 450,000 slaves in Delaware, Kentucky, Maryland, and Missouri; 275,000 in Union-occupied Tennessee; and tens of thousands in occupied portions of Virginia and Louisiana.

By 1864, the Senate approved the 13th amendment, abolishing slavery throughout the Union, but it failed to receive the necessary two-thirds majority in the House. Eventually, in January 1865, this amendment narrowly won House approval and was sent to the states for ratification. Although several Southern legislatures were reluctant to lend their support, this amendment was ratified by the end of the year. To some, this not only ended one of America's most shameful institutions but offered the hope of the beginning of a nation where North and South, black and white, were ruled by one law impartial over all. As we know with historical hindsight, such an interpretation was far too optimistic.

Even at the time, questions were raised about the practical implications of the amendment. James A. Garfield asked, "What is freedom? Is it the bare privilege of not being chained? . . . If this is all, then freedom is a bitter mockery, a cruel delusion." More to the point, Frederick Douglass maintained, "Slavery is not abolished until the black man has the ballot."[25]

In fact, a political vacuum developed between 1865 and 1867 in which the opponents of the extension of full citizenship to blacks were able to exercise great influence. President Andrew Johnson, with hopes of receiving the support of his fellow Southerners in the election in 1868, left the definition of black rights to the individual states. They accepted the opportunity with a vengeance. In addition to prohibiting black suffrage, the provisional legislatures passed the Black Codes, a series of state laws intended to define the freedmen's new rights and responsibilities.

Mississippi and South Carolina enacted the first and most severe Black Codes toward the end of 1865. Mississippi required all blacks to possess, each January, written evidence of employment for the coming year. Laborers leaving their jobs before the contract expired would forfeit wages already earned and, as under slavery, be subject to arrest by any white citizen. A person offering work to a laborer already under contract risked imprisonment or a fine. Blacks were forbidden to rent land in urban areas. Vagrants—under whose definition fell the idle, disorderly, and those who "misspend what they earn"—could be punished by fines or involuntary plantation labor; other criminal offenses included "insulting" gestures or language, "malicious mischief," and preaching the Gospel without a license. In case anything had been overlooked, the legislature declared all existing penal codes defining crimes by slaves and free blacks "in full force" unless specifically altered by law. South Carolina's Code barred blacks from any occupation other than farmer or servant except by paying an annual tax ranging from $10 to $100.[26]

Virtually all of the former Confederate States enacted such laws. Blacks protested most bitterly, however, against apprenticeship laws, which seized upon the consequences of slavery—the separation of families and the freedmen's poverty—to provide planters with the unpaid labor of black minors. Generally, these laws allowed judges to bind to white employers black orphans and those whose parents were deemed unable to support them. The former slave owner usually had first preference, the consent of the parents was not required, and the law permitted "moderate corporal chastisement."[27]

This entire complex of Black Codes was enforced:

> . . . by a police apparatus and judicial system in which blacks enjoyed virtually no voice whatever. Whites staffed urban police forces as well as state militias, intended, as a Mississippi white put it in 1865, to "keep good order and discipline amongst the negro population."[28]

Sheriffs, justices of the peace, and other local officials proved extremely reluctant to prosecute whites accused of crimes against blacks. In those rare cases in which they did prosecute, convictions were infrequent and sentences were far more lenient than blacks received for the same crimes. For example, Texas courts indicted some 500 white men for the murder of blacks in 1865 and 1866, but not one was convicted.[29]

Largely in response to the Black Codes, Congress passed, over President Johnson's veto, the Civil Rights Act of 1866. This act defined all persons born in the United States (except Indians) as national citizens and spelled out rights they were to enjoy equally without regard to race—making contracts, bringing lawsuits, and enjoying "full and equal benefit of all laws and proceedings for the security of person and property." No state law or custom could deprive any citizen of these rights. Furthermore, Federal officials were authorized to bring suit against violations and made all persons, including local officials, who deprived a citizen of a civil right liable to fine or imprisonment.

To institutionalize the legal implications of the Civil War beyond the reach of shifting political majorities and presidential vetoes, Congress, after a long struggle, passed the 14th amendment, providing, among other things, that equal protection under the law be afforded to every citizen. Although it implicitly acknowledged the right of states to limit voting because of race, they could do so only at the expense of losing a significant portion of their congressional representation.

The 1866 congressional election essentially became a referendum on the 14th amendment—Republicans in favor, President Johnson and the Democrats opposed. The Republicans won an overwhelming victory, large enough to give them well over the two-thirds majority required to override a veto. In contrast, all Southern legislatures except Tennessee repudiated the amendment by enormous majorities.

Frustrated, and sensing its political strength, the Congress passed, again over Johnson's veto, the Reconstruction Act of 1867. This act divided the eleven Confederate States, except Tennessee, into five military districts and stipulated the process by which new state governments could be created and recognized. This process required the ratification of the 14th amendment, writing of new constitutions providing for manhood suffrage, and approval of these constitutions by a majority of registered voters.

After two years of "Presidential Reconstruction," characterized by a lack of commitment to the extension of full rights to blacks, the era of "Radical Reconstruction" began. Given the right to vote, many blacks participated in—and won—election to the new state legislatures. To allay any concerns that the issue had not been addressed completely, Congress passed the 15th amendment, providing the right to vote to all persons, regardless of "race, color, or previous state of servitude," and prohibited the abridgement of that right by federal and state governments. The Civil Rights Act of 1875 outlawed the exclusion of blacks from hotels, theaters, railroads, and other public accommodations.

The results of black suffrage on policing were not long in coming. Blacks appeared in several southern police departments soon after Radical Reconstruction began, especially where Republicans were in office and where blacks constituted a large percentage of the population. Black police appeared in Selma, Alabama, in 1867; Houston, Texas, in 1870; and Jackson, Mississippi, in 1871.[30] In New Orleans, a majority of whose population was black, a police board composed of three black members out of five appointed a police force that included 177 blacks by 1870.[31]

Such change was not always easy, however. In July 1868, in Raleigh, North Carolina, under the headline "The Mongrel Regime!! Negro Police!!" the Conservative *Daily Sentinel* announced the appointment of four black police officers and concluded that "this is the beginning of the end."[32] Race riots occurred in Jackson and Meridian, Mississippi, because black police attempted to use their police authority over whites.[33]

In 1872, a Republican mayor in Chicago appointed the first black policeman in the North, where black suffrage was not required by Congress. Three years later, a mayor belonging to the People's Party replaced that officer with another black. In 1880, the Republicans won the mayor's office again, resulting in the appointment of four more black policemen. These officers all worked in plain clothes—in part not to offend the sensibilities of racist whites—and were assigned to black neighborhoods, practices adopted in most departments that hired blacks at that time. By 1894 there were 23 black policemen in Chicago.[34] Blacks were appointed in other cities in the North soon after those in Chicago: in Washington, D.C., in 1874; in Indianapolis in 1876; in Cleveland in 1881; in Boston in 1885.[35]

Lane provides one of the most thorough and fascinating analyses of the political complexities involved in appointing the first black police officers.[36] The approximately 7,000 blacks in Philadelphia's Seventh Ward had become a consistent Republican constituency, accounting for more than 10 percent of the party's vote. During the 1880 mayoral campaign, however, the black vote became a target of both parties' attention. Although the Seventh Ward voted overwhelmingly for the Republican candidate, the winner was Samuel King, a reform Democrat. Mayor King then appointed Alexander Davis and three other black men to the police department.

The selection criteria applied in appointing these Philadelphia officers reflect a common pattern in the choice of the earliest black officers. As Lane points out:

> In an era before any sort of civil service, when many officers were semiliterate at best, the four blacks chosen, although currently trapped in unskilled jobs, were characteristically overqualified.[37]

Davis, although born a slave, had graduated from Lincoln University, worked as a schoolteacher, and founded a newspaper. Only one of the other blacks appointed at that time had no experience beyond "laboring work."

Despite their qualifications, the appointment of the first black police officers in Philadelphia produced the same responses as were seen in many other cities. Several officers quit the force in protest. The new men were assigned to beats in or near black neighborhoods and immediately attracted crowds of spectators, saying such things as "Ain't he sweet?" or "Is the thing alive?"

As in Philadelphia, most departments, to appease the racial attitudes of whites, did not allow black officers to arrest whites or to work with white officers. Even as late as 1961, a study reported by the President's Commission on Law Enforcement and Administration of Justice found that 31 percent of the departments surveyed restricted the right of blacks to make felony arrests; the power of black officers to make misdemeanor arrests was even more limited.[38]

Miami established a different designation for the two races: blacks were "patrolmen" and whites were "policemen." In Chicago, blacks were largely confined to the Southside districts; in St. Louis, the "black beats" ranged from the central downtown area to the Northside. Los Angeles established a special "black watch" for the predominantly black Newton Station district.

After the initial dramatic changes brought about by the effects of Radical Reconstruction, the situation for blacks—and policing—began to revert to the *status quo ante*. As early as 1867, black suffrage went down to defeat in referendums in Minnesota, Ohio, and Kansas. Moderates within the Republic party began to back away from "extreme radical measures" such as egalitarianism. The Ku Klux Klan, founded in 1866 in Tennessee as a social club, launched a reign of terror against Republican leaders, black and white. In some parts of the South, armed whites blocked blacks from voting. Violence spread, especially in Georgia and Louisiana where, unable to hold meetings, Republicans abandoned their presidential campaign. By 1868, Republicans, the stalwart supporters of black rights, began to lose some of their strength in the South.[39]

By 1872, the presidential election focused on southern policy, the Democrats emphasizing the evils of Reconstruction and the need to restore local self-government. Although the Republicans won, a significant number of former Radicals supported the Democratic ticket, indicating that their campaign themes were more powerful than the returns would indicate.

While political support for Radical Reconstruction waned, debate about whether the 14th amendment applied only to states raged throughout the nation—and has continued to do so even in the last decade. Presidents Grant and Hayes retreated from strict enforcement of the so-called "Reconstruction Amendments." The Supreme Court began to shift away from the broad interpretation of the 13th amendment to the narrower 14th and 15th. This shift, in turn, encouraged legislators to narrow their concerns as well.

In 1874, a long-awaited compilation of the United States laws, known as the *Revised Statutes*, was produced. This document rearranged the nation's laws into supposedly relevant, logical categories. Inexplicably, however, this rearrangement failed to list the Civil Rights Act of 1866 either in the published text or in the "historical" documentation. Instead, various parts of the 1866 law were scattered throughout the document, under various chapter headings. Civil rights as an independent subject worthy of the attention of lawyers, judges, law professors, and an entire generation of law students was neither easily researched nor, by implication, important. One by one, case by case, the legal rights of blacks were ruled away.

Against this already ominous backdrop came the Compromise of 1877, by which the Federal Government agreed to end Reconstruction, withdraw military forces from the South, and cease enforcing civil rights laws. In exchange, the election of the Republican candidate for president, Rutherford B. Hayes, was assured. The dike that had laboriously been constructed against racist retaliation was suddenly broken. The stage was set for a massive reversal of the gains made in the previous 20 years.

In 1883, the Supreme Court, in deciding five litigations joined as the *Civil Rights Cases*, declared the Civil Rights Act of 1875 unconstitutional. Reflecting the earlier debates over the Reconstruction amendments, the ruling was based on the premise that those amendments prohibited only states, not individuals, from infringing on the equal protection and due process guaranteed to individuals by the Constitution.

Moreover, in 1896, the Supreme Court, in the landmark decision of *Plessy v. Ferguson*, found state laws that required segregation of the races in public accommodations to be constitutional, thereby endorsing the proposition that public facilities could be "separate but equal." This decision virtually completed the quarter-century-long process of standing the law established by the Reconstruction amendments on its head. The effects were quickly seen in police departments. In department after department, blacks lost their jobs, either by dismissal or by being forced to resign. The disappearance of blacks from the New Orleans police department serves as the most dramatic example of this trend. From a high of 177 black officers in 1870, the number dropped to 27 in 1880. By 1900, only five black officers remained; by 1910 there were none. The city did not appoint another black to the police force until 1950.

It is in this context that the Kelling and Moore discussion of the reform era must be interpreted. They argue that police reformers, led by August Vollmer and O. W. Wilson, changed the basic orientation of American policing in response to the excesses of the political era. The paradigm thus adopted, they contend, rejected politics as the source of authority for the police, replacing it with law and professionalism.

In an effort to curtail the close relationship between local political leaders and police, civil service replaced patronage and influence in the selection, assignment, and retention of police officers. Individual police officers were expected to avoid becoming closely associated with, and therefore contaminated by, the areas in which they patrolled. In some cases, they were prohibited from living in their beats. To further eliminate local political influence, functional control was centralized. By the time this era had reached its peak, during the 1950s and 1960s, police departments had become largely autonomous agencies, led by professionals guided by law, immune from political influence.

As dramatic as this change must have appeared to the white middle-class inhabitants of America's major cities, the transition to the reform era was barely noticeable to blacks and other minorities. Relying on law, rather than politics, as the source of police authority had many desirable aspects for those provided full protection by the law. Once again, however, for those who lacked both political power and equal protection under the law, such a transformation could have little significance.

Even the particular mechanisms implemented to bring about reform proved to be of little avail to blacks and other minorities. Civil service examinations, for example, designed to avoid the influence of patronage and nepotism, provided slight consolation for those who had been denied access to quality education. These examinations, which according to some experts, reveal less about the qualifications of the applicants than about the cultural biases of the examiners, winnowed out a far higher proportion of blacks than whites. In Boston, for example, the examiners failed 75 percent of the blacks as opposed to 35 percent of the whites in 1970. In Atlanta, in the same year, 72 percent of the blacks and only 24 percent of the whites failed. In New York, in 1968, 65 percent of the blacks as opposed to 31 percent of the whites failed. Mexicans and Puerto Ricans fared even worse, perhaps because the tests were given in English.[40]

Background investigations, which blacks and other minorities are more likely to fail than whites, also served as a barrier to inclusion. Fogelson reports evidence indicating that investigators rejected 41 percent of black applicants as opposed to 29 percent of whites in St. Louis in 1966; 68 percent of the blacks, as opposed to 56 percent of the whites, were rejected in Cleveland in 1966; and 58 percent of the blacks, as opposed to 32 percent of the whites, in Philadelphia in 1968.[41] He concludes that these disparities were a function of two things, notwithstanding racial prejudice. First, many departments were unwilling to accept any applicant who had been arrested or convicted for any criminal offense, no matter how trivial—the President's Crime Commission showed that blacks were more likely to have a criminal record than whites.[42] Second, most departments were reluctant to hire anyone who was truant from school, changed jobs too often, associated with known criminals, or had broken military regulations, all of which are more prevalent among blacks and other minorities than among whites.[43] Regardless of the merits of these criteria, their effect was the same—the exclusion of minorities.

Centralization of control also provided little help for minorities, inasmuch as it meant that already strained relations with the police officer on the beat translated into even more strained relations with a distant government downtown. Reduced contacts with local officers meant that limited opportunities to bridge the racial barrier became even more limited.

In their efforts to attract qualified recruits, the reformers not only raised salaries, increased benefits, and improved working conditions, they also extended their recruitment efforts. One method of expanding the pool of applicants was to abolish residency requirements. This reform, although defended by reformers on professional grounds, handicapped the blacks, Hispanics, and other minorities by slowing down the ethnic turnover in police departments. Without such a change, as whites fled from the inner cities, the increasing percentage of minorities remaining could have been expected to have been more readily reflected in the ranks of the police. Furthermore, despite heavy immigration of minorities to the nation's urban centers, the competitive edge that had been experienced earlier by the Irish and other white ethnic minorities no longer held sway.

Despite its limitations, the reform era provided, for members of the majority, a marked improvement in the delivery of professional police services. For members of minority groups, however, the change from the political era, in which they lacked political power, to the reform era, in which they lacked the support of the law, meant, for the most part, more of the same. In only 7 of the 26 cities for which the Kerner Commission collected data was the percentage of nonwhite police officers equal to as much as one-third of the percentage of nonwhites in the city.[44]

❖ THE COMMUNITY ERA ❖
POLICING DISINTEGRATING COMMUNITIES

By the late 1970s and early 1980s, according to Kelling and Moore, we had entered the era of community policing. Although law remained a source of authority, the police began once again to recognize that, ultimately, they are dependent on neighborhood, or community, support to achieve their goals. Turning to the citizens they serve for consultation, the police realized that more was expected of them than simply enforcing the law. Looking at people as clients of their services, the police found that they were also being judged on their ability to maintain order, resolve conflict, protect rights, and provide other services. In order to be able to remain responsive to community concerns, organizational decentralization was necessary. To remain even more flexible, officers were given authority and discretion to develop responses appropriate to local needs.

To organized, empowered communities, this strategy of policing offered extraordinary opportunities to participate in structuring the nature of police services delivered. As a result of community demands, for example, programs such as foot patrol were revived, long before they were found to be effective in reducing fear and, in some cases, crime. Despite the popularity of such initiatives, a closer examination of the areas in which such foot beats were created reveals one of the serious problems with this approach. In the state of New Jersey, for example, where foot patrol was funded by the Safe and Clean Neighborhoods Program, most foot beats were instituted in areas with strong community or business organizations— or both—with strong support from and access to political leaders. Those without such resources—and those most in need of police services—often found themselves in a long queue.

Although the 1954 Supreme Court decision in *Brown v. Board of Education of Topeka* began to provide blacks and other minorities with their just share of legal rights and remedies, that provision came only with "all deliberate speed." As this glacially slow process continued, something more virulent occurred in minority communities, especially in the inner cities. Those who could afford to do so moved into less crowded, more comfortable, neighborhoods, leaving behind vacant houses—and those who could not afford an alternative. Businesses closed. Tax bases eroded. Among those who remained, unemployment, especially among minority youths, grew markedly higher than among whites. The incomes of employed minorities was significantly lower than that of whites. The quality of education deteriorated. School dropout rates rose precipitously. Infant mortality rates reached alarming levels. Decent, affordable housing became scarce. More and more children were born to unwed mothers. Drug and alcohol use became endemic. Crime and the fear of crime soared out of control.

The convergence of these factors produced a vicious circle. The police, regardless of the era or the strategic paradigm, must, along with families and other community institutions, concern themselves with crime and the fear of crime. The inner cities, where families, schools, jobs, and other community institutions were disintegrating at a rapid pace, presented the police with the most serious crime problems of all. But the police, because of a gross underrepresentation of minorities among their ranks, a lack of sensitivity and understanding of minority concerns and culture, and, therefore, a lack of community support, were least able to deal effectively in the inner cities—precisely where they were needed most.

Frustrated and angry, many blacks came to see the police as symbolizing the entire "system"—those institutions and resources that had been so unresponsive to their needs. Tensions rose, culminating in the series of riots in America's inner cities during the middle and late 1960s. Many Americans had their first glimpse of ghettos as they burned through the night. Reflecting the nature and extent of the underlying problems, Senator Robert Kennedy observed, after visiting the scene of the Watts riot, "There is no point in telling Negroes to observe the law . . . It has almost always been used against them." Despite the tragic destructiveness of those riots, they did concentrate the minds of the nation's leaders wonderfully. In 1967, President Johnson appointed the National Advisory Commission on Civil Disorders (the Kerner Commission) to investigate the causes of the disorder and to recommend solutions. In a trenchant analysis, the commission report concluded that "Our nation is moving toward two societies, one black, one white—separate and unequal."[45] Essentially, they said, what lay behind the riots was a long historical pattern of racism on the part of whites in America. In one of the most forceful passages of their report, the commissioners observed:

> What white Americans have never fully understood—but what a Negro
> can never forget—is that white society is deeply implicated in the

ghetto. White institutions created it, white institutions maintain it, and white society condones it.[46]

Specifically, the Kerner Commission found that many of the riots had been precipitated by police actions, often cases of insensitivity, sometimes incidents of outright brutality. They saw an atmosphere of hostility and cynicism reinforced by a widespread belief among many blacks in a "double standard" of justice and protection. More generally, they concluded that:

> In many ways the policeman only symbolizes much deeper problems.
> The policeman in the ghetto is a symbol not only of law, but of the entire system of law enforcement and criminal justice.[47]

The report offered five basic suggestions to address this situation:

- Change operations in the inner city to ensure proper officer conduct and to eliminate abrasive practices.
- Provide adequate police protection to inner city residents to eliminate the high level of fear and crime.
- Create mechanisms through which citizens can obtain effective responses to their grievances.
- Produce policy guidelines to assist police in avoiding behaviors that would create tension with inner city residents.
- Develop community support for law enforcement.

Fearful that new conflagrations would occur otherwise, and responding in many cases to newly elected black and progressive white mayors, many departments followed the commission's recommendations. As a result, a number of improvements have occurred that have reduced the barriers between the police and the inner city. Many more blacks and other minorities are now patrolling our streets. Strict rules against the unnecessary use of weapons, brutality, harassment, verbal abuse, and discourtesy have been promulgated and enforced. The use of aggressive patrol techniques has been curtailed, restricted to those situations in which it is justified. Steps have been taken to ensure adequate patrol coverage and rapid response to calls for service from inner city areas. Open, impartial, and prompt grievance mechanisms have been established. Policy guidelines have been implemented to direct officers' discretion in potentially tense situations. New approaches—storefront offices, adopting (or even organizing) neighborhood groups, addressing the causes of fear—have been put into effect to improve relations with the community.

Because of these changes, the relationship between the police and citizens has improved considerably in the last several years—to a large extent in white middle-class neighborhoods, to a lesser extent in the inner city. Any transition to an era of community policing will be both a cause and an effect of these improvements. But such a transition is far from complete in the inner city. A recent assessment by the Commission on the Cities found that, despite a brief period of improvement, the conditions that produced the dissolution of ghetto communities are actually getting worse. "Quiet riots," the report concludes, are occurring in America's central cities: unemployment, poverty, social disorganization, segregation, housing and school deterioration, and crime are worse now than ever before.[48] These "quiet riots," although not as alarming or as noticeable to outsiders as those of the 1960s, are even more destructive of human life. Under such conditions, it is unreasonable to expect that the residents of the inner city will have the characteristics—whether social, economic, or political—that are required to sustain the partnership required of the community policing approach.

Furthermore, although the police are better prepared to deal with residents of the inner city than they were 20 years ago, they are far from having totally bridged the chasm that has separated them from minorities—especially blacks—for over 200 years. There are still too few black officers, at all levels. Racism still persists within contemporary police departments. Regardless of rules and guidelines, inappropriate behavior on the streets still occurs. Complaints about differential treatment, patrol coverage, and response time persist. And empirical studies have shown that community-oriented approaches that are effective in most neighborhoods work less well, or not at all, in areas inhabited by low-income blacks and other minority groups.

We welcome the prospect of entering the community era of policing. In a dramatic way, this represents a return to the first principles of policing as established in London in 1829. As Critchley so aptly put it, "From the start, the police was to be . . . in tune with the people, understanding the people, belonging to the people, and drawing its strength from the people."[49] Once community policing becomes a pervasive reality, we will have finally approximated the attainment of that goal. We have begun to bring such fundamental changes about in many of our nation's police departments. But because of the devastation afflicting our inner cities and the inability of our police to relate to those neighborhoods, the areas that most require a transition to the community era will unfortunately be the last to experience such a change.

❖ SUMMARY ❖

Kelling and Moore have contributed a valuable addition to our repertoire of concepts for understanding the strategic history of American policing.

Their interpretation of the shifts in policing from a political to a reform to a community era provides useful insights. It is our contention, however, that the applicability of this interpretation is confined largely to the white majority communities of our nation. For blacks, and to a lesser extent other minority groups, the utility of this analysis is quite limited. During the political era, for example, blacks were completely powerless, leaving them unable to exert the influence necessary to affect police strategy. According to the paradigm Kelling and Moore posit to have prevailed in the reform era, police strategy was determined largely on the basis of law, which left blacks almost completely unprotected. Finally, the community era requires an empowered, cohesive community to be able to deal with a sensitive, responsive police agency; neither precondition prevails in many contemporary minority neighborhoods.

Significant progress has been made, however. Large numbers of blacks and other minorities have joined—and in many cases have become leaders of—our major departments. The use of violence by police against minorities has declined dramatically in the last decade. Special efforts have been made to provide training to make our police officers sensitive to the needs and concerns of minority communities. Enlightened, better educated police leadership has opened the profession to new approaches and ideas. The rising popularity of community-oriented policing will undoubtedly further improve the relationship between the police and minorities.

We think it is a particularly hopeful sign in this regard that many of the most articulate proponents of community policing are themselves African-American police executives. Their unswerving emphasis, in their statements of values, on the protection of constitutional rights and the protection of all citizens, gives us reason to be optimistic about the future of policing.

Nevertheless, the history of American police strategies cannot be separated from the history of the nation as a whole. Unfortunately, our police, and all of our other institutions, must contend with many bitter legacies from that larger history. No paradigm—and no society—can be judged satisfactory until those legacies have been confronted directly.

Notes

[1] Howard Zinn, *The Politics of History* (Boston: Beacon Press, 1970), 102.

[2] George L. Kelling and Mark H. Moore, "The Evolving Strategy of Policing," *Perspectives on Policing*, No. 4. (Washington, D.C.: National Institute of Justice and Harvard University, November 1988).

[3] Robert M. Fogelson, *Big City Police* (Cambridge: Harvard University Press, 1977); J. F. Richardson, *Urban Police in the United States* (Port Washington, New York: National University Publications, 1974).

[4] Roger Lane, *Policing the City: Boston, 1822–1885* (Cambridge: Harvard University Press, 1967); E. A. Savage, *A Chronological History of the Boston Watch and Police, from 1631–1865*. Available on Library of American Civilization fiche 13523, 1865.

[5] J. Flinn, *History of the Chicago Police from the Settlement of the Community to the Present Time* (Montclair, New Jersey: Patterson Smith, 1975).

[6] J. Schneider, *Detroit and the Problem of Order, 1830–1880: A Geography of Crime, Riot, and Policing* (Lincoln: University of Nebraska, 1980).

[7] J. F. Richardson, *The New York Police: Colonial Times to 1901* (New York: Oxford University Press, 1970).

[8] Samuel Walker, *A Critical History of Police Reform: The Emergence of Professionalism* (Lexington, Massachusetts: Lexington Books, 1977), 4–6.

[9] Richardson, *Urban Police*, op. cit. supra, Note 3, p. 19.

[10] Walker, *A Critical History*, op. cit. supra, Note 8.

[11] P. L. Reichel, "Southern slave patrols as a transitional police type," *American Journal of Policing*, 7, (2): 51–77.

[12] T. Cooper, ed., *Statutes at Large of South Carolina*, v. 3, part 2 (Columbia, South Carolina: A. S. Johnston, 1838), 568.

[13] A. Candler, ed., *The Colonial Records of the State of Georgia*, v. 18 (Atlanta: Chas. P. Byrd, State Printer, 1910), 225.

[14] Alabama: W. L. Rose, ed., *A Documentary History of Slavery in North America* (New York: Oxford University Press, 1976). Arkansas: O. W. Taylor, *Negro Slavery in Arkansas* (Durham, North Carolina: Duke University, 1958). Georgia: R. B. Flanders, *Plantation Slavery in Georgia* (Cos Cob, Connecticut: John E. Edwards, 1967); B. Wood, *Slavery in Colonial Georgia* (Athens: University of Georgia Press, 1984). Kentucky: J. W. Coleman, Jr., *Slavery Times in Kentucky* (New York: Johnson Reprint Company, 1940); I. E. McDougle, *Slavery in Kentucky 1792–1865* (Westport, Connecticut: Negro Universities Press, 1970). Louisiana: S. Bacon, *The Early Development of American Municipal Police: A Study of the Evolution of Formal Controls in a Changing Society*, unpublished dissertation, Yale University, University Microfilms No. 66-06844 (1939); J. G. Taylor, *Negro Slavery in Louisiana* (New York: Negro Universities Press, 1963); E. R. Williams, Jr., "Slave patrol ordinances of St. Tammany Parish, Louisiana, 1835–1838," *Louisiana History*, v. 13 (1972), 399–411. Mississippi: C. S. Sydnor, *Slavery in Mississippi* (New York: Appleton Century Co., 1933). Missouri: H. A. Trexler, "Slavery in Missouri: 1804–1865," in H. Trexler, *Slavery in the States: Selected Essays* (New York: Negro Universities Press, 1969). North Carolina: G. G. Johnson, *Ante-bellum North Carolina: A Social History* (Chapel Hill: University of North Carolina, 1937). Tennessee: C. P. Patterson, *The Negro in Tennessee, 1790–1865* (New York: Negro Universities Press, 1968); C. C. Mooney, *Slavery in Tennessee* (Westport, Connecticut: Negro Universities Press, 1971). Virginia: J. Ballagh, Jr., *A History of Slavery in Virginia* (New York: Johnson Reprint Co., 1968); A. Stewart, "Colonel Alexander's slaves resist the patrol," in W. L. Rose, ed., *A Documentary History of Slavery in North America* (New York: Oxford University Press, 1976).

[15] B. Wood, op. cit. supra, Note 14, pp. 123–4.

[16] P. S. Foner, *History of Black Americans: From Africa to the Emergence of the Cotton Kingdom* (Westport, Connecticut: Greenwood, 1975), 206.

[17] Richardson, *Urban Police*, op. cit. supra, Note 3, p. 21.

[18] I. Berlin, *Slaves Without Masters: The Free Negro in the Antebellum South* (New York: Pantheon Books, 1974), 316–17.

[19] *Ibid.*, p. 319.

[20] L. F. Litwack, *North of Slavery: The Negro in the Free States, 1790–1860* (Chicago: University of Chicago Press, 1961), 3.

[21] Berlin, *op. cit. supra*, Note 18, p. 330.

[22] Litwack, *North of Slavery, op. cit. supra*, Note 20, p. 97.

[23] C. V. Woodward, *The Strange Career of Jim Crow* (New York: Oxford University Press, 1966), 17.

[24] E. F. Foner, *Reconstruction: America's Unfinished Revolution, 1863–1877* (New York: Harper and Row, 1988), 4–5.

[25] *Ibid.*, pp. 66–67.

[26] *Ibid.*, pp. 199–200.

[27] *Ibid.*, p. 201.

[28] *Ibid.*, p. 203.

[29] *Ibid.*, p. 204.

[30] M. Delaney, "Colored brigades, 'negro specials' and colored policemen: A history of blacks in American police departments," unpublished manuscript, no date: 12.

[31] J. W. Blassingame, *Black New Orleans, 1860–1880* (Chicago: University of Chicago Press, 1973), 244.

[32] H. N. Rabinowitz, *Race Relations in the Urban South, 1865–1890* (Urbana: University of Illinois Press, 1980), 41.

[33] V. L. Wharton, *The Negro in Mississippi, 1865–1890* (New York: Harper and Row, 1965), 167.

[34] Walker, *A Critical History, op. cit. supra*, Note 8, p. 10.

[35] Delaney, "Colored brigades," *op. cit. supra*, Note 30, p. 20.

[36] R. Lane, *Roots of Violence in Black Philadelphia: 1860–1900* (Cambridge: Harvard University Press, 1986), 60–67.

[37] *Ibid.*, pp. 64–65.

[38] President's Commission on Law Enforcement and Administration of Justice, *Task Force Report: The Police* (Washington, D.C.: U.S. Government Printing Office, 1967), 170.

[39] E. F. Foner, *Reconstruction, op. cit. supra*, Note 24, p. 342.

[40] Fogelson, *Big City Police, op. cit. supra*, Note 3, p. 250.

[41] *Ibid.*, p. 251.

[42] President's Commission on Law Enforcement and Administration of Justice, *Task Force Report: Science and Technology* (Washington, D.C.: U.S. Government Printing Office, 1967), 216–28.

[43] Fogelson, *op. cit. supra*, Note 3, p. 251.

[44] *Report of the National Advisory Commission on Civil Disorders* (Washington, D.C.: U.S. Government Printing Office, 1968), 321.

[45] *Ibid.*, p. 1.

[46] *Ibid.*, p. 2.

[47] *Ibid.*, p. 299.

[48] F. R. Harris and R. Wilkins, *Quiet Riots: Race and Poverty in the United States* (New York: Pantheon Books, 1988).

[49] T. A. Critchley, *A History of Police in England and Wales, 1900–1966* (London: Constable and Company, Ltd., 1967), 46.

"Broken Windows" and Fractured History
The Use and Misuse of History in Recent Police Patrol Analysis

Samuel Walker

A fresh burst of creativity marks current thinking about police patrol in the United States. This revival follows a period of doubt and disorientation in the late 1970s when recent research shattered traditional assumptions about patrol strategy. The most notable proposal for a reorientation of police patrol is set forth in ''Broken Windows'' by James Q. Wilson and George L. Kelling. Drawing partly on recent patrol experiments and partly on a rethinking of police history, Wilson and Kelling propose a return to what they see as an older ''watchman'' style of policing (Wilson and Kelling, 1982).

This article examines the use of history by Wilson and Kelling in their proposal for reorienting police patrol. Because the historical analysis is central to their argument, its viability may well depend upon how well they have interpreted police history. Kelling develops his view of police history even more explicitly in a subsequent article co-authored with Mark H. Moore (Moore and Kelling, 1983).

We shall argue here that Wilson, Kelling and Moore have misinterpreted police history in several important respects. Their proposal calls for a restoration—a return to a former tradition of police patrol. Joe

Justice Quarterly, 1(1): 75–90. Reprinted with permission of the Academy of Criminal Justice Sciences.

McNamara, Chief of the San Jose police, has already responded to the "broken windows" thesis by arguing that the good old days weren't all that good (McNamara, 1982). This article elaborates upon that point and argues that the tradition of policing cited by Wilson, Kelling and Moore never existed. This does not necessarily mean that the broken windows thesis is completely invalid. But if there is merit in the style of police patrol Wilson and Kelling propose, that style will have to be created anew. There is no viable older tradition to restore. Obviously, this is a far more difficult and challenging proposition than they have suggested.

❖ POLICING AND BROKEN WINDOWS ❖

Broken windows are a metaphor for the deterioration of neighborhoods. A broken window that goes unrepaired is a statement that no one cares enough about the quality of life in the neighborhood to bother fixing the little things that are wrong. While a broken window might be a small thing in and of itself, left unrepaired it becomes an invitation to further neglect. The result is a progressive deterioration of the entire neighborhood. Wilson and Kelling cite research in social psychology where abandoned cars were rapidly vandalized when some sign of prior vandalism invited further destructive acts (Zimbardo, 1969).

Policing in America has failed, Wilson, Kelling and Moore argue, because it has neglected "the little things," the law enforcement equivalents of broken windows. This neglect is the product of the development of an efficiency-oriented, crime control-focused style of policing over the past fifty years. Eric Monkkonen argues that the shift toward crime control began even earlier and was substantially complete by 1920 (Monkkonen, 1981).

Two developments in the 1930s launched a radical reorientation of police patrol. The first was the greatly increased use of the patrol car, which took the patrol officer off the street and isolated him from the public. The second was the development of the Uniform Crime Reports system which then became the basic measure of police "success."

By themselves, these two developments might not have exerted such a profound effect on policing. The crucial difference was the influence of O. W. Wilson who forged a coherent theory of police management in the late 1930s. Wilsonian theory emphasized the suppression of crime as the primary mission of policing. Fulfillment of this mission depended upon maximizing the efficiency of patrol coverage. The automobile allowed a patrol officer to cover his beat more often during one tour of duty, and to do so in a more unpredictable fashion than foot patrol.

Wilson became the leading proponent of one-officer cars, claiming that two single-officer patrol cars were twice as efficient as one two-officer car. He recommended that patrol beats should be organized according to a workload formula which distributed the work evenly among patrol officers. Finally, he concluded that rapid response time would increase apprehensions and generally enhance public satisfaction with police service (Walker, 1977; Fogelson, 1977).

Wilson tirelessly propounded his gospel of efficiency from the late 1930s onward. His text *Police Administration* became "the bible" of police management and instructed an entire generation of police executives (Wilson and McLaren, 1977). Police departments converted almost entirely from foot to automobile patrol, invested enormous sums of money in sophisticated communications equipment, and encouraged members of the public to avail themselves of their service.

Lost in this process were the personal aspects of routine policing. The car isolated officers from the people in the neighborhoods, which became nothing more than a series of "beat assignments" to the officers. The most professionalized departments, in fact, took extra measures to de-personalize policing. Frequent rotation of beat assignments was adopted as a strategy to combat corruption.

The crime control orientation meanwhile caused the police to concentrate on more serious crimes—primarily, the seven felonies that comprised the Crime Index. Significantly, the police actively adopted the UCR system as the measure of their performance. It was not something imposed on them (Manning, 1977). The police lost interest in lesser violations of the law and routine nuisances because they just did not count. These nuisances included drunks, loud and intimidating groups of teenagers, public drug dealing, and the like.[1]

According to Wilson, Kelling and Moore, these nuisances are the "broken windows," the little things that convey the message that no one cares about the quality of life in this neighborhood. Wilson, Kelling and Moore base much of their argument on the recent Newark Foot Patrol Experiment (The Police Foundation, 1981). The presence of officers on foot patrol did not reduce crime, but did make people feel safer. Officers were able to establish and enforce informal rules of behavior for the neighborhood. It was alright to be intoxicated in public but not to pass out in the gutter, for example. Wilson and Kelling also cite with apparent approval the technique used by some Chicago police officers to maintain order in public housing projects: if groups of teenagers were troublesome, the officers would simply chase them away. "We kick ass," one officer explained (Wilson and Kelling, 1982:35).

The "Broken Windows" article argues that policing should be neighborhood-oriented. More officers should be deployed on foot, and those officers should concentrate less on catching criminals and more on enforcing informal neighborhood norms of behavior. To a certain extent it advocates a form of team policing, although with some important differences.

Team policing experiments in the 1970s did not emphasize foot patrol, gave insufficient attention to street-level patrol tactics, and maintained the traditional crime control focus. Indeed, the incompatibility of some elements of team policing with the prevailing organizational structure and management philosophy was one of the factors in the failure of early team policing experiments (Sherman, 1973; U.S. Department of Justice, 1977; Schwartz and Clarren, 1977).

"Broken Windows" offers an alternative model precisely because it focuses on what officers would actually do. It characterizes the recommended style of policing as a return to an earlier (pre-1930s) style of "watchman" or "constabulary" policing. At this point we turn our attention to the historical analysis that underpins this argument.

❖ THE HISTORICAL FRAMEWORK ❖

The historical framework presented by Wilson, Kelling and Moore consists of three components: the near-term, which embraces the last fifteen years; the middle-term, which includes the last fifty years; and the long-term, which involves all of police history before the last fifty years.

Their reading of near-term history is excellent. One of the most important developments of the past fifteen years has unquestionably been the enormous expansion of our knowledge about all aspects of policing. We can now discuss in an informed fashion issues that were *terra incognita* to the staff of the President's Crime Commission (Walker, 1983). The most important findings constitute a systematic demolition of the assumptions underlying O. W. Wilson's approach to police management. We have learned that adding more police or intensifying patrol coverage will not reduce crime and that neither faster response time nor additional detectives will improve clearance rates. Few authorities on policing today could endorse the basic Wilsonian idea that improved management in the deployment of patrol officers or detectives is likely to reduce the crime rate.

Wilson's, Kelling's and Moore's reading of the last fifty years of police history is mixed. They recognize the most significant developments in the period but misinterpret them in important respects. There are substantial implications of this misinterpretation for their proposed style of policing.

The development of American policing from the 1930s through the 1960s was a far more complex process than historians have lead us to believe. Wilson, Kelling and Moore can be excused in large part because they have simply drawn upon the available historical scholarship. We will focus here on two aspects of police history since the 1930s which have not received sufficient attention. The first involves the impact of the patrol car and the second concerns the crime control orientation of policing.

❖ THE TECHNOLOGICAL REVOLUTION ❖

It is indeed true that American police departments largely converted from foot to automobile patrol between the 1930s and the present. We should, of course, be cognizant of the enormous variations that exist even today. Some departments are almost wholly motorized while others, primarily Eastern cities, still make heavy use of foot patrol (Police Executive Research Forum, 1981). And it is also true that car patrols remove officers from the sidewalks, isolate them from casual contacts with ordinary citizens, and damage police-community relations. This analysis is part of the conventional wisdom about policing.

The impact of technology was paradoxical, however. The mid-century revolution in American policing involved not just the patrol car, but the car in conjunction with the telephone and the two-way radio. These served to bring police officers into far more intimate contact with people than ever before. While the patrol car isolated police officers in some respects, the telephone simultaneously increased the degree of contact in other respects. Let us examine this paradox in detail.

In the days of foot patrol, officers had extensive casual contacts with people. But they occurred primarily on the streets or in other public places. The police did not often obtain entry to private residences. The reason for this is obvious: there was no mechanism whereby the ordinary citizen could effectively summon the police. The telephone radically altered that situation with profound ramifications for both policing and public expectations about the quality of life. Stinchcombe (1963) has discussed the impact of privacy considerations on routine police work.

The telephone made it possible for the ordinary citizen to summon the police, and the combination of the two-way radio and the patrol car allowed the police to respond quickly. As we know, the more professional departments acquired a fetish for responding as quickly as possible to all calls. The development of the 911 telephone number was simply the logical conclusion of this effort to advertise and encourage people to use police service. People have in fact availed themselves of this service. The number of calls for service has escalated to the point where serious attention has been given to the idea of restricting or otherwise managing those requests in the last few years (Gay, 1977).

Technology radically alters the nature of police-citizen contacts. Most of those contacts now occur in private residences. Albert Reiss reports that 70% of all police-citizen contacts occur in private places, 12% in semi-public, and 18% in open public places (Reiss, 1971:16). The police not only gain access to private places, but observe the most intimate aspects of peoples' lives, and are asked to handle their most personal problems.

Research has confirmed that the bulk of police work involves domestic disputes and other problems arising from alcohol, drugs, mental illness, and poverty. Officers refer to all this as "bullshit" or "social work" because it is unrelated to what they believe to be their crime control mission.

Police-citizen contacts became increasingly skewed. The police lost contact with "ordinary" people and gained a great deal of contact with "problem" people, who included not just criminal offenders but those with multiple social problems. David Bayley and Harold Mendelsohn once observed that police officers had more direct knowledge about minorities than did the members of any other occupation. This knowledge was a direct product of the heavy demands upon police service placed by low-income and racial minorities (Bayley and Mendelsohn, 1969:156).

Our understanding of the full impact of the telephone on policing remains problematic. Not all experts on policing accept the argument advanced here. Some argue that the police were indeed intimately involved in people's lives prior to the advent of the telephone.[2] Unfortunately, there is no empirical evidence that would permit the resolution of this question. Prior to the late 1950s, there were no observational studies of police patrol activities and thus we have no reliable evidence on what American police officers did on patrol in the pre-telephone era.[3]

❖ THE REVOLUTION IN PUBLIC EXPECTATIONS ❖

One consequence of the technological revolution in policing has been a parallel revolution in public expectations about the quality of life. The availability of police service created and fed a demand for those services. The establishment of the modern police in the early nineteenth century was an initial phase of this process, which created the expectation that a certain level of public order would, or at least should, prevail (Silver, 1967).

The technological revolution of the mid-twentieth century generated a quantum leap in those expectations. Because there was now a mechanism for getting someone (the police) to "do something" about minor disorders and nuisances, people came to expect that they should not have to put up with such minor irritations. Thus, the general level of expectations about the quality of life—the amount of noise, the presence of "strange" or "undesirable" people—has undergone an enormous change. Three generations of Americans have learned or at least have come to believe that they should not have to put up with certain problems.

The police are both the source and the victims of this revolution. They have stimulated higher levels of public expectations by their very presence and their policy of more readily available services. At the same time they are the prisoners of their own creation, swamped with an enormous service call workload. The recent effort to restrict or somehow manage this workload faces the problem of a public that expects rapid police response for any and every problem as a matter of right.

Documenting changes in public expectations concerning the police is difficult given the absence of reliable data about public attitudes or police practices prior to the late 1950s and early 1960s. Several indicators do provide evidence of short-term changes in public expectations. The development of three-digit (911) emergency phone numbers for the police increased the number of service calls. In Omaha, Nebraska, for example, the number of patrol car dispatches increased by 36% between 1969 and 1971, presumably as a result of a new 911 phone number (Walker, 1983:110). These figures represent the dispatch of a patrol car, not the number of incoming calls. Omaha police officials estimate that about 35% of all calls do not result in a dispatch.

Additional evidence is found in data on the number of civilian complaints about police misconduct. In New York City, for example, the number of complaints filed with the Civilian Complaint Review Board (CCRB) increased from about 200 per year in 1960–62 to just over 2000 per year in 1967–68 and more than 3000 annually in 1971–74. It would be difficult to believe that the conduct of New York City police officers deteriorated by a factor of 10 or 15 during this period. Rather, the increase is probably the result of a lower threshold of tolerance for police misconduct on the part of citizens and the increased availability of an apparent remedy for perceived misconduct.

During the period under discussion, the procedures of the New York CCRB were reorganized several times. Each reorganization facilitated complaint filing and at the same time heightened public awareness of the availability of this particular remedy (Kahn, 1975:113). The data on civilian complaints supports the argument made herein concerning police services generally: the availability of a service or remedy stimulates demand for that service, thereby altering basic expectations.

❖ THE MYTHOLOGY OF CRIME CONTROL ❖

The conventional wisdom states that police organize their efforts around the goal of crime control. Wilson, Kelling and Moore restate this conventional wisdom, but the matter is a bit more complex.

There is an important distinction between the self-image of the police and the day-to-day reality of routine policing (Goldstein, 1977). The emphasis on crime control is and has been largely a matter of what the police say they are doing. Peter Manning argues persuasively that the police consciously created and manipulated this self-image as a way of establishing greater professional and political autonomy (Manning, 1977).

As we have seen, however, the day-to-day reality of policing contradicted this self-image. The sharp contrast between the crime-fighting imagery of the police and the peacekeeping reality of police activities was one of the first and most important findings of the flood of police research that began in the 1960s. When Wilson, Kelling and Moore suggest that the police are completely crime control-oriented they seriously misrepresent the nature of contemporary policing.

The discrepancy between crime control imagery and operational reality also becomes evident when we look more closely at how police departments utilize their resources. The most recent Survey of Police Operational and Administrative Practices reveals enormous variations among departments (Police Executive Research Forum, 1981). Many still distribute their patrol officers equally among three shifts, ignoring even the most rudimentary workload formulas, which were first developed by O. W. Wilson over forty years ago (Wilson and McLaren, 1977: Appendix J). Departments typically do not revise the boundaries of their patrol districts on a regular basis. Districts remain unchanged for ten or twenty years, or longer. Meanwhile, the composition of the urban environment changes radically, as older areas are depopulated, new residential areas created, and so on.

❖ THE QUESTION OF LEGITIMACY ❖

The most important long-term development in American policing, according to Wilson, Kelling and Moore, has been the loss of political legitimacy. There can be little doubt that legitimacy, by which we mean acceptance of police authority by the public, is a major problem today.

The interpretation of police history offered by Wilson, Kelling and Moore, which purports to explain how that legitimacy was lost, is seriously flawed. The evidence completely contradicts the thrust of their argument.

The police in the nineteenth century were not merely the "adjuncts" of the machine, as Robert Fogelson (1977) suggests, but were central cogs in it. Wilson, Kelling and Moore maintain that this role offered certain benefits for the police, which reformers and historians alike have overlooked.

As cogs in the machine, the police served the immediate needs of the different neighborhoods. Political control was highly decentralized and local city councilmen or ward bosses exercised effective control over the police. Thus, the police carried out a wide range of services. Historians have rediscovered the social welfare role of the police, providing food and lodging for vagrants (Walker, 1977; Monkkonen, 1981). The police also performed political errands and were the means by which certain groups and individuals were able to corrupt the political process. These errands included open electioneering, rounding up the loyal voters, and harassing the opponents. Police also enforced the narrow prejudices of their constituents, harassing "undesirables" or discouraging any kind of "unwelcome" behavior.

Wilson, Kelling and Moore concede that there was a lack of concern for due process, but argue there was an important trade-off. By virtue of serving the immediate needs and narrow prejudices of the neighborhoods, the police gained an important degree of political legitimacy. They were perceived as faithful servants and enjoyed the resulting benefits. All of this was destroyed by the reforms of the twentieth century. The patrol car removed officers from the streets, while the new "professional" style dictated an impersonal type of policing. Legal concerns with due process denied officers the ability to use the tactics of rough justice by which they had enforced neighborhood community norms.

This historical analysis is central to the reorientation of policing presented in the "Broken Windows" article. Wilson, Kelling and Moore propose that the lost political legitimacy could be re-established by what they view as the older "watchman" style of policing. Unfortunately, this historical analysis is pure fantasy.

Historians are unanimous in their conclusion that the police were at the center of urban political conflict in the nineteenth century. In many instances policing was the paramount issue and in some cases the only issue. Historians disagree only on their interpretation of the exact nature of this political conflict. The many experiments with different forms of administrative control over the police (the last of which survives only in

Missouri) were but one part of this long and bitter struggle for political control (Walker, 1977; Fogelson, 1977).

To say that there was political conflict over the police means that the police lacked political legitimacy. Their authority was not accepted by the citizenry. Wilson, Kelling and Moore are seriously in error when they suggest that the police enjoyed substantial legitimacy in the pre-technology era.

The lack of legitimacy is further illustrated by the nature of the conflicts surrounding the police. Non-enforcement of the various laws designed to control drinking was the issue that most often roused the so-called "reformers" to action. Alcohol consumption was a political issue with many dimensions. In some respects it was an expression of ethnic conflict, pitting sobersided Anglo-Saxons against the heavy-drinking Irish and Germans. Drinking was also a class issue. Temperance and, later, prohibition advocates tended either to come from the middle class or at least define themselves in terms of the values of hard work, sobriety, thrift and upward mobility (Gusfield, 1963). When nineteenth century Americans fought over the police and the enforcement of the drinking laws, that battle expressed the deepest social conflicts in American society.

In one of the finest pieces of historical scholarship on the American police, Wilbur Miller explores the question of legitimacy from an entirely different angle (Miller, 1977). The great difference between the London and New York City police was precisely the extent to which officers in New York were denied the grant of legitimacy enjoyed by their counterparts in London. Miller further argues that the problem of legitimacy was individualized in New York City. Each officer faced challenges to his personal authority and had to assert his authority on a situational level.

Miller does not argue that challenges to police legitimacy were patterned according to class, ethnicity or race. Thus, an Irish-American cop was just as likely to be challenged by a fellow countryman as he was by someone of a different ethnic background. To be sure, the poor, political radicals, blacks, and other people deemed "undesirable" were victimized more often by the police than were other groups, but it does not follow that the police enjoyed unquestioned authority in the eyes of those people who were members of the same class and ethnic groups as police officers.

❖ THE MYTH OF THE WATCHMAN ❖

With their argument that the nineteenth century police enjoyed political legitimacy, Wilson, Kelling and Moore have resurrected in slightly different garb the old myth of the friendly cop on the beat. They offer this older "watchman" style of policing as a viable model for contemporary policing. Quite apart from the broader question of political legitimacy, their argument turns on the issue of on-the-street police behavior.

Historians have not yet reconstructed a full picture of police behavior in the nineteenth century. At best, historians can make inferences about this behavior from surviving records. None of the historical accounts published to date presents a picture of policing that could be regarded as a viable model for the present.

What do we know about routine policing in the days before the patrol car? There is general agreement that officers did not necessarily do much work at all. Given the primitive state of communications technology, patrol officers were almost completely on their own and able to avoid effective supervision (Rubinstein, 1974). Evidence suggests that evasion of duty was commonplace. We also know that corruption was the norm. Mark Haller (1976) suggests that corruption was possibly the primary objective of all of municipal government, not just the police department.

Wilbur Miller (1977), meanwhile, places the matter of police brutality in a new and convincing light. His argument that brutality was a response to the refusal of citizens to grant the police legitimacy speaks directly to the point raised by Wilson, Kelling and Moore.

Recently some historians have attempted to draw a more systematic picture of police law enforcement activities. The most convincing picture is drawn by Lawrence Friedman and Robert Percival (1981) in their study of the Oakland police between 1870 and 1910. They characterize police arrest patterns as a giant trawling operation. The typical arrestee was a white, working class adult male who was drunk and was arrested for intoxication, disturbing the peace, or some related offense. But there was nothing systematic about police operations. The people swept up into their net were simply unlucky—there was no reason why they should have been arrested rather than others whose behavior was essentially the same. Nor was it apparent, in Friedman's and Percival's view, that the police singled out any particular categories of people for especially systematic harassment.

The argument offered by Wilson, Kelling and Moore turns in part on the question of purpose: what the police saw themselves doing. Historians have established that police officers had a few purposes. The first was to get and hold the job. The second was to exploit the possibilities for graft that the job offered. A third was to do as little actual patrol work as possible. A fourth involved surviving on the street, which meant establishing and maintaining authority in the face of hostility and overt challenges to that authority. Finally, officers apparently felt obliged to go through the motions of "real" police work by arresting occasional miscreants.

We do not find in this picture any conscious purpose of fighting crime or serving neighborhood needs. That is precisely the point made by Progressive era reformers when they indicted the police for inefficiency. Wilson, Kelling and Moore have no grounds for offering this as a viable model for contemporary policing. Chief McNamara is right: the good old days were not that good.

The watchman style of policing described by Wilson, Kelling and Moore can also be challenged from a completely different perspective. The idea that the police served the needs of local neighborhoods and thereby enjoyed political legitimacy is based on a highly romanticized view of nineteenth century neighborhood life. Urban neighborhoods were not stable and homogeneous little villages nestled in the city. They were heterogeneous, and the rate of geographic mobility was even higher than contemporary rates. Albert Reiss (1971:209–210) in *Police and the Public* critiques recent "community control" proposals on these very grounds: they are based on the erroneous impression that neighborhoods are stable, homogeneous and relatively well-defined.

❖ SUMMARY AND CONCLUSIONS ❖

In "Broken Windows," James Q. Wilson and George Kelling offer a provocative proposal for reorienting police patrol. Their argument is based primarily on an historical analysis of American policing. They propose a return to a watchman style of policing, which they claim existed before the advent of crime control oriented policing in the 1930s. This historical analysis is further developed in a subsequent article by Kelling and Moore (1983).

In this article we have examined the historical analysis used by these three authors. We find it flawed on several fundamental points.

First, the depersonalization of American policing from the 1930s onward has been greatly exaggerated. While the patrol car did isolate the police in some respects, the telephone brought about a more intimate form of contact between police and citizen by allowing police officers to enter private residences and involving them in private disputes and problems.

Second, the crime control orientation of the police has been greatly exaggerated. Crime control is largely a matter of police rhetoric and self-image. Day-to-day policing is, on the other hand, primarily a matter of peacekeeping.

Third, there is no historical evidence to support the contention that the police formerly enjoyed substantial political legitimacy. To the contrary, all the evidence suggests that the legitimacy of the police was one of the major political controversies throughout the nineteenth century and well into the twentieth.

Fourth, the watchman style of policing referred to by Wilson, Kelling and Moore is just as inefficient and corrupt as the reformers accuse it of being. It does not involve any conscious purpose to serve neighborhood needs and hardly serves as a model for revitalized contemporary policing.

Where does this leave us? We should not throw the proverbial baby out with the bath water. The fact that Wilson and Kelling construct their "Broken Windows" thesis on a false and heavily romanticized view of the past does not by itself invalidate their concept of a revitalized police patrol. They correctly interpret the lessons of recent police research. Suppression of crime is a will-of-the-wisp which the police should no longer pursue. Enhancement of public feelings of safety, however, does appear to be within the grasp of the police. A new form of policing based on the apparent lessons of the Newark Foot Patrol Experiment, the failures of team policing experiments, and the irrelevance of most official police-community relations programs seems to be a goal that is both worth pursuing and feasible.

Our main point here is simply that such a revitalized form of policing would represent something entirely new in the history of the American police. There is no older tradition worthy of restoration. A revitalized, community-oriented policing would have to be developed slowly and painfully.

There should be no mistake about the difficulty of such a task. Among other things, recent research on the police clearly demonstrates the enormous difficulty in changing either police officer behavior and/or the structure and process of police organization. Yet at the same time, the history reviewed here does suggest that fundamental long-term changes in policing are indeed possible. Change is a constant; shaping that change in a positive way is the challenge.

Notes

[1] James Fyfe argues that prosecutorial and judicial indifference to minor "quality of life" offenses is also responsible for neighborhood deterioration and that the police should not be singled out as the major culprits. By implication, he suggests that reorienting the police role would be futile without simultaneously reorienting the priorities of prosecutors and judges. Personal correspondence, James Fyfe to Walker.

[2] Lawrence W. Sherman accepts this view and dissents from the argument advanced in this article. Personal correspondence, Lawrence W. Sherman to Walker.

[3] The debate is conducted largely on the basis of circumstantial evidence. Sherman, for example, believes that literary evidence is a reliable guide to past police practices and cites *A Tree Grows in Brooklyn* as one useful example. Personal correspondence, Sherman to Walker.

References

Bayley, D., & Mendelsohn, H. (1969). *Minorities and the Police*. New York: The Free Press.

Fogelson, R. (1977). *Big City Police*. Cambridge: Harvard University Press.

Friedman, L. M., & Percival, R.V. (1981). *The Roots of Justice*. Chapel Hill: University of North Carolina Press.

Gay, W. (1977). Improving Patrol Productivity. *Routine Patrol*, Vol. I. Washington D.C.: Government Printing Office.

Goldstein, H. (1977). *Policing a Free Society*. Cambridge: Ballinger.

Gusfield, J. (1963). *Symbolic Crusade: Status Politics and the American Temperance Movement*. Urbana: University of Illinois Press.

Haller, M. (1976). Historical roots of police behavior: Chicago, 1890-1925. *Law and Society Review*, 10 (Winter):303-324.

Kahn, R. (1975). Urban reform and police accountability in New York City, 1950-1974. In Lineberry, R. L., and Masotti, L. H. (eds.). *Urban Problems and Public Policy*. Lexington: Lexington Books.

McNamara, J. D. (1982). Dangerous nostalgia for the cop on the beat. *San Jose Mercury-News*, May 2.

Manning, P. K. (1977). *Police Work*. Cambridge: MIT Press.

Miller, W. (1977). *Cops and Bobbies*. Chicago: University of Chicago Press.

Monkkonen, E. (1981). *Police in Urban America, 1860-1920*. Cambridge: Cambridge University Press.

Moore, M.H., & Kelling, G.L. (1983). To serve and protect: learning from police history. *The Public Interest*, 70:49-65.

Police Executive Research Forum (1981). *Survey of Police Operational and Administrative Practices—1981*. Washington: Police Executive Research Forum.

Police Foundation (1981). *The Newark Foot Patrol Experiment*. Washington D.C.: The Police Foundation.

Reiss, A. (1971). *The Police and the Public*. New Haven: Yale University Press.

Rubinstein, J. (1974). *City Police*. New York: Ballantine Books.

Schwartz, A. I., & Clarren, S. N. (1977). *The Cincinnati Team Policing Experiment*. Washington D.C.: The Police Foundation.

Sherman, L. W. (1973). *Team Policing: Seven Case Studies*. Washington D.C.: The Police Foundation.

Silver, A. (1967). The demand for order in civil society. In Bordua, David J. (ed.). *The Police: Six Sociological Essays*. New York: John Wiley.

Stinchcombe, A. (1963). Institutions of privacy in the determination of police administrative practice. *American Journal of Sociology*, 69 (September):150-160.

U.S. Department of Justice (1977). *Neighborhood Team Policing*. Washington D.C.: Government Printing Office.

Walker, S. (1983). *The Police in America: An Introduction*. New York: McGraw-Hill.

———— (1977). *A Critical History of Police Reform: The Emergence of Professionalization*. Lexington: Lexington Books.

Wilson, J. Q., & Kelling, G.L. (1982). Broken windows: police and neighborhood safety. *Atlantic Monthly*, 249 (March):29–38.

Wilson, O. W., & McLaren, R. C. (1977). *Police Administration*, 4th ed. New York: McGraw-Hill.

Zimbardo, P. G. (1989). The human choice: individuation, reason, and order versus deindividuation, impulse, and chaos. In Arnold, W. J., & Levine, D. (eds.). *Nebraska Symposium on Motivation*. Lincoln: University of Nebraska Press.

4

Revising the Histories and Futures of Policing

Victor G. Strecher

$\mathbb{A}$ generation ago it could be said that policing was an occupation without a written, generally known history and its academic counterpart a field with a one-book theoretical foundation. What was commonly known of policing penetrated the past barely beyond the collective memories of elderly police practitioners and journalists on the police beat. Elements of history are as subject to impediments to long-term retention as are elements of human memory. That is, even if the historical perceptions were documented in their time, it remains to find them and bring them into historical annals.

Learning history is generally considered indispensable to our understanding of the "present," which is little more than an elusive knife-edge between past and future—or in a practical sense, a thin, recent slice of the past. Although we may be unconsciously motivated by a wish to predict, to extrapolate the strands of change, we more often claim to read history for itself rather than as prelude to the future. On the other hand, the study of history can be oriented explicitly toward applications. Social policy analysis and formulation, for example, often rest on an understanding of antecedent policies and events, which, if rigorously documented, may be termed histories.

Police Forum, 1991, 1(1): 1–9. Reprinted with permission of the Academy of Criminal Justice Sciences.

The few published works of the 19th century (e.g. Baker, Savage, Costello, Flinn, Hale, Roe) and early 20th century (e.g. Fosdick, Fuld, Hamilton, Hickey, Maltby, Peck, Russell) were largely anecdotal, richly subjective and occasionally self-serving glimpses rather than systematic histories. The contemporary, serious study of police history had not yet commenced (although Hale, Fosdick and Fuld did provide cross-sectional views of policing in their times). Fortunately, the past fifteen years have seen the beginnings of a significant history of policing in the works of Gene and Elaine Carte, Robert Fogelson, Mark Haller, Sidney Harring, David Johnson, Roger Lane, Wilbur Miller, Eric Monkkonen, James Richardson, Richard Terrill and Samuel Walker. Collateral historical insights have derived from works of Egon Bittner, Peter Manning, Arthur Niederhoffer, Louis Radelet, Albert Reiss, Thomas Repetto, Jerome Skolnick and others.

Contributing to the available body of knowledge is The Executive Session on Policing, a panel of distinguished thinkers in the field of policing, which meets periodically at Harvard. The series of monographs resulting from these sessions has an explicit policy analysis focus. However, historical materials are referenced almost continuously as the series describes the past, present and possible future of American policing. The fourth monograph in the series, "The Evolving Strategy of Policing," by George L. Kelling and Mark H. Moore, depends heavily on interpretations of history.

But histories are not written equally, nor are the subsequent uses of historical materials. Both can differ in depth, scope, methodology and quality of insight. The focus of this article is an examination of the extent to which uses of history differ in purpose and whether these differences affect our understanding of history. "The Evolving Strategy of Policing" may best exemplify the *revising* of police history. If history is misread, there is a potential for distortion of our understanding of the present and of correspondingly inappropriate policy recommendations for the future.

The Kelling/Moore monograph will be assessed in relation to the accuracy of its use of historical materials in support of policy analysis and development. One of the questions to be raised is whether historical depictions which are impelled by an explicit interest in policy applications might not become inherently distorted by that interest. This discussion should be considered an exploratory probe of this question and some of its related issues.

❖ HISTORIES AND "ERAS" ❖

As in the case of many other histories of American policing, the Kelling/Moore article discovers, labels and characterizes "eras" in the development of law enforcement. The article describes three periods in the development of policing: "political," "reform," and "community." Before treating in detail the characterizations of the "eras," a comment is offered about the three-era framework itself. The assertion that early American policing (1840s—early 1900s) was political stirs no objections, considering the very creation of the United States and its formation of governmental institutions was intensely political, as any revolution and its aftermath are apt to be. However, the implication of the authors' sequence—"political" policing supplanted by an era of reform, in turn replaced by a sharp turn toward bonding with the community—seems historiographically unsound, whether referring to ideas, events or practices. These "eras" have the appearance of three neatly encased sausages linked tenuously or not at all by social continuities of American history. There is little reference to social context and no clear recognition of the interplay of change and continuity in social institutions, roles, values, structures, economics, technology and political development. The authors delineate three discrete pieces of police history, each somehow isolated from the other and from all other elements of social history. Williams and Murphy sharply criticized the Kelling/Moore scheme for ignoring much of the social context of the three periods, particularly rural and minority social history.

Another objection to the three-era model is that nothing in the nature of the first two suggests the third—community policing—should follow. There is no sense of progression or culmination of a social change trend, no building toward this sudden re-emergence of "community" in America's cities. Is there, in fact, evidence of this trend beyond the assertions of the Harvard panel?

❖ THE POLITICAL ERA ❖

There are two implications of this labeling of the period covering the formation of the first urban police agencies through the early 1900s. First, it raises the question of whether policing was deviantly political or simply part of an era which was inherently political. Policing, after all, was merely one of many governmental services, functions and processes being devised throughout that period. Was the emergence of services such as sanitation, waste disposal, water supply, fire protection, parks and recreation, street construction, welfare, public health, social services and education also beset by political struggles? Were the associated functions of taxation, budgeting, public personnel administration, the emergence of civil service, land-use controls and licensing politicized? The histories of the development of these governmental services and processes are replete with examples of intense, protracted political influences and conflicts.

Secondly, this labeling implies that politics was uniquely manifest only in the political era—that in later eras the influence of politics was eliminated, reduced or displaced by some other social mechanism. The authors failed to distinguish between the primitive sorts of corrupt and machine politics prevalent during the formative years of American local governments and the (only slightly) more subtle but no less prevalent political incursions into policing known throughout the subsequent periods termed "reform" and "community."

"Politics" in the context of the structure of American government (three branches of government and their interdependent accountability model) is an essential element of American local governance and thus necessarily part of the administration of policing. The question is not whether politics has a role in policing, but only what that role should be and when it is legitimately to be exercised. City councils have the duty to appropriate funds but generally not a duty or right to decide who will be promoted to internal police ranks. Councils can pass licensing ordinances but should not tamper with police inspection reports on licensed premises.

The failure of Kelling and Moore to distinguish between this kind of legitimate political involvement and the primitively corrupt machine politics of the 19th and early 20th centuries introduces serious confusion into any discussion of a "political era" and the succeeding eras. If they merely meant the amount, nature and intensity of political intrusion into policing changed, they should have stated that—but then added that inappropriate intrusions continued long into the two subsequent eras. They could have mentioned that the design of American government requires politics at the executive level of policing. The pejorative labeling of "politics" during these early developmental times was carried forward and institutionalized in policing. It eventually became a straw-man symbol around which to organize policing's resistance to any form of political influence over their practices. This symbol of "politics"—assumed to be corrupt and inimical to the proper functioning of dedicated police officers— persists not only in the thinking of police officials but in the beliefs of middle-American culture as well. This earliest period of police development might aptly be renamed the "primitive era," if naming is necessary, and applied equally to all institutions of American local government, rather than singling out the police.

An alternative view of history would assert that cultural knowledge does not somehow disappear on the emergence of new ideas. History (and social change theory) teaches that social innovation is overlaid on existing culture rather than causing it to disappear. Culture is not thrown away. New ideas are continuously joined with old ideas in myriad combinations; values not only change but become more diverse, subtle and shaded in meanings. New institutions emerge from powerful social values (e.g. public education, paid policing) and then endlessly reorganize to reflect shifting values. Social innovation emerges out of complex interactions of technology, institutions, values, creative roles and the human environment. An accurate reading of history would find social change to be a restless network of interaction among variables such as these.

❖ REFORM ERA ❖

Labeling the years between 1930 and 1970 as a period of "police reform" raises several objections. First, the span of the "era" is incorrect at both ends. General governmental reform (including policing) began much earlier, during the 1880s. Popular revulsion to the fiscal and personnel excesses of the Grant administration generated pressures for reform which eventuated in ethical constraints on national, state and local governmental practices. The Pendleton Act, the first attempt to bring civil service and merit principles into federal government (1883), was merely one of the signals of this movement. Fiscal reforms were set in motion, although they were not effective until 1910 in the case of New York City and 1920 in the case of the U.S. Government. These years were notable for the number of police scandals which resulted in the removal of chiefs and moves to bring police operations under more central, executive branch control in the cities. George Hale's Prison and Police Cyclopedia of 1893 contains an astonishing set of commentaries from police chiefs in response to his survey of 1890. Although there is plenty of rough and ready stuff here (as there would be today), it is more than offset by the articulate, socially pragmatic and reform-minded tone of many chiefs' statements. A reading of Hale's exquisite sampling of the criminal justice system of his time will leave no serious doubt that the reform of government, including the police, had begun before the time of his survey.

Varieties of reform—in pursuit of ethical constraints, competence, technological advancement, utility and efficiency, and the setting of governmental priorities—have now continued into the last decade of the twentieth century. If anything, governmental reform appears to have gained momentum by engaging the interest of the electorate, whether or not an "era" of community policing has, in the meantime, begun.

Second, to abstract from this span of years one occupation, policing, and a certain few phenomena in a certain few organizations, seems intended to establish the idea that policing was, by itself, being urged or moved toward reform. The social context continues to be ignored.

Third, this monograph shares a characteristic of many police histories: the failure to distinguish between the ostensible knowledge base and the practices of policing. In this sense, historical accounts often move freely among disparate elements of practices and knowledge without noting whether they are connected with their ideational/activity counterparts. In many cases, it is suspected, no distinction is made because none is recognized or even suspected. In our time, all that is required to establish a distinction between knowledge and practice is to observe the variety of police operational forms and quality to be found among agencies within a single metropolitan area. Within a few miles of each other in many parts of the country departments range from primitive to state-of-the-art modern, from corrupt, brutal and inept to professional policing.

Last, Kelling/Moore imply the reform era has faded and given over to a community policing era. Three questions are provoked:

1. Are professional and community policing mutually exclusive? Could community policing be no more than a recent development in the reform movement?

2. Have efforts to reform the police continued during the past few years and, in particular, since the end of the reform era as described by the authors?

3. Has reform been realized? Did the years of police reform produce a durable effect?

One might re-phrase the first question by asking whether the effort to professionalize the police had to wither and die before the police could establish a closer relationship with the community. Was reform in itself antagonistic to the establishment of a better relationship between police and community? Critics of the police reform movement often imply that efforts of reformers to separate policing from machine politics inherently erected barriers between the police and the public. These critics, however, fail to note that Woodrow Wilson, long before his election to the presidency, advocated isolating the administration of public services from machine politics. This is not to say that either Woodrow Wilson or O.W. Wilson seriously advocated separating government services from the communities they served.

It should not be so hard to understand that both Woodrow and O.W. Wilson were seeking ways to preserve the intended constitutional distinctions among the three branches of government. The executive branch institutions, they were saying, should be permitted to do their work unimpeded by narrow, partisan, corrupt machine politics. Also, the line between legislative policy-making and executive administration was to be preserved. The tendency of policing early in the reform days to define all politics as bad politics was an aberration of a time when nearly all politics was corrupt. But "politics," even at that time, did not refer to the whole electorate. Reformers were not as concerned about their officers associating with the mass of householders and business people on their beats as with ward-bosses and their thugs and runners. It has been too facile an interpretation to assume that insulation from dirty politics included all the people living in the police jurisdiction. Perhaps a few police officials saw it that way, but the more cogent concern of reformers was with dirty political interference in internal police administrative matters.

The second question can be addressed by searching for continuing efforts to reform and professionalize policing. If the Kelling/Moore date (1930) for the beginning of reform were accepted, it could be observed that a mere two generations is not very long for the development of major social institutions. Has the effort to reform policing in fact ended? To answer affirmatively, one would have to ignore developments in police administration between 1970 and 1988, the year of their publication. Where the Kelling/Moore monograph dwells on the over-reliance of the police on radio car patrols "to create an impression of omnipresence, and to respond rapidly to incidents of crime" and on criminal investigations, it ignores the many continuing efforts to "professionalize" policing.

- It ignores the NIJ police executive development programs administered by the University Research Corporation and the Police Management Association which, ironically, were based in part on excellent research conducted by one of the authors, Kelling.
- It ignores the research agenda of the Police Division of the National Institute of Justice, LEAA, during the 1970s and 1980s, which addressed virtually every major issue of police operations and administration.
- It ignores the wide-ranging attempts to convert patrol from the random, blunt instrument Kelling reported on in the early 1970s, into a focused, goal-oriented but not necessarily community-oriented strategy. The following are only a few of the studies engendered by skepticism about random patrol and called-for-service management:
  — New Haven Directed Patrol
  — Kansas City Directed-Interactive Patrol
  — Wilmington's Split Force Patrol Experiment
  — San Diego Field Interrogation Experiment

- San Diego One-Officer, Two-Officer Patrol Experiment
- Three Approaches to Criminal Apprehension in Kansas City
- Differential Police Response in Birmingham
- Crime analysis in support of crime control developments
- Police Car Allocation Model
- Hypercube beat design model
- Police Performance Measures research project

- It ignores the effects of the RAND Study of the Investigative Process, which set in motion:
  - The SRI case screening model
  - The Rochester investigations management model
  - Investigative screening/optimization models
  - Offender-based investigative methods
  - Case purging criteria
  - Crime analysis in support of investigations
  - Concepts to integrate patrol and investigative operations

The answer to the third question (Did police reform produce durable effects?) is simply stated: policing now involved science. Here we are not speaking of microscopes and X-ray diffraction, but rather of bringing the traditional standards and methods of the sciences to the description, analysis, and planning of police operations. The management of policing would continue to be an art based on sciences, but the old-fashioned cookbook versions of police administration would now yield ground to a more rigorous way of thinking about policing. George Kelling's Kansas City Preventive Patrol Study deserves recognition as the first carefully designed and executed scientific analysis of a long-standing police doctrine. Systems analysts often say that in order to ask the right question you have to know half the answer. That, indeed, was the situation in the early 1970s when Kelling undertook his important research; many observant police managers were already questioning the utility of random patrol.

William Bieck's stunning analysis of response time in Kansas City not only upset rapid response doctrines but also produced findings which dramatically overhauled our ways of visualizing the response time continuum and its implications. The most critical response delays were found not to be those in processes controlled by the police—dispatching and travel time, in which millions of dollars had been invested—but in complainants' delays in calling the police. The response time problem was suddenly deflected away from computer-assisted dispatch, automatic vehicle locator systems, mini-radios, fast cars, sirens and lights, and optimum response beat designs toward the problem of educating the victimized public to call sooner, if able. More scientific thinking was the durable effect of the reform and so-called professionalizing years. More to the point, this effect is one that continues and thus contradicts the notion that police reform has ended. Science suffuses not only the knowledge base of policing but also its more recent approaches to operational analysis and development. The universities and colleges are no longer teaching rote doctrine about patrol being the back-bone of policing but instead are instructing students to consider the issues and problems of crime, order and the delivery of services. They make use of the rigorous studies which have been conducted in analyzing these issues and problems. Gone is the old belief in doctrines. In its place resides a skepticism that raises hard questions for hard analyses.

Some of the science is not very good (particularly the failure to replicate major studies whose findings seemed to disparage traditional methods), and the loss of federal support for research has been unfortunate. But a corner has been turned in two respects by the years of LEAA and LEEP:

- rigorous thinking has found a place in policing, and
- a market for higher education has been established within the police occupation, even without LEEP support.

❖ COMMUNITY POLICING ERA ❖

Where the criticisms of the three-era scheme and the first two "eras" were based on misreadings of the more distant past, this present/future "era" raises formidable issues of sociological credibility. The very mention of "community" raises multiple, complex questions.

How can the Kelling/Moore analysis attribute the beginning of a "community problem-solving era" to anything other than the work of Louis Radelet and his police community relations programming which started in 1955? It is incredible that the significance of Radelet's annual, international conferences attended by thousands of police administrators, and his pioneering publications should be ignored in the monograph. There is almost no other way of explaining the origins of the Detroit mini-stations, store-front centers, and other measures to increase contact between the police and their communities. This is a serious lapse in the authors' presentation of historical materials.

Is the new vision of community policing simply a turn away from one type of process-oriented policing (patrol, investigation) toward another? The substance of community-oriented policing is difficult to pin down. When officers assigned in the COP mode are asked what they do, they paw the ground, shrug, and give answers such as, "walk and talk," "grin and chin," "chat and charm," "schmooze," and often, "maybe the brass will let us know." Peter Manning, in a recent presentation at Sam Houston State University, described community-oriented policing as more of an *ethos* than a method or concept, an ethos driven by the academic establishment rather than by developments in policing. Others refer to it as a *philosophy* of policing. Either term leaves unanswered the question of what community-oriented officers actually do, how their activities differ from those of traditional patrol officers, and how these activities might be evaluated.

The most serious question, however, remains, where is "community" coming from at this point in the development of American society? This question can be subdivided into a number of others.

- Is American society moving toward "community" and carrying policing along with it?
- Is American government moving toward "community" outside the context of the general social trend, and carrying policing along with it?
- Is policing (some 17,000 local agencies) moving toward "community" on its own, outside the context of American society and government?
- Is academic Criminal Justice moving toward "community" on its own?

An "American community" is a warm, comforting phrase. In this concept there is the overtone of the small society—the community of neighbors who know each other (to the third generation), and whose offspring develop their self-awareness in an atmosphere of warmth, trust and a wish to become like those who have gone before. Here is Toennies' *gemeinschaft* and Durkheim's mechanical solidarity of society. The small, simple, pre-industrial, consensual, almost primitive aspect of community does not require much secular law (especially *mala prohibita* law)—not much beyond the Ten Commandments. There is no big government, no regulatory laws and agencies (certainly nothing as secular or commercialized as the Code of Hammurabi), no tension between the sermons heard in church and the high school curriculum. "Community" is a realization of the romanticized melting pot.

Where do we find this small, uncomplicated, unspecialized, unstratified colony of believers who are clustered around an agreeable moral code? Chicago? Miami? San Francisco? Minneapolis? Maybe those are too large. Bangor? Rocky Mount? Wausau? Dothan? Waco? Nogales? Butte? Poplar Bluff? Bakersfield? Boulder? Eugene? Take a look at one of these smaller places. Determine for yourself whether any one of them has a basis for "community." Is there a moral consensus, a definition of social order that will guide the police department—the "forces of order"—in its daily activities?

Indicators show the United States becoming more, not less, of a *mass* society. There is increasing cultural pluralism and moral fragmentation. The underclass is growing; the middle class diminishing. High-transiency poor neighborhoods are known to be much harder to organize for purposes of community crime prevention and cooperative programs with the police than affluent neighborhoods. These poorer neighborhoods usually have higher rates of violent street crime than middle- and upper-class areas, and are most in need of police services. Add to that the traditional mistrust the poor have for the police and you have the unlikeliest of social settings for "community" policing.

American government, similarly, seems to be growing more distant from the mass society it serves. Smaller proportions of the electorate vote, and those strata which vote least are the poorest, the most victimized by crime, and most productive of offenders. Local, state and national governments are increasingly polarized and cross-cut on a variety of issues. The trend is away from moral consensus. Although polls sometimes indicate a consensual concern over an issue such as crime, education, health care, transportation or environmental damage, there is an abyss among advocates of conflicting policies and measures. There is nothing in the conduct of our many local governments to indicate they are carrying themselves—or policing—toward a more intimate relationship with their communities.

Is policing, then, moving closer to the community on its own, unsupported by a social or governmental trend? There is no example from history to suggest this is even possible, much less probable in our conflicted times. In almost all cases the police have been creatures of their social systems and times. Rarely if ever do they present institutional forms, technologies, processes or values different from those of their parent governments. Therein lies the most serious implication for Kelling/Moore's earlier fallacy of defining the two prior eras as distinct phenomena isolated from their general social/governmental context. If eras in policing were conceivable as isolated phenomena, then projecting a trend toward community policing might be possible. Seen in the broader context of social/governmental change, however, true community policing seems an unlikely future.

There is no joy in this observation. The prospect of a stronger bond between community and police is intrinsically attractive. Sadly, however, one can visualize a whole new episode of the Keystone Cops rushing down the street to meet their "community," only to find a bewildering array of mini-communities, each with widely divergent demands and expectations.

There *is* the possibility that academic Criminal Justice is defining an era of community policing on its own—making sure of a collection of police experiments and innovations to support the hypothesis. Community-oriented policing is sometimes said to include elements of foot patrol, vertical patrol, mini-stations, sub-stations, store-front centers, special purpose patrols, fear-reduction efforts, premise security crime prevention programs, citizen patrols, problem-oriented policing, location-oriented policing, and a variety of other operations. On close inspection, community-oriented policing seems diffuse, difficult to define and describe, comprised of too great a variety of operational forms to be considered a typology. Most probably it is, as Manning has stated, an ethos which has yet to be defined operationally. Even among academics who would support its emergence, community policing provokes endless debate about its format, operations, its utility and whether it includes problem-oriented policing, location-oriented policing, neighborhood oriented policing, known-offender-oriented policing, or is, conversely, an element in one of the others.

If community policing is largely a reified concept at this time, a creature of the academic literature rather than a defined, measurable and widespread approach among the 17,000 local policing agencies, a reason for the academic explosion on its behalf should be found. The energy being expended in producing community-policing literature may be greater than the energy of community policing being expended on the streets of America's cities. Is there, in fact a clamor for foot patrol, for a closer relationship between community and police? In our age of highly specialized division of work, of cooly distant "professionals," the idea of more personalized, intimate government services has a romantic and nostalgic note in it. There is more reason to believe citizens simply want to be protected, by whatever means, have lost faith in the capacity of government to provide that protection, and want the situation corrected. There is less reason to believe citizens want to become involved actively with the police in order to protect themselves. Every attempt to sustain citizen motivation in community/police programming has verified the tenuous nature of citizen participation. What, then, motivates the community-policing movement, if not verifiable success or social trend?

❖ ROBERT MERTON'S "UNANTICIPATED CONSEQUENCES" ❖

More than half a century ago, Robert Merton wrote his now classic "Unanticipated Consequences of Purposive Social Action," the essence of which holds that deliberate social action often produces alternative or additional results to those intended, because of ignorance, error, habit and the "imperious immediacy of interest." His scheme involves (A) an assessment of the present condition, (B) an imagined, preferable future condition, and (C) a means of getting from A to B.

Ignorance, defined as "incomplete information," seems a most unlikely driving force for an academic redefinition of policing or for the misreading of history. The authors of the monograph and their conferees have access to the knowledge base of the field and make use of it. We have no doubt The Executive Session was well-acquainted with Radelet's work, which opened the door to the community-policing concept. Error, defined as incorrect reasoning about available information, is also unlikely as a primary explanation, although misjudgments about the meanings of historical events are evident in the monograph (e.g., confused treatments of police reform). Habit, in the sense of proceeding outside of accustomed areas of study, may explain methodological lapses connected with the authors' unsound treatment of social history. The imperious immediacy of interest is defined as a focus on a desired outcome or a method of producing it that is so compelling that it brushes aside all indications which might contravene it. It is this last characteristic which seems to present a most likely explanation for Kelling/Moore's treatment of their topic.

There is in this monograph (and in some others of the series) a zeal to redefine policing as a community endeavor that takes the analysis beyond evidence, particularly in portraying the immediate future of policing. There is conviction and dedication rather than dispassionate examination of historical and recent experimental information. The tone of the presentation is persuasive, as if marketing is the intent. The driving force could simply be that which impels so many scholars: the wish to be the first to recognize and describe phenomena. On the other hand, this monograph and some of its companions may be seen as an initiative toward the molding of ideas among a skeptical and diffuse police leadership and eventually the influencing of public opinion favorably toward community policing. This, of course, turns the corner from policy analysis to policy development and advocacy. There is nothing improper in advocating public policy, unless history has been misread and/or misstated in the service of advocacy.

❖ References ❖

Baker, L. C. (1867). *History of the United States Secret Service.* Philadelphia: L.C. Baker.

Carte, G. E. & Carte, E. E. (1975). *Police Reform in the United States. The Era of August Vollmer, 1905–1932.* Berkeley: University of California Press.

Costello, A. E. (1885). *Our Police Protectors: History of the New York Police from the Earliest Period to the Present Time.* Reprint, 1970. Montclair, NJ: Patterson Smith.

Flinn, J. J. & Wilkie, J. E. (1887). *History of the Chicago Police*. Reprint, 1973. Montclair, NJ: Patterson Smith.
Fogelson, R. M. (1977). *Big City Police*. Cambridge: Harvard University Press.
Fosdick, R. (1920). *American Police Systems*. Reprint, 1969. Montclair, NJ: Patterson Smith.
Fuld, L. (1909). *Police Administration*. New York: G.P. Putnam.
Hale, G. W. (1892). *Police and Prison Cyclopaedia*. Cambridge, MA: Riverside Press.
Haller, M. "Historical Roots of Police Behavior: Chicago, 1890-1925." *Law and Society Review*. (Winter, 1976): 303-324.
Hamilton, M. E. (1924). *The Policewoman, Her Service and Ideals*. New York: Fredrick A. Stokes Co.
Harring, S. L. (1983). *Policing a Class Society: The Experience of American Cities, 1865-1915*. New Brunswick, NJ: Rutgers University Press.
Hickey, J. J. (1925). *Our Police Guardians: History of the Police Department of the City of New York*. New York: Author.
Johnson, D. R. (1981). *American Law Enforcement: A History*. St. Louis: Forum Press.
Kelling, G. L. & Moore, M. H. (1988). "The Evolving Strategy of Policing." No. 4, *Perspectives on Policing*. Washington, DC: U.S.G.P.O.
Lane, R. (1967). *Policing the City: Boston, 1822-1885*. Cambridge: Harvard University Press.
Maltby, W. J. (1906). *Captain Jeff; or, Frontier Life in Texas with the Texas Rangers; Some Unwritten History and Facts in the Thrilling Experiences of Frontier Life*. Colorado, Tex. Whipkey.
Merton, R. K. (1936). "The Unanticipated Consequences of Purposive Social Action." No. 1, *American Sociological Review*.
Miller, W. R. (1976). *Cops and Bobbies: Police Authority in New York and London, 1830-1870*. Chicago: University of Chicago Press.
Monkkonen, E. H. (1981). *Police in Urban America, 1860-1920*. Cambridge: Harvard University Press.
Peck, W. F. (1903). *History of the Police Dept. of Rochester, New York, from the Earliest Time to May 1, 1903*. Rochester, NY: Police Benevolent Association.
Radelet, L. A. (1973). *The Police and the Community*. Beverly Hills: Glencoe Press.
Richardson, J. F. (1978). *The New York Police: Colonial Times to 1901*. New York: Oxford University Press.
Roe, G. M. (1976). *Our Police: A History of the Cincinnati Police Force, from the Earliest Period until the Present Day*. 1890. Reprint. New York: AMS Press.
Russell, F. (1975). *A City in Terror: 1919, the Boston Police Strike*. New York: Viking Press.
Strecher, V. G. (1971). *The Environment of Law Enforcement*. Englewood Cliffs, NJ: Prentice-Hall.
Terrill, R. J. (1989). "Police History: 1920 to the Present." In William G. Bailey, editor, *Encyclopedia of Police Science*, pp. 447-453. New York: Garland Publishing, Inc.
Walker, S. (1977). *A Critical History of Police Reform: The Emergence of Professionalism*. Lexington, MA: Lexington Books.
Williams, H. & Murphy, P. V. (1990). "The Evolving Strategy of Police: A Minority View." No. 13, *Perspectives on Policing*. Washington, DC: U.S.G.P.O.

5

The Iron Fist and the Velvet Glove

Crime and Social Justice Associates

There must be something in the very core of a social system which increases its wealth without diminishing its misery, and increases in crime even more rapidly than in numbers.

Karl Marx

In the past, the police forces in this country were, for the most part, fragmented and scattered in many different levels and jurisdictions, uncoordinated with each other, without central planning or comprehensive strategies. Relatively little money was spent on strengthening local police forces and little attention was given to developing new concepts and techniques of police practice. In the 1960s all this began to change. . . .

Even more significant than the general increase in the size and fiscal importance of the police is the growing centralization and sophistication of the police system—and the criminal justice system generally—over the last few years. . . . Most spending on criminal justice still comes from the local level—but the share of the states and especially of the Federal

Excerpted from Institute for the Study of Labor and Economic Crisis, *The Iron Fist and the Velvet Glove: An Analysis of the U.S. Police (3rd Ed)*. San Francisco: Crime and Social Justice Associates, 1982, 7–18. Reprinted with permission of *Social Justice*, a project of Global Options. Footnotes renumbered.

government is rising fast. Federal spending on criminal justice shot up by 62 percent between 1971-1974, and on police in particular by about 52 percent.[1] For the first time in U.S. history, the Federal government has become deeply involved in the police system, mainly through the creation of the massive Federal Law Enforcement Assistance Administration (LEAA), devoted primarily to standardizing and centralizing the police and other criminal justice agencies, and to funding the development of new and increasingly sophisticated police strategies. At the same time, the 1960s saw the rise of a whole "police-industrial complex," a rapidly growing industry that took technical developments originally created for overseas warfare or for the space program and, backed by government funds, applied them to the problems of domestic "order" in the United States.

In addition to the rise of new, sophisticated technologies, another striking development in the U.S. police apparatus during the sixties was the growth of new strategies of community penetration and "citizen participation" that sought to integrate people into the process of policing and to secure the legitimacy of the police system itself. Along with this has been a dramatic increase in the money and attention given to various kinds of "police education" programs and other efforts designed to give a new "professional" look to the police. The Federal government in the early 1970s began spending about $20 million annually on police education in the universities, colleges, and even high schools, and today . . . colleges and universities offer degrees or courses in "police science or criminal justice."[2] On the other side of the coin, the police have developed a variety of new "tough" specialized units—special anti-riot and tactical patrol forces, "special weapons" teams, and highly sophisticated intelligence units. And the growth and spread of the U.S. police apparatus has not stopped at the national boundaries; since the sixties, the United States has been actively exporting its police concepts, technologies, and personnel to the far corners of the American empire. Finally, the government effort to beef up and streamline the police system has been matched by an equally dramatic increase in the number of private police, security guards, and private corporations engaged in producing and selling all kinds of complicated security hardware and services.

. . . What happened to cause this sudden growth in the size and significance of the police? Most importantly, the 1960s and early 1970s have been a time of great crisis for American capitalism—not the first crisis the U.S. capitalist system has undergone, but one of the most severe. The crisis has had many different aspects, economic, social, and political, but in terms of the growth of the police, the most important is the erosion of the popular acceptance of the corporate system and of the political power that supports it, both at home and abroad. During the last ten years, this crisis in legitimacy has been manifested in many ways—not only in the widespread resistance and rebellion . . . but in the rapidly and steadily rising rates of street crime. The combined rates of the seven "serious" crimes as defined by the FBI (murder, rape, robbery, burglary, aggravated assault, larceny, and auto theft) rose by 158 percent between 1960 and 1971.[3] Crime became a central preoccupation and fear for many people during this period, and emerged as a crucial political issue of the sixties. It became especially critical in the "inner cities," where by the early seventies one person in every five was being victimized by some form of serious crime each year.[4]

The new emphasis on strengthening and streamlining the police is one of the most important responses of the American government to the widespread challenge to its legitimacy. It goes along with other, similar attempts to refurbish the "correctional" system, to harness the public schools more tightly to corporate values and interests, and to rationalize the "mental health" and welfare systems in the face of the growing disintegration of the "consensus" that was supposed to exist in the U.S. in the 1940s and 1950s. How successful the state[5] is in developing such means of integration and repression will depend on how effectively we are able to resist that development.

❖ THE ROLE OF THE POLICE ❖

Why are we so concerned about the growth of the police in the first place? Why don't we welcome it as a step toward a safer and more decent society? The answer lies in our basic view of the functions that the police perform in the U.S. today, and have performed throughout U.S. history. Although the actual role of the police at any given time—like the role of the state in general in advanced capitalist societies—is complex and should not be oversimplified, it is clear that the police have *primarily* served to enforce the class, racial, sexual, and cultural oppression that has been an integral part of the development of capitalism in the U.S.[6] As long as this function remains, any strengthening of the powers of the police, any movement toward greater efficiency or sophistication in their methods, must be seen as inherently contrary to the interests and needs of the majority of people in this country, and in other countries where the U.S. police system penetrates.

Our position is very different from that of most people who write about the police. Whether "liberal" or "conservative," most commentators on the police share a common assumption: they all take the existence of the police for granted. They assume that any modern society necessarily has to have a large and ever-present body of people whose purpose is to use coercion and force on other people. "Conservatives" usually point to such things as the decline in respect for authority, the breakdown of traditional values or of family discipline, as the source of the need for the police, who are seen as a "thin blue line" holding back the forces of evil and destruction that lurk just beneath the surface of civilization. This view is often found within police departments (and was promoted for decades by the FBI under J. Edgar Hoover) and in many popular movie and TV portrayals of the police. A more "liberal" approach—increasingly evident among academic and professional police reformers—sees the need for police in the growing complexity and diversity of modern urban society. Liberal commentators often point to social and economic conditions— especially poverty and unemployment—as factors underlying the crime and social disorder that make the police necessary. But these conditions are usually accepted, in the liberal view, as either inevitable or as problems that can only be solved in the "long run." In the meantime, we have to accept the basic role of the police for the indefinite future, although we can do something about correcting police abuses and inefficiency. A classic example of this kind of thinking can be found in the (1967) Report of the President's Crime Commission, a standard source for modern liberal platitudes about the police. The Commission recognized that "the police did not create and cannot resolve the social conditions that stimulate crime," and went so far as to acknowledge that "the economy is not geared to provide (criminals) with jobs." But the Commission did not go on to examine in detail the particular conditions that cause crime, or how these conditions are related to the most basic structures of the U.S. economy.[7] It did not ask, for example, why the economy has not been able to provide enough jobs throughout the entire twentieth century. The larger social and economic issues were raised, but then conveniently dropped, and the rest of the Report deals with ways of improving the functional capacity of the criminal justice system.

To accept the basic role of the police in this way is to accept the system of social, political, and economic relations that role supports. Behind both the liberal and conservative views of the police there is a basic pessimism about the possibilities for human liberation and cooperation, a pessimism that we do not share. We believe that a society that must be held together by constant force or the threat of force is an oppressive society, and we do not believe that oppression is inevitable. Around us there are examples of societies that have done much to eliminate the sources of exploitation and suffering that generate crime. A main premise of our approach to the police, then, is that we believe things *can* be different;

that we can build a society without grinding poverty, ill-health, mutual exploitation and fear—and, therefore, without a vast, repressive police apparatus.

How do the present police enforce the oppressive social and personal relations of capitalist society? There are two different, but related ways in which this is accomplished. (1) The laws that define what is and what is not "crime"—and thus what is or is not a concern of the police—have been primarily defined in U.S. history by and for the people who benefit most from the capitalist system; (2) Even within the inherently one-sided system of laws the police have been used *selectively*, enforcing *some* of the laws against *some* kinds of people, while allowing other laws to fall into disuse and letting other kinds of law-breakers go free, or nearly free.

(1) *The Definition of Crime*

The most violent and socially harmful acts in the history of the U.S. have been carried out by the government and the wealthy rulers of the corporate economy. Whether measured in human lives or dollars, these acts constitute the most severe crimes of all, though they are not labeled as such in the criminal codes. The overwhelming number of killings in the 1960s were committed by the U.S. armed forces in Southeast Asia. The largest thefts in U.S. history were carried out by the U.S. government against the lands of Mexicans and the various Native American tribes. The most brutal kidnapping since Blacks were forced into slavery was carried out by the U.S. government, against the Japanese-Americans in the 1940s, when they were stripped of their belongings and held in camps during World War II.[8] Perhaps most importantly, the process of getting rich off the labor of other people, far from being considered a crime, is the basis of normal economic life in the U.S., and people who do it successfully have great prestige and power.

Historically, the *main* function of the police has been to protect the property and well-being of those who benefit most from an economy based on the extraction of private profit. The police were created primarily in response to rioting and disorder directed against oppressive working and living conditions in the emerging industrial cities (see below, sections II and III for history). They were used consistently to put down striking workers in the industrial conflicts of the late 19th and early 20th centuries. The police did not shoot or beat the corporate executives of Carnegie Steel, the Pullman Company, or the Pennsylvania Railroad who subjected their workers to long hours, physical danger, and low pay; instead, they shot and beat the workers who protested against that exploitation. In the 1960s, the police did not arrest the men who planned and directed the U.S.

aggression in Southeast Asia; they arrested the people who protested against that aggression. And in the ghetto revolts of Harlem, Watts, and Newark, the police did not use tear gas and shotguns on slumlords or on merchants who sold shoddy and overpriced goods; they used them on the Black people who rebelled against that victimization.

All of this is often conveniently forgotten in discussions of the police. It adds up to the simple fact that the police were not created to serve "society" or "the people," but to serve *some* parts of society and *some* people at the expense of others. Sometimes, this means that things like racism, sexism, economic exploitation, or military aggression are defined as worthy rather than criminal. In other cases, something more subtle happens. Many of the most socially and personally damaging acts that *are* forbidden in U.S. law are handled as "civil" rather than "criminal" issues. This is often true, for example, for such things as denying people jobs on the grounds of sex or race, or violating safety or anti-pollution regulations. Generally, the executives of corporations and other institutions that violate these laws are not visited by armed police, handcuffed and thrown in patrol wagons, and taken to jail. Instead, a long, drawn out, and expensive process of litigation takes place, during which "business as usual" goes on as before. This distinction, like the basic definition of crime, is not natural or inevitable, but reflects the social priorities and sources of political power in a society built on private profit.

(2) *Selective Enforcement*

Even when the actions of the wealthy and powerful are defined as criminal and detected, the penalties they face are usually relatively mild and rarely applied in practice. Offenses such as embezzlement, fraud, tax fraud, and forgery resulted in a loss of $1.73 billion in 1965. In the same year, robbery, burglary, auto theft, and larceny resulted in a loss of $690 million—less than half as much. Although the "crime in the suites" represented much more stolen wealth, it was much less severely punished. Less than 20 percent of those convicted of tax fraud in 1969 (which averaged $190,000) served prison terms, and these terms averaged only 9 months. At the same time, over 90 percent of those convicted of robbery were sentenced to prison, where they served an average of 52 months.[9]

Alongside this systematic leniency toward white-collar or corporate offenders, there is considerable evidence showing that underneath the formal structure of the criminal law there is an unofficial but systematic pattern of selective use of the police to coerce and intimidate oppressed people. Studies of police street practices consistently show that the police use their discretion to arrest more often against working-class people than others.

For example, middle-class youth are much more likely to be let off with a reprimand for many kinds of crimes, while working-class youth are far more likely to be formally arrested and charged, for the same kinds of offenses.[10] More dramatically, it has been shown that the police systematically use their ultimate weapon, deadly force, much more against . . . [minorities] than against whites. . . . The police response to the crime of rape is another example of this pattern, for although rape—unlike most expressions of sexism—is considered in law as a serious crime, it is typically dealt with in ways that serve to degrade and further victimize women and to enforce oppressive and stereotypical conceptions of women's roles.[11] In these and other ways too numerous to mention here, the routine operation of the police creates an informal system of criminal law that, even more than the formal one, is designed to support the fundamentally oppressive social relations of capitalism. It should be emphasized that this is not just a question of easily correctable police "abuses." The selective use of the police has been a systematic and constant feature of the whole pattern of "social control" in the U.S., and its consistency shows how tightly it is tied in to the repressive needs of the system as a whole.

❖ DEALING WITH CRIME ❖

Even though we believe that the most dangerous criminals sit in corporate and government offices, we recognize that the more conventional kinds of crime—"street crimes"—are a real and frightening problem which must be confronted. The Left in the United States has neglected, with few notable exceptions, to deal with the problem of street crime as the serious social problem that it is. In the United States people are faced every day with the danger of theft or personal violence. . . .

We know, however, that many, if not most, crimes are not even reported to police. This is confirmed by a recent series of "victimization" studies which are based on systematic interviews with representative samples of the urban population. In these studies, people are asked about the number and types of crimes in which they have been the victim. This provides a much more accurate picture of the extent of crime than the FBI Reports which are primarily based on crimes reported to the police. One such victimization study conducted in 1973 showed that less than one out of five people reported to police instances of personal larceny without contact.[12] Some experts estimate that only 10 percent of all rapes are reported,[13] and the reporting rate for wife-beating is even lower. The primary reason for not contacting police is the belief that police cannot do anything.[14] The victims of crime are overwhelmingly poor people, particularly . . . [minorities] and those living in urban areas. . . .

While the greatest fear of crime exists in poor and . . . [minority] communities because most street crime is committed by the poor against the poor . . . the concern with crime as a political issue is concentrated in the middle and upper classes.[15] In 1948, only 4 percent of the population felt crime was their community's worst problem but in 1972 the figure in large cities was 21 percent. The state has used this issue of street crime as a mask to encourage fear and racist attitudes and to divert people's attention away from corporate and government crime. Since street crime is an authentic issue that easily arouses people, the promise to establish law and order and make the streets safe is an appealing one. Because the fear of crime is a demoralizing and oppressive fact of life, many people believe the police should be supported and encouraged since it is theoretically their job to provide protection against this type of crime. In reality, however, the police have been ineffective in dealing with street crimes and do not protect the property or lives of poor and . . . [minority] people. The solutions proposed by law and order politicians and the state include harsher treatment of criminals, more police with less legal restrictions and more technological equipment, and a strong moral order based on family and religion; but politicians cannot offer *viable* solutions to crime because they do not discuss the real causes.

The reasons why there is so much street crime in the United States are complex, but they are rooted in the material deprivations, personal alienation and misery that capitalism produces. Under the capitalist system, emphasizing high profits at the expense of people's needs, workers are prevented from developing cooperative social relations that grow in the process of producing needed services and goods with fellow workers. A large part of the alienation and insecurity results from the tenuous position of many individuals in the labor force, to unemployment and underemployment, to dead-end jobs and job instability. Divisively pitting people against each other for scarce jobs is integral to the capitalist system since the fear of unemployment weakens resistance. . . . [Minorities] are the most victimized by this, feeling it through racism from both the people in the labor market and by the employers' need to keep people divided.[16]

Crime is caused not only by economic policies which result in direct material suffering for millions of people, but also by the individualistic, competitive and cynical values which are endemic to capitalist social relations and ideology. The ideological function of unfulfilling, alienated work is to dehumanize workers; and this condition makes it difficult for workers to discover the socialist alternative. Although street criminals do constitute a real danger to many of us, the basic crime problem originates with the ruling class whose control of and profit from capitalism perpetuates oppressive social relationships.

No "war on crime" can provide a truly enduring solution to the problem of crime unless it directly attacks the sources of that misery and alienation. Strengthening the existing police does not do this; but only helps to strengthen the system that generates crime in the first place. Flooding the society with more and better-equipped police—putting a cop on every corner—could have some effect on the rate of crime. But this kind of "solution" would not touch the underlying roots of crime, and could only be done at tremendous economic, political and social costs.

To deal with crime by strengthening the police is to accept the inevitability of crime and the permanence of the oppressive social system which breeds it. We believe that the real solution to ending street crime is in the struggle for a society that can meet people's basic needs. We have a right to live in a society where labor without profit and equitable social relationships can set the conditions for eradicating crime. . . .

To understand the specific pattern of crime in any particular capitalist system, we must examine the concrete historical conditions and development of each society. The United States has much higher rates of crime than all other "developed" capitalist countries, for example Sweden, Switzerland, or England. In the United States, the historical patterns of racism help to explain the specific types and amount of crime. U.S. capitalist development has depended heavily on the super-exploitation of . . . [minority] people. The resulting special oppression of . . . [minorities] contributes to higher rates of U.S. street crime. However, the oppression itself which is characterized also by higher rates of disease, infant mortality, unemployment, etc. is the more fundamental and harmful crime.

While the long-term struggle for socialism is waged, people have a right and need to make political and economic demands on the state. The rich can afford private police and security systems to protect their interests; working people have to fight for the right to a decent standard of living and to exercise our constitutional freedoms. We think that it is crucial for crime control programs to be linked with an analysis of the political economy. To do less than this is to feed into corporate reforms and to give people the illusion that exploitation can be conquered under capitalism. These struggles for immediate demands should not be minimized, partly because they serve to expose the hypocrisy of bourgeois democracy and partly because they provide important support for the institutions and rights that the working class has gained. . . .

❖ FRAMEWORK FOR ANALYSIS ❖

Up to now, there has been insufficient analysis of changes in the police system to provide a basis for effective understanding and resistance. For the most part, analysis of the new developments in the police has been made by liberal commentators. But the liberal analysis of the police . . . is basically misleading and mystifying, and more often than not has served as a main means of ideological justification for the growth and power of the new police forces.

The starting point for any analysis of the police is the nature of the state. The Marxist analysis, developed most thoroughly by Lenin in *State and Revolution*,[17] has seen the police in capitalist society as one part— along with the military and the penal system—of the apparatus of state force and violence, which directly serves the interests of the capitalist class. The capitalist state serves to facilitate the accumulation of capital in the hands of this ruling class. It helps to concentrate profits in the hands of the rich in a number of ways: by directly financing a number of key industries, by regulating destructive competition, by purchasing and absorbing surplus production, by maintaining a large segment of the working class through various social welfare expenditures, and by preserving the stability of the existing social order and existing class relations. All social institutions combine to serve various aspects of this capital accumulation function. The police, however, serve as the front line mechanism of repression. As such, the central function of the police is to control the working class. This class control takes a number of forms, ranging from strikebreaking, to helping divide . . . [minority] and white workers, to infiltrating working class political activities, to repressing working class culture and recreational activities. . . . [Minority] communities, which include the most exploited sectors of the working class, have historically experienced the most severe forms of repression. In addition to being victimized by the class-related functions of the criminal justice system, they are further oppressed by its racist double standards and practices. This accounts for the disproportionate representation of Blacks, Chicanos, Puerto Ricans, Native Americans, and Asians in arrest statistics as well as in the jails and prisons.

Overtly repressive police action (the *Iron Fist*) functions within a liberal democratic framework because the ruling class in an advanced capitalist society generally finds democracy as the best state form. This framework provides a greater potential for cooptation of the working class and for mystification of power relationships. The capitalist state places a great emphasis on the legitimation of state power.[18] Powerful ideology-producing institutions—such as the educational system, the mass media and organized religion—mystify the nature of state power. It is presented as being separate and above class conflict and representing the interests of all segments of the population, rather than an instrument of control for the ruling class. Social welfare institutions (social security, unemployment compensation, welfare) work to reinforce this mystification by ameliorating some of the most exploitative aspects of capitalism, chiefly poverty and unemployment. The extent of this amelioration depends on the balance of class power at a given time: during the 1930s, the government devoted a major proportion of its resources to public welfare expenditures, while during the 1970s these expenditures are proportionately much lower.[19]

The police institution masks its central class control function behind various kinds of public service—helping people in trouble, solving a few dangerous crimes, directing traffic and providing public information. These and other "community relations" activities constitute the *Velvet Glove* side of police work. It is important to see both sides as integrally intertwined. The legitimating functions provided by the public service programs of the police enables them to increase the level of violent repression. Moreover, the mystification of the class control nature of policing, and the mass dissemination of ruling class ideological justification of the police, such as "law and order" rhetoric, is in itself repressive, and serves important class control functions. . . .

Notes

[1] U.S. Department of Justice, Law Enforcement Assistance Administration, *Trends in Expenditure and Employment Data for the Criminal Justice System, 1971-1974* (Washington, D.C., U.S. Government Printing Office, 1976), pp. 11, 8 respectively.

[2] Richard Quinney, *Critique of Legal Order* (Boston: Little, Brown, and Co., 1973), 74.

[3] LEAA, *Sourcebook of Criminal Justice Statistics* (Washington, D.C.: Government Printing Office 1973), 198.

[4] National Advisory Commission on Criminal Justice Standards and Goals, *A National Strategy to Reduce Crime* (Washington, D.C.: Government Printing Office, 1973), 19.

[5] Our use of the word "state" may be unclear to some readers. By "state," we refer to the whole range of political institutions—including not only the courts, military and police but also such things as the schools and the welfare system—through which the structure of the capitalist system is maintained.

[6] There is presently a considerable amount of debate among radical theorists about the exact way the state functions in modern capitalist societies. For a good description of the issues involved, see David Gold et al., "Recent Developments in Marxist Theories of the Capitalist State," *Monthly Review*, 27 (5); (6) (October, November 1975), 29-43; 36-51.

[7] President's Crime Commission, *The Challenge of Crime in a Free Society* (Washington, D.C.: Government Printing Office, 1967), 1.

8 This is a somewhat modified version of the statement in American Friends Service Committee, *Struggle for Justice* (New York: Hill and Wang, 1970), 11.

9 Erik Wright, *The Politics of Punishment* (New York: Harper and Row, 1973), 28–30.

10 For some studies, see any criminology text, for example, Richard Quinney, *The Social Reality of Crime* (Boston: Little, Brown, and Co., 1970).

11 For an analysis of stereotypical responses to rape, see Julia R. Schwendinger and Herman Schwendinger, "Rape Myths: In Legal, Theoretical, and Everyday Practice," *Crime and Social Justice*, 1, (Spring-Summer 1974).

12 Michael J. Hindelang et al., *Sourcebook of Criminal Justice Statistics—1974* (U.S. Government Printing Office), 233.

13 This is an unofficial estimate by Bay Area Women Against Rape in Berkeley, California.

14 Hindelang, *op. cit.*, p. 242.

15 Hindelang, *op. cit.*, p. 171.

16 For a more extensive discussion of this issue, see Editorial, "The Politics of Street Crime," *Crime and Social Justice*, No. 5 (Spring-Summer 1976), 1–4.

17 Lenin's classic work, written at the time of the Russian Revolution, is available in many editions.

18 Ralph Miliband, *The State in Capitalist Society* (New York: Basic Books, 1969).

19 Frances Fox Piven and Richard A. Cloward, *Regulating the Poor: The Functions of Public Welfare* (New York: Random House, 1971).

Part II

The Role
of the Police
in Society

The Police
Mandate, Strategies, and Appearances

Peter K. Manning

All societies have their share of persistent, chronic problems—
problems of life, of death, problems of property and security, problems
of man's relationship to what he consecrates. And because societies have
their quota of troubles, they have developed ways in which to distribute
responsibility for dealing with them. The division of labor that results is
not only an allocation of functions and rewards, it is a moral division as
well. In exchange for money, goods, or services, these groups—such as
lawyers or barbers or clergymen or pharmacists—have a *license* to carry
out certain activities that others may not. This license is a legally defined
right, and no other group or groups may encroach upon it.[1]

The right to perform an occupation may entail the permission to pick
up garbage or to cut open human bodies and transfer organs from one
to another. What it always involves, however, is a series of tasks and
associated attitudes and values that set apart a specialized occupational
group from all the others. Further, the licensed right to perform an
occupation may include a claim to the right to define the proper conduct
of others toward matters concerned with the work. The claim, if granted,
is the occupation's *mandate*. The mandate may vary from a right to live
dangerously to the right to define the conditions of work and functions
of related personnel.

Peter K. Manning and John Van Maanen (Eds.), *Policing: A View from the Street*, (1978)
pp. 7–32. Reprinted with permission of the editors. Footnotes renumbered.

The professional mandate is not easily won, of course, for clients are often unwilling to accept the professional definition of their problem. Professions claim a body of theory and practice to justify their right to discover, define, and deal with problems. The medical profession, for example, is usually considered the model of a vocation with a secure license and mandate. Yet even in medicine the client may refuse to accept the diagnosis; he may change physicians or fail to follow doctor's orders or insist upon defining his troubles as the product of a malady best cured by hot lemonade or prayer. The contraction and expansion of an occupation's *mandate* reflects the concerns society has with the services it provides, with its organization, and with its effectiveness. In times of crisis, it is the professions that are questioned first.[2]

Some occupations are not as fortunate as others in their ability to delimit a societal "trouble" and deal with it systematically. The more power and authority a profession has, the better able it is to gain and maintain control over the symbolic meanings with which it is associated in the public's mind. As we have become less concerned with devils and witches as causes of mental illness, clergymen have lost ground to psychiatrists who have laid claim to a secular cure for madness; in this sense, mental illness is a product of the definitions supplied by psychiatry. A profession, therefore, must not only compete with its clientele's definitions, it must also defend itself against the definitions of competing groups. Is a backache better treated by a Christian Scientist, an osteopath, a chiropractor, a masseuse, or an M.D.? Professional groups whose tools are less well-developed, whose theory is jerry-built or unproved, and who are unable to produce results in our consumer-oriented society will be beset with public doubt, concern, and agitation. In other words, these are the groups that have been unable to define their mandate for solving social "troubles" in such a way that it can be accomplished with ease and to the satisfaction of those they intend to serve.

The police have trouble. Among the many occupations now in crisis, they best symbolize the shifts and strains in our changing socio-political order. They have been assigned the task of crime prevention, crime detection and the apprehension of criminals. Based on their legal monopoly of violence, they have staked out a mandate that claims to include the efficient, apolitical, and professional enforcement of the law. It is the contention of this article that the police have staked out a vast and unmanageable social domain. And what has happened as a result of their inability to accomplish their self-proclaimed mandate is that the police have resorted to the manipulation of *appearances*.

We shall attempt to outline the nature of the police mandate, or their definition of social trouble, their methods of coping with this trouble, and the consequences of their efforts. After developing a sociological analysis of the paradoxes of police work and discussing the heroic attempts—*strategies*—by police to untangle these paradoxes, we shall also consider the recommendations of the President's crime commission[3] and assess their value as a means of altering and improving the practical art of managing public order.

To turn for the moment to "practical matters," the same matters to which we shall return before concluding, the troubles of the police, the problems and paradoxes of their mandate in modern society, have become more and more intense. Police today may be more efficient in handling their problems than were the first bobbies who began to patrol London in 1829. Or they may not be. There may or may not be more crime. Individual rights may or may not be greatly threatened by crime or crime-fighters, and the enforcement of law in view of recent Supreme Court decisions may or may not be a critical issue in crime control. The police may or may not have enough resources to do their job, and they may or may not be allocating them properly. Peace-keeping rather than law enforcement may or may not be the prime need in black communities, and the police may or may not need greater discretionary powers in making an arrest. But however these troubles are regarded, they exist. They are rooted deeply in the mandate of the police.

❖ SOME SOCIOLOGICAL ASSUMPTIONS ❖

This article makes several assumptions about occupations, about people as they execute occupational roles, about organizations as loci or structures for occupational activities, and about the nature of society. Not all activity taking place "on the job" can be construed as "work"; goldbricking is not unknown in American society and some professionals have even been known to use their places of work to conduct business somewhat outside the mandate of their organization. An individual's "organizational" behavior varies with what the organization is said to require or permit, with his particular place in the organizational hierarchy, and with the degree of congruence between the individual's personal definition of his role and the organization's definition of his role. In a given situation, then, organizational rules and regulations may be important sources of meanings ("He's working hard"), or other criteria may provide more relevant meanings of behavior ("He can't be expected to work. His wife just had a baby"). The ways in which people explain or account for their own organizational activities and those of others are problematic. How do people refer to their organizational roles and activities? How do they construct their moral obligations to the organization? What do they think they owe the organization? How does this sense of obligation and commitment pattern or constrain them in another role—the role of golfer or father or politician?

People as they perform their roles are actors. They are alert to the small cues that indicate meaning and intention—the wink, the scowl, the raised eyebrow. Those who attend to these behavioral clues are the audience. All actors try to maximize the positive impression they make on others, and both experience and socialization provide them with a repertoire of devices to manage their appearance.

People as actors in roles must also make assumptions about their audience. The politician, for example, must make certain assumptions about his constituency, the lawyer certain assumptions about clients. Assumptions are an important part of urban life. Some actors with white faces, for instance, may make certain assumptions about others with black faces, that they will be ill-mannered or badly educated and that any request for directions is a prelude to a holdup. Assumptions are not simply individual in nature; they are shared, patterned, and passed on from one social group to the next.

One of the most important aspects of assumptions, however, is that they are the basis for strategies.[4] Strategies arise from the need of organizations and individuals to cope with persistent social problems about which assumptions have been made. Strategies are often a means of survival in a competitive environment; they can be inferred from the allocation of resources or from the behavior and pronouncements of an organization. In short, strategies assist any organization within the society in managing its appearance and in controlling the behavior of its audience.

All organizations and individuals, we assume, are bent on maximizing their impressions in order to gain control over an audience.[5] The audience for the police is diverse; it should be considered many audiences. For the police must convince the politicians that they have used their allocated resources efficiently; they must persuade the criminals that they are effective crimefighters; they must assure the broader public that they are controlling crime. Rather than a single rhetoric—the "use of words to form attitudes or induce actions in other human agents"[6]—directed toward convincing one audience, the police must develop many rhetorics. Linguistic strategies to control audience are only one of many ploys used by the police organization to manage its impression. Not all the results of the use of rhetorics are intended; the consequence of the rhetorical "war on crime" in Detroit in the fall of 1969, to cite one example, was a continued advance in the city's downtown crime rate. Moreover, rhetoric can take on different meanings even within the organizational hierarchy. To patrolmen, the term "professionalism" means control over hours and salary and protection from arbitrary punishment from "upstairs"; to the chief and the higher administrators, it relates to the public-administration notions of efficiency, technological expertise, and standards of excellence in recruitment and training.

Tactics are the means by which a strategy is implemented. If the strategy is to mount a war on crime, then one tactic might be to flood the downtown area with scooter-mounted patrolmen. Tactics, in other words, are the ways in which one group of people deals with others in face-to-face encounters. How does the policeman handle a family quarrel in which the wife has the butcher knife and the husband already knows how sharp it is? Strategies pertain to general forms of action or rhetoric while tactics refer to the specific action or the specific words used to best meet a specific, problematic situation.[7] The tactic of flattery may be far more effective—and safer—in wresting the butcher knife than a leap over the kitchen table.

All occupations possess strategies and tactics, by means of which they attempt to control their most significant audiences. However, our analysis must do more than describe the existence of such means of creating impressions. So far as the police are concerned, impression management, or the construction of appearances, cannot substitute for significant control of crime. To maintain the dramaturgic metaphor, we suggest that there are significant flaws and contradictions in the performance of the police that cast a serious doubt on the credibility of their occupational mandate.

The mandate of the police is fraught with difficulties, many of them, we shall argue, self-created. They have defined their task in such a way that they cannot, because of the nature of American social organization, hope to honor it to the satisfaction of the public. We will argue that the appearances that the police create—that they control crime and that they attain a high level of efficiency—are transparent on close examination, that they may, in fact, be created as a sop to satisfy the public's impossible expectations for police performance. By utilizing the rhetoric of crime control, the police claim the responsibility for the social processes that beget the illegal acts. They cannot control these social processes that are embedded in American values, norms, and cultural traditions. Creating the appearance of controlling them is only a temporizing policy; it is not the basis for a sound, honorable mandate.

The police mandate and the problems it creates in American society are our central concern. We will rely on the concepts of actor, organization, and audience, of mandate, and of strategy and appearances. We will show that the police mandate, as presently defined, is full of contradictions. We will further demonstrate that the strategies and tactics of the American police are failing in a serious way to meet the need of controlling crime.

❖ THE OCCUPATIONAL CULTURE OF THE POLICE ❖

Before beginning an analysis of the police mandate, a brief comment is necessary about the occupational culture of our law enforcers. The American police act in accord with their assumptions about the nature of social life, and their most important assumptions originate with their need to maintain control over both their mandate and their self-esteem. The policeman's self is an amalgam of evaluations made by the many audiences before whom he, as social actor must perform: his peers, his family, his immediate superiors and the higher administrators, his friends on and off duty. His most meaningful standards of performance are the ideals of his *occupational culture*. The policeman judges himself against the ideal policeman as described in police occupational lore and imagery. What a "good policeman" does is an omnipresent standard. The occupational culture, however, contains more than the definition of a good policeman. It contains the typical values, norms, attitudes, and material paraphernalia of an occupational group.

An occupational culture also prompts the *assumptions* about everyday life that become the basis for organizational strategies and tactics. Recent studies of the occupational culture of the police allow the formulation of the following postulates or assumptions, all of which are the basis for police strategies to be discussed later:

1. People cannot be trusted; they are dangerous.
2. Experience is better than abstract rules.
3. You must make people respect you.
4. Everyone hates a cop.
5. The legal system is untrustworthy; policemen make the best decisions about guilt or innocence.
6. People who are not controlled will break laws.
7. Policemen must appear respectable and be efficient.
8. Policemen can most accurately identify crime and criminals.
9. The major jobs of the policeman are to prevent crime and to enforce laws.
10. Stronger punishment will deter criminals from repeating their errors.[8]

Some qualifications about these postulates are in order. They apply primarily to the American noncollege-educated patrolman. They are less applicable to administrators of urban police departments and to members of minority groups within these departments. Nor do they apply accurately to nonurban, state, and federal policemen.

We shall now describe the paradoxes of the police mandate, the strategies of the police in dealing with their troubles, and some of the findings and recommendations of the President's crime commission as they bear on the current attempt by the police to make a running adjustment to their problems.

❖ THE "IMPOSSIBLE" MANDATE ❖

The police in modern society are in agreement with their audiences— which include their professional interpreters, the American family, criminals and politicians—in at least one respect: they have an "impossible" task. Certainly, all professionals have impossible tasks insofar as they try to surmount the problems of collective life that resist easy solutions. The most "successful" occupations, however, have managed to construct a mandate in terms of their own vision of the world. The policeman's mandate, on the other hand, is defined largely by his publics—not, at least at the formal level, in his own terms.

Several rather serious consequences result from the public's image of the police. The public is aware of the dramatic nature of a small portion of police work, but it ascribes the element of excitement to all police activities. To much of the public, the police are seen as alertly ready to respond to citizen demands, as crime-fighters, as an efficient, bureaucratic, highly organized force that keeps society from falling into chaos. The policeman himself considers the essence of his role to be the dangerous and heroic enterprise of crook-catching and the watchful prevention of crimes.[9] The system of positive and negative sanctions from the public and within the department encourages this heroic conception. The public wants crime prevented and controlled; that is, it wants criminals caught. Headlines herald the accomplishments of G-Men and FBI agents who often do catch dangerous men, and the reputation of these federal authorities not infrequently rubs off on local policemen who are much less adept at catching criminals.

In an effort to gain the public's confidence in their ability, and to insure thereby the solidity of their mandate, the police have encouraged the public to continue thinking of them and their work in idealized terms, terms, that is, which grossly exaggerate the actual work done by police. They do engage in chases, in gunfights, in careful sleuthing. But these are rare events. Most police work resembles any other kind of work: it is boring, tiresome, sometimes dirty, sometimes technically demanding, but it is rarely dangerous. Yet the occasional chase, the occasional shoot-out, the occasional triumph of some extraordinary detective work have been seized upon by the police and played up to the public. The public's response has been to demand even more dramatic crook-catching and crime prevention, and this demand for arrests has been converted into an index for measuring how well the police accomplish their mandate. The public's definitions have been converted by the police organization into distorted criteria for promotion, success, and security. Most police departments promote men from patrol to detective work, a generally more desirable duty, for "good pinches"—arrests that are most likely to result in convictions.[10] The protection of the public welfare, however, including personal and property safety, the prevention of crime, and the preservation of individual civil rights, is hardly achieved by a high pinch rate. On the contrary, it might well be argued that protection of the public welfare could best be indexed by a low arrest rate. Because their mandate automatically entails mutually contradictory ends—protecting both public order and individual rights—the police resort to managing their public image and the indexes of their accomplishment. And the ways in which the police manage their appearance are consistent with the assumptions of their occupational culture, with the public's view of the police as a social-control agency, and with the ambiguous nature of our criminal law.

The Problematic Nature of Law and Order

The criminal law is one among many instrumentalities of social control. It is an explicit set of rules created by political authority; it contains provisions for punishment by officials designated with the responsibility to interpret and enforce the rules which should be uniformly applied to all persons within a politically defined territory."[11] This section discusses the relationships between the laws and the mores of a society, the effect of the growth of civilized society on law enforcement, and the problematic nature of crime in an advanced society. The differential nature of enforcement will be considered as an aspect of peace-keeping, and will lead to the discussion of the police in the larger political system.

A society's laws, it is often said, reflect its customs; it can also be said that the growth of the criminal law is proportionate to the decline in the consistency and binding nature of these mores. In simpler societies, where the codes and rules of behavior were well known and homogeneous, sanctions were enforced with much greater uniformity and predictability. Social control was isomorphic with one's obligations to family, clan, and age group, and the political system of the tribe. In a modern, differentiated society, a minimal number of values and norms are shared. And because the fundamental, taken-for-granted consensus on what is proper and respectable has been blurred or shattered or, indeed, never existed, criminal law becomes a basis of social control. As Quinney writes, "Where correct conduct cannot be agreed upon, the criminal law serves to control the behavior of all persons within a political jurisdiction."[12]

Social control through the criminal law predominates in a society only when other means of control have failed. When it does predominate, it no longer reflects the mores of the society. It more accurately reflects the interests of shifting power groups within the society. As a result, the police, as the designated enforcers of a system of criminal laws, are undercut by circumstances that accentuate the growing differences between the moral order and the legal order.

One of these complicating circumstances is simply the matter of social changes, which further stretch the bond between the moral and the legal. The law frequently lags behind the changes in what society deems acceptable and unacceptable practice. At other times, it induces changes, such as those pertaining to civil rights, thereby anticipating acceptable practice. The definition of crime, then, is a product of the relationship between social structure and the law. Crime, to put it another way, is not a homogeneous entity.

The perspective of the patrolman as he goes about his daily rounds is a legalistic one. The law and the administrative actions of his department provide him with a frame of reference for exercising the mandate of the police. The citizen, on the other hand, does not live his life in accordance with a legalistic framework; he defines his acts in accordance with a moral or ethical code provided him by his family, his religion, his social class. For the most part, he sees law enforcement as an intervention in his private affairs.

No matter what the basis for actions of private citizens may be, however, the patrolman's job is one of practical decision-making within a legalistic pattern. His decisions are expected to include an understanding of the law as a system of formal rules, the enforcement practices emphasized by his department, and a knowledge of the specific facts of an allegedly illegal situation. The law includes little formal recognition of the variation in the private arrangement of lives. Even so, the policeman is expected to take these into account also. No policeman can ever be provided with a handbook that could tell him, at a moment's notice, just what standards to apply in enforcing the law and in maintaining order. Wilson summarizes the difficulty inherent in law enforcement as follows:

> Most criminal laws define *acts* (murder, rape, speeding, possessing narcotics), which are held to be illegal; people may disagree as to whether the act should be illegal, as they do with respect to narcotics, for example, but there is little disagreement as to what the behaviour

in question consists of. Laws regarding disorderly conduct and the like assert, usually by implication, that there is a condition ("public order") that can be diminished by various actions. The difficulty, of course, is that public order is nowhere defined and can never be defined unambiguously because what constitutes order is a matter of opinion and convention, not a state of nature. (An unmurdered person, an unraped woman, and an unpossessed narcotic can be defined so as to be recognizable to any reasonable person.) An additional difficulty, a corollary of the first, is the impossibility of specifying, except in the extreme case, what degree of disorder is intolerable and who is to be held culpable for that degree. A suburban street is quiet and pleasant; a big city street is noisy and (to some) offensive; what degree of noise and offense, and produced by whom, constitutes disorderly conduct?[13]

The complexity of law enforcement stems from both the problem of police "discretion" and the inherent tensions between the maintenance of order and individual rights. The law contains rules on how to maintain order; it contains substantive definitions of crime, penalties for violations, and the conditions under which the commission of a crime is said to have been intended.[14] Further, the law contains procedures for the administration of justice and for the protection of the individual. The complexities of law enforcement notwithstanding, however, the modern policeman is frequently faced with the instant problem of defining an action as either legal or illegal, of deciding, in other words, whether to intervene and, if so, what tactic to use. He moves in a dense web of social action and social meanings, burdened by a problematic, complex array of ever-changing laws. Sometimes the policeman must quickly decide very abstract matters. Though a practitioner of the legal arts, his tools at hand are largely obscure, ill-developed, and crude. With little formal training, the rookie must learn his role by absorbing the theories, traditions, and personal whims of experienced patrolmen.

Police Work as Peace Keeping [15]

The thesis of two recent major works on the police, Wilson's *The Varieties of Police Behavior* and Skolnick's *Justice Without Trial*, can be paraphrased as follows: the policeman must exercise discretion in matters involving life and death, honor and dishonor, and he must do so in an environment that he perceives as threatening, dangerous, hostile, and volatile. He sees his efficiency constrained by the law and by the police organization. Yet, he must effectively manage "disorder" in a variety of unspecified ways, through methods usually learned and practiced on the job. As a result of these conditions, the policeman, in enforcing his conception of order, often violates the rights of citizens.

Many observers of police work regard the primary function of a policeman as that of a *peace-keeper*, not a *law enforcer*. According to this view, police spend most of their time attending to order-maintaining functions, such as finding lost children, substituting as ambulance drivers or interceding in quarrels of one sort or another. To these observers, the police spend as little as 10 to 15 percent of their time on law enforcement—responding to burglary calls or trying to find stolen cars. The large-scale riots and disorders of recent years accounted for few police man-hours. Wilson illustrates the peace-keeping (order maintenance) and law-enforcement distinction this way:

> The difference between order maintenance and law enforcement is not simply the difference between "little stuff" and "real crime" or between misdemeanors and felonies. The distinction is fundamental to the police role, for the two functions involve quite dissimilar police actions and judgments. Order maintenance arises out of a dispute among citizens who accuse each other of being at fault; law enforcement arises out of the victimization of an innocent party by a person whose guilt must be proved. Handling a disorderly situation requires the officer to make a judgment about what constitutes an appropriate standard of behavior; law enforcement requires him only to compare a person's behavior with a clear legal standard. Murder or theft is defined, unambiguously, by statutes; public peace is not. Order maintenance rarely leads to an arrest; law enforcement (if the suspect can be found) typically does. Citizens quarreling usually want the officer to "do something," but they rarely want him to make an arrest (after all, the disputants are usually known or related to each other). Furthermore, whatever law is broken in a quarrel is usually a misdemeanor, and in most states, an officer cannot make a misdemeanor arrest unless one party or the other will swear out a formal complaint (which is even rarer)[16]

The complexity of the law and the difficulty in obtaining a complainant combine to tend to make the policeman underenforce the law—to overlook, ignore, dismiss, or otherwise erase the existence of many enforceable breaches of the law.

Some researchers and legalists have begun to piece together a pattern of the conditions under which policemen have a tendency not to enforce the law. From a study of police in three Midwestern states, LaFave has concluded that two considerations characterize a decision not to arrest. The first is that the crime is unlikely to reach public attention—for example, that it is of a private nature or of low visibility—and the second is that underenforcement is unlikely to be detected or challenged.[17] Generally, the conditions under which policemen are less likely to enforce the law are those in which they perceive little public consensus on the law, or in which the law is ambiguous. LaFave found that policemen are not apt to enforce rigorously laws that are viewed by the public as dated, or that are used on the rare occasions when the public order is being threatened.

There is a certain Benthamic calculus involved in all arrests, a calculus that is based on pragmatic considerations such as those enumerated by LaFave. Sex, age, class, and race might also enter into the calculus of whether the law should be enforced. In a case study of the policeman assigned to skid row, Bittner illustrates the great degree of discretion exercised by the policeman. Yet the law, often reified by the policeman, is rarely a clear guide to action—despite the number of routine actions that might be termed "typical situations that policemen perceive as *demand conditions* for action without arrest."[18]

In the exercise of discretion, in the decision to enforce the law or to underenforce, the protection of individual rights is often at stake. But individual rights are frequently in opposition to the preservation of order, as a totalitarian state exemplifies in the extreme. The police try to manage these two contradictory demands by emphasizing their peace-keeping functions. This emphasis succeeds only when a consensus exists on the nature of the order (peace) to be preserved. The greater the difference in viewpoint between the police and the public on the degree and kind of order to be preserved, the greater will be antagonism between the two; the inevitable result of this hostility will be "law breaking."

The resolution of the contradictions and complexities inherent in the police mandate, including the problems of police discretion, of individual rights, of law enforcement and peace-keeping, is not helped, however, by the involvement of police in politics. Politics only further complicates the police mandate. The law itself is a political phenomenon, and at the practical level of enforcing it, the local political system is yet another source of confusion.

The Police in the Political System

In theory, the American police are apolitical. Their own political values and political aims are supposed to be secondary to the institutional objective of law enforcement. In practice, however, police organizations function in a political context; they operate in a public political arena and their mandate is defined politically. They may develop strategies to create and maintain the appearance of being apolitical in order to protect their organizational autonomy, but they are nonetheless a component of American political machinery. There are three reasons why the police are inextricably involved in the political system, the first and most obvious being that the vast majority of the police in this nation are locally controlled. . . . Responsibility for maintaining public order in America is decentralized, and law-enforcement officers are largely under the immediate control of local political authorities.

The second reason why the police are an integral part of the political system is this: law is a political entity, and the administration of criminal law unavoidably encompasses political values and political ends. The police are directly related to a political system that develops and defines the law, itself a product of interpretations of what is right and proper from the perspective of different politically powerful segments within the community.

The third reason why the police are tied to the political system emanates from the second: the police must administer the law. Many factors pattern this enforcement, but they all reflect the political organization of society. The distribution of power and authority, for example, rather than the striving for justice, or equal treatment under the law, can have a direct bearing on enforcement.

Because law enforcement is for the most part locally controlled, sensitivity to local political trends remains an important element in police practice. Since the police are legally prohibited from being publicly political, they often appeal to different community groups, and participate sub rosa in others, in order to influence the determination of public policy. Community policy, whether made by the town council or the mayor or the city manager, affects pay scales, operating budgets, personnel, administrative decisions, and, to some extent, organizational structure. The police administrator must, therefore, be responsive to these controls, and he must deal with them in an understanding way. He must be sensitive to the demands of the local politicians—even while maintaining the loyalty of the lower ranks through a defense of their interests.

There are several direct effects of the political nature of the police mandate. One is that many policemen become alienated; they lose interest in their role as enforcers and in the law as a believable criterion. The pressures of politics also erode loyalty to the police organization and not infrequently lead to collusion with criminals and organized crime.

The policeman's exposure to danger, his social background, low pay, low morale, his vulnerability in a repressive bureaucracy all conspire to make him susceptible to the lures of the underhanded and the appeals of the political. Studies summarized by Skolnick[19] reveal a political profile of the policeman as a conservative, perhaps reactionary, person of lower-class or lower-middle-class origin, often a supporter of radical right causes, often prejudiced and repressive, often extremely ambivalent about the rights of others. The postulates, or assumptions of the police culture, the suspiciousness, fear, low self-esteem, and distrust of others are almost diametrically opposed to the usual conception of the desirable democratic man.

Thus, the enforcement of some laws is personally distasteful. Civil-rights legislation, for example, can be anathema. Or truculence can be the reaction to an order relaxing controls in ghettos during the summer months. It is the ambivalence of policemen toward certain laws and toward certain local policies that fragments loyalty within a department and causes alienation.

There is another consequence of the political nature of the police mandate: the police are tempted. They are tempted not to enforce the law by organized crime, by the operators of illegal businesses such as prostitution, and by fine "law-abiding," illegally parked citizens. All too frequently, the police submit to temptations, becoming in the process exemplars of the corruption typical of modern society, where the demand for "criminal services" goes on at the station house.

Police and politics within the community are tightly interlocked. The sensitivity of the police to their political audiences, their operation within the political system of criminal justice, and their own personal political attitudes undermine their efforts to fulfill their contradictory mandate and to appear politically neutral.

The Efficient, Symptom-Oriented Organization

The Wickersham report, the Hoover administration's report on crime and law enforcement in the United States, was published in 1931. This precursor of the Johnson administration's *The Challenge of Crime in a Free Society* became a rallying point for advocates of police reform. One of its central themes was the lack of "professionalism" among the police of the time—their lack of special training, their corruption, their brutality, and their use of illegal procedures in law enforcement. And one of its results was that the police, partly in order to demonstrate their concern with scientific data gathering on crime and partly to indicate their capacity to "control" crime itself, began to stress crime statistics as a major component of professional police work.

Crime statistics, therefore—and let this point be emphasized—became a police construction. The actual amount of crime committed in a society is unknown—and probably unknowable, given the private nature of most crime. The *crime rate*, consequently, is simply a construction of police activities. That is, the crime rate pertains only to "crimes known to the police," crimes that have been reported to or observed by the police and for which adequate grounds exist for assuming that a violation of the law has, in fact, taken place. (The difference between the *actual* and *known crimes* is often called the "dark figure of crime.") Of course, the construction of a crime rate placed the police in a logically weak position in which they still find themselves. If the crime rate is rising, they argue that more police support is needed to fight the war against crime; if the crime rate is stable or declining, they argue that they have successfully combated the crime menace—a heads-I-win-tails-you-lose proposition.

In spite of their inability to control the commission of illegal acts (roughly, the actual rate), since they do not know about all crime, the police have claimed responsibility for crime control, using the crime rate as an index of their success. This use of the crime rate to measure success is somewhat analogous to their use of a patrolman's arrest rate as an indication of his personal success in law enforcement. Questions about the actual amount of crime and the degree of control exercised are thus bypassed in favor of an index that offers great potential for organizational or bureaucratic control. Instead of grappling with the difficult issue of defining the ends of police work and an operational means for accomplishing them, the police have opted for "efficient" law-enforcement defined in terms of fluctuations of the crime rate. They transformed concern with undefined ends into concern with available means. Their inability to cope with the causes of crime—which might offer them a basis for defining their ends—shifts their "organizational focus" into symptomatic concerns, that is, into a preoccupation with the rate of crime, not its reasons.

This preoccupation with the symptoms of a problem rather than with the problem itself is typical of all bureaucracies. For one characteristic of a bureaucracy is goal-displacement. Bureaucratic organizations tend to lose track of their goals and engage in ritual behavior, substituting means for ends. As a whole, bureaucracies become so engrossed in pursuing, defending, reacting to, and, even, in creating immediate problems that their objective is forgotten. This tendency to displace goals is accelerated by the one value dear to all bureaucracies—efficiency. Efficiency is the be-all and end-all of bureaucratic organizations. Thus, they can expend great effort without any genuine accomplishment.

The police are burdened with the "efficiency problem." They claim to be an efficient bureaucratic organization, but they are unable to define for themselves and others precisely what it is they are being efficient about. In this respect, they do not differ from other paper-shuffling organizations. The police's problem is that the nature of their work is uncertain and negatively defined. It is uncertain in the absence of a consensus not only between the police and the public but also among themselves as to what the goals of a police department should be. It is defined in the negative because the organization punishes its members—patrolmen—for violating departmental procedures but offers no specifications on what they should do or how they should do it.

What do the police do about the problematic nature of law, about the problems arising from their involvement with politics, about their preoccupation with the symptoms of crime rather than the causes? Do they selectively adopt some strategies at the expense of others? Do they vacillate? Are the roles of the organization's members blurred? Before answering these questions, let us examine how the police, through various strategies, manage their appearance before the public. The questions will then be easier to answer.

❖ MAJOR STRATEGIES OF THE POLICE ❖

The responsibilities of the police lead them to pursue contradictory and unattainable ends. They share with all organizations and occupations, however, the ability to avoid solving their problems. Instead, they concentrate on managing them through strategies. Rather than resolving their dilemmas, the police have manipulated them with a professional eye on just how well the public accepts their dexterity. Thus, law enforcement becomes a self-justifying system. It becomes more responsive to its own needs, goals, and procedures than to serving society. In this section, we will show the ways in which the police have followed the course of most other bureaucratic institutions in society, responding to their problems by merely giving the appearance of facing them while simultaneously promoting the trained incapacity to do otherwise.

The two primary aims of most bureaucracies, the police included, are the maintenance of their organizational autonomy and the security of their members. To accomplish these aims, they adopt a pattern of institutional action that can best be described as "professionalism." This word, with its many connotations and definitions, cloaks all the many kinds of actions carried out by the police.

The guise of professionalism embodied in a bureaucratic organization is the most important strategy employed by the police to defend their mandate and thereby to build self-esteem, organizational autonomy, and occupational solidarity or cohesiveness. The professionalization drives of the police are no more suspect than the campaigns of other striving, upwardly mobile occupational groups. However, since the police have a monopoly on legal violence, since they are the active enforcers of the public will, serving theoretically in the best interests of the public, the consequences of their yearnings for prestige and power are imbued with far greater social ramifications than the relatively harmless attempts of florists, funeral directors, and accountants to attain public stature. Disinterested law enforcement through bureaucratic means is an essential in our society and in any democracy, and the American police are certainly closer to attaining this ideal than they were in 1931 at the time of the Wickersham report. Professionalism qua professionalism is unquestionably desirable in the police. But if in striving for the heights of prestige they fail to serve the altruistic values of professionalism, if their professionalism means that a faulty portrait of the social reality of crime is being painted, if their professionalism conceals more than it reveals about the true nature of their operations, then a close analysis of police professionalism is in order.

Police professionalism cannot be easily separated in practice from the bureaucratic ideal epitomized in modern police practice. The bureaucratic ideal is established as a means of obtaining a commitment from personnel to organizational and occupational norms. This bureaucratic commitment is designed to supersede commitments to competing norms, such as obligations to friends or kin or members of the same racial or ethnic group. Unlike medicine and law, professions that developed outside the context of bureaucracies, policing has always been carried out, if done on a full-time basis, as a bureaucratic function.

Modern police bureaucracy and modern police professionalism are highly articulated, although they contain some inherent stresses that are not our present concern. The strategies employed by the police to manage their public appearance develop from their adaptation of the bureaucratic ideal. These strategies incorporate the utilization of *technology* and *official statistics* in law enforcement, of *styles of patrol* that attempt to accommodate the community's desire for public order with the police department's preoccupation with bureaucratic procedures, of *secrecy* as a means of controlling the public's response to their operations, of *collaboration* with criminal elements to foster the appearance of a smoothly run, law-abiding community, and of a *symbiotic relationship* with the criminal justice system that minimizes public knowledge of the flaws within this largely privately operated system.

❖ THE EFFECTIVENESS OF POLICE STRATEGIES ❖

The police have developed and utilized the strategies outlined above for the purpose of creating, as we have said, the appearance of managing their troublesome mandate. To a large extent, they are facilitated in the use of these strategies, in being able to project a favorable impression, by a public that has always been apathetic about police activity. Moreover, what activity the public does observe is filtered through the media with its own special devices for creating a version of reality. The public's meaning of police action is rarely gathered from first-hand experience, but from the constructed imagery of the media—which, in turn, rely upon official police sources for their presentation of the news. The police for their part, understandably, manipulate public appearances as much as they possibly can in order to gain and maintain public support.

The specific strategies used by the police to create a publicly suitable image . . . described [earlier were]: the guise of professionalism; the implementation of the bureaucratic ideal of organization; the use of technology, official statistics, and various styles of patrol; secrecy; collaboration with corrupt elements; and the establishment of a symbiotic relationship with the courts. This section will present evidence by which to evaluate these strategies. The term "effectiveness" is used only in the context of how well these devices accomplish the ends which the public and the police themselves publicly espouse; the recommendations and evaluations of the President's crime commission will be central in making judgments of police effectiveness. This appraisal of how well the police manipulate their appearance will also be a guideline for evaluating the recommendations of the commission's task force report on the police.

Professionalism and the Bureaucratic Ideal

The assumptions of professionalism and of a bureaucratic organization include a devotion to rational principles and ends that may then be translated into specific work routines having predictable outcomes. The police are organized in a military command fashion, with rigid rules and a hierarchy governing operations. However, the patrolman, the lowest man in the hierarchy—and usually the least well-trained and educated—is in the key position of exercising the greatest amount of discretion on criminal or possibly criminal activities. Especially in his peace-keeping role and in dealing with minor infractions (misdemeanors), the patrolman has wide discretionary power concerning if, when, why, and how to intervene in private affairs.

Police work must both rely on discretion and control it. Excessive inattention and excessive attention to infractions of the law are equally damaging to a community. However, the complexity of the law, its dynamic and changing properties, the extensiveness of police department regulations, policies, and procedures, and the equivocal, relativistic nature of crime in regard to certain situations, settings, persons, and groups make it impossible to create a job description that would eliminate the almost boundless uncertainty in police patrol.

Neither professionals nor bureaucrats, however, have yet found an effective means of controlling discretion. If an organization cannot control those of its members with the greatest opportunity to exercise discretion, it flounders in its attempts to accomplish its stated purposes. Two general principles suggest why the police have not been able to control discretion. The first has to do with the general problem of control and the second with the specific nature of police work.

Men are unwilling to submit completely to the will of their organizational superiors. Men will always attempt to define and control their own work. Control means the right to set the pace, to define mistakes, to develop standards of "good" production and efficiency. But as surely as superiors seek to control the quality and the extent of work performed by their subordinates in a hierarchy, just as surely will they meet with attempts to reshape and subvert these controls.

In the specific instance of police bureaucracies, the patrolman conceives of himself as a man able to make on-the-spot decisions of guilt or innocence. He does not think of himself as a bureaucratic functionary nor as a professional. Further, since the police organization itself has become far more interested in efficiency than in purpose, since it is unable to specify its overall objectives, the patrolman finds it difficult, if not impossible, to demonstrate that necessary devotion to rational ends required of professionalism and bureaucratic organizations. Until police departments are able to control the amount and kind of discretion exercised by their members, and until the police are able, with the help of lawyers and other citizens, to develop positive means of motivation and reward in line with clear, overall policy directives, the failure of what we have called the professionalism-bureaucracy strategy is an absolute certainty.

Technology, Statistics, and the Crime Rate

This section will evaluate the strategy of technology in the control and prevention of crime, the use of statistics, and the significance of the so-called crime rate. Given the sociological nature of crime, let it be said immediately that present technology deals with unimportant crime and that the FBI index of crimes, by which we base judgments of police effectiveness, is biased and an unrealistic reflection of the actual crime rate.

One of the striking aspects of the President's crime commission report is the thoroughly sociological nature of the document. The discussion of the causes of crime in the first two chapters points to the growth of urbanism, anonymity, the breakdown in social control, and the increasing numbers of frustrated and dissatisfied youth who have always constituted the majority of known lawbreakers. There are no labels such as "evil people," "emotionally disturbed," "mentally ill," or "criminally insane." The first set of recommendations under prevention in the summary pages of the report are "sociological": strengthen the family, improve slum schools, provide employment, reduce segregation, construct housing. All these matters are patently and by definition out of the control of the police.

There is every evidence that the police themselves subscribe to a thoroughly social, if not sociological, definition of the causes of crime—that is, that crime is the manifestation of long-established social patterns and structures which ensnare and implicate the police and the criminals as well as the general public. And they are doubtless correct.

Surveys done by the President's crime commission revealed that there are always contingencies in the information police receive about a crime even before they are able to investigate it. These contingencies involve such matters as the nature of the relationship between the victim and the offender and whether or not the victim believes the police are competent to investigate and solve the crime. Computer technology depends on informational "input." On that point, the police seem both unable to define what sort of information would be useful and unable to obtain, and probably never can obtain in a democratic society, information that would make them better able to enforce the law.

The facts in the problem of "crime prevention" overwhelmingly doom the present professionally based notion that the application of science and technology will begin to ease the distress the police feel as they face the escalating demands of their audiences. Also, it would be easier to assess the value of the technology strategy if we were able to define exactly to what end the technology would be applied and in what ways it could be expected to work.

Styles of Patrol

Police strategy is subject to many contingencies. It is a basic principle of public administration that policy made at the higher echelons of an organization will be effective only if each successively lower level of the organization complies with that policy and is capable of carrying it out. It is also a truism that participants at the lowest level in the hierarchy are the most "difficult" to mobilize and integrate into the organization. A style of patrol is basically the manner in which an administrative police policy is executed. The policy may prescribe that the patrolman overlook certain types of illegal acts; it may order that he minimally enforce particular laws or be sensitive to and strictly enforce others. If the administrative order setting a patrol style does not win the cooperation of the patrolman it is certain to fail. Thus, the success of any high-echelon policy that involves the performance of the patrolman is contingent upon his compliance with that policy. If the administrator's orders are not binding on the patrolman, no distinctive style of patrol will result; all that will be demonstrated will be the responses of the patrolman to other aspects of his social environment, especially, how his fellow patrolmen perform.

The success of this strategy is dependent upon the capacity of the administrator to create loyalty to his internal policies. With the rise of police unions, the discontent of the black patrolman, low pay, and relatively less security for the policeman, organizational control is a major problem in all the large police departments. . . .

The effectiveness of the watchman, legalistic, and service styles of patrol will also depend on the degree of political consensus among the community groups patrolled, the clarity of the boundaries of community neighborhoods, competition between the police and self-help or vigilante groups, and the relative importance of nonoccupational norms in enforcement practice—that is, the importance of racial or ethnic similarities between the patrolman and the people in his neighborhood. If a clear social consensus on the meaning of the law and what is expected of the police can be established within a community, a well-directed policy of control over police patrol is the most logical and rational approach to police work. In some communities, largely suburban and middleclass, the police can carry out what their public demands and a degree of harmony exists. This consensus is absent in our inner cities.

Secrecy and Collaboration

The use of secrecy by the police is, as we have pointed out, a strategy employed not only to assist them in maintaining the appearance of political neutrality but to protect themselves against public complaints. Secrecy also helps to forestall public efforts to achieve better police service and to secure political accountability for police policy. Police collaboration with criminal elements—corruption, in other words—has much the same effect since it decreases the pressure to enforce ''unenforceable'' laws against certain segments of the police's clientele.

These two strategies were among the major concerns of the President's crime commission task force on police. The task force's report devoted major attention to the fact that political forces influence police actions and policies. The report affirmed the political nature of police work; what concerned the writers of the report was the nature and type of political influence on police actions. Their recommendations, furthermore, were based on their recognition of the fact that the police have been fairly successful in managing the appearance of being apolitical.

There are several reasons why the police strategies of secrecy and collaboration will continue in force: (1) as long as the client—the public—is seen as the enemy, the police will treasure their secrecy and use it to engineer public consent to their policies and practices; (2) as long as a new political consensus is not formed on the nature and type of police control necessary in society as a whole, the organized, self-serving survival aims of police organizations will emerge victorious. Any well-organized consensual, secretive organization can resist the efforts of an unorganized public, managed by rhetoric and appearances, to reform it; (3) as long as there remains a lack of consensus on the enforcement of our "moralistic" laws, police corruption and selective law enforcement will continue. Collaboration to reduce adversary relationships with the criminal segment of society will always be an effective strategy—providing a sudden upsurge in public morality doesn't temporarily subject the police to a full-scale "housecleaning." Replacements would, of course, be subject to the same pressures and would, in all likelihood, eventually take the same line of least resistance.

One solution to corruption is said to be better educated, more professional policemen. By recruiting better educated men, the more professionalized police departments also seek to diminish the expression of political attitudes on the job and the tendency of policemen to form political power groups based on their occupation. These are also assumptions made by the crime commission's task force on police. There is, however, no evidence that college-educated or better-paid policemen are "better policemen"; nor is there any evidence that "better men" alone will solve the essentially structural problems of the occupation.

We can tentatively conclude from this review that corruption will remain with us as long as laws remain which stipulate punishments for actions on which a low public consensus exists. It will remain when there is likely to be a low visibility of police performance, and it will remain while there is a high public demand for illegal services—gambling, prostitution, abortion—and the concomitant need of the police for information on these services from the practitioners themselves.

Symbiosis and Justice

Although the police have the principal discretion in the field with reference to the detection, surveillance, and appraisal of alleged offenders, the final disposition of a criminal case must be made in the courts. The police are thus dependent on the courts in a very special way for their successes. The ideal model of the criminal justice system makes the police essentially the fact gatherers and apprehenders, while the courts are to be the decision-makers.

The police attempt to appear efficient has led them as we have noted before to seek the good pinch, the arrest that will stand up in court. With victimless crimes, such as those involving gambling or drugs or prostitution, the police control the situation since they alone decide whether an offense has been committed and whether they have a legal case against the offender. To control the success rate in these cases, the police create a gaggle of informants, many of whom are compelled to give the police evidence in order to stay free of a potential charge against themselves for a violation similar to the one they are providing information about. In the case of more serious crimes, the problems are more complex; in these cases the police must rely on other informants, and their discretion on arrests and charges are more often exercised by administrators and prosecuting attorneys.

In the prosecution stage, the bureaucratic demands of the court system are paramount. Abraham Blumberg describes these demands and the tension between efficiency and ''due process'':

> The dilemma is frequently resolved through bureaucratically ordained shortcuts, deviations and outright rule violations by the members of the courts, from judges to stenographers, in order to meet production norms. Because they fear criticism on ethical as well as legal grounds, all the significant participants in the court's social structure are bound into an organized system of complicity. Patterned, covert, informal breaches, and evasions of ''due process'' are accepted as routine—they are institutionalized—but are nevertheless denied to exist.[20]

The net effect of this strain within the court system is to produce a higher rate of convictions by means of encouraging a plea of guilty to a lesser charge. As far as the police are concerned, then, the strategy of symbiosis is sound.

There are several undesirable effects of this symbiosis. First, it encourages corruption by permitting the police to make decisions about the freedom of their informants; it gives them an illegal hold and power over them, and thus it undercuts the rule of law. Second, many offenders with long criminal records are either granted their freedom as informants or allowed to plead guilty to lesser charges in return for the dismissal of a more serious charge. Skolnick calls this the ''reversal of the hierarchy of penalties,'' because the more serious crimes of habitual criminals are prosecuted less zealously than the minor violations of first offenders. Third, it helps blur the distinction between the apprehension and prosecution aspects of our criminal-justice system.

❖ CONCLUSIONS AND PROPOSED REFORMS ❖

The allocation of rewards in a society represents both its division of labor and its configuration of problems. Ironically, the allocation of rewards is also the allocation of societal trouble. Societal trouble in a differentiated society is occupational trouble. The ebb and flow of rewards emanating from the division of labor becomes structured into persistent patterns that are sustained by continuous transactions among organizations and occupational groups. Occupational structures reflect societal structures, but they reflect them in ways that have been negotiated over time. The negotiation is based upon the universal human proclivity to differentiate roles, organizations, and occupations. The more dependent an organization is upon its environment for rewards, the more likely it is to rely on the management and presentation of strategies to establish the appearance of autonomy.

Organizations without a high degree of autonomy in the environments in which they operate are greatly constrained by the internal pressure of competing aims and roles of members. The agreement on problems, goals, values, and self-concepts that emerges from occupational socialization and functioning is a strong basis for influencing organizational direction. The occupational standards in this case subvert the rule of law as a system of norms outside the informal norms of the occupation. The policeman's view of his role and his occupational culture are very influential in determining the nature of policing. The basic source of police trouble is the inability of the police to define a mandate that will minimize the inconsistent nature of their self-expectations and the expectations of those they serve.

The problems derived from a contradictory mandate remain unaffected by the efforts of the institution to solve them; they do, however, take the shape into which they have been cast by institutional functionaries. Cooley long ago discussed the process of institutional ossification, the process by which institutions stray from serving the needs of their members and their publics, thereby losing the loyalty of those within and the support of those without. The consequences of institutional ossification as related to the police are twofold. First, the police begin to search for a so-called higher order of legitimacy; they make appeals to morality, to patriotism, to "Americanism," and to "law and order" to shore up eroded institutional charters and to accelerate their attempts to control and manipulate their members and clients. Second, the police, as they develop a far greater potential for controlling those they serve through their presentational strategies, come to serve themselves better than ever before.

The problem of the police is essentially, the problem of the democratic society, and until the central values and social structures of our society are modified (and I think we are seeing such a modification), there can be no real change in the operation of social control. The needed changes are, by and large, not those dealt with in the crime commission report. And this is telling. For an eminently sociological document, it did not focus on the heart of the problem: our anachronistic, moralistic laws, with which the police are burdened, and our dated political system, which is unable to bring political units into a state of civil accountability. The focus of the report and recommendations was predictably on symptoms of crime, not on causes of crime. The "managerial focus" of the report, or its public-administration bias, outlined needed reforms, but not ways in which to implement them, and the problem of efficiency was never really faced.

Not surprisingly for a political document having a variety of public functions, the report has little to say about the nature of the present criminal laws. It dwells, like the police themselves, on means, not ends. As Isidore Silver points out in a critique of the report, more than one-half the crimes committed do not harm anyone: more than one-third are for drunkenness, and a small but important portion are for other "crimes without victims." Most crimes are committed by juveniles who inexplicably "grow out" of their criminality. In 1965, 50 percent of the known burglaries and larcenies were committed by youths under 18.[21] The report does note what was a central point of our discussion of the political nature of crime, that police corruption is, in almost every instance, a consequence of trying to enforce admittedly unenforceable laws. The demand for services provided by homosexuals, by gamblers [and] prostitutes . . . is high, and the supply is legally made unavailable to anyone who wants to remain in the so-called "law-abiding" category. The laws, in effect, create the crime and the criminals.

Changes in laws to reduce their absolutistic element and to free people who deviate with little harm to others from the onus of criminalization cannot be accomplished without a parallel change in the nature of police accountability. As we have seen, the strategies of secrecy and rhetoric used by the police play on the fears of society and provide a basis for police control. The managerial reforms contained in the task force report—more public debate on and greater internal and external control over police actions—are needed. Even more urgently required are specific ways in which the cities can control the police and make them strictly accountable for their actions—methods, that is, which go a good deal further than merely disposing of the chief or convening a judicial review board. To give city governments this kind of control over the police, however, entails the reorganization of police departments themselves so that their goals are clear and defined and so that the occupational rewards within the police organization are aligned with public goals.

Three interrelated organizational changes must be made to insure that police attend to the job of maintaining public order. One is to reorganize police departments along functional lines aimed at peace-keeping rather than law enforcement; the second is to allocate rewards for keeping the peace rather than for enforcing the law; the third is to decentralize police functions to reflect community control without the diffusion of responsibility and accountability to a central headquarters.

Present police departments are organized in a military fashion; orders move down the line from the chief to departmental sections assigned law-enforcement functions. These sections usually include such divisions as traffic, patrol, records, detective, juvenile, intelligence, crime-lab, and communications. The principal basis for the assignment of functions, however, is law enforcement;[22] what is needed is a new set of organizational premises so that the basis for the assignment of functions is not law enforcement but the maintenance of order. As Wilson explains:

> If order were the central mission of the department, there might be a "family disturbance squad," a "drunk and derelict squad," a "riot control squad," and a "juvenile squad"; law enforcement matters would be left to a "felony squad." Instead, there is a detective division organized, in the larger departments, into units specializing in homicide, burglary, auto theft, narcotics, vice, robbery, and the like. The undifferentiated patrol division gets everything else. Only juveniles tend to be treated by specialized units under both schemes, partly because the law requires or encourages such specialization. The law enforcement orientation of most departments means that new specialized units are created for every offense about which the public expresses concern or for which some special technology is required.[23]

What is called for, then, is a new organizational pattern that will provide a domestic unit (as is now being tried in New York City), a juvenile unit, and a drunk unit with a detoxification center, all with a peace-keeping orientation and peace-keeping functions. Only a felony squad and perhaps a riot squad should be used to enforce the law.

One of the obvious ways in which to improve the morale of the patrolman is to let him do a greater amount of investigative work and to take on the responsibility for "solving" some of the crimes originating with his patrol. Rewards could then be allocated in accord with the more limited ends of peace-keeping—for instance, in rewarding a patrolman for a decline in the number of drunks who reappear in court. Since no comprehensive policy can be imagined to guide order maintenance, limited ends for various departments must be developed and subjected to public review. The key is to allow the policeman to develop judgment about the motives and future intentions of people with whom he comes in contact, and to reward him for peace-keeping, not "good pinches" alone.

This reappraisal of the allocation of rewards means, of course, that there must be greater coordination of police and other agencies within the criminal-justice system in order to increase the benefits to the client (the offender or the criminal) and break down the isolation of the police.[24] To allow the policeman to assume greater peace-keeping responsibilities would allow him to play a functional role parallel to that of the better general practitioner of medicine: the referral specialist, the coordinator of family health, the source of records and information, and the family friend and counselor. Such an organizational change in the policemen's function would, naturally enough, make community control of the police a greater possibility. It would begin to bridge the chasm between the police and many hostile segments within the public, a process that could be facilitated by the creation of a community-relations division within police departments.

The third needed modification of the present structure of police work is the development of decentralized operations. One of the major social trends of the last ten years has been the increase in the lack of attachment people have for their major institutions. Police today suffer from a crisis of legitimacy, and this crisis is heightened by their failure to promote a sense of commitment to their operations by the citizens they serve. One way in which to introduce commitment and a sense of control over the police by members of a community is to make the police more accessible. St. Louis, for example, has experimented with "storefront" police stations, staffed by a few men who are available as advisers, counselors, protectors, and friends of the people in the immediate neighborhood. If the police should begin to differentiate the role of the patrolman to include the functions of a peace-keeping community agent, the control of these agents should reside in the community. Thus public participation in the decision-making processes of the police would begin at the precinct or neighborhood level; it would not be simply in the form of a punitive civilian review board or a token citizen board at headquarters.

We began with the notion of trouble, police trouble, the troublesome mandate of the policeman. There will be little succor for him as long as our social structure remains fraught with contradictory value premises, with fragmented political power and the consequent inadequate control of the police, with the transformation of public trusts into institutional rights. There will be little succor for him as long as our political agencies resist moving to de-moralize our criminal laws. As it is, we can expect that the management of crime through police strategies and appearances will continue to be a disruptive element in American society.

Notes

[1] See Everett C. Hughes, *Men and Their Work* (New York: The Free Press, 1958), chap. 6; idem, "The Study of Occupations," in *Sociology Today*, ed. R. K. Merton, Leonard Broom, and L. S. Cottrell (New York: Basic Books, 1959), 442–458.

[2] Hughes, *op. cit.*

[3] The President's Commission on Law Enforcement and Administration of Justice (hereafter cited as President's Commission). *The Challenge of Crime in a Free Society* (Washington, D.C.: U.S. Government Printing Office, 1967); and idem. *Task Force Report: The Police* (Washington, D.C.: United States Government Printing Office, 1967).

[4] The important, sociological notions of "strategy" and "tactics" come from military theory and game theory. See, for example, Erving Goffman, *The Presentation of Self in Everyday Life* (Garden City, NY: Doubleday, 1959).

[5] *Ibid.*

[6] Kenneth Burke, *A Grammar of Motives and a Rhetoric of Motives* (New York: Meridian Books, 1962), 565.

[7] D. W. Ball makes this distinction between rhetoric and what he terms "situated vocabularies" in "The Problematics of Respectability," in Jack D. Douglas, ed., *Deviance and Respectability* (New York: Basic Books, 1970).

[8] These postulates have been drawn from the work of Michael Banton, *The Policeman in the Community* (New York: Basic Books, 1965); the articles in *The Police: Six Sociological Essays*, ed. David Bordua (New York: John Wiley & Sons, 1967), esp. those by Albert J. Reiss and David Bordua, and John H. McNamara; Arthur Niederhoffer, *Behind the Shield* (Garden City, NY: Doubleday, 1967); Jerome Skolnick, *Justice Without Trial* (New York: John Wiley & Sons, 1966); and William A. Westley, "Violence and the Police," *American Journal of Sociology*, 59 (July 1953), 34–41; idem, "Secrecy and the Police," *Social Forces*, 34 (March 1956), 254–257; idem, "The Police: Law, Custom and Morality," in Peter I. Rose, ed. *The Study of Society* (New York: Random House, 1967). See also James Q. Wilson, *Varieties of Police Behavior: The Management of Law and Order in Eight Communities* (Cambridge: Harvard University Press, 1968); idem, "The Police and Their Problems: A Theory," *Public Policy*, 12 (1963), 189–216; idem, "Generational and Ethnic Differences Among Police Officers," *American Journal of Sociology*, 69 (March 1964), 522–528.

[9] Although the imagery of the police and their own self-definition coincide on the dangers of being a policeman, at least one study has found that many other occupations are more dangerous. Policemen kill six times as many people as policemen are killed in the line of duty. In 1955, Robin found that the rate of police fatalities on duty, including accidents, was 33 per 100,000, less than the rate for mining (94), agriculture (55), construction (76), and transportation (44). Between 1950 and 1960, an average of 240 persons were killed each year by policemen—approximately six times the number of policemen killed by criminals. Gerald D. Robin, "Justifiable Homicide by Police Officers," *Journal of Criminal Law, Criminology and Police Science*, 54 (1963), 225–231.

[10] Niederhoffer, *Behind the Shield*, 221.

[11] See Richard Quinney, "Is Criminal Behavior Deviant Behavior?" *British Journal of Criminology*, 5 (April 1965), 133. The material in this section draws heavily from Quinney. See also R. C. Fuller, "Morals and the Criminal Law," *Journal of Criminal Law, Criminology and Police Science*, 32 (March-April 1942), 624–630.

12 Quinney, *op. cit.*, 133.

13 Wilson, *op. cit.*, 21–22.

14 Skolnick, *op. cit.*, 7–8, 9.

15 This perspective on police work is emphasized by Wilson *op. cit.*; Banton, *op. cit.*; and Skolnick, *op. cit.* In addition, see the more legalistically oriented work of Wayne R. LaFave, *Arrest*, ed. F. J. Remington (Boston: Little, Brown, 1965); Joseph Goldstein. "Police Discretion Not to Invoke the Legal Process: Low-Visibility Decisions in the Administration of Justice." *Yale Law Journal*, 69 (1960), 543–594; and Herman Goldstein, "Police Discretion: The Ideal Versus the Real," *Public Administration Review*, 23 (September 1963), 140–148.

16 James Q. Wilson, "What Makes a Better Policeman?" *Atlantic*, 223 (March 1969), 131.

17 LaFave, *op. cit.*

18 Egon Bittner, "The Police on Skid-Row: A Study of Peace-Keeping." *American Sociological Review*, 32 (October 1967), 699–715.

19 Jerome Skolnick, ed., *The Politics of Protest* (New York: Simon & Schuster, 1969), 252–253.

20 Abraham Blumberg, *Criminal Justice* (Chicago: Quadrangle Press, 1967), 69.

21 Isidore Silver, Introduction to *The Challenge of Crime in a Free Society* (New York: Avon Books, 1968), 25. The President's Commission, *Task Force Report: The Courts*, discusses substantive criminal law, however, and does make some suggestions for legal change.

22 President's Commission, *Task Force Report: The Police*, charts on 46–47.

23 Wilson, *op. cit.*, 69.

24 See John P. Clark, "The Isolation of the Police: A Comparison of the British and American Situations," in John Scanzoni ed., *Readings in Social Problems* (Boston: Allyn & Bacon, 1967), 384–410. See also David Bordua, "Comments on Police-Community Relations," mimeographed (Urbana: University of Illinois, n.d.).

7

The Capacity to Use Force as the Core of the Police Role

Egon Bittner

Our society recognizes as legitimate three very different forms of responsive force. First, we are authorized to use force for the purpose of self-defense. Though the laws governing self-defense are far from clear, it appears that an attacked person can counterattack only after he has exhausted all other means of avoiding harm, including retreat, and that the counterattack may not exceed what is necessary to disable the assailant from carrying out his intent. These restrictions are actually enforceable because harm done in the course of self-defense does furnish grounds for criminal and tort proceedings. It becomes necessary, therefore, to show compliance with these restrictions to rebut the charges of excessive and unjustified force even in self-defense.[1]

The second form of authorization entrusts the power to proceed coercively to some specifically deputized persons against some specifically named persons. Among the agents who have such highly specific powers are mental hospital attendants and prison guards. Characteristically, such persons use force in carrying out court orders; but they may use force only against named persons who are remanded to their custody and only to the extent required to implement a judicial order of confinement. Of course, like everybody else, they may also act within the provisions governing self-defense. . . .

Reprinted courtesy of the author from *The Functions of the Police in Modern Society*. (1970), pp. 36–47. Footnotes renumbered.

The third way to legitimize the use of responsive force is to institute a police force. Contrary to the cases of self-defense and the limited authorization of custodial functionaries, the police authorization is essentially unrestricted. Because the expression "essentially" is often used to hedge a point, we will make fully explicit what we mean by it. There exist three formal limitations of the freedom of policemen to use force, which we must admit even though they have virtually no practical consequences. First, the police use of deadly force is limited in most jurisdictions. Though the powers of a policeman in this respect exceed those of citizens, they are limited nevertheless. For example, in [all] jurisdictions policemen are empowered to shoot to kill [some] fleeing felony suspects, but not fleeing misdemeanor suspects. It is scarcely necessary to argue that, given the uncertainties involved in defining a delict under conditions of hot pursuit, this could hardly be expected to be an effective limitation.[2] Second, policemen may use force only in the performance of their duties and not to advance their own personal interest or the private interests of other persons. Though this is rather obvious, we mention it for the sake of completeness. Third, and this point too is brought up to meet possible objections, policemen may not use force maliciously or frivolously. These three restrictions, and nothing else, were meant by the use of the qualifier "essentially." Aside from these restrictions there exist no guidelines, no specifiable range of objectives, no limitations of any kind that instruct the policeman what he may or must do. Nor do there exist any criteria that would allow the judgment whether some forceful intervention was necessary, desirable, or proper. And finally, it is exceedingly rare that police actions involving the use of force are actually reviewed and judged by anyone at all.

In sum, the frequently heard talk about the lawful use of force by the police is practically meaningless and, because no one knows what is meant by it, so is the talk about the use of minimum force. Whatever vestigial significance attaches to the term "lawful" use of force is confined to the obvious and unnecessary rule that police officers may not commit crimes of violence. Otherwise, however, the expectation that they may and will use force is left entirely undefined. In fact, the only instructions any policeman ever receives in this respect consist of sermonizing that he should be humane and circumspect, and that he must not desist from what he has undertaken merely because its accomplishment may call for coercive means. We might add, at this point, that the entire debate about the troublesome problem of police brutality will not move beyond its present impasse, and the desire to eliminate it will remain an impotent conceit, until this point is fully grasped and unequivocally admitted. In fact, our expectation that policemen will use force, coupled by our refusals to state clearly what we mean by it (aside from sanctimonious homilies), smacks of more than a bit of perversity.

Of course, neither the police nor the public is entirely in the dark about the justifiable use of force by the officers. We had occasion to allude to the assumption that policemen may use force in making arrests. But the benefit deriving from this apparent core of relative clarity is outweighed by its potentially misleading implications. For the authorization of the police to use force is in no important sense related to their duty to apprehend criminals. Were this the case then it could be adequately considered as merely a special case of the same authorization that is entrusted to custodial personnel. It might perhaps be considered a bit more complicated, but essentially of the same nature. But the police authority to use force is radically different from that of a prison guard. Whereas the powers of the latter are incidental to his obligation to implement a legal command, the police role is far better understood by saying that their ability to arrest offenders is incidental to their authority to use force.

Many puzzling aspects of police work fall into place when one ceases to look at it as principally concerned with law enforcement and crime control, and only incidentally and often incongruously concerned with an infinite variety of other matters. It makes much more sense to say that the police are nothing else than a mechanism for the distribution of situationally justified force in society. The latter conception is preferable to the former on three grounds. First, it accords better with the actual expectations and demands made of the police (even though it probably conflicts with what most people would say, or expect to hear, in answer to the question about the proper police function); second, it gives a better accounting of the actual allocation of police manpower and other resources; and, third, it lends unity to all kinds of police activity. These three justifications will be discussed in some detail in the following.

The American city dweller's repertoire of methods for handling problems includes one known as "calling the cops." The practice to which the idiom refers is enormously widespread. Though it is more frequent in some segments of society than in others, there are very few people who do not or would not resort to it under suitable circumstances. A few illustrations will furnish the background for an explanation of what "calling the cops" means.[3]

> Two patrolmen were directed to report to an address located in a fashionable district of a large city. On the scene they were greeted by the lady of the house who complained that the maid had been stealing and receiving male visitors in her quarters. She wanted the maid's belongings searched and the man removed. The patrolmen

refused the first request, promising to forward the complaint to the bureau of detectives, but agreed to see what they could do about the man. After gaining entrance to the maid's room they compelled a male visitor to leave, drove him several blocks away from the house, and released him with the warning never to return.

In a tenement, patrolmen were met by a public health nurse who took them through an abysmally deteriorated apartment inhabited by four young children in the care of an elderly woman. The babysitter resisted the nurse's earlier attempts to remove the children. The patrolmen packed the children in the squad car and took them to Juvenile Hall, over the continuing protests of the elderly woman.

While cruising through the streets a team of detectives recognized a man named in a teletype received from the sheriff of an adjoining county. The suspect maintained that he was in the hospital at the time the offense alleged in the communication took place, and asked the officers to verify his story over their car radio. When he continued to plead innocence he was handcuffed and taken to headquarters. Here the detectives learned that the teletype had been cancelled. Prior to his release the man was told that he could have saved himself grief had he gone along voluntarily.

In a downtown residential hotel, patrolmen found two ambulance attendants trying to persuade a man, who according to all accounts was desperately ill, to go to the hospital. After some talk, they helped the attendants in carrying the protesting patient to the ambulance and sent them off.

In a middle-class neighborhood, patrolmen found a partly disassembled car, tools, a loudly blaring radio, and five beer-drinking youths at the curb in front of a single-family home. The homeowner complained that this had been going on for several days and the men had refused to take their activities elsewhere. The patrolmen ordered the youths to pack up and leave. When one sassed them they threw him into the squad car, drove him to the precinct station, from where he was released after receiving a severe tongue lashing from the desk sergeant.

In the apartment of a quarreling couple, patrolmen were told by the wife, whose nose was bleeding, that the husband stole her purse containing money she earned. The patrolmen told the man they would "take him in," whereupon he returned the purse and they left.

What all these vignettes are meant to illustrate is that whatever the substance of the task at hand, whether it involves protection against an undesired imposition, caring for those who cannot care for themselves, attempting to solve a crime, helping to save a life, abating a nuisance, or settling an explosive dispute, police intervention means above all making use of the capacity and authority to overpower resistance to an attempted solution in the native habitat of the problem. There can be no doubt that this feature of police work is uppermost in the minds of people who solicit police aid or direct the attention of the police to problems, that persons against whom the police proceed have this feature in mind and conduct themselves accordingly, and that every conceivable police intervention projects the message that force may be, and may have to be, used to achieve a desired objective. It does not matter whether the persons who seek police help are private citizens or other government officials, nor does it matter whether the problem at hand involves some aspect of law enforcement or is totally unconnected with it.

It must be emphasized, however, that the conception of the centrality of the capacity to use force in the police role does not entail the conclusion that the ordinary occupational routines consist of the actual exercise of this capacity. It is very likely, though we lack information on this point, that the actual use of physical coercion and restraint is rare for all policemen and that many policemen are virtually never in the position of having to resort to it. What matters is that police procedure is defined by the feature that it may not be opposed in its course, and that force can be used if it is opposed. This is what the existence of the police makes available to society. Accordingly, the question, "What are policemen supposed to do?" is almost completely identical with the question, "What kinds of situations require remedies that are non-negotiably coercible?"[4]

Our second justification for preferring the definition of the police role we proposed to the traditional law enforcement focus of the role requires us to review the actual police practices to see to what extent they can be subsumed under the conception we offered. To begin we can take note that law enforcement and crime control are obviously regarded as calling for remedies that are non-negotiably coercible. According to available estimates, approximately one-third of available manpower resources of the police are at any time committed to dealing with crimes and criminals. Though this may seem to be a relatively small share of the total resources of an agency ostensibly devoted to crime control, it is exceedingly unlikely that any other specific routine police activity, such as traffic regulation, crowd control, supervision of licensed establishments, settling of citizens' disputes, emergency health aids, ceremonial functions, or any other, absorb anywhere near as large a share of the remaining two-thirds. But this is precisely what one would expect on the basis of our definition. Given the likelihood that offenders will seek to oppose apprehension and evade punishment, it is only natural that the initial dealings with them be assigned to an agency that is capable of overcoming these obstacles. That is, the proposed definition of the role of the police as a mechanism for the distribution of non-negotiably coercive remedies entails the priority of crime control by direct inference. Beyond that, however, the definition also encompasses other types of activities, albeit at lower level of priority.

Because the idea that the police are basically a crimefighting agency has never been challenged in the past, no one has troubled to sort out the remaining priorities. Instead, the police have always been forced to justify activities that did not involve law enforcement in the direct sense by either linking them constructively to law enforcement or by defining them as nuisance demands for service. The dominance of this view, especially in the minds of policemen, has two pernicious consequences. First, it leads to a tendency to view all sorts of problems as if they involved culpable offenses and to an excessive reliance on quasi-legal methods for handling them. The widespread use of arrests without intent to prosecute exemplifies this state of affairs. These cases do not involve errors in judgment about the applicability of a penal norm but deliberate pretense resorted to because more appropriate methods of handling problems have not been developed. Second, the view that crime control is the only serious, important, and necessary part of police work has deleterious effects on the morale of those police officers in the uniformed patrol who spend most of their time with other matters. No one, especially he who takes a positive interest in his work, likes being obliged to do things day-in and day-out that are disparaged by his colleagues. Moreover, the low evaluation of these duties leads to neglecting the development of skill and knowledge that are required to discharge them properly and efficiently.

It remains to be shown that the capacity to use coercive force lends thematic unity to all police activity in the same sense in which, let us say, the capacity to cure illness lends unity to everything that is ordinarily done in the field of medical practice. While everybody agrees that the police actually engage in an enormous variety of activities, only a part of which involves law enforcement, many argue that this state of affairs does not require explanation but change. Smith, for example, argued that the imposition of duties and demands that are not related to crime control dilutes the effectiveness of the police and that the growing trend in this direction should be curtailed and even reversed.[5] On the face of it this argument is not without merit, especially if one considers that very many of those activities that are unrelated to law enforcement involve dealing with problems that lie in the field of psychiatry, social welfare, human relations, education, and so on. Each of these fields has its own trained specialists who are respectively more competent than the police. It would seem preferable, therefore, to take all those matters that belong properly to other specialists out of the hands of the police and turn them over to those to whom they belong. Not only would this relieve some of the pressures that presently impinge on the police, but it would also result in better services.[6]

Unfortunately, this view overlooks a centrally important factor. While it is true that policemen often aid sick and troubled people because physicians and social workers are unable or unwilling to take their services where they are needed, this is not the only or even the main reason for police involvement. In fact, physicians and social workers themselves quite often "call the cops." For not unlike the case of the administration of justice, on the periphery of the rationally ordered procedures of medical and social work practice lurk exigencies that call for the exercise of coercion. Since neither physicians nor social workers are authorized or equipped to use force to attain desirable objectives, the total disengagement of the police would mean allowing many a problem to move unhampered in the direction of disaster. But the non-law-enforcement activities of the police are by no means confined to matters that are wholly or even mainly within the purview of some other institutionalized remedial specialty. Many, perhaps most, consist of addressing situations in which people simply do not seem to be able to manage their own lives adequately. Nor is it to be taken for granted that these situations invariably call for the use, or the threat of the use, of force. It is enough if there is need for immediate and unquestioned intervention that must not be allowed to be defeated by possible resistance. And where there is a possibility of great harm, the intervention would appear to be justified even if the risk is, in statistical terms, quite remote. Take, for instance the presence of mentally ill persons in the community. Though it is well known that most live quiet and unobtrusive lives, they are perceived as occasionally constituting a serious hazard to themselves and others. Thus, it is not surprising that the police are always prepared to deal with these persons at the slightest indication of a possible emergency, Similarly, though very few family quarrels lead to serious consequences, the fact that most homicides occur among quarreling kin leads to the preparedness to intervene at the incipient stages of problems.

In sum, the role of the police is to address all sorts of human problems when and insofar as their solutions do or may possibly require the use of force at the point of their occurrence. This lends homogeneity to such diverse procedures as catching a criminal, driving the mayor to the airport, evicting a drunken person from a bar, directing traffic, crowd control, taking care of lost children, administering medical first aid, and separating fighting relatives.

There is no exaggeration in saying that there is topical unity in this very incomplete list of lines of police work. Perhaps it is true that the common practice of assigning policemen to chauffeur mayors is based on the desire to give the appearance of thrift. . . . But note, if one wanted to make as far as possible certain that nothing would ever impede His Honor's freedom of movement, he would certainly put someone into the driver's seat of the auto who has the authority and the capacity to overcome all unforeseeable human obstacles. Similarly, it is perhaps not too farfetched to assume that desk sergeants feed ice cream to lost children because they like children. But if the treat does not achieve the purpose of keeping the youngster in the station house until his parents arrive to redeem him, the sergeant would have to resort to other means of keeping him there.

. . . [A] stigma attaches to police work because of its connection with evil, crime, perversity, and disorder. Though it may not be reasonable, it is common that those who fight the dreadful end up being dreaded themselves. Second, because the police must act quickly and often on mere intuition, their interventions are lacking in those aspects of moral sophistication which only a more extended and more scrupulous consideration can afford. Hence their methods are comparatively crude. Third, because it is commonly assumed that the risks of the kinds of breakdowns that require police action are much more heavily concentrated in the lower classes than in other segments of society, police surveillance is inherently discriminatory. That is, all things being equal, some persons feel the sting of police scrutiny merely because of their station in life. Insofar as this is felt, police work has divisive effects in society.

. . . [O]ne cannot understand how the police "found themselves" in this unenviable position without taking into consideration that one of the cultural trends of roughly the past century-and-a-half was the sustained aspiration to install peace as a stable condition of everyday life. Though no one can fail being impressed by the many ways the attainment of this ideal has been frustrated, it is possible to find some evidence of partially effective efforts. Many aspects of mundane existence in our cities have become more pacific than they have been in past epochs of history. More importantly for our purposes, in the domain of internal statecraft, the distance between those who govern and those who are governed has grown and the gap has been filled with bureaucratically symbolized communication. Where earlier compliance was secured by physical presence and armed might, it now rests mainly on peaceful persuasion and rational compliance. We found the trend toward the pacification in governing most strongly demonstrated in the administration of justice. The banishment of all forms of violence from the criminal process, as administered by the courts, has as a corollary the legalization of judicial proceedings. The latter reflects a movement away from peremptory and oracular judgment to a method in which all decisions are based on exhaustively rational grounds involving the use of explicit legal norms. Most important among those norms are the ones that limit the powers of authority and specify the rights of defendants. The legalization and pacification of the criminal process was achieved by, among other things, expelling from its purview those processes that set it into motion. Since in the initial steps, where suspicions are formed and arrests are made, force and intuition cannot be eliminated entirely, purity can be maintained by not taking notice of them. This situation is, however, paradoxical if we are to take seriously the idea that the police is a law enforcement agency in the strict sense of legality. The recognition of this paradox became unavoidable as early as in 1914, in the landmark decision of *Weeks v. U.S.* In the following decades the United States Supreme Court issued a series of rulings affecting police procedure which foster the impression that the judiciary exercises control over the police. But this impression is misleading, for the rulings do not set forth binding norms for police work but merely provide that *if* the police propose to set the criminal process into motion, *then* they must proceed in certain legally restricted ways. These restrictions are, therefore, conditional, specifying as it were the terms of delivery and acceptance of a service and nothing more. Outside of this arrangement the judges have no direct concerns with police work and will take notice of its illegality, if it is illegal, only when offended citizens seek civil redress.

Because only a small part of the activity of the police is dedicated to law enforcement and because they deal with the majority of their problems without invoking the law, a broader definition of their role was proposed, After reviewing briefly what the public appears to expect of the police, the range of activities police actually engage in, and the theme that unifies all these activities, it was suggested that *the role of the police is best understood as a mechanism for the distribution of non-negotiably coercive force employed in accordance with the dictates of an intuitive grasp of situational exigencies.*

It is, of course, not surprising that a society committed to the establishment of peace by pacific means and to the abolishment of all forms of violence from the fabric of its social relations, at least as a matter of official morality and policy, would establish a corps of specially deputized officials endowed with the exclusive monopoly of using force contingently where limitations of foresight fail to provide alternatives. That is, given the melancholy appreciation of the fact that the total abolition of force is not attainable, the closest approximation to the ideal is to limit it as a special and exclusive trust. If it is the case, however, that the mandate of the police is organized around their capacity and authority to use force, i.e., if this is what the institution's existence makes available to society, then the evaluation of that institution's performance must focus on it. While it is quite true that policemen will have to be judged on other dimensions of competence, too—for example, the exercise of force against criminal suspects requires some knowledge about crime and criminal law—their methods as society's agents of coercion will have to be considered central to the overall judgment.

The proposed definition of the police role entails a difficult moral problem. How can we arrive at a favorable or even accepting judgment about an activity which is, in its very conception, opposed to the ethos of the polity that authorizes it? Is it not well nigh inevitable that this mandate be concealed in circumlocution? While solving puzzles of moral philosophy is beyond the scope of this analysis, we will have to address this question in a somewhat more mundane formulation: namely, on what terms can a society dedicated to peace institutionalize the exercise of force?

It appears that in our society two answers to this question are acceptable. One defines the targets of legitimate force as enemies and the coercive advance against them as warfare. Those who wage this war are expected to be possessed by the military virtues of valor, obedience and *esprit de corps*. The enterprise as a whole is justified as a sacrificial and glorious mission in which the warrior's duty is "not to reason why." The other answer involves an altogether different imagery. The targets of force are conceived as practical objectives and their attainment a matter of practical expediency. The process involves prudence, economy, and considered judgment, from case to case. The enterprise as a whole is conceived as a public trust, the exercise of which is vested in individual practitioners who are personally responsible for their decisions and actions.

Reflection suggests that the two patterns are profoundly incompatible. Remarkably, however, our police departments have not been deterred from attempting the reconciliation of the irreconcilable. Thus, our policemen are exposed to the demand of a conflicting nature in that their actions are supposed to reflect military prowess and professional acumen. . . .

Notes

1 "Justification for the Use of Force in the Criminal Law," *Stanford Law Review,* 13 (1961), 566–609.

2 "At common law, the rule appears to have been that an officer was entitled to make a reasonable mistake as to whether the victim had committed a felony, but a private person was not so entitled. Thus strict liability was created for the private arrester, and he could not justifiably kill, if the victim had not actually committed a felony. Several modern cases have imposed this standard of strict liability even upon the officer by conditioning justification of deadly force on the victims actually having committed a felony, and a number of states have enacted statutes which appear to adopt this strict liability. However, many jurisdictions, such as California, have homicide statutes which permit the police officer to use deadly force for the arrest of a person 'charged' with felony. It has been suggested that this requirement only indicates the necessity for reasonable belief by the officer that the victim has committed a felony." *Ibid.,* 599–600.

3 The illustrations are taken from field notes I have collected over the course of fourteen months of intensive field observations of police activity in two large cities. One is located in a Rocky Mountain state, the other on the West Coast. All other case vignettes used in the subsequent text of this report also come from this source.

4 By "non-negotiably coercible" we mean that when a deputized police officer decides that force is necessary, then, within the boundaries of this situation, he is not accountable to anyone, nor is he required to brook the arguments or opposition of anyone who might object to it. We set this forth not as a legal but as a practical rule. The legal question whether citizens may oppose policemen is complicated. Apparently resisting police coercion in situations of emergency is not legitimate; see Hans Kelsen, *General Theory of Law and State* (New York: Russel & Russel, 1961), 278–279, and H. A. L. Hart, *The Concept of Law* (Oxford: Clarendon Press, 1961), 20–21. Common law doctrine allows that citizens may oppose "unlawful arrest," 6 *Corpus Juris Secundum,* Arrest #13, 613; against this, the Uniform Arrest Act, drafted by a committee of the Interstate Commission on Crime in 1939, provides in Section 5, "If a person has reasonable grounds to believe that he is being arrested by a peace officer, it is his duty to refrain from using force or any weapons in resisting arrest regardless of whether or not there is a legal basis for the arrest." S. B. Warner, "Uniform Arrest Act," *Vanderbilt Law Review,* 28 (1942), 315–347. At present, at least twelve states are governed by case law recognizing the validity of the Common Law doctrine, at least five have adopted the rule contained in the Uniform Arrest Act, and at least six have case law or statutes that give effect to the Uniform Arrest Act rule. That the trend is away from the Common Law doctrine and in the direction of the Uniform Arrest Act rule is argued in Max Hochanadel and H. W. Stege, "The Right to Resist an Unlawful Arrest: An Outdated Concept" *Tulsa Law Journal,* 3 (1966), 40–46. I am grateful for the help I received from 35 of the 50 state Attorney General Offices from whom I sought information concerning this matter.

5 Bruce Smith, *Police Systems in the United States* (New York: Harper & Row, 1960, second rev. ed.), 3.

6 The authors of the *Task Force Report: Police* note that little has been done to make these alternative resources available as substitutes for police intervention; President's Commission on Law Enforcement and Administration of Justice (Washington, D.C.: U.S. Government Printing Office, 1967), 14.

Street Justice
A Moral Defense of Order Maintenance Policing

Gary W. Sykes

T he police in the United States developed as a community-based, politically decentralized institution (Bittner, 1971; Lane, 1967; Johnson, 1981; and Klockars, 1985a). One increasingly essential role in the early years was social regulation, supplementing other norm-maintaining institutions when they performed less effectively as communities became more cosmopolitan (Black, 1980 and Kelling, 1985). As part of this role, police commonly provided informal peacekeeping services in response to a general failure of local governments to establish integrative and supportive social-economic programs in the wake of the ravages brought about by urbanization in a market-based society (see Walker, 1980 and Cumming, et al., 1965). The traditional police officer in the most disorderly parts of American cities became an ''institution'' who responded to a ''moral mandate'' for informal distributive and retributive justice in situations where individuals violated community norms and impinged on the personal and property rights of others (see Van Maanen, 1974 and 1980).

For discussion purposes, this role is referred to as the ''street justice'' function and is used in a limited sense. It will not be used to describe police behavior related to or associated with personal bias, such as racial prejudice, or psychological factors, such as authoritarian predispositions. Its primary

Justice Quarterly, 3 (4) (December 1986): 497–512. Reprinted with permission of the Academy of Criminal Justice Sciences.

use in this article is related to police behavior that is responsive to situational and organizational factors arising from the nature of the police role itself. Studies of police discretion largely reinforce the view that street decisions to intervene, arrest, use force or issue traffic citations are primarily a function of situational and organizational factors that reflect interpretations of community needs and expectations by police. "Street justice" in this sense is a response to a community mandate that something be done about situations where formal institutions cannot or will not respond for a variety of reasons (see, Bittner, 1971; and especially Klockars, 1983 and 1985a for a discussion of the police role and the studies which elaborate its implicit peacekeeping nature).

This "street justice" function created widespread concern in the past (and causes much concern in the present), especially when linked to ethnic and racial prejudice inherent in the inequalities of the market-based urban context; and it became the target for decades of reform. An over-arching concern that motivated many attempts to reform police practices—changes designed in many ways to subordinate police to administrative and legal due process (see, for example, Brown, 1981)—was that such an "institution" violated the basic liberal understanding of how governmental power should be held accountable in a liberal democratic society.

❖ THE ROOTS OF "REFORM" ❖

"Street justice" appeared to be an anomaly and was targeted for reform on many fronts, most effectively by the "professional paradigm" which emphasized the enforcement role of the police (see Wilson, 1968; Brown, 1981; and Kelling, 1985 for a discussion of the dilemmas of "order maintenance" versus "enforcement" policing). In recent years, a challenge to the liberal reformers emerged which questioned the efficacy of these reforms. This challenge can be referred to as the "order maintenance paradigm" which alleges that many discretionary police activities cannot be reduced to bureaucratic due process without a costly trade-off in crime control effectiveness (Sykes, 1985).

The most prominent images of traditional policing in the United States, constructed by many liberal reformers concerned with the issue of accountability, focused on the problems of corruption, brutality, racism, inefficiency and political repression. Samuel Walker (1984), for example, challenged the recent "order maintenance paradigm" and took exception to reviving the traditional peacekeeping role outlined by James Q. Wilson and George Kelling (1982). He maintained that the limited historical evidence available supported the view that traditional city police were corrupt and lazy and handled challenges to their authority repressively. Walker asserted that the advocates of order maintenance policing mistakenly based their view of traditional officers on a "highly romanticized view of nineteenth century neighborhood life."

To some extent, Walker's critique of order maintenance policing focused the issue in such a manner that it missed a major point. What many early cities attempted to achieve was some measure of stability and order in the midst of continuous social upheaval resulting in part from their failure to develop adequate services and institutions to deal effectively with the problems of social integration. The police institution was one of many responses by rapidly growing cities to the constant threat of disintegration caused by the impact of industralization on community institutions—e.g, the family. The question is less whether the police successfully performed in such turbulent times, but why the police "idea" was proposed and widely adopted as a solution to the chaos of early urban life. Without systematic evidence, it can be assumed that the police institution provided an important social support function in the face of failing communality (Erickson, 1966 and Cumming, *et al.*, 1965).

Thus, the establishment of the police institution attempted to buttress the new heterogeneous society (*gesellschaft*) through order maintenance policing. The alleged problems of traditional policing that Walker outlined do not inevitably support the conclusion that police failed. Rather they show that the dimensions of the problems were enormous and traditional policing was a limited function that had difficulty living up to its expectations as a mechanism for social integration.

The establishment of communality (*gemeinschaft*) was a continuing problem in many cities of American society as well as a major theme of political thought (e.g., Jacobson, 1963 and Macpherson, 1962). The success of the police "idea" varied widely from one city to another, but its proliferation constituted one measure of its utility in solving some of the early problems of disorder. It may also be the case that the police response to these problems was inadequate, from the standpoint that most cities also failed to develop the corollary support services, in order to smooth the transition to liberal industrial society. Early cities simply relied on the police to handle the problems created by disorder as best they could. As Wilson suggested (1968:412–413):

> . . . Abusive practices or indifference to citizen needs (by the police) can be eliminated, but it typically requires a community that . . . is small, expensive, and cooperative. In short, it requires a middle- or upper-middle class suburb. Some advocates of community control over the police argue that it is the close supervision of the police (account-ability through administration and legal due process) . . . that

accounts for the good relations between police and citizens to be found there; if one duplicates those political conditions in the central city—if one, in short, 'suburbanizes' the central-city neighborhoods—comparable improvements in police-citizen relations may well occur. My research suggests that it is not the degree or kind of control that produces this effect in the suburbs, it is the class composition of the community.

One implication of Wilson's conclusion is that reformers tend to "blame the victim." The victim in this sense is the police institution which is given the functional role of responding to an intractable situation. The problems of disorder are lodged in the class structure as a product of change; and the police role is not adequately supplemented by social, economic and political reforms which might help ameliorate the conditions. Blaming the police focuses attention away from these failures and may blind reformers to the positive contributions of the police in maintaining the norms of lower class neighborhoods.

In sum, the "worst case" images of traditional policing promoted by reformers fueled decades of reform and culminated in the nationalization of the procedural rights in the U.S. Constitution, *professional* movements and administrative programs aimed at subordinating police discretion to bureaucratic and legal norms (Sykes, 1985). Professionalizing the police meant limiting line-officer discretion to primarily enforcement activities which resulted in peacekeeping and order maintenance activities being denied legitimacy. As Wilson and Kelling (1982) summarized:

> Over the past two decades, the shift of police from order maintenance to law enforcement has brought them increasingly under the influence of legal restrictions, provoked by media complaints and enforced by court decisions and departmental orders. As a consequence, the order-maintenance functions of the police are now governed by rules developed to control police relations with suspected criminals (p. 65).

The legal authority of police in peacekeeping activities remains unclear and ambiguous in liberal culture (Kelling, 1985; and Goldstein, 1977) and is described by some as an "anomaly." Although there is widespread recognition of the difficulties of "structuring discretion," there is a virtual silence in the literature when it comes to constructing a moral defense of informal police practices as an important social function.

Egon Bittner (1971) confronted this "anomaly" by characterizing these activities as "beyond the rule of law" and suggested that police exhibit a "love-hate" relationship with the legal system partly because it denies legitimacy to many routine peacekeeping practices. He suggested that in the past the courts responded to these activities by "sweeping them under the rug," or simply "looking the other way," an implicit recognition of both their important functional role as well their anomalous nature in liberal society.

Assuming that some reforms achieved a measure of success in reducing the police role to bureaucratic and legal due process as part of the professional movement, the question remained—how extensively did such reforms penetrate agency culture? When looking at the line officer's role, some researchers concluded that the professional movement was superficial, a strategy designed to create the appearance without the substance of effectiveness (Fogelson, 1977; and Manning, 1978).

Whatever the case may be, it is safe to assume that professionalization varied across departments and depended on factors which are not completely understood. Some recent evidence suggests, however, that there are limits to professional reforms and that currently the movement may be at an impasse (Brown, 1981; Van Maanen, 1982; Fogelson, 1977; and Sykes, 1985). The rise of the order maintenance paradigm must be related to some extent to the failure of professionalism to increase police effectiveness against crime.

One of the missing elements in the current debate over order maintenance policing is an understanding of its functional role in relation to community expectations, and the informal use of police powers to supplement social integration. The proponents of order maintenance policing justify this approach as part of the strategy to increase effectiveness against crime, although most evidence indicates that it only reduces the fear of crime. For example, Wilson and Kelling (1982) suggested that it might be possible to more effectively control crime through personal contact policing (e.g., foot patrol) by creating an atmosphere in a community where "somebody's in charge" and "somebody cares." Consequently, they argued, serious crime can be denied an environment conducive to its development.

More recently, Kelling (1985) justified peacekeeping activity as a way to prevent the escalation of disorder into crime through preventive intervention. In other words, the primary justification for the revival of peacekeeping strategies rest essentially on police effectiveness in crime control. By salvaging the crime control function *via* order maintenance, the moral arguments in support of peacekeeping are not explored.

❖ THE POLICE AS A COMMUNITY-BASED INSTITUTION ❖

The creation of a sense of community is at least partially dependent on boundary maintaining institutions which define cultural space and develop an "ethos."

> The people of a community spend most of their lives in close contact
> with one another, sharing a common sphere of experience which
> makes them feel that they belong to a special "kind" and live in a
> special "place." . . . Now people who live together in communities
> cannot relate to one another in any coherent way or even acquire a
> sense of their own stature as group members unless they learn some-
> thing about the boundaries of the territory they occupy in social space,
> if only because they need to sense what lies beyond the margins of
> the group before they can appreciate the special quality of the
> experience which takes place within it. . . . (Erickson, 1966:9)

Although social control is often thought of as essentially punitive in
nature in liberal society—i.e., institutions vs. individual freedom
(Macpherson, 1972)—the function of social control in human associations
also provides for cultural integrity, stability, sense of purpose and an
antecedent for other cherished values (Erickson, 1966).

A moral dilemma created by due process reforms can be stated as
follows: "freedom," or more accurately "liberty," is culturally defined
in liberal society as limiting government powers through legal and
bureaucratic due process. The practical result is the enhancement of personal
license because the legitimacy of government action is always open to
question. However, since many government functions actually serve to
protect, support and maintain other essential values, a distortion of the
social control function is created by this idea of "freedom" because of
the implicit liberal assumption that the exercise of governmental power
is inherently repressive. This assumption of repression ignores the positive
side of government in which it actually creates "freedom" through
regulation, intervention on behalf of the less powerful and the reallocation
of values on behalf of the common good. The classical liberal (the
contemporary "conservative") tends to view the state as primarily punitive
(Macpherson, 1965) and a threat to "freedom," largely ignoring the
repressive potential of private power. There is a significant body of literature
that discusses the problem of private power left uncontrolled through "non-
decision making" in liberal society (see for example, McConnell, 1966;
and Bachrach and Baratz, 1967; Macpherson, 1962 and 1972; Ricci, 1971;
and Wolff, 1968).

The difficulty with the classical liberal view of the state as punitive
is exemplified in the issue of the police role and the physical abuse of
women. Many state jurisdictions rely on the common law and codified
principle that misdemeanor offenses, including simple assault and battery,
lack probable cause for immediate arrest unless a police officer personally
witnesses the offense (although police and citizens theoretically may "swear
out" a warrant which leaves to the prosecutor and courts the discretion

to dispose of the case). However, in recent years, many women's and crime victims' groups successfully expanded the statutory powers of the police to make arrests as an exception to the traditional requirements of probable cause in misdemeanor situations. In achieving such changes in the law, women were provided with some protection from the physical domination by men and the intimidation which heretofore limited their role and options in personal relationships. From the viewpoint of abused women, the role of the state was not inherently repressive, but expansive, when broader powers to protect them from physical assault and abuse were granted.

By inference, the peacekeeping role of the police in regulating human relationships can take on a different character than provided by the liberal view of the state. The use of force or threat of force by the police in maintaining order can be understood in functional terms as expanding human "freedom" rather than being inherently repressive. As a community-based mechanism for order, it provides for protection and regulation necessary for civilization. In broader terms, it provides the articulation of community norms when other supporting institutions fail or are inadequately developed to insure social peace.

By defining police activities on the bases of due process criteria and by focusing on the professionalized enforcement role we ignore the functions that provide supportive services and protection from the physically powerful who take advantage of the disintegration of traditional institutions. Evidence that police continue to play this role is ubiquitous in the literature on policing. Skolnick (1966) described peacekeeping-type activities as "justice without trial," implicitly raising the moral issue of whether such activities violated the canons of liberal legal culture, but at the same time acknowledging the existence of a definition of justice different from due process. Van Maanen (1978) not only recognized the essential nature of the peacekeeping role, but he developed a model of the decision-making process police officers employ when determining the appropriate response in situations where their authority is challenged. He also found that flowing from the community was a "moral mandate" creating an expectation that officers will "take care" of troublemakers and others who cause community problems. Implicit in these studies was the suggestion that officers responded to a retributive community-based idea, rather than a due-process-based idea of justice, and that community cooperation and support rested essentially on problem-solving effectiveness.

Historically speaking, traditional societies evolved boundary maintaining functions within the institutional framework of the family, tribe and clan. Urbanization resulting from massive economic changes during the periods of industrialization required communities to develop the police institution partially for purposes of social integration (Klockars,

1983). Admittedly, the police role relies more on coercion than community-based support institutions and, consequently, entails serious problems of efficacy given the impossible nature of the task (Wilson, 1968).

Initially, local police in the United States performed both controlling and supporting roles in the urban setting (Walker, 1980). Given the lack of political and social development in a society committed to individualism and privatism, practical necessity required a community-based, omni-functional institution to deal with the constant problems of a changing urban milieu. In many cases, police agencies were *the* local government response to the ravages of change in the initial phases of industrialization and subsequent urbanization.

The evolution of American police differed substantially from other cultural settings. As Wilbur Miller (1975) pointed out, not only was policing decentralized and geographically dispersed, it was idiosyncratic (highly personalized) in nature. "Calling the cops" meant most often a request for someone able to forcefully intervene and solve a variety of human problems, especially when these conflicts threatened others. The police institution evolved partially as service-oriented, especially in lower class communities, when societal resources were scant for developing needed social and economic services (Cumming, *et al.*, 1965). As a consequence, police officers as individuals sometimes became "institutions" within many communities (Wambaugh, 1973). Police were and remain the last resort institution for many problems in lower class communities, partly because of the political failure to develop adequate supportive services available to, or affordable by, more affluent groups (Cumming, *et. al.*, 1965).

In the early urban context, accountability was maintained by judging police on the basis of meeting community needs, not by the extent to which they conformed to some due process standards (Wilson and Kelling, 1982). The crime control function remained largely a citizen-based and collective community responsibility. The traditional response to crime prevailed in the cities: *watching, walking, wariness* and mustering citizens to apprehend (Sherman, 1983). In broad terms, urban development required a local institution to maintain ordered social relationships as well as provide support and protection for groups vulnerable to the socially destructive conditions of city life where communality was problematic.

Even popular fictional accounts of policing, such as the works of Joseph Wambaugh (1973), recognized not only that discretion was inherent in the police role, but that police officers acted out of a sense of moral indignation when intervening in peacekeeping situations. Wambaugh described street ethics in which police officers were motivated by an idea of justice that the courts failed to explicitly recognize, leaving the officer in an ambiguous "double-bind" in which he was expected to handle the "dirty work" of society (see also Bittner, 1971).

In short, there is widespread recognition in the academic and fictional literature that police often express a commitment to moral and ethical codes that are in conflict with officialdom and its liberal tenets. One of the major ambiguities of the police task is that officers are caught between two profoundly compelling moral systems: justice as due process as part of the liberal society *gesellschaft*, and conversely, justice as righting a wrong as part of defining and maintaining community norms *gemeinschaft*.

In responding to the mandate for order maintenance, the police create a sense of community that makes social life possible. Where police are unwilling or unable to play this moral leadership role or define the community boundaries of right conduct, the quality of life declines and the existence of every other cherished value may be jeopardized. Where the civil libertarian fears repression and the denial of due process, others see the emancipation from fear and the creation of community as the result of police peacekeeping activities.

Klockars (1985b) implicitly argued that enhancing the police role to suppress "annoying," "offensive" and "disruptive" behavior, to which so-called "respectables" objected and which were not illegal, created a threat to civil liberties. The image was one of police repression, conjuring up the fear of unbridled social and economic prejudice being acted out against social deviants who were not engaged in illegal behavior. On the other hand, he recognized the difficulty in reducing this type of policing discretion. In other words, Klockars recognized that peacekeeping was inherent in the role, and there were few practical limits. Implicitly, however, he also was disturbed by the arguments to expand and legitimize the peacekeeping function through the revival of order maintenance strategies.

The costs of the enforcement approach must be taken into account, since it seeks to deny to police this social regulatory function as a community-based institution (Wilson and Kelling, 1982; Sykes, 1985). It must be realized that the suffering produced by communal decay is not equally endured across the societal landscape. The more affluent can geographically and economically insulate themselves from the central urban context where disorder is most pronounced. The result is that the poor—mostly women, children (mostly minorities) and elderly who cannot afford to follow urban flight—must "cope" with the "annoying offensive and disruptive" behavior prevalent in lower class life. In other words, a major problem with Klockars' characterization of peacekeeping and the implicit fear of the police performing order maintenance is that it is not necessarily the "respectables" who are "annoyed" or "disrupted," but the remaining members of the community who must face the disorganized and threatening life of a normless environment.

The reductionist liberal image of policing, i.e., essentially punitive, nurtures the concern and fear of repression. To reinforce this concern, one need only emphasize the "worst case" examples of traditional policing (e.g. Walker, 1984). Such proponents of "professional" and/or enforcement-oriented policing are reluctant to grant legitimacy to the functional role of "street justice" in creating freedom from fear and the possibility of its crime control effectiveness (Klockars, 1985b). The question that many opponents of peacekeeping do not address is the means by which a community can achieve order if its police institution is limited by the administrative and procedural due process.

Evidence to support the social support function of the police is implicit not only in the studies of foot-patrol experiments, but also in the oft-noted findings that residents of less affluent communities are more concerned about the lack of police protection than about the occasional episodes of police brutality or corruption (Black, 1980). When youthful male "troublemakers" loiter on street corners, harass elderly citizens, intimidate passersby and generally add to the fear and uncertainty of urban life, the police become the only institution available for remedy. Urban dwellers find themselves imprisoned by fear, and other rights become meaningless if they confront unregulated terrorism in the streets. "Street justice" continues to be a community service demanded by citizens, and the failure to provide it might be related to the disenchantment and declining legitimacy of formal criminal justice institutions.

De-criminalizing offenses such as public intoxication, public drinking, vagrancy and other forms of disorderly conduct may actually contribute to the repression of the less fortunate by the physically powerful by removing important peacekeeping tools from police officers (Kelling, 1985). Without police intervention, the idea of a free society remains problematic. It is this understanding of the police function which is missing from the discussion about the police role in modern society.

In summary, the liberal reformers fear police repression and overlook the functional role of "street justice" in creating a sense of community. They choose to emphasize justice defined as due process over the community-based idea of justice as righting a wrong and protecting the physically weak from the powerful. Police accountability remains a problem, and order maintenance continues to create the potential for abuse of power. However, the answer provided by the professional model, which emphasizes the enforcement role, leaves many citizens without the means to civilize their community. The trade-off must be recognized and provides an on-going moral dilemma in liberal society.

❖ CONCLUSION ❖
LAISSEZ-FAIRE POLICING VS REGULATORY POLICING

> . . . a (liberal) democratic government, like any other, exists to uphold
> and enforce a certain kind of society, a certain set of relations between
> individuals, a certain set of rights and claims that people have on each
> other both directly, and indirectly through their rights and property.
> These relations themselves are relations of power—they give different
> people, in different capacities, power over others (Macpherson,
> 1965:4).

It is conventional among reformers to describe the police function
using the liberal democratic assumption that individuals are free to the
extent that government does not intervene in their personal choices—a
negative idea of freedom more accurately described as *liberty*. As a
consequence, the police role is defined as "anomalous" in a "free" society
precisely because the use of arrest, force and detention constitute a denial
of individual liberty (Goldstein, 1977). The legitimacy of the police role,
therefore, rests on limiting its functions to essential enforcement activities—
and only when such activities are subject to review under administrative
and legal rules.

The critics of order maintenance policing, reflecting this punitive
assumption, seek to reduce the police role to its nominal enforcement
function and raise the spectre of unbridled police power menacing the civil
liberties of citizens. In effect, they deny to police an essential regulatory
function growing out of the need, expressed most clearly in urban
communities, to establish norms and ordered social relations. In
emphasizing the concept of due process over other ideas of justice, the
police role is left without effective tools for social regulation and the ability
to protect the physically powerless from the powerful. When it comes to
the police role, the solution is *laissez-faire* policing. This is reminiscent
of classical liberal assumptions, denigrating the functional role that remains
at the center of many police activities, along with the right of the community
to define and maintain its normative boundaries.

Walker (1984) was concerned that the gains of recent reform efforts
will be sacrificed by the implementation of order maintenance policing.
What he failed to explore was the socially functional role of police as a
community institution. Individuals' perceptions of the police when they
"call the cops" involve situations, in which "something—ought—not—
to—be—happening—about—which—something—ought—to—be—done—
Now!" (to use Klockars' (1985) creative elaboration of Bittner's view of
the police). Most often, such situations are minimally crime-related, and
the complaining citizen will not or cannot use the formal legal system to

deal with the repressive behavior of others. What the complainant wants and needs is an officer who is empowered to solve immediate problems and establish norms of right conduct. On the other hand, the "professional" officer under such circumstances is likely to relay to the citizen all of the legal reasons for non-intervention. Thus, citizen disenchantment with the police is often characterized by the phrase, "I've called the cops many times, but they didn't do anything!"

An order-maintenance oriented officer responding to a request for help is likely to emphasize the "moral mandate" of his role by threatening, persuading, intimidating and thereby imposing some solution (maybe only temporary) on the disorder problems of an urban community. In doing so, the officer is acting as a community-based, social support agent.

The refusal to administer street justice can be viewed as allowing normlessness to prevail, fostering a sense of injustice by the complainant and leaving victims without protection against those who intimidate and violate the rights of others. Where the police appear to be helpless by limiting their activities to official due process responses, the atmosphere is created that essentially tells the marginal members of the community that anarchy prevails.

It was customary in the past to recognize implicitly the informal authority of police officers to use their discretion to discipline and regulate social relationships on behalf of the community or specific victims. As with *laissez-faire* economics, it is not the powerful who suffer from the lack of regulatory actions, but the powerless—in this case primarily women, children and the elderly in urban areas.

The police officer, in responding to community demands for justice in the sense of retribution or righting a wrong, plays the role of judge, jury and in some cases punisher. Caught between the official definition of justice as due process and the community mandate, the officer can opt out of the "double-bind" through withdrawal, as the "professional" approach advocates. This response to the conflict between official and street justice may be a form of moral abdication and has profound consequences for the quality of the lives of victims and for the viability of the community as a whole.

The reformers will still raise the concern of who will guard the guardians and the question of how the police will be held accountable. Kelling (1985) suggests that the recent emphasis on professional ethics may act as an internal mechanism of restraint. But such a response will not satisfy the liberal yearning for formal controls and external limits to police discretion. There are no easy or simple answers, but the limits must be defined very broadly within the context of the community itself. With decentralized police as the arm of local government, the abuse of police discretion must ultimately rest with the political process.

One brief illustrative example might indicate in a general way how the political process changes the nature of police policies and behavior. Many Americans still recall the image of Chief ''Bull'' Connor, the police dogs and fire hoses used against peaceful demonstrators during the civil rights struggle in the South. Most would agree that such abuses of police power are less likely to recur in Birmingham today. Perhaps the reason is less police professionalism and due process-related reforms than the fact that the Alabama city has a black mayor and black leadership in the police department. What makes the difference may be more a function of political rights, e.g., the Voting Rights Act of 1965, than procedural due process. Whatever the case, formal institutional restraints reflective of the liberal reformist approach may be only one avenue for accountability—and the least efficacious when compared to other political processes. In short, the key to police accountability may rest more with the First Amendment (substantive due process) than with the Fourth, Fifth, Sixth or Fourteenth Amendments (procedural due process) of the U.S. Constitution.

Order maintenance policing is the central function of police at the local level and can be justified on moral grounds as part of the community building and maintaining functions. To deny to citizens this police role has profound moral consequences and abandons those less capable of protecting themselves to the unchecked forces of private power. If there is a linkage between order maintenance policing and crime control, as Wilson and Kelling allege, then there should be a sense of urgency to legitimizing the street justice function. At the very least, the benefits of social regulatory policing should be explored before more victims are left to the uncertainties of *laissez-faire* policing.

References

Bachrach, P. (1967). *The Theory of Democratic Elitism: A Critique*. Boston: Little Brown and Company.

Bachrach, P., & Baratz, M. (1963). ''Decisions and nondecisions: An analytical framework.'' *American Political Science Review*, 57:632–642.

Banton, M. (1964). *The Policeman in the Community*. New York: Basic Books.

Berkely, G. F. (1969). *The Democratic Policeman*. Boston: Beacon Press.

Bittner, E. (1971). *The Functions of the Police in Modern Society*. Washington, D.C.: U.S. Government Printing Office.

_____ (1967). ''Police discretion in emergency apprehension of mentally ill persons.'' *Social Problems*, 14:278–92.

Black, D. J. (1980). *The Manners and Customs of the Police*. New York: Academic Press.

Brown, M. K. (1981). *Working the Street*. New York: Russell Sage Foundation.

Chevigny, P. (1969). *Police Power*. New York: Pantheon Books.

Critchley, T. A. (1972). *A History of Police in England and Wales*. 2nd ed. Montclair, NJ: Patterson Smith.

Cumming, E., Cumming, I., & Edell, L. (1965). "Policeman as philosopher, guide, and friend." *Social Problems*, 12, 3:276-86.

Davis, K. C. (1975). *Police Discretion*. St. Paul, MN: West Publishing Co.

Douthit, N. (1975). "Police professionalism and the war against crime in the United States, 1920s-30s." In Mosse, George, L. (ed.). *Police Forces in History*, pp. 317-33. Beverly Hills: Sage.

Erickson, K. T. (1966). *Wayward Purtians: A Study in the Sociology of Deviance*. New York: John Wiley & Sons.

Farris, E. A. (1982). "The path to professionalism: Five decades of American policing—1932-1982." *Police Chief*, November: 30-36.

Fogelson, R. M. (1977). *Big-City Police*. Cambridge: Harvard University Press.

Garner, G. W. (1984). *The Police Meet the Press*. Springfield, IL: Charles C. Thomas.

Goldstein, H. (1979). "Improving policing: A problem-oriented approach." *Crime and Delinquency*, 25 (April): 236-58.

—————— (1977). *Policing a Free Society*. Cambridge, MA: Ballinger.

—————— (1960). "Police discretion not to invoke the criminal process: Low-visibility decisions in the administration of justice." *Yale Law Journal*, 69:543.

Jacobson, N. (1963). "Political science and political education." *American Political Science Review*, 60 (September): 562-573.

Johnson, D. R. (1981). *American Law Enforcement: A History*. St. Louis, MO: Forum Press.

Kelling, G. L. (1985). "Order maintenance, the quality of urban life, and police: A different line of argument." In Geller, William A., *Police Leadership in America: Crisis and Opportunity*. New York: Praeger: 296-308.

Klockars, C. B. (1980). "The Dirty Harry problem." *Annals of the American Academy of Political and Social Science*, 452 (November): 33-47.

—————— (1983). *Thinking About Police: Contemporary Readings*. New York: McGraw-Hill.

—————— (1985a). *The Idea of Police*. Beverly Hills: Sage Publications.

—————— (1985b). "Order maintenance, the quality of urban life, and police: A different line of argument." In Geller, William A., *Police Leadership in America: Crisis and Opportunity*. New York: Praeger: 309-321.

Lane, R. (1967). *Policing the City: Boston 1822-1885*. Cambridge: Harvard University Press.

Macpherson, C. B. (1962). *The Political Theory of Possessive Individualism*. London: Oxford University Press.

—————— (1972). *The Real World of Democracy*. New York: Oxford University Press.

Manning, P. K. (1978). "The police: Mandate, strategies and appearances." In Manning, Peter K., & Van Maanen, John (eds.). *Policing: A View from the Street.* Santa Monica: Goodyear Publishing Co.

McConnell, G. (1966). *Private Power and American Democracy.* New York: Alfred A. Knopf.

Muir, Jr., W. K. (1980). "Power attracts violence." *Annals of the American Academy of Political and Social Science*, 452 (November): 48–52.

Neiderhoffer, A. (1967). *Behind the Shield: The Police in Urban Society.* New York: Doubleday.

Ostrom, E., R. B. Parks, & Whitaker, G. P. (1978). *Patterns of Metropolitan Policing.* Cambridge, MA: Ballinger.

Police Foundation (1983). "Experiments in fear reduction: Program and evaluation plans" (report on file at the National Institute of Justice, Washington, D.C.).

Reiss, Jr., A. J. (1971). *The Police and the Public.* New Haven: Yale University Press.

Ricci, D., and Keynes, E. (1971). *Community Power and Democratic Theory: The Logic of Political Analysis.* New York: Random House.

Rubenstein, J. (1973). *City Police.* New York: Farrar, Straus and Giroux.

Sherman, L.W. (1974). "The sociology and the social reform of the American police: 1950–1973." *Journal of Police Science and Administration*, 2(3): 255–62.

_____ (1978). "National Advisory Commission on Higher Education for Police Officers." *The Quality of Police Education.* San Francisco: Jossey-Bass.

Silberman, C. E. (1978). *Criminal Violence, Criminal Justice.* New York: Random House.

Skolnick, J. (1966). *Justice Without Trial: Law Enforcement in a Democratic Society.* New York: John Wiley & Sons.

Sykes, G. W. (1978). "Images of power in academia: A critical view." In *Power and Empowerment in Higher Education.* Lexington: University Press of Kentucky.

_____ (1985). "Saturated enforcement: The efficacy of deterrence in drunk driving." *Journal of Criminal Justice*, 12, 2:185–195.

_____ (1985). "The functional nature of police reform: The 'myth' of controlling the police." *Justice Quarterly*, 2, 1:51–65.

Van Maanen, J. (1974). "Working the street: A developmental view of police behavior." In Jacob, Herbert (ed.). *The Potential for Reform of Criminal Justice*, pp. 83–130. Beverly Hills: Sage.

_____ (1977). *A Critical History of Police Reform: The Emergence of Professionalism.* Lexington, MA: Lexington Books.

_____ (1980). "Street Justice." In Lundman, Richard J. (ed.). *Police Behavior*, pp. 296–311. New York: Oxford University Press.

Walker, S. (1980). *Popular Justice.* New York: Oxford University Press.

_____ (1984). "Broken windows and fractured history: The use and misuse of history in recent police patrol analysis." *Justice Quarterly* 1(1): 75–90.

_____ (1985). "Setting the standards: The efforts and impact of blue-ribbon commissions on police." In Geller, William A. *Police Leadership in America; Crisis and Opportunity.* New York: Praeger.

Wambaugh, J. (1973). *The Blue Knight.*, Boston: Little, Brown and Co.

Westley, W. A. (1970). *Violence and the Police.* Cambridge: MIT Press.

Wilson, J. Q. (1968). "Dilemmas of police administration." *Public Administration Review* 28, 5:407–17.

Wilson, J. W. (1978). *Varieties of Police Behavior; The Management of Law and Order in Eight Communities.* Cambridge: Harvard University Press.

Wilson, J. Q., & Kelling, George L. (1982). "Police and neighborhood safety: Broken windows." *Atlantic Monthly*, 249 (March): 29–38.

Wolff, R. P. (1968). *The Poverty of Liberalism.* Boston: Beacon Press.

Street Justice
Some Micro-Moral Reservations
Comment on Sykes

Carl B. Klockars

Over the past few years, the dialogue surrounding order maintenance policing has grown rather fuzzy. Partly, this is because different speakers in the dialogue promote very different images of what order maintenance policing actually involves. Partly, this is because different speakers in the dialogue share different notions of what order maintenance policing is supposed to achieve. And partly, this is because no speaker in the dialogue is prepared to confront squarely the question of how the potential for abuse in order maintenance policing is to be managed and controlled.

Gary Sykes' "Street Justice: A Moral Defense of Order Maintenance Policing" contributes a clear and quite important thesis to this fuzzy dialogue: that order maintenance policing is a good thing (i.e., morally justifiable and socially desirable) because it helps the poor and the disadvantaged. This thesis is probably true, if only because most policing in this country, whether it be strict law enforcement, dispute settlement, attending to medical emergencies, or order maintenance, is done at the request of the poor and disadvantaged.

However, while Sykes' thesis is probably true, it is, I think, flawed in two important ways. First, the thesis suffers from being so abstract and general that it is not very helpful in distinguishing types of order

Justice Quarterly, 3 (4) (December 1986): 513–516. Reprinted with permission of the Academy of Criminal Justice Sciences.

maintenance policing which are good and should be encouraged from those which are bad and should not. Sykes leaves us with a thesis that says all order maintenance policing is a good thing; and that, I believe Sykes would agree, is just not true.

Secondly, Sykes' thesis commits the error of mistaking a specific case for a very general one. That is, Sykes finds the moral motive for order maintenance policing to be located in the need to support community norms, particularly in communities that are beginning to fall apart. Even if we grant that all community norms in all communities should be supported—a questionable assumption indeed and the source of the first flaw in Sykes' thesis—it does not follow that supporting community norms is the only motive for order maintenance policing, or in fact the most important one from the point of view of the officers who police them.

I believe that the proper way to correct the flaws in Sykes' thesis is to approach the problem of street justice from the bottom up, rather than from the top down, to examine its micro- rather than its macro-morality. Doing so helps guard against the error of assuming that the moral motives of those who dish out street justice are always the same as our own. Within the space provided to me for a response to "Street Justice," it is not possible to play out this alternative approach systematically. Hopefully, the little sketch which follows may be helpful in suggesting some directions for further discussion of the moral dimensions of order maintenance policing.

❖ STREET JUSTICE: WHAT IT IS ❖

If order maintenance policing is, as Sykes suggests in his article, the incapacitation, punishment and treatment of offenders by police without judicial review or due process, this definition squares fairly well with what I have come to understand police mean when they speak of "street justice." When a cop says that a situation calls for "a little street justice," I understand the phrase to mean that someone should be hurt a bit for what they did or were about to do. In my experience police understand "street justice" to be appropriate and necessary (i.e., morally justifiable and socially desirable) in situations where the law and courts would be likely to refuse to punish with the severity that police themselves believe the offense warrants.

Offenses against police officers are the most widely appreciated, the most general and the most morally basic provocation for street justice. Any act which openly defies police authority, insults a police officer or causes a police officer to lose face merits "street justice" to even up the score and teach the offending party a lesson. Street justice has both retributive and utilitarian dimensions. For example, running away from a policeman and making him give chase through back yards, over fences and down back alleys is an offense that warrants the "little street justice" of at least one or two good punches when the offender is finally caught. By extension, police morality also holds that the more serious the offense against police authority, the more severe the street justice that is warranted. Assaulting a police officer justifies street justice severe enough to require a trip to the hospital. Shooting or shooting at a police officer justifies street justice severe enough to require a trip to the morgue.

When looked at from the bottom up, what Sykes sees as the community mandate for street justice is, I believe, better understood as a special case of this most general moral justification for street justice. When an officer is given regular responsibility for policing a specific area, and if that area is small enough, he typically develops a sense that the area is **his** territory and what goes on there is a reflection on **him**. Under such conditions, a violation of the established order in that territory becomes an affront to the officer. The officer assumes an active *moral* interest in his territory because he has an active moral interest in himself.

❖ STREET JUSTICE: WHAT IT SEEKS TO ACHIEVE ❖

Understanding the moral mandate for street justice in this way leads us to see the moral relationship between police officers and the areas they police in terms quite different from those which Sykes suggests. From a micro-morality perspective, it really does not matter whether an area is characterized by *gemeinschaft* or *gesellschaft* relations to the questions of whether a police officer takes an active moral interest in maintaining order in that area. In fact, foot patrol, the kind of policing most often associated with order maintenance and the kind of policing most likely to encourage officer intimacy and identity with a specific territory, is most frequently used in the most *gesellschaftlich* areas of modern cities. What matters is that the officer comes to identify with that area and see disorder in it as a challenge to his authority. It is maintaining that authority, which officers believe they have the moral right and obligation to do, that street justice seeks to achieve.

❖ STREET JUSTICE: HOW IT CAN BE CONTROLLED ❖

One of the most remarkable things about street justice is how infrequently officers actually do carry through on its moral recommendations. In part, this is so because the general moral premises of street justice justifications are subject to a whole host of usually unspoken, common sense restrictions. For example, though the morality of street justice provides for a punch or two for the suspect who runs when told to stop, this does not apply to children, women, crazy people or old people—all of whom it would be unbecoming for an officer to punch.

In part as well, the morality of street justice is often not realizable in situations where it is likely to be misinterpreted by observers. To a great degree this is solely a matter of timing. In order to appreciate the moral drama of street justice, one must be in on it from the very first act and stay with it until its final scene. If one is not aware of all the circumstances which led up to and justify a particular act of street justice, the act alone appears vicious and brutal. The general public cannot be counted on to be sympathetic witnesses to the administration of street justice for the simple reason that they do not know its rationale.

Finally, while street justice is limited in its use by the two internal and inherent controls mentioned above, a most important control is external. It is that administering street justice, particularly if it is severe, is going to put the officer through a lot of hassle. If street justice results in someone being hurt enough to require a trip to the hospital, it is the police officer who is going to take that person there. After that, arrest reports will have to be written. After that, reports will have to be written justifying the use of force. The officer is going to have to write; the officer's supervisor is probably going to have to write; and internal affairs may have to write too, if someone files a formal complaint. The country is full of underemployed lawyers advertising everyday that they will take almost any case on a contingency fee basis. The department is not going to appreciate having to spend money defending the officer in a civil suit, even if police morality holds that his actions were completely justified. From the street policeman's point of view, this is a fairly hefty price to pay for giving somebody the street justice he morally deserves.

The happy consequence of all of this potential hassle is, of course, that it encourages police officers to minimize the use of force in administering street justice. If a threat to use force will work as well as force itself, in the face of all of the potential hassle, an officer would be a fool to resort to its actual use. The unhappy consequence of all of this potential hassle is that some officers may choose to "take a hike," to walk away from a situation in which street justice is morally required. The way to guard against this happening is to attach officers to the areas they police so tightly that there is nowhere else they can hike to.

10

Acquiring a Taste for Order
The Community and Police

George L. Kelling

I n recent writings (Kelling, 1981; Wilson and Kelling, 1983; Moore and Kelling, 1983; Kelling, 1986) I have discussed and advocated aggressive order maintenance activities by the police. Implicit in such advocacy are assumptions about the source of authority for police activity. The purpose of this article is to explore in more detail a particular source of police authority: neighborhoods and communities. The article begins with a brief description of an event I witnessed in Chicago.

> It was a late warm afternoon on north Michigan Avenue: Chicago's Gold Coast. Two young rollerskaters were taking advantage of Michigan Avenue's long slope toward the Watertower, John Hancock Building, and ultimately Lake Shore Drive. As they gyrated, dipped, and wove among pedestrians they appeared able to turn and stop on a dime. Whether intended or not, they were the center of attention and a source of some fear: some citizens moved against buildings; others stepped off of the sidewalk into the street; still others "froze" in place; and a few tried to ignore the whole thing.

Reflecting on this observation, I assume the skaters were reasonably intelligent high-spirited young people who, in their own minds, were doing

Reprinted by permission of Sage Publications, Inc. from *Crime & Delinquency*, Vol. 33, No. 1 (January), pp. 90–102. Copyright © 1987.

nothing more than "showboating." Taken by itself the event was not particularly noteworthy. It had some dangerous potential, especially for the elderly who could not move quickly and for whom an accident could be serious, but given the catalogue of evils that afflict cities, it was a minor event.

Had a police officer seen the skaters, he or she might have asked them to stop skating in such a crowded area. Most citizens would have appreciated such an intervention. In other places or times, they may well have intervened on their own. Undoubtedly, some citizens would cluck their indignation at the youths (or, at least, feel like doing so) and hope that an officer would "run them in"; others would feel empathy with the youths, but would understand the need for intervention and hope the officer would exercise good humor and patience; a few, and I suspect a *very* few, would object to police action. In any case, odds are that the skaters would have acquiesced to the officer's request.

But alas, there's a rub. Despite the relative unimportance of such events, they have within them the seeds of mischief. What if the youths had not been of good spirit? What if they would not stop or slow down and had refused the officer's request or skated away in an insulting fashion? After all, what legal right does a police officer have to order roller skaters to slow down and what recourse does the officer have if the request is ignored or defied?

If the only issue at stake were two youths roller skating on a busy street, then most of us might be quite content for the officer to do nothing if he or she were ignored or defied. Other values are at stake, however. Earlier I mentioned the danger of injury to elderly persons. Other people, less at jeopardy but equally committed to being able to walk on sidewalks, might wish to do so without having to dodge fast-moving roller skaters. What if other youths decided that Michigan Avenue was a great place for roller skating and inundated the area? Do we want civil requests from police officers to be ignored with impunity? What about bystanders who would witness disrespect for a police officer and decide that they too, perhaps in more serious circumstances, could choose whether or not to abide by an officer's request? What of the response of the police officer to being ignored? Do we want police officers to develop a "What the hell" attitude toward disorderly or dangerous behavior, even if it is not technically illegal?

❖ MAINTAINING ORDER IN CITIES ❖

At stake in the roller skating incident is whether reasonable levels of order can be maintained on city streets—that is, whether citizens and government can define, through tradition and law, what order is and devise methods to maintain it—without substantially threatening essential rights of citizens. This is an important, but controversial issue. It is important because civility, order, and predictability in daily contacts with strangers are important values in all aspects of urban life: commerce, industry, transportation, communication, education, and public safety. It is controversial because order maintenance lies at the heart of the tension between individual freedom and communal security.

The Importance of Maintaining Order

Citizens in public areas, especially city streets, are obligated by a common sense of propriety. Civility allows citizens both to move safely through city streets and to enjoy street life—the simple freedom from the intimacy of homes and intensity of domestic relationships. Without civility—the sense of reciprocity with strangers—every stranger would be a source of fear and no basis would exist for resolving conflicts.

Street life since the early 1960s has been characterized by an erosion of reciprocity. Streets have become stages for the drama of what Wilson (1983) has called "the psychology of radical individualism and the philosophy of individual rights" and, more cryptically, what Tom Wolfe has labeled the "Me Decade." This era has emphasized individual liberty over communal security, privilege over responsibility, self-expression over restraint, and egalitarianism over meritocracy.[1]

Public policy has fostered this individualistic ethos. Drunkenness, vagrancy, loitering, and minor drug use have been decriminalized. Emotionally disturbed persons have been turned out onto city streets and juvenile courts have backed away from controlling obstreperous youth. The ideology of radical individualism and preoccupation with mounting crime has kept us from fully comprehending the consequences of these public policies. While government policy and police concentrated on serious crime during the 1960s and 1970s, prostitutes, gangs, hustlers, drunks, and others lacking commitment to civic virtue increasingly behaved in outrageous ways. Despite professional and academic absorption with crime, citizens were bothered by the consequences of radical individualism and public policy: increasingly outrageous street disorder. Police officials recall that citizens' groups meeting with police during this period were concerned primarily about "quality of life" problems in their neighborhoods—drunks, gangs, unruly youth, and other sources of disorder. Yet public policy concentrated on crime: It was not unusual for police and other government officials to attempt to "educate" citizens about the *real* problem—crime— and convince them of the need to concentrate police resources on it.

In the early 1980s research caught up with public sentiment when it recognized that public fear stemmed more from disorder than from serious crime (Kelling, 1981; Skogan and Maxfield, 1981; Trojanowicz, 1981). Research showed that maintaining order—keeping subways free of graffiti or keeping dirty and messy people off the street—was not merely a cosmetic treatment. Drunks, gangs, prostitutes, obstreperous youth, as well as panhandling and other behaviors considered disorderly, were linked in citizens' minds to personal danger and serious crime. Moreover, as James Q. Wilson and I have argued, citizens may be right: Just as unrepaired broken windows in buildings may signal that nobody cares and lead to additional vandalism and damage, so untended disorderly behavior may also communicate that nobody cares (or that nobody can or will do anything about disorder) and thus lead to increasingly aggressive criminal and dangerous predatory behavior (Wilson and Kelling, 1982).

Whether or not Wilson and I are correct in this latter point, the consequences of fear for both citizens and cities have been dramatic: Citizens have abandoned neighborhoods, cities, shopping areas, public transportation systems, churches, and other public and private facilities. Even areas once rejuvenated—Chicago's Old Town, for example—are again troubled due primarily to street disorder. And, citizens have become increasingly skeptical of government's ability to ameliorate these problems.

One final point about the importance of order maintenance: it is deceptive to think that the majority of urban residents who are intolerant of street barbarism and support protecting neighborhood and traditional values are white, conservative, and middle class. Those demanding increased order are people of all races wanting to walk streets or ride buses without feeling under constant siege by others asserting their "rights" to say anything or behave any way they wish. These people have a deep concern for propriety and civility.

Even in the most crime ridden and disorderly neighborhoods, a majority of citizens are deeply troubled about the quality of neighborhood life. Many of these people are minorities. Despite the contrary belief of some citizens and police that minority residents do not respect police, the great majority do. For many of them, police presence is the difference between being a prisoner in their own homes and being free to move about and conduct their daily business. Some minorities are indeed frustrated with police, as police have sensed, but their frustration is different from that portrayed by journalistic and professional elites who have focused on police brutality and abuse of authority. Most urban minorities are frustrated because police have been strangers in their communities, whisking in and out and responding to calls for service in a brusque fashion. They believe that police have not been a tangible presence, engaged with citizens to develop neighborhood peace and security. A sadness of contemporary policing is its alienation from good people in minority neighborhoods.

The Controversial Aspects of Maintaining Order

Despite the importance of maintaining order, it is also controversial—for at least two reasons. First, there is no clear and consistent definition of disorder. Unlike criminal laws that define *acts*, public disorder is a *condition*. Criminal acts are relatively easy to define (threatening someone with a weapon and taking his or her money, for example) and there is almost universal agreement among citizens of all social classes that such activities are indeed reprehensible, threaten communal life, and deserve drastic public response.

Disorder as a condition may depend on the number of persons or events involved. One prostitute or one person drinking on the street may not create disorder in any community; two prostitutes or drunks may. Every community has perceptual thresholds that when approached threaten basic order. The perception of disorder may be caused by the timing of behavior. Revelry and noisemaking that are appropriate on New Year's Eve, Halloween, and the Fourth of July (indeed, often sanctioned and promoted by communities and cities), usually are not appropriate at other times. More commonly, behavior considered tolerable Friday and Saturday nights may not be condoned on other nights. Location is also important: Partying and noisemaking are commonplace and accepted in some neighborhoods, but rare and unacceptable in others.

Disorder then, is a condition resulting from behavior that, depending on location, time, and local traditions, is offensive in its violation of local expectations for normalcy and peace in a community. Whether malevolent or innocent in intent, disorderly behavior powerfully shapes the quality of urban life and citizens' views both of their own safety and the ability of government to ensure it.

The relativity and ambiguity that characterize definitions of disorder lead to the second controversial aspect of order maintenance: that is, the basis upon which responses to it are justified. The justification for intervening in serious criminal events is clear: there is evidence of the commission of a crime, or else it has been committed in view of a police officer. With elaborate procedural safeguards for the alleged perpetrator, the police officer can make an arrest, detain the suspect, and initiate prosecution. Maintenance of order is different: many behaviors that may create disorder are not illegal. Those that *are* illegal present, at least in theory, little difficulty for the police officer who can order the behavior stopped and make an arrest if the person will not desist. However, many disruptive behaviors have never been illegal (roller skating for example), and over the past 20 years the list of disorderly behaviors categorized as illegal has shrunk considerably (vagrancy, drunkenness, and so on).

When activities of individuals threaten order but are not illegal, perplexing problems arise for citizens and police officers. On the one hand, we all respect constitutional principles that prevent police interference with citizens' essential rights. Yet whether disorder originates from lack of civic virtue or sheer meanness, it demands action of limited scope and duration by citizens or police. The fact that public drunkenness has been decriminalized does not change the situation for police—it is a social problem about which something must be done. Likewise, deinstitutionalization of the emotionally disturbed may have been conceptually wise, but lack of community resources has resulted in the addition of one more source of urban disorder and fear: the mentally ill—another police problem. Gangs are an additional example. There is nothing illegal about the existence of a gang or its meeting on a street corner. Nevertheless, depending on where members congregate and what they do, their very presence may terrorize many citizens. And citizens may well demand, in fact *do* demand, that police respond to gangs and gang activities, as well as drunkenness and the mentally ill. To the extent that police do respond—except when gangs, drunks, or mentally ill are involved in illegal behaviors, and for the most part they are not—police are involved in order maintenance activities that have as their goal the establishment and maintenance of some vision of civic morality.

❖ AUTHORIZING ORDER MAINTENANCE ACTIVITIES ❖

Many citizens as well as police are squeamish about acknowledging police involvement in establishing and maintaining civic morality. Yet, every shred of empirical evidence is that police are deeply involved in order maintenance (Wycoff, 1982). It is not a question of whether police have been involved in such activities or whether they will continue to be, it is instead a question of whether they are going to acknowledge and manage their activities fully and properly to maintain order. George Will's comment, "Government would do better what it does if it would admit what it is doing" (1983), is especially apt for police. The deep-seated American inclination to be suspicious of government and especially distrustful of police ought not to divert citizens and police from the real world. Since police, as part of government, are inextricably involved in the business of defining and maintaining civic morality, it is important that police and policymakers be clear about the sources of their authority to do so. Certainly law is important. Professional wisdom is as well. What has been lost, however, is the realization and acknowledgment that community traditions are also a basic source of public authority.

The Origins of Civic Responsibility

Political theory from Aristotle to contemporary times has affirmed the centrality of the community in the development of individual character and morality. This concept has been especially important in the shaping of American political thought. De Tocqueville (1945, p. 71) describes the link between community life and good citizenship in his description of political life in New England townships.

> The native of New England is attached to his township because it is independent and free: his cooperation in its affairs ensures his attachment to its interests; the well-being it affords him secures his affection; and its welfare is the aim of his ambition and of his future expectations. He takes a part in every occurrence in the place; he practices the art of government in the small sphere within his reach; he accustoms himself to those forms without which liberty can only advance by revolutions; he imbibes their spirit; he acquires a taste for order, comprehends the balance of powers, and collects clear practical notions on the nature of his duties and the extent of his rights.

Assertion of the primacy of the community as a force shaping citizen duties and rights shifts attention from the current emphasis on the constitution and law as basic or sole repositories of society's values and virtues. That we should have come to emphasize legal sources of social control in our attempts to find a base for moral action in America is not hard to understand. During periods of rapid social change, both the constitution and laws represent a broad political and moral consensus about the role of government in economic and social life and acceptable limits on official and citizen behavior. Yet the foundations of moral and civic life are more complicated: legal codes represent a small portion of the norms, mores, taboos, and traditions that define goodness, propriety, and ultimately, legal codes. Any human society, and certainly a society as pluralistic as the United States, is characterized by both a relatively monolithic formal legal system and informal social control systems that complement and compete with the formal system.

Moreover, powerful institutions encourage and enforce adherence to both formal legal and informal social control codes: The constitution and laws are shored up by the police and courts; other basic values and norms are buttressed by the family, church, neighborhood, and community.

The power of these later institutions of social control to encourage and enforce morality is found in their capacity to provide care, nurture, education, and opportunity, as well as structure and discipline. Despite the potential of neighborhoods and communities to mold and shape behavior, it can be argued that public policy has weakened many informal institutions of social control. Of particular interest here are those deliberate political, governmental, and professional policies that have weakened the political and moral authority of neighborhoods and communities.

Opposition to and elimination of powerful neighborhood governance can be traced to turn-of-the-century reformers. For the most part white Anglo-Saxon Protestants confronted by ethnic minorities and wishing to maintain their political control and traditional values, reformers came to see political methods of maintaining values, resolving disputes, and allocating services to communities as ineffective and inherently distasteful. That they should have wished to change those methods is not surprising: Consensus was not hard to achieve in the relative homogeneous New England villages described by De Tocqueville. Later, when ethnic minorities claimed their rights to their own values and used the decentralized political system to their advantage, it was another matter. Reformers moved to protect their urban vision and interests by "freeing" cities from politics. Politics became synonymous with corruption, and neighborhood and community power became equated with "ward bosses." City management came to be seen as primarily a technical matter.

According to this view, fire and police protection, garbage collection, and other urban services could best be planned and administered by professional managers serving the city at large rather than local neighborhoods. Touting efficiency and clean government, and motivated by moral zeal, reformers advocated removing control of service functions from neighborhoods and assigning them to the city at large, and when all else failed—as in the case of the police in many cities—transferring city functions to the state.

During the 1950s, urban renewal and highway construction further eroded neighborhoods. Many administrators of such programs openly claimed that social good came from the obliteration of ethnic neighborhoods. When I was a student in Milwaukee during the early 1960s, for example, a former director of urban renewal justified the eradication of an Italian neighborhood for an expressway on the basis that it was "time" for second- and third-generation Italians to be integrated into the community at large. The wide dispersal of these citizens throughout Milwaukee and its suburbs suggested to administrators that Italians had been ready and wanted to disperse, rather than that these citizens had no choice but to disperse.

Preemption of political authority from neighborhoods has radically separated urban service systems from neighborhoods. While this separation was characteristic of all services, it became the keystone of the police version of professionalism. Independence from neighborhood, community, and, ultimately, city government became so central to police orthodoxy that most police administrators viewed any political attempts to influence them as tantamount to corruption. To ensure maximum separation of police officers from neighborhoods, many cities enforced legislation that police officers could not live in the neighborhoods they patrolled. "Good" services were seen as those delivered by remote professionals acting independently with little or no investment in, or accountability to, neighborhoods. This model has dominated urban administration and ideals to the present time.

In actuality, neighborhoods and communities were not easily subdued and in many cities, including Boston, New York, Philadelphia, Chicago, San Francisco, and others, they have maintained considerable political authority. For example, in New York City neighborhood representatives have regularly monitored allocation of police personnel and precluded administrative attempts to alter them appreciably. It is for this reason that it is not unlikely that when New York City allocates the 1,500 officers it is now hiring, the current district proportions will be perpetuated. Likewise, citizens in Boston have prevented neighborhood fire and police stations from closing despite the "efficiencies" to be gained from centralization. The strength of Chicago's traditional ethnic neighborhoods is well known. But generally, neighborhood political activity has been considered a throwback to earlier, less progressive forms of government— inefficient, perhaps having a particular charm, but certainly not in accord with reformers' perceptions of proper urban administration.

It is arguable whether centralizing control of urban service has resulted in the efficiencies both hoped for and promised by reformers. Perhaps in the case of fire protection and garbage collection, it has—although even that is debatable. In the case of neighborhood protection and safety, it has not. Despite increases in the number of police, narrowed responsibilities, improved management, reduced corruption, and most recently, improved treatment of minorities, police have not notably improved their record with respect to crime rates, citizen fear, disorder, or service delivery. Although police have developed an impressive capacity to respond rapidly to calls for service, the primary result of this ability has been an increase in the demand for rapid response to calls for service without any measurable impact. It has, however, widened the chasm between the police and citizens: If police are to respond rapidly to calls for service, they must remain on standby in their cars—not out of their cars with citizens.

The removal of control of police services from neighborhoods is felt most acutely when the informal controls exercised by families and neighborhoods break down and are in need of buttressing. If the breakdown in a neighborhood consists primarily of serious crime, police are increasingly positioned to know it and target an impressive array of resources at the problem. Although serious crime is a common problem in many neighborhoods, most often residents are troubled by less dramatic but, from a citizen's point of view, a more vexatious problem: chronic and demoralizing disorder. Yet rarely have police routinely collected data about chronic disorder and citizens' response to it or used such data to formulate personnel allocations or police tactics. As a result, neighborhoods 'have often been left to their own devices to deal with disorder. Some communities have had the resources to do so; but in other communities citizens could not make a significant impact on disorder without substantial police assistance. Indeed, disorder has become so severe in certain communities it would have been foolhardy for citizens to try. Under such circumstances, residents want and need assistance from police—not necessarily to arrest those creating disorder, but to bring them in line with community ideas of appropriate behavior. Centralizing police authority and narrowing police functioning have preempted the authority of neighborhoods and left them bereft of back-up force when things start to get out of control.

Today, circumstances are changing. Neighborhood political awareness is growing stronger and spreading—not just in the cities mentioned above that have maintained a strong sense of neighborhoods, but also in cities like Houston, Columbia (SC), Detroit, Milwaukee, Seattle, Minneapolis, Washington, D. C., and others not generally known for having politically viable neighborhoods. Neighborhoods are organizing both to provide their own neighborhood security and to structure new relations with local politicians, police, fire departments, prosecutors' offices, courts, and other agencies responsible for citizen safety. As these groups coalesce, they become means by which citizens collectively press their interests and demands on the police.

And, just as nineteenth-century Progressives were fueled by moral zeal and civic virtue, so too are the new generation of reformers. To be sure, their vision of cities is different than the Progressive view, but it is no less fervent. At its core is a sense that citizens are no longer prepared to tolerate their own lack of control over urban services, especially given the level of urban incivility and barbarity and the apparent helplessness of centralized government to cope with it.

Increasingly, neighborhood political groups are rejecting protective services that are remote and not accountable to them. Citizens do not want to delegate social control to strangers in their communities. This is not limited to the police: It explains the recent conflicts between the Guardian

Angels and citizens in the Mattapan area of Boston. Stranger guardians may be fine in neutral and impersonal territories like subways, but citizens want to know and have significant influence over anyone exercising authority in their territory. The persistence of small-town police departments, despite their "inefficiencies" evidences the same political fact: Residents of small towns are simply not prepared to give power over police to outsiders. Neighborhoods are slowly, but inexorably, learning this basic political reality. Police are starting to adjust to it.

Does this mean that local residents should completely control neighborhood standards, police should be accountable solely to communities, and police behavior should be circumscribed by neighborhood interests? Clearly, the answer is no. Such an orientation has gotten police into much difficulty in the past. Communities exist within cities, states, and the country, and alongside other communities. Each polity imposes obligations and opportunities on citizens as well as the police. Values compete with and contradict each other. For example, constitutional rights of strangers to express themselves freely can conflict with community rights of citizens to determine the character of their neighborhoods. No easy or fully satisfactory resolutions to such contradictions are available. They are inherent in a liberal democracy with competing interests and values. As much as police may want to avoid such ambiguities, the very nature of our society and its problems ensures that they cannot. Paraphrasing George Will (1983:93), do we want citizens to enjoy freedom of expression? Yes, up to a point. Do we want police to encourage self-expression? Up to a point. Do we want police to control citizen behavior that offends and frightens other persons? Up to a point. Identifying excesses and encouraging citizen restraint is the honor, privilege, and duty of police. The fact that it is hard to define standards, reconcile competing values, and prescribe police activities to enforce them does not mean that individual citizens, groups, collectives, and police and other representatives of government should be free from the responsibility of trying to do so. If the police do become involved in such processes earnestly, their contributions may be small and indirect; but they stand a chance of strengthening those institutions that have the primary task of social control—family and community.

Notes

[1] Such trends have contributed much to our society. They have reduced the consequences of racism, sexism, and other forms of inequality based on personal characteristics. They have also fostered creative thinking and expression. The same trends, however, have

given rise to selfishness, incivility, and unlimited behavior. Unfortunately, city streets have borne the brunt of radical individualism. And, they have been seriously, if not irreparably, harmed.

References

Kelling, George L. (1986). "Order maintenance, the quality of urban life, and the police: A line of argument." In Geller, William A. (ed.). *Police Leadership in America: Crisis and Opportunity*. New York: Praeger.

Moore, Mark H., & Kelling, George L. (1983). "To serve and protect: Learning from police history." *The Public Interest*, 76 (Winter): 49–65.

The Newark Foot Patrol Experiment (1981). Washington, D.C.: Police Foundation. (See especially, Conclusions, pp. 111–129.)

Skogan, Wesley G., & Maxfield, Michael G. (1981). *Coping with Crime: Individual and Neighborhood Reactions*. Beverly Hills: Sage.

Tocqueville, Alexis de (1945). *Democracy in America*. Vol. I. New York: Vintage.

Trojanowicz, Robert C. Unpublished. An Evaluation Report: The Flint Neighborhood Foot Patrol.

Will, George F. (1983). *Statecraft as Soulcraft: What Government Does*. New York: Simon & Schuster.

Wilson, James Q. (1983). "Crime and American culture." *The Public Interest*, 70 (Winter): 22–48.

Wilson, James Q., & Kelling, George L. (1983). "Broken windows." *The Atlantic Monthly*, (March): 29–38.

Wycoff, Mary Ann. (1982). "The Role of Municipal Police: Research as a Prelude to Changing it." Washington, D.C.: Police Foundation.

Part III

The Society
of Police

11

The Quasi-Military Organization of the Police

Egon Bittner

The conception of the police as a quasi-military institution with a war-like mission plays an important part in the structuring of police work in modern American departments. The merits of this conception have never been demonstrated or even argued explicitly. Instead, most authors who make reference to it take it for granted or are critical only of those aspects of it, especially its punitive orientation, that are subject [to] aspersion even in the military establishment itself.[1] The treatment the topic receives in the Task Force Report on the Police of the President's Commission on Law Enforcement and Administration of Justice is representative of this approach. The authors note that "like all military and semi-military organizations, a police agency is governed in its internal management by a large number of standard operating procedures."[2] This observation is accompanied by remarks indicating that the existence of elaborate codes governing the conduct of policemen relative to intra-departmental demands stands in stark contrast to the virtual absence of formulated directives concerning the handling of police problems in the community. The imbalance between proliferation of internal regulation and the neglect of regulations relative to procedures employed in the field leads to the inference that the existing codes must be supplemented by substantive instructions

Reprinted courtesy of the author from *The Functions of the Police in Modern Society*. (1970), pp. 52–62. Footnotes renumbered.

and standards in the latter area. The question whether such an expansion of regulation might not result in a code consisting of incompatible elements is not considered. Instead, it is implicitly assumed that policemen can be instructed how to deal with citizens by regulations that will not affect the existing system of internal disciplinary control.

The lack of appreciation for the possibility that the development of professional discretionary methods for crime control and peacekeeping may conflict with the enforcement of bureaucratic-military regulations is not merely a naive oversight; more likely, it represents an instance of wishful thinking. For the military is immensely attractive to police planners, and not without reason. In the first place, there exist some apparent analogies between the military and the police and it does not seem to be wholly unwarranted to expect methods of internal organization that work in one context to work also in the other. Both institutions are instruments of force and for both institutions the occasions for using force are unpredictably distributed. Thus, the personnel in each must be kept in a highly disciplined state of alert preparedness. The formalism that characterizes military organization, the insistence on rules and regulations, on spit and polish, on obedience to superiors, and so on, constitute a permanent rehearsal for "the real thing." What sorts of rules and regulations exist in such a setting are in some ways less important than that there be plenty of them and the personnel be continually aware that they can be harshly called to account for disobeying them.[3] Second, American police departments have been, for the greater part of their history, the football of local politics, and became tainted with sloth and corruption at least partly for this reason. Police reform was literally forced to resort to formidable means of internal discipline to dislodge undesirable attitudes and influences, and the military model seemed to serve such purposes admirably. In fact, it is no exaggeration to say that through the 1950s and 1960s the movement to "professionalize" the police concentrated almost exclusively on efforts to eliminate political and venal corruption by means of introducing traits of military discipline. And it must be acknowledged that some American police chiefs, notably the late William Parker of Los Angeles, have achieved truly remarkable results in this respect. The leading aspiration of this reform was to replace the tragicomic figure of the "flatfoot cop on the take" by cadres of personally incorruptible snappy operatives working under the command of bureaucrats-in-uniform. There is little doubt that these reforms succeeded in bringing some semblance of order into many chaotic departments and that in these departments "going by the book" acquired some real meaning.

Finally, the police adopted the military method because they could not avail themselves of any other options to secure internal discipline. For all its effectiveness, the military method is organizationally primitive. At least, the standard part of the method can be well enough approximated with a modicum of administrative sophistication. Moreover, since most of the men who go into police work have some military experience, they need not go to outside resources to obtain help in building a quasi-military order. This is important because a century of experience taught American police forces that outside intervention into their affairs—known as the "shake-up"—was almost always politically inspired. Because the suspicion of high-level chicanery is still very much alive, and not without reasons, the police is the only large scale institution in our society that has not benefited from advances in management science. In the absence of lateral recruitment into supervisory positions and developed technical staff skills, changes had to be achieved mainly by means of rigid enforcement of regulations of internal procedure and by emphasizing external trappings of discipline. In a situation where something had to be done, with little to do it with, this was no mean accomplishment.[4]

Acknowledging that the introduction of methods of military-bureaucratic discipline was not without some justification, and conceding that it helped in eliminating certain gross inadequacies, does not mean, however, that the approach was beneficial in larger and longer range terms. Even where the cure succeeded in suppressing many of the diseases of earlier times, it brought forth obstacles of its own to the development of a model of a professional police role, if by professional role is meant that practice must involve technical skill and fiduciary trust in the practitioner's exercise of discretion. The reason for this is simple. While in early police departments there existed virtually no standards of correct procedure at all and no inducement to do well—since rewards were scant and distributed along lines of personal favoritism—one can now distinguish between good and bad officers, and engaging in what is now defined as correct conduct does carry significant rewards. But since the established standards and the rewards for good behavior relate almost entirely to matters connected with internal discipline, the judgments that are passed have virtually nothing to do with the work of the policeman in the community, with one significant exception. That is, the claims for recognition that have always been denied to the policeman are now respected, but recognition is given for doing well in the department, not outside where all the real duties are located.

The maintenance of organizational stability and staff morale require that praise and reward, as well as condemnation and punishment, be distributed methodically, i.e., predictably in accordance with explicit rules. Correspondingly, it is exceedingly difficult to assign debits and credits for performances that are not regulated by rule. Because the real work of the policeman is not set forth in the regulations, it does not furnish his superior a basis for judging him.[5] At the same time, there are no strongly compelling reasons for the policeman to do well in ways that do not count in terms of official occupational criteria of value. The greater the weight placed on compliance with internal departmental regulation, the less free is the superior in censoring unregulated work practices he disapproves of, and in rewarding those he admires, for fear that he might jeopardize the loyalty of officers who do well on all scores that officially count—that is, those who present a neat appearance, who conform punctually to bureaucratic routine, who are visibly on the place of their assignment, and so on. In short, those who make life easier for the superior, who in turn is restricted to supervising just those things. In fact, the practical economy of supervisory control requires that the proliferation of intra-departmental restriction be accompanied by increases in license in areas of behavior in unregulated areas. Thus, one who is judged to be a good officer in terms of internal, military-bureaucratic codes will not even be questioned about his conduct outside of it. The message is quite plain: the development of resolutely careful work methods in the community may be nice, but it gets you nowhere!

There is one important exception to the priority of intra-departmental quasi-military discipline in the judging of the performances of policemen. Police departments have to produce visible results of their work. The most visible results are arrested persons who keep the courts busy. This demand naturally devolves on individual officers. The question about the expected contribution of individual policemen to the statistical total of crimes cleared, summonses delivered, and arrests made is a matter of heated controversy. The problem is usually addressed as to whether or not there exist quotas officers must meet. Of course, the question can always be so framed that one can answer it truthfully either way.[6] But more fundamentally it is quite clear that individual policemen must contribute to the sum total of visible results, unless they have some special excuse, such as being assigned to a desk job. Moreover, how could any police superior under present conditions of supervision ever know whether the men assigned to the traffic division or to the vice squad are on the job at all, if they did not produce their normal share of citations or arrests?

Clearly, therefore, there is added to the occupational relevance of the military-bureaucratic discipline the demand to produce results.[7] While the emphasis on stringent internal regulation, taken alone, merely discourages the elaboration of careful approaches to work tasks, it exercises in combination with production demands a truly pernicious influence on the nature of police work. There are several reasons for this but the most important is based on the following consideration. Though the explicit departmental regulations contain little more than pious sermonizing about police dealings with citizens, whether they be offenders, an unruly crowd, quarreling spouses, accident victims, or what not, it is possible that a policeman could, despite his discretionary freedom, act in some such way as to actually come into conflict with some stated rule, even though the rule is not topically relevant to the situation at hand. Since he knows that his conduct will be judged solely with respect to this point he must be attuned to it, avoiding the violation even if that involves choosing a course of action that is specifically wrong with respect to the realities of the problem. For example, it is far from unusual that officers decide whether to make an arrest or not on the basis of their desire to live within departmental regulation rather than on the merits of the case at hand. In these situations the military-bureaucratic discipline regulates procedure speciously; it does not provide that in such-and-such a situation such-and-such a course of action is indicated. On the contrary, the regulations are typically silent about such matters; but in insisting on specific ways for officers to keep their noses clean they limit the possibilities of desirable intervention and they encourage transgression. Thus, it has been reported that in the New York Police Department, known for its stringently punitive discipline, officers who violate some official rules of deportment while dealing with citizens simply arrest potential complainants, knowing the complaints of persons charged with crimes are given no credence. Incongruously, while in New York the Police Department is much more likely to discipline an officer for brutalizing a citizen than elsewhere, it in fact rarely gets a chance to do it. For whenever there is a situation in which it is possible that an officer could have an infraction entered in his record, an infraction against an explicit regulation, he will redefine it into an instance of police work that is not regulated. Thus, while citizens everywhere run the risk of receiving a beating when they anger a policeman, in New York they run the added risk of being charged with a crime they did not commit, simply because its officers must keep their records clean.[8]

As long as there are two forms of accounting, one that is explicit and continually audited (internal discipline), and another that is devoid of rules and rarely looked into (dealings with citizens), it must be expected that keeping a positive balance in the first might encourage playing loose with the second. The likelihood of this increases proportionately to pressures to produce. Since it is not enough that policemen be obedient soldier-bureaucrats, but must, to insure favorable consideration for advancement, contribute to the arrest total, they will naturally try to meet this demand in ways that will keep them out of trouble. Thus, to secure the promotion from the uniformed patrol to the detective bureau, which is highly valued and not determined by civil service examinations, officers feel impelled to engage in actions that furnish opportunities for conspicuous display of aggressiveness. John McNamara illustrates this tactic by quoting a dramatic expression of cynicism, "If you want to get 'out of the bag' into the 'bureau' shoot somebody."[9] Leaving the exaggeration aside, there is little doubt that emphasis on military-bureaucratic control rewards the appearance of staying out of trouble as far as internal regulations are concerned, combined with strenuous efforts to make "good pinches," i.e., arrests that contain, or can be managed to appear to contain, elements of physical danger. Every officer knows that he will never receive a citation for avoiding a fight but only for prevailing in a fight at the risk of his own safety. Perhaps there is nothing wrong with that rule. But there is surely something wrong with a system in which the combined demands for strict compliance with departmental regulation and for vigorously productive law enforcement can be met simultaneously by displacing the onus of the operatives' own misconduct on citizens. This tends to be the case in departments characterized by strong militaristic-bureaucratic discipline where officers do not merely transgress to make "good pinches," but make "good pinches" to conceal their transgressions.[10]

No matter how elaborate and no matter how stringently enforced codes of internal regulations are, they do not impinge on all segments of police departments with equal force. By and large the highly visible uniformed patrol is exposed to far greater disciplinary pressures than personnel in the detective bureaus, which Arthur Niederhoffer aptly described as "mock bureaucracies."[11] While this situation is viewed as unavoidable, because the conduct of detectives cannot be as closely scrutinized as the conduct of patrolmen, and necessary because detectives need more freedom than patrolmen,[12] it tends to demean uniformed assignments. Because patrolmen perceive military discipline as degrading, ornery, and unjust, the only motive they have for doing well—which, of course, involves, among others, the devious practices we have just described—is to get out of the uniformed assignments.[13] Thus, the uniformed patrol suffers from a constant drain of ambitious and enterprising men, leaving it generally understaffed and, incidentally, overstaffed with men who are regarded as unsuitable for more demanding tasks. Though by no means all competent personnel take advantage of opportunities to leave the patrol for the detective bureaus, those who remain are dispirited by the conditions under which they are obliged to work and by the invidiously low level of prestige connected with their performance.[14] In consequence the outwardly snappy appearance of the patrol hides a great deal of discontent, demoralization, and marginal work quality.

Another complex of mischievous consequences arising out of the military bureaucracy relates to the paradoxical fact that while this kind of discipline ordinarily strengthens command authority it has the opposite effect in police departments. This effect is insidious rather than apparent. Because police superiors do not direct the activity of officers in any important sense they are perceived as mere disciplinarians.[15] Not only are they not actually available to give help, advice, and direction in the handling of difficult work problems, but such a role cannot even be projected for them. Contrary to the army officer who is expected to lead his men into battle—even though he may never have a chance to do it—the analogously ranked police official is someone who can only do a great deal *to* his subordinates and very little *for* them. For this reason supervisory personnel are often viewed by the line personnel with distrust and even contempt.[16] It must be understood that this character of command in police departments is not due solely to its administrative incompetence. It is exceedingly rare that a ranking police officer can take positive charge of police action, and even in the cases where this is possible, his power to determine the course of action is limited to giving the most general kinds of directions.[17] But like all superiors, police superiors, do depend on the good will of the subordinates, if only to protect their own employee interests within the institution. Thus, they are forced to resort to the only means available to insure a modicum of loyalty, namely, covering mistakes. The more blatantly an officer's transgression violates an explicit departmental regulation the less likely it is that his superior will be able to conceal it. Therefore, to be helpful, as they must try to be, superiors must confine themselves to white-washing bad practices involving relatively unregulated conduct, that is, those dealings with citizens that lead up to arrests. In other words, to gain compliance with explicit regulations, where failings could be acutely embarrassing, command must yield in unregulated or little regulated areas of practice. It is almost as if patrolmen were told, "Don't let anyone catch you sleeping on the job; if they do I'll get it in the neck and you will too. So, please, keep walking; in return I'll cover for you if you make a false arrest." Superiors, needless to say, do not speak in such terms. They probably do not even communicate the message covertly. Indeed, it is quite likely that most police officials would honestly view the suggestion with contempt. But this is the way things work out and the more a department is organized along military-bureaucratic lines the more likely it is that they will work out this way. Naturally, the situation is not conducive to the development of relations of genuine trust, respect, and loyalty.

Finally, emphasis on elaborate codes of internal regulation of a military kind tends to subvert police training, at least wherever this training is administered in departments, as is commonly the case. In the very best existing training programs, instruction consists of three parts. There are some lectures concerning criminology, criminal law, human relations, mental health, etc., given by visiting social scientists and lawyers. The second part consists largely of homilies about the social importance and dignity of police work, which emphasize that the occupation makes the highest demands on integrity, wisdom, and courage. The third part, to which the bulk of instructional time is devoted, relates to the teaching of departmental regulations. Since this is the only practical part of the course of instruction, it is abundantly clear that the overall purpose of the training is to turn tyros into compliant soldier-bureaucrats rather than competent practitioners of the craft of peacekeeping and crime control.[18] But since there exists no direct relation between knowing the regulations and maintaining the appearance of complying with them, the first thing graduates learn on their first assignment is that they must forget everything they have been taught in the academy. The immediate effect of the "reality shock" is a massive increase in the attitude of cynicism among first year policemen, not surprisingly since their introduction to the occupation was not only inadequate as far as their work duties are concerned, but also misleading.[19]

It could be said, of course, that the argument proposed thus far merely shows that efforts to professionalize police work by means of importing traits of outward military discipline is apt to create tendencies to displace misconduct into unregulated areas because the pertinent regulations have not yet been formulated. In time, these areas too will come under the scope of the existing discipline. It is our view that it is exceedingly unlikely that this development will take place. The charting of realistic methods of peacekeeping and crime control is profoundly incompatible with the style of current regulations of internal discipline. One simply cannot bring under the same system of control rules relating to dress and bureaucratic formalities, on the one hand, and norms governing the discretionary process of handling an instance of disorderly conduct on the streets, on the other. Emphasis on the first defeats care for the other. This does not imply that all presently existing regulations must be rescinded to encourage a methodical approach to police work tasks. Quite the contrary, the majority of present expectations will probably retain value in any alternative system of control. But their relevance, mode of presentation, and enforcement will have to be made subsidiary to a system of procedure that charts professionally responsible decisionmaking under conditions of uncertainty, In simplest terms, if policemen can be induced to face problems in the community and to deal with citizens in ways that meet at once criteria of purposeful efficiency and will correspond to the expectations of the kind of public trust commonly associated with the exercise of professional expertise, then there will be no need to treat them like soldier-bureaucrats. Correspondingly, as long as policemen will be treated like soldier-bureaucrats, they cannot be expected to develop professional acumen, nor value its possession.

It must be said, however, that the true professionalization of police work, in and of itself, is no weapon against sloth and corruption, no more than in the case of medicine, the ministry, law, teaching, and social work. That is, the professionalization of police work still leaves open the matter of its control. But if we are not willing to settle for having physicians who are merely honest, and who would frankly admit that in curing diseases and dealing with patients they have to rely entirely on "playing by ear," it is difficult to see why we would devote all our energies to trying to make the police honest without any concern whatever for whether or not they know, in a technical sense, how to do what they are supposed to do. Some people say it is foolish to demand technical proficiency and professional ethics where none exists. This view is certainly premature and probably wrong. We know far too little about the way police work is actually done to say with assurance that what we desire does not exist. What we know is that policemen have not written any scholarly tracts about it. We also know that presently good and bad work practices are not distinguishable, or, more precisely, are not distinguished. Worst of all, we have good reasons to suspect that if some men are possessed by and act with professional acumen, they might possibly find it wiser to keep it to themselves lest they will be found to be in conflict with some departmental regulation. The pending task, therefore, has less to do with putting external resources of scholarship at the disposal of the *police departments*, than with discovering those good qualities of police work that already exist in the skills of *individual practitioners*. It is not enough to discover them, however, they must be liberated and allowed to take their proper place in the scheme of police organization. By making the possession and use of such skills the controlling consideration in the distribution of rewards, we will have a beginning of a professional system for controlling police practices. The prospect of such a control is in strict competition with presently existing methods of military-bureaucratic regulation.[20]

Notes

1 Recently some authors have expressed doubts about the merits of organizing the police along military lines. J. Q. Wilson takes issue with Smith's assertion that the police have "disciplinary requirements of a quasi-military body." Wilson, *Varieties of Police Behavior: The Management of Law and Order in Eight Communities* (Cambridge: Harvard University Press), 79, n. 24. Similarly, A. J. Reiss and D. J. Bordua have questioned the adequacy of the idea of the police as a military organization; see "Environment and Organization: A Perspective on the Police," in Bordua (ed.), *The Police: Six Sociological Essays* (New York: John Wiley & Sons, 1967), 46 ff.

2 *Task Force Report: The Police* (Washington, D.C.: U.S. Government Printing Office, 1967), 16.

3 The tendency of police departments to adopt outward military rigidities has been frequently emphasized; see *Task Force Report: The Police, ibid.*, p. 29; J. D. Lohman and G. E. Misler, *The Police and the Community*, A Report Prepared for the President's Commission on Law Enforcement and Administration of Justice, (Washington, D.C.: U.S. Government Printing Office, 1966), Vol. I, 152, Vol. II, 196; Michael Banton reports that American police chiefs admire Scottish officers who "bore themselves well, and were smartly and uniformly dressed," Banton, *The Policeman in the Community* (New York: Basic Books, 1964), 123.

4 In addition to the rigors of outward discipline, military establishments also rely on "command charisma," a feature observed in American police departments by D. J. Bordua and A. J. Reiss; see their "Command, Control and Charisma: Reflections on Police Bureaucracy," *American Journal of Sociology*, 72 (1966), 68–76. The term indicates a leadership principle in which subordinates are moved to obedience by a high regard for, and trust in, the person in command.

5 See *Task Force Report: The Police, op. cit. supra*, Note 2, p. 20; Herman Goldstein, "Administrative Problems in Controlling the Exercise of Police Authority," *Journal of Criminal Law, Criminology and Police Science*, 58 (1967), p. 162; and Wilson, *op. cit. supra*, Note 1, p. 16.

6 Arthur Niederhoffer, *Behind the Shield: The Police in Urban Society* (New York: Anchor Books, 1969), 68–69.

7 The most illuminating and extensive discussion of pressures to produce is contained in J. H. Skolnick, *Justice Without Trial: Law Enforcement in Democratic Society* (New York: John Wiley & Sons, 1967), 164–181.

8 Paul Chevigny explains that New York policemen sometimes rebut allegations of brutality by maintaining that they are obviously fabrications since the complainant would have been arrested had the officer laid hands on him. Chevigny reports numerous instances of arrests following altercations with citizens which were ineptly or deviously provoked by policemen, and he comments, "Many lawyers think it a triumph for a felony to be reduced to a mere offence, but the truth is that it requires only two simple ingredients: guiltless clients and infinite patience." Chevigny, *Police Power: Police Abuses in New York City* (New York: Pantheon Books, 1969), 167.

9 J. H. McNamara (p. 189) of "Uncertainties in Police Work: The Relevance of Police Recruits' Background and Training," in Bordua (ed.) *op. cit. supra*, Note 1, pp. 163–252.

10 McNamara cites the following case at p. 171, *ibid.*: "a patrolman directing traffic in the middle of an intersection . . . fired his revolver and hit an automobile whose driver had not heeded the officer's hand signals. The driver immediately pulled over to the side of the street and stopped the car. The officer realized the inappropriateness of his action and began to wonder what he might offer as an explanation to his supervisor and to the citizen. The patrolman reported that his anxiety was dissipated shortly upon finding that the driver of the car was a person convicted of a number of crimes. The reader should understand that departmental policy did not specify that any person convicted of crimes in New York City thereby became a target for police pistol practice." Nevertheless, as the officer's feeling of relief indicates, the transgression was apparently construable as an instance of aggressive crime control.

11 Niederhoffer, *op. cit. supra*, Note 6, p. 85.

12 Wilson notes, however, that this view is probably mistaken. The patrolman deals with matters that are ill defined and ambiguously emergent, while detectives deal with more precisely defined crimes and only after they have been committed; *op. cit. supra*, Note 1, pp. 8–9.

13 "A high arrest record reinforces the cynicism that inspired it in the first place, while often establishing a policeman's reputation for initiative and efficiency. His superiors recommend him for assignment to the detective division. This route to promotion appeals to many young policemen who have little hope of passing a written competitive test for promotion, and impels many of them to adopt cynicism as a rational and functional way to advancement." Niederhoffer, *op. cit., supra*, Note 6, pp. 76–77.

14 "At present the principal rewards are promotion, which takes a patrolman off the street, or reassignment to a detective or specialized unit, which takes him out of order maintenance altogether; not surprisingly, patrolmen wanting more pay or status tend to do those things . . . that will earn them those rewards." Wilson, *op. cit. supra*, Note 1, pp. 292–293.

15 On the pervasiveness of purely punitive discipline, see McNamara *op. cit. supra*, Note 9, pp. 178–183. Wilson reports that regulations are so framed that they do not instruct but "give the brass plenty of rope with which to hang us." *op. cit. supra*, Note 1, p. 279.

16 McNamara, *op. cit. supra*, Note 9, pp. 187–188, reports attitudes of patrolmen towards their superiors and concludes, "Regardless of their accuracy, these assertions strongly support the feeling that the 'bosses' of the department do not deserve the respect which the organization requires or demands."

17 Banton views the absence of instructions and supervision as a main characteristic distinguishing American police from their British counterpart, *op. cit. supra*, Note 3, pp. 115–116. The absence of supervision is frequently noted; see McNamara, *op. cit. supra*, Note 9, p. 183; and *Task Force Report: The Police, op. cit. supra*, Note 2, pp. 28, 52, *et passim*.

18 McNamara speaks about the dilemma, "whether to emphasize training strategies aimed at the development of self-directed and autonomous personnel or to emphasize strategies aimed at developing personnel over whom the organization can readily exercise control. It appears that the second strategy is the one most often emphasized." *op. cit. supra*, Note 9, p. 251. Niederhoffer similarly states that, "At the Academy he [the recruit] masters and simultaneously succumbs to, the web of protocol and ceremony that characterizes any quasi-military hierarchy." *op. cit, supra*, Note 6, p. 45.

19 Niederhoffer, *ibid.*, speaks about the "reality shock" and documents the rapid rise of cynicism among first year policemen; see especially p. 239.

20 The competitive nature of ideals of military discipline and methodical discretion has been noted in a survey of the Boston police department undertaken in 1934: "Too often the military aspect of organization pushes the "essentially individual character of police work into the background." cited in *Task Force Report: The Police, op. cit. supra*, Note 2, p. 136.

12

The Informal "Code" of Police Deviancy
A Group Approach to "Blue-coat Crime"

Ellwyn R. Stoddard

It has been asserted by various writers of criminology, deviant behavior, and police science that unlawful activity by a policeman is a manifestation of personal moral weakness, a symptom of personality defects, or the recruitment of individuals unqualified for police work. In contrast to the traditional orientation, this article is a sociological examination of "blue-coat" crime[1] as a functioning informal social system whose norms and practices are at variance with legal statutes. Within the police group itself, this pattern of illicit behavior is referred to as the "code."

Following an examination of these contrasting viewpoints, this case study will provide data to ascertain the existence of the "code," its limitations and range of deviancy, and the processes through which it is maintained and sanctioned within the group. The guiding hypothesis of this study is that illegal practices of police personnel are socially prescribed and patterned through the informal "code" rather than being a function of individual aberration or personal inadequacies of the policeman himself.

❖ THE INDIVIDUALISTIC APPROACH ❖

Three decades ago August Vollmer emphasized that the individual being suited to police work was the factor responsible for subsequent deviancy

The Journal of Criminal Law, Criminology and Police Science, 59 (2) (1968): 201–213. Reprinted with permission of the author.

among officers. This approach implicitly assumes inherent personality characteristics to be the determinant which makes a police recruit into a good officer or a bad one.[2] A current text of police personnel management by German reaffirms the individualistic orientation of Vollmer and suggests that the quality of police service is ultimately dependent upon the individual police officer. There is no evidence of an awareness of group pressures within his analysis.[3]

A modified version of this individualistic approach is the view that perhaps the individual chosen had already become "contaminated" prior to being hired as a member of the force, and when presented with chances for bribery or favoritism, the "hard core guy, the one who is a thief already, steps in."[4]

A third factor, stressed by Tappan,[5] is the poor screening method at the recruitment stage. Such an officer might have had inadequate training, insufficient supervision, and poor pay and is ripe for any opportunity to participate in lucrative illicit enterprises. This author then goes into great detail to show the low intelligence and educational level of police officers. Another author adds that improved selection and personality evaluation have improved the quality of the police considerably over the past 20 years,[6] thereby attacking this problem directly. One recent author wrote that low salaries make more difficult the attraction of applicants with the moral strength to withstand temptations of "handouts" and eventual corruption.[7] Sutherland and Cressey, although aware that graft is a characteristic of the entire police system[8] rather than of isolated patrolmen, stress the unqualified appointments of police officials by corrupt politicians as the source of police deviancy. They state:

> Another consequence of the fact that police departments often are organized for the welfare of corrupt politicians, rather than of society, is inefficient and unqualified personnel. This is unquestionably linked with police dishonesty, since only police officers who are "right" can be employed by those in political control. Persons of low intelligence and with criminal records sometimes are employed.[9]

❖ THE GROUP APPROACH ❖

In contrast to the individualistic approach of these foregoing authors, the emphasis on the social context in which police deviancy flourishes has preoccupied the sociological criminologists. The present case study would clearly reflect this latter orientation.

Barnes and Teeters mention police deviancy in conjunction with organized, syndicated crime.[10] Korn and McCorkle,[11] Cloward,[12] and

Merton[13] see political and police corruption as a natural consequence of societal demands for illegal services. When these desired services are not provided through legal structures, they are attained through illegal means. However, documentation in support of these theoretical explanations is sketchy and limited in scope. Bell suggests that "crime is an American way of life." In the American temper there exists a feeling that "somewhere, somebody is pulling all the complicated strings to which this jumbled world dances." Stereotypes of big crime syndicates project the feeling that laws are just for "the little guys." Consequently, while "Americans have made such things as gambling illegal, they don't really in their hearts think of it as wicked."[14] Likewise, the routine discovery of an average citizen in overt unlawful activity rarely inflames the public conscience to the degree that it does when this same deviant behavior is exhibited by a police officer. Thus, the societal double standard demands that those in positions of trust must exhibit an artificially high standard of morality which is not required of the average citizen.

A measure of role ambivalence is an inevitable part of the policeman occupation in a democratic society. While he is responsible to protect the members of his society from those who would do them harm, the corresponding powers for carrying out this mandate are not delegated.[15] To perform his designated duties, the conscientious policeman often must violate the very laws he is trying to enforce. This poses a serious dilemma for the police officer since his attempt to effectively discourage violation of the law among the general public is often hinged to extra-legal short-cut techniques[16] which are in common practice by his law enforcement cohorts. For example, the use of "illegal" violence by policemen is justified by them as a necessary means to locate and harass the most vicious criminals and the Organized Syndicates.[17] These procedures are reinforced through coordinated group action.

> The officer needs the support of his fellow officers in dangerous situations and when he resorts to practices of questionable legality. Therefore, the rookie must pass the test of loyalty to the code of secrecy. Sometimes this loyalty of colleagues has the effect of protecting the law-violating, unethical officer.[18]

Such illegal practices which are traditionally used to carry out a policeman's assigned tasks might well be readily converted to the aims of personal gain.

In these tight informal cliques within the larger police force, certain "exploratory gestures"[19] involving the acceptance of small bribes and favors can occur. This is a hazy boundary between grateful citizens paying their respects to a proud profession and "good" citizens involved in corruption wishing to buy future favors. Once begun, however, these practices can become "norms" or informal standards of cliques of policemen. A new recruit can be socialized into accepting these illegal practices by mild, informal, negative sanctions such as the withholding of group acceptance. If these unlawful practices are embraced, the recruit's membership group—the police force—and his reference group—the clique involved in illegal behavior—are no longer one and the same. In such circumstances the norms of the reference group (the illegal-oriented clique) would clearly take precedence over either the formal requisites of the membership group (police department regulations) or the formalized norms (legal statutes) of the larger society.[20] When such conflicts are apparent a person can "1) conform to one, take the consequences of non-conformity to the other. 2) He can seek a compromise position by which he attempts to conform in part, though not wholly, to one or more sets of role expectations, in the hope that sanctions applied will be minimal."[21]

If these reference group norms involving illegal activity become routinized with use they become an identifiable informal "code" such as that found in the present study. Such codes are not unique to the police profession. A fully documented case study of training at a military academy[22] in which an informal pattern of behavior was assimilated along with the formal standards clearly outlined the function of the informal norms, their dominance when in conflict with formal regulations, and the secretive nature of their existence to facilitate their effectiveness and subsequent preservation. The revelation of their existence to those outside the cadet group would destroy their integrative force and neutralize their utility.

This same secrecy would be demanded of a police "code" to insure its preservation. Although within the clique the code must be well defined, the ignorance of the lay public to even its existence would be a requisite to its continuous and effective use.[23] Through participation in activity regimented by the "code" an increased group identity and cohesion among "code" practitioners would emerge.

> Group identity requires winning of acceptance as a member of the inner group and, thereby, gaining access to the secrets of the occupation which are acquired through informal contacts with colleagues.[24]

Lack of this acceptance not only bars the neophyte from the inner secrets of the profession, but may isolate him socially and professionally from his colleagues and even his superiors. There is the added fear that, in some circumstance in which he would need their support, they would avoid becoming involved, forcing him to face personal danger or public ridicule alone.

The social structure in which law enforcement is maintained has a definite bearing on what is considered normal and what is deviant behavior. The pattern of "blue-coat crime" (i.e., the "code") seems far more deviant when compared to the dominant middle-class norms of our society as when compared to lower class values. Whyte maintains that in the Italian slum of Cornerville, the primary function of the police department is not the enforcement of the law, but the regulation of illegal activities . . .

> . . . an outbreak of violence arouses the "good people" to make demands for law enforcement . . . even when they disturb police racketeer relations. Therefore, it is in the interest of the department to help maintain a peaceful racket organization. . . . By regulating the racket and keeping peace, the officer can satisfy the demands for law enforcement with a number of token arrests and be free to make his adjustment to the local situation.[25]

Since an adjustment to the local situation might well involve adopting some of the "code" practices, the successful police rookie is he who can delicately temper three sets of uncomplimentary standards: 1) the "code" practices adopted for group acceptance, 2) the societal standards regulating the duties and responsibility of the police profession and 3) his own system of morality gained from prior socialization in family, religious, educational and peer-group interaction.

Methodological Considerations

The difficulties connected with any intensive investigation into the "code" are self evident. The binding secrecy which provides the source of its power would be disrupted if the "code" were revealed to an "outsider." Thus, standard sociological research methods were ineffective in this type of investigation. The traditional ethnographic technique of using an informant familiar with the "code" and its related practices made available the empirical data within this study. Obviously, data from a single informant do not begin to meet the stringent scientific criteria of reliability for the purpose of applying the conclusions from this case to police agencies in general. It is assumed that subsequent research will establish whether this is a unique episode or more of a universal phenomenon. However, the decision to enrich the literature with this present study in spite of its methodological deficiencies was felt to be justified inasmuch as an intensive search through the professional literature revealed no empirical accounts dealing directly with deviant policemen."[26]

Because of the explosive nature of such materials on the social, political and economic life of the persons involved, the use of pseudonyms to maintain complete anonymity is a precaution not without precedent, and was a guarantee given by the director of this study in return for complete cooperation of the informant.[27] The informant was a police officer for three and one-half years before he was implicated in charges of robbery and grand larceny. He was subsequently tried and convicted, serving the better part of a year in prison. At the time of these interviews, he had been released from prison about three years.

The initial design of this study attempted to correlate these empirical data with two journalistic accounts[28] but the subjective handling of those stories neutralized any advantage gained from an increased number of informants. The present design is based exclusively on the single informant.

The Code and Its Practices

Some of these terms used to describe police deviancy are widely used, but because of possible variations in meaning they are defined below.[29] These practices are ordered so that those listed first would generally elicit the least fear of legal prosecution and those listed last would invoke major legal sanctions for their perpetration.

Mooching—An act of receiving free coffee, cigarettes, meals, liquor, groceries, or other items either as a consequence of being in an underpaid, undercompensated profession *or* for the possible future acts of favoritism which might be received by the donor.

Chiseling—An activity involving police demands for free admission to entertainment whether connected to police duty or not, price discounts, etc.

Favoritism—The practice of using license tabs, window stickers or courtesy cards to gain immunity from traffic arrest or citation (sometimes extended to wives, families and friends of recipient).

Prejudice—Situations in which minority groups receive less than impartial, neutral, objective attention, especially those who are less likely to have ''influence'' in City Hall to cause the arresting officer trouble.

Shopping—The practice of picking up small items such as candy bars, gum, or cigarettes at a store where the door has been accidentally unlocked after business hours.

Extortion—The demands made for advertisements in police magazines or purchase of tickets to police functions, or the ''street courts'' where minor traffic tickets can be avoided by the payment of cash bail to the arresting officer with no receipt required.

Bribery—The payments of cash or "gifts" for past or future assistance to avoid prosecution; such reciprocity might be made in terms of being unable to make a positive identification of a criminal, or being in the wrong place at a given time when a crime is to occur, both of which might be excused as carelessness but no proof as to deliberate miscarriage of justice. Differs from mooching in the higher value of a gift and in the mutual *understanding* regarding services to be performed upon the acceptance of the gift.

Shakedown—The practice of appropriating expensive items for personal use and attributing it to criminal activity when investigating a break-in, burglary, or an unlocked door. Differs from shopping in the cost of the items and the ease by which former ownership of items can be determined if the officer is "caught" in the act of procurement.

Perjury—The sanction of the "code" which demands that fellow officers lie to provide an alibi for fellow officers apprehended in unlawful activity covered by the "code."

Premeditated Theft—Planned burglary, involving the use of tools, keys, etc. to gain forced entry or a pre-arranged plan of unlawful acquisition of property which cannot be explained as a "spur of the moment" theft. Differs from shakedown only in the previous arrangements surrounding the theft, not in the value of the items taken.

Mooching, chiseling, favoritism and *prejudice* do not have rigid interpretations in the "code." Their presence appears to be accepted by the general public as a real fact of life. Since the employment of one of these practices can be done while in the normal routine of one's duties, such practices are often ignored as being "deviant" in any way. Ex-officer Smith sees it in this light:

> . . . the policeman having a free cup of coffee? I have never thought of this as being corrupt or illegal because this thing is just a courtesy thing. A cup of coffee or the old one—the cop on the beat grabbing the apple off the cart—these things I don't think shock too many people because they know that they're pretty well accepted.

But when asked about the practice of *mooching* by name, it assumed a different character of increased importance to Smith!

> I think mooching is accepted by the police and the public is aware of it. My opinion now, as an ex-policeman, is that mooching is one of the underlying factors in the larger problems that come . . . it is one of the most basic things. It's the easiest thing to accept and to take in stride because it's so petty. I think that it is the turning point a lot of times.

The "Sunday Comics" stereotype of policemen initiating mooching, bribery and favoritism is incorrect according to Smith's experience:

> Generally, the policeman doesn't have to ask for things, he just finds out about them. Take for example the theaters. I know the Roxy theaters would let the policeman in on his badge, just about anytime. It's good business because it puts the owner in a closer relationship with the policeman, and the policeman is obligated to him. If they had a break-in, a fire, or a little favor such as double parking out front to unload something, they'd expect special consideration from the policeman.

> When I walked the east side beat the normal thing was for bartenders to greet me and offer me a pack of cigarettes or a drink. When I walked the beat I was pretty straightlaced, there were a few bartenders that I felt were just trying to get along with me, and I loosened up a little with those people. One bartender gave me cigars when he found out that I didn't smoke cigarettes. I always accepted them; he always pointed out that there wasn't any obligation. Some of the beat men accepted cigarettes, some cigars, some took cash, and these men know when they're dealing with bootleggers, and why they're being paid. Different businessmen in the loop area give policemen Christmas presents every year.

Shopping and *shakedown, extortion* and *bribery* are all clearly unlawful, but in these practices the manner in which they are carried out contains a measure of safety to the policeman should his presence or behavior be questioned. A policeman's investigative powers allow him entry into an open building in which a "suspected robbery" has occurred, and various types of articles such as cigarettes and the like cannot be traced to any given retail outlet. Hence, his presence on such *occasions* is not suspected; rather, it is *expected*! Also, should a clumsy job of *shopping* or *shakedown* result in witnesses reporting these unlawful practices, the "code" requires that participating officers must commit *perjury* to furnish an alibi for those colleagues observed in illegal activities. This is both for the protection of the deviant officer and to preclude public disclosure of the widespread involvement of fellow officers in "code" practices. How extensive is *shopping* and *shakedown* as practiced by a department?

> As far as the Mid-City department is concerned I would say that 10 percent of the department would go along with anything, including deliberate forced entries or felonies. But about 50 percent of them would openly go along with just about anything. If they found a place open or if there had been a break-in or if they found anything they could use and it was laying there, they'd help themselves to it.

> Whenever there's an open door or window, they call for all the cars and they shake the whole building down—loot it!

Would those policemen involved in shopping and shakedown participate in something more serious? According to ex-officer Smith, they would.

> Most of the policemen who shop or go along with shopping would go along with major theft, if it just happened. I think where you've got to draw the line is when you get into premeditated, deliberate thefts. I think this is where the big division comes. In shopping, the theft just happens. Premeditated theft is a cold, deliberate, planned thing.

Here Smith points out the limits of the "code" which, though condoning any level of theft that "just happens," cannot fully support *premeditated theft*.

> I think in premeditated theft that the general police attitude is against it, if for no other reason just for the matter of self-preservation, and survival. When you get to a premeditated, deliberate thing, then I think your police backing becomes pretty thin.

At the time when Smith was engaged in the practice of *premeditated theft* in Mid-City, it looked somewhat different to him than it did later. When he took an objective look, he was aware of just how little this extreme deviancy *actually was practiced.*

> When I was involved in it, it seemed like all the people around me were involved in it, and participating in it. It looked more to me like the generally accepted thing then, than it does now, because actually the clique that I was in that did this sort of thing was a small one. I'm not discounting the fact that there may have been a lot of other small cliques just like this.

Looking at his behavior as an outsider, after his expulsion, Smith saw it in this light:

> After taking a long, hard look at my case and being real honest about it, I'd have to say that this [Premeditated theft like mine] is the exception. The longer I'm away from this thing the more it looks like this.

In Mid-City, *extortion* was not generally practiced and the "code" prescribed "street courts" (i.e., bribery for minor traffic offenses) as outside the acceptable pattern.

> [Extortion is] something that I would classify as completely outside the law [here in Mid-City], something that in certain areas has been accepted well on the side of both the public and the police. There's

a long standing practice that in Chicago if you are stopped for a traffic violation if you have a five dollar bill slipped in your plastic holder, or your billfold, the patrolman then asks for your license, and if that's in there you'll very rarely be issued a summons. Now this thing was something that was well known by truck-drivers and people who travel through that area.

Smith maintains that the "code" is widespread, although from the above analysis of extortion it can be clearly seen that specific practices have been traditionally practiced and accepted in certain areas, yet not found acceptable in another community. Would this mean that the bulk of these "code" practices occur in police departments other than the one in which Smith served his "apprenticeship" in "Blue-Coat Crime"? Our informant says "yes" and offers the following to substantiate his answer:

> I think generally the Mid-City police department is like every police department in the world. I think the exceptions are probably in small towns or in a few cities that have never been touched by corrupt politics, if there are any. But I think that generally they are the same everywhere,[30] because I have talked to policemen from other cities. I know policemen in other cities that I've had contact with that were in those things. I've discussed open things, or out and out felonies, with policemen from Kansas City on. And I know that at least in that city that it happens, and it's a matter of record that it happens in Denver and Chicago. And I think that this happens in all cities.

From a scientific point of view, other than the incidence of police scandals from time to time, there is no evidence to confirm or deny this one ex-officer's opinion regarding the universal existence of the "code."

The Recruit's Initiation into the "Code" Clique

Bucher describes a profession as a relatively homogeneous community whose members share identity, values, definitions of role, and interest. Socialization of recruits consists of inducting them into the "common core."[31] This occurs on two levels: the formal, or membership group, and the informal, or the reference group.

In the Mid-City police department the failure to socialize most of the new recruits into the "code" would constitute a threat to those who presently practice it. Thus, all "code" practitioners have the responsibility of screening new recruits at various times to determine whether they are "alright guys," and to teach by example and mutual involvement the limitations of "code" practices. If the recruit accepts such training, he is welcomed into the group and given the rights and privileges commensurate with his new status. If he does not, he is classified as a "goof" and avoided by the rest.

In a journalistic account of police deviancy, it was argued that if corruption exists in the political structures controlling police department appointments, this "socialization" into deviancy begins at the point of paying for the privilege of making an application or of buying an appointment.[32] Although Smith did not "buy" his appointment, he cited the existence of factions having influence in recruit appointments, even within the structure of a Civil Service Commission.

> There are four different requirements to the whole thing. One is your written test, one is your agility, one is your physical examination, and the fourth is the oral examination which is given by the civil service commission. I really crammed before I took the test. When I took the test it was a natural for me, it was a snap. I scored a 94 on my test for the police department. With my soldiers preference, which gives you 5 points, I scored a 99.[33] I passed my agility test and my physical. I could have had a 100 score, I could have been a gymnast, gone through the agility test and made everyone else look silly and still I could have failed in the oral exam. And this is the kicker where politics comes in.

> There are three old men that are aligned with different factions, different people on and off the department, different businessmen that have power, different groups, different lodges and organizations and all these things influence these men, these three people that make up the civil service board.

The existence of the "code" had hurt the level of morale generally in the Mid-City department. In fact, the breakdown of each new recruit's morale is an important step in gaining his acceptance of the "code."[34]

> The thing that hurt the morale was the fact that a large percentage of the people on the department were involved in illegal practices to some degree. And actually you take a man that has just joined the department, has good intentions[35] and is basically honest, and in this, to a man that's never been dishonest and hasn't stepped over the line, there aren't degrees. It's all either black or white. And the illegal activity I know shocks a lot of these young men . . . because it was the thing to do. It's a way to be accepted by the other people. It's a terrible thing the way one policeman will talk about another. Say an old timer will have a new man working with him and he'll tell you, "You've got to watch him, because *he's honest!*"

For a recruit to be accepted in the Mid-City police department he must accept the informal practices occurring in the department. Illegal activity is pursued within the police force as the dominant "norm" or standard.

To illustrate the group pressure on each policeman who dares to enforce the law as prescribed in the legal statutes, the following account is typical.

> We'll take a classic example—Mr. Sam Paisano. Now when I was on the force I knew that whenever I worked in the downtown area, I could go into Sam's restaurant and order my meal and never have to pay a dime. I think that just about every patrolman on the force knew that. If I had run across Sam doing anything short of murder, I think I would have treaded very lightly. Even if I hadn't accepted his free meals. Say I had turned it down; still, if I stopped this man for a minor traffic violation, say I caught him dead to rights, I'd be very reluctant to write this man a ticket because I'd suffer the wrath of the other men on the force. I'd be goofing up their meal ticket. Now he in turn knows this. The rest of the officers wouldn't waste any words about it, they'd tell you right off—"You sure fouled up our meal ticket." The old timers would give you a cold shoulder. If it came to the attention of the gold braid, your immediate superiors, they'd make sure you had a little extra duty or something. In most cases if you did this just to be honest, just to be right, it would go badly for you.
>
> This special treatment of Mr. Paisano wasn't something that you concealed, or that you were ashamed of because it was the normal accepted thing to do. I'd have been more ashamed, and I'd have kept it quiet if I'd stopped such a man as this, because I'd have felt like some kind of an oddball. I would have been bucking the tide, I'd been out of step.

Yet, such general practices must be converted to individual participation at some point, and to be effective this involvement must be on a primary group relationship basis. Smith's account of his introduction to the "code" follows the first steps of the assimilating process.

> The first thing that I recall seeing done [which was illegal] was on the night shift when I first went on patrol. The old timers were shaking buildings down and helping themselves to whatever was in the building. The first time I saw it happen I remember filing through the check-out counter at a supermarket, seeing all the officers grabbing their cigarettes or candy bars, or whatever they wanted and I passed through without anything.
>
> I got in the car and this old timer had, of all the petty things, two of these 25 or 30 cent candy bars and he sat them down in the seat and told me to have some. I told him I really didn't want any. And

he asked me if "that shook me up" or something. And I told him, "Well, it sort of surprised me." He said that everybody did it and that I should get used to that.

And as it went on it progressed more. Well, in fact, he justified it at the time by telling me he had seen the same market one time, when there had been a legitimate break-in and one particular detective had been so busy loading the back seat of his car full of hams and big pieces of beef that he was stumbling and falling down back and from the cooler to the alley, and he didn't even know who was around him he was so busy carrying things out. And he named this officer and I don't doubt it because I've seen the same officer do things in the same nature. And this was the first direct contact I had with anything like this.

The old timers would test the new recruits with activities which could be laughed off if they were reported, such as the 30 cent candy bar taken from the supermarket in the above account.

The old timers would nose around 'til they found out whether a young guy was going to work with them and "be right" as far as they were concerned, or whether he was going to resist it and be straight as far as the rest of the world was concerned.

If the recruit cooperated, the practices were extended and the rookie became involved. Once he was involved there was no "squealing" on fellow policemen breaking the law. Then he could have some personal choice as to how far he personally wished to go. However, those who were straightlaced and wanted to stay honest had their problems too. Social isolation appears to be a powerful sanction as can be seen from Smith's information.

There are a few policemen that are straightlaced all the way. I can remember one policeman who might have made an issue of another policeman taking something. He had that attitude for the first six months that he was on the force but by that time, he had been brow beaten so bad, he saw the writing on the wall. He knew better than to tell anything. In addition to brow beating, this man in very short order was put in a position where they had him on the information desk, or kicked around from one department to another, 'cause nobody wanted to work with him. This kind of a man they called "wormy," because anything that would happen he'd run to the braid.

This fellow, I knew, wanted to be one of the boys, but he wanted to be honest, too. As it turned out, this guy was finally dismissed from the force for having an affair with a woman in his squad car.

Just a couple of years before that he would have had a fit if he thought that somebody was going to take a drink on duty, or fool around with a woman, or steal anything. For this reason this man spent a lot of time on the information desk, working inside, and by himself in the squad car.

Negative sanctions were applied against "goofs" who advocated following the legitimate police ethic. Group acceptance by senior officers was the reward to a recruit accepting the "code," and the "code" was presented to the recruit as the police way of life having precedence over legal responsibilities.

This small fraction that . . . are honest and would report illegal activity, are ostracized. Nobody will work with them. They look at them like they're a freak, talk about them like they're a freak, and they are a freak.

The goofs that would talk about doing things the way they should be done, they had to be ignored or put down. There were older policemen that as they found out I would go along with certain things, pressed to see how much further I would go. And showed me that they went farther, whether I cared to or not. So naturally I went along quite a ways with some of them. And I don't really remember how we first became aware of how far the other person would go. I think this is just a gradual thing.

The existence of a social system of an informal nature working quietly under the facade of the formal police department regulations has been clearly demonstrated in Mid-City. One further note in explaining the motivations of policemen toward illegal activities involves the condition of low salaries. Smith's department pay scale and working conditions would suggest that economic pressures were a factor in condoning or rationalizing "code" practices.

The pay wasn't good. I went on the department and earned $292 a month. The morale of the force was as low as that of any group that I've ever been around. There was constant complaining from all them about everything.

The training programs were set up so that you would have to come in on your own time and weren't compensated for it. . . . They dictated to you how you lived your whole life, not only what you did during the eight hours you were a policeman but how you'd live your whole life. This as much as anything hurt the morale.

But when Smith was asked directly, "With the policeman's low salary, do illegal activities become necessary to keep up financially?" he discounted it as a major factor.[36]

I don't think this is the case. I don't think there are very many policemen that I knew, and I knew all of them, that were social climbers or that tried to keep up with the Jones, by illegal activities anyway.

Actually most of the police officers think that they are even above those people that have money, because they have power. Those people with money are pretty well forced to cater to a policeman. And you'll find that very few people ever tell a policeman what they think of him, whether they like him or not. They know that a policeman will do him harm. The businessmen, especially the bigger businessmen, pamper the policemen. They will treat them with respect when they face them.

Sanctions for Preservation of the "Code"

Normally, practitioners of the "code" would consist of a united group working to protect all fellow patrolmen from prosecution. However, Smith had exceeded the "code" limits[37] by committing *premeditated theft*, and in order to protect the "code" from being exposed during the scandal involving Smith and two accomplices, the "clique" socially and spatially isolated themselves from the three accused policemen.

Everybody ran for cover, when the thing hit the front page of the newspapers. I've never seen panic like there was at that time. These people were all ready to sell out their mother to save their own butts. They knew there was no holding back, that it was a tidal wave. They were grabbing just anything to hang on. The other policemen were ordered to stay away from us, myself and the other men involved. They were ordered to stay away from the trials. They were told to keep their noses out of this thing, that it would be handled.

There were a few policemen who came around during this time. Strangely the ones who came around were the ones who didn't go in for any of the illegal activity. They didn't have anything to worry about. Everybody else ran and hid.

During a time like this, group consensus is required to preserve the "code." A certain amount of rationalization is necessary to mollify past illicit activity in light of present public exposure. Smith continues:

I think if they had really gone by the book during the police scandal, that 25 percent of the policemen would have lost their jobs. I've talked to some of them since, and the worst violators all now have themselves convinced that they weren't guilty of a thing.

> I've never referred to myself as this before, but I was their goat, their scapegoat. The others stuck together and had support. I got what I deserved, but if I compare myself with the others, I got a real raw deal.

Preservation of the "code" occurs when policemen work with another person who has similar intentions and begin to "trust" one another in illegal activities without fear of the authorities being informed. A suggestion of rotating young officers from shift to shift to weaken the "code" had been given public discussion. To this, Smith reacted thusly:

> I think the practice of rotating young officers will serve a purpose. It will eliminate a lot of things because you just can't take a chance with somebody that you don't know. If you don't know but what the next person they throw you with might be a CID . . . short for Criminal Investigation Department. They're spies! Say there are just 10 percent of the men on the department that wouldn't go along with anything, and they are switching around with the new system, you don't know when you're going to catch one of them, and if you do you're a cooked goose. The old system you were 90 percent sure of the people you were with.

This same process used to preserve the illegal "code" as a group phenomenon is also the same process used to develop and promote the acceptable professional ethics of the police. A situation in which it is "normal" for a policeman to "squeal on his fellow patrolmen," would undermine professional ethics. Personal insecurity would mount with the constant fear of just being accused with or without supporting evidence. Such an anarchical system lends itself to intrigue, suspicion and an increased possibility of each officer being "framed." Thus, these same procedures which would effectively reduce the continuation of the "code" would also prove dysfunctional to the maintenance of the ethics which are the core of the police profession itself. These concurrent processes reflect the dual standards extant in society at large.

Difficulties Involved in Breaking the "Code"

If a "code" does exist in a law enforcement agency, one of the major factors which protects it from attack is secrecy. This factor is compounded by public acceptance of the traditional view of illegal behavior as only an individualistic, moral problem.

Another shield of the "code" from attack is the apathy resulting from the myriad of complex demands and responsibilities placed upon the average citizen. So many things touch him with which he *must* become involved that he does not pursue problems which do not directly concern him.

Inextricably connected with this is the realistic fear of retaliation, either through direct harassment by the police or indirectly through informal censures.[38]

Smith says that only a real big issue will provoke an apathetic public to action.

> Everybody's looking out for number one. And the policeman can do you harm. It's such a complex thing, there are so many ways, so many different people are affected by the police—most people will back off. Most people are afraid to do anything, if it looks like it's going to affect them adversely.

If the police have carefully practiced *prejudice*, in their day-to-day operations, the chances are slim that the persons against whom these illegal practices were committed possess either the social or political power to break the "code" before the system could retaliate. Knowing this fact keeps most of the persons with any knowledge of the "code's" operation silent indeed.

The rigid procedures of obtaining legal evidence and the dangers of committing a *false arrest* are gigantic deterrents to bringing accusations against any suspicious person, especially a policeman. Ex-officer Smith discusses the realistic problems involved in attempting to enforce legal statutes against *shopping* or other aspects of the "code":

> I think that any law against *shopping* would be hard to enforce against a police officer. You'd really have to have the evidence against him and really make it public, 'cause it would be soft pedalled all the way otherwise. Let's say you see a police officer in a restaurant taking a pack of cigarettes or let's say it's something other than a pack of cigarettes, something that you can prove came from the restaurant. And along comes a radio news unit and you stop the unit and say you just saw a policeman steal a pack of cigarettes or something bigger. When other police arrive on the scene the newsman would probably pull the other policemen off to the side and tell them that their buddy just took a pack of cigarettes and that goofball [the informer] wants to make trouble about it. You insist that they shake down the policeman and they find the item. Here you're in pretty good shape. In this case you'd have a policeman in a little bit of trouble. I don't think he'd lose his job or do any time over it, but I'd say there would be some scandal about it. Unless you were real hard headed they'd soft pedal it.
>
> Let's back up a little and say the policeman threw the item back into the restaurant, and then you made your accusation. Then you're in trouble, 'cause when they shake him down and he doesn't have a thing.

Now you're a marked man, because every policeman in town will know that you tried to foul up one of their boys. Even the honest policemen aren't going to like what you did. In other words, they are tightly knit, and they police this city by fear to a certain extent.

In Mid-City only those who are involved in practicing the "code" are equipped with the necessary information to expose its operations. Whether one *can* inform on his fellow officers is directly connected with the degree of his illegal involvement prior to the situation involving the unlawful event.

It all depends upon how deeply you are involved. If you've been a guy who has gone along with a free cup of coffee, the gratuities, the real petty things and you'd happen to drive up on a major theft, drive up on another policeman with his shoulder against the door, then you might take action. However, if you had gone a little farther, say you'd done some shopping, then you're forced to look the other way. It's like a spider spinning a web, you're drawn in toward the center.

It appears obvious that those who are involved in the "code" will be the least useful instruments for alleviating the problem. Only the professionally naive would expect a "code" practitioner to disclose the "code's" existence, much less reveal its method of operation, since his own position is so vulnerable.

❖ SUMMARY OF FINDINGS ❖

From data furnished by a participant informant, an informal "code" of illegal activities within one police department was documented. The group processes which encouraged and maintained the "code" were identified. It was found that the new recruits were socialized into "code" participation by "old timers" and group acceptance was withheld from those who attempted to remain completely honest and not be implicated. When formal police regulations were in conflict with "code" demands among its practitioners, the latter took precedence. Since the "code" operates under conditions of secrecy, only those who participate in it have access to evidence enough to reveal its method of operation. By their very participation they are implicated and this binds them to secrecy as well. In this study the public indignation of a police scandal temporarily suspended the "code" but it flourished again when public apathy returned.

Although some individual factors must be considered in explaining police deviancy, in the present study the sanction of group acceptance was paramount. This study clearly demonstrates the social genesis of the "code," the breeding ground for individual unlawful behavior. From evidence contained herein, an individualistic orientation to police deviancy may discover the "spoiled fruit" but only when the "code" is rooted out can the "seedbed" of deviancy be destroyed.

From related research in group deviancy, it can be stated that the social organization of a given community (including its respectable citizens) is the milieu in which a "code" flourishes. Thus, a police department is an integral element of that complex community structure, and deviancy found in an enforcement agency is a reflection of values which are habitually practiced and accepted within that community. This was found to be true in the present study.

The findings of this case study should not be interpreted as applicable to all police departments nor should it be a rationalization for the existence of an illicit "code" anywhere. Rather, it is a very limited effort to probe the very sensitive area of "Blue-Coat Crime" and describe its operation and method of perpetuation in one enforcement agency.

Notes

[1] This concept is a restricted modification of Sutherland's term "White Collar Crime." Edwin H. Sutherland, "White Collar Criminality," *American Sociological Review* 5 (1940), 1–12. However, the stress of Sutherland's thesis is the lowering of social morale *of the larger society* by the violation of trust by those holding these social positions. The present emphasis is upon the group participating in those violations and *their* reactions, morale and behavior, rather than the consequences accruing the larger society as a result of these illegal actions. The same violation of trust might produce a degree of disorganization and lowering of morale among nonparticipants, while producing a heightened morale and cohesion among all of those in the norm-violating clique.

[2] August Vollmer, *The Police and Modern Society* (1936), 3–4.

[3] A. C. German, *Police Personnel Management* (1958), 3–4.

[4] Mort Stern, "What Makes a Policeman Go Wrong? An Ex-Member of the Force Traces the Steps on Way from Law Enforcement to Violating," by a Former Denver Police Officer as told to Mort Stern, *Denver Post*, October 1, 1961. Reprinted in *Journal of Criminal Law, Criminology and Police Science* 53 (1962), 97–101.

A similar reaction is given by James F. Johnson, a former state trooper, Secret Service Agent, security officer and private investigator in *World Telegram and Sun*, March 10, 1953, quoted in Tappan, *Crime, Justice, and Correction* (1960), 290.

[5] Tappan, *Ibid.* p. 390ff.

[6] Wilson, "Progress in Police Administration," *Journal of Criminal Law, Criminology, and Police Science* 42 (1951), 141.

[7] Johnson, *Crime, Correction and Society* (1964), 452.

[8] The Lexow Committee in New York (1894–1895) and the Seabury Committee a generation later found the same situation of *departmental* corruption quoted in Sutherland and Cressey, *Principles of Criminology*, 6th ed. (1960), 338.

[9] *Ibid.*

[10] Barnes and Teeters, *New Horizons in Criminology*, 2d. ed. (1958), 245–247.

[11] Korn and McCorkle, *Criminology and Penology* (1959), 85–86, 125–136.

[12] Richard A. Cloward, "Illegitimate Means, Anomie, and Deviant Behavior," *American Sociological Review* 24 (1959), 167.

[13] Merton, *Social Theory and Social Structure*, Revised and enlarged ed. (1958), chapters 1, 4 and 5.

[14] Bell, "Crime as an American Way of Life," *Antioch Review* 13 (1953), 140–144.

[15] Sutherland & Cressey, *op. cit.*, p. 331.

[16] This dilemma is presently being compounded by recent Supreme Court decisions involving police powers and personal civil rights. The fear of an emergent police state (which may or may not be valid) leads the present Justices to feel that freedom of the individual will result when police powers no longer encroach upon individual rights. The paradox is that the police are required to fulfill their traditional protection duties in spite of these new formal procedures designed to limit their investigative activities. To fulfill the social expectations of "catching criminals, dope peddlers, etc.," the policeman must adopt certain extra-legal procedures strictly on an informal basis, while appearing on the surface to be adhering to the formal limitations imposed upon him. See Arthur Niederhoffer's recent monograph, *Behind the Shield: The Police in Urban Society* (1967).

[17] Westley, "Violence and the Police," *American Journal of Sociology* 59 (1953), 34–41.

[18] Westley, "Secrecy and the Police," *Social Forces* 34 (1956), 254–257.

[19] This concept was taken from Cohen, *Delinquent Boys: The Culture of the Gang* 60 (1955).

[20] Sherif & Sherif, *An Outline of Social Psychology*, revised edition (1956) 630–631, 638. For a sophisticated treatment of reference group theory see chapters 4, 16, and 18.

[21] Stouffer, "An Analysis of Conflicting Social Norms," *American Sociological Review* 14 (1949), 707.

[22] Dornbush, "The Military Academy as an Assimilating Institution," *Social Forces* 33 (1955), 316–321.

[23] Moore & Tumin, "Some Social Functions of Ignorance," *American Sociological Review* 14 (1949), 791.

[24] Johnson, *op. cit.*, pp. 445–446.

[25] Whyte, *Street Corner Society*, Enlarged ed. (1955), 138–139. Another author conceptualized this problem by delineating it as two separate police functions. "Law enforcement" has specific formal legal procedures whereas "keeping the peace" is vague and without a clear-cut mandate. This study updates by three decades the classic work of Whyte. See Egon Bittner, "The Police on Skid-Row: A Study of Peace Keeping," *American Sociological Review* 32 (1967), 699–715.

[26] Many authors have written of police deviancy as tangential to their central theme. However, persistent search failed to reveal recent empirical studies focusing directly on the deviant policeman himself. Most applicable were Westley's "Violence and the Police," *op. cit.*, and "Secrecy and the Police," *op. cit.*, although even here the data were gained from policemen still "in favor," who might well have reservations about revealing the full extent to which the "code" was practiced.

[27] A graduate assistant from the Department of Sociology, Mr. Ivy L. Gilbert approached ex-officer "Smith" as a friend, and under guidance of the present author was able to gain "Smith's" cooperation for a scientific study. Taped interviews over a period of

several months were recorded and transcribed by Gilbert. Many of these materials were used in Gilbert's Master's Thesis, "A Case Study of Police Scandal: An Investigation into Illegitimate Norms of a Legitimate Enforcement Agency (June, 1965).

[28] One article is a composite of personal experience as a police reporter, David G. Wittles, "Why Cops Turn Crooked," *Saturday Evening Post*, April 23, 1949, p. 26ff; the other is an account of a former Denver policeman as retold by a news editor, Mort Stern, *op. cit. supra*, Note 4.

[29] The majority of these terms and definitions are modified from those listed by Gilbert, *op. cit.* pp. 3–4, and discussed by German, *op. cit. supra*, Note 3, p. 173.

[30] Smith's evaluations are heavily influenced by his experience. He was a patrolman in a police department totaling about 250 personnel, serving a metropolitan area of a quarter of a million persons. However, other sources have suggested that when a community gets larger than 80,000 people, political corruption and graft are inevitable. Wittels, *op. cit.*, p. 26.

[31] Rue Bucher and Anselm Strauss, "Professions in Progress," *American Journal of Sociology* 64 (1961), 325–326.

[32] One policeman reported having paid $300.00 to take the police examination. He also was required to pledge his family's vote to the "right" party. After some wait, he took a "special exam," then more waiting lists, and a final $300.00 to the party fund was required before he was hired. Then he had to purchase his own uniform on contract at the "right" store. Before this man became a member of the department, by his participation in the recruitment process, he was an involved member practicing the "code." Wittels, *op. cit.*, pp. 105–107, 111.

[33] In spite of Smith's remarkable test level, he was left off a list of highest 10 eligible applicants, and some three months later was put on the list through the influence of his father, a respected member of the police department with many years of unblemished service. Otherwise, he may never have been placed on the appointment list.

[34] This is not unlike the planned removal of old civilian standards and values when a new soldier recruit is given basic training. The formal regulations are presented to him, but in company with "old Salts" he learns how the system can be worked and what a person must do to participate in it.

[35] One writer corroborates this by stating that young recruits who show traits of being ambitious, as well as those with family responsibilities, are the most susceptible to graft. The pressures toward success and achievement are clearly indicated by either or both of these factors. Wittels, *op. cit.*, p. 27.

[36] To evaluate Smith's statement on economic pressures, an additional personal datum is relevant. Smith used most of his money from *premeditated theft* for his "habit"—a racing car. He later declared he probably wouldn't have participated in this crime so *much* had it not been for the "habit." His responses did not seem to indicate that he *began* theft for racing money, but that he *continued* it to counter the economic drain created by owning and driving the racing machine.

[37] One officer reports that he wondered why he was not promoted—perhaps they thought he was lazy. He was tagging cars of all violators, and even reported a broken sidewalk belonging to an "organization" man. He couldn't get ahead. He made a couple of outstanding arrests and was made a detective. Later, he ran a "vice" raid against a "protected" place, and was back as a rookie on a beat in "Siberia." He finally took some payoffs and cooperated and eventually became a Police Captain, but exceeding

the "code" limits, was caught and prosecuted. Either not accepting the "code" or exceeding its limits, had negative effects. Wittels, *op. cit.*, pp. 111–122.

[38] The campaigning attack on the "untouchable" image of J. Edgar Hoover and the FBI has made political news. The very act of exposing methods used by Hoover's organization, which though admittedly effective were clearly unlawful, caused the political downfall of an otherwise popular politician in the November 1966 Nevada election.

13

People Who Don't Even Know You

Victor G. Strecher

Transactions involving uniformed police officers and citizens occur primarily between social roles rather than between individual human beings, although the human carriers of the roles do not escape the consequences of the interaction. This is an exaggerated way of making the point that while on duty a police officer is rarely able to function solely as a person. An officer's role easily overwhelms his or her personal characteristics and identity as an individual human being. The positive side of role behavior provides a form of social efficiency useful in everyday life. It is a form of social shorthand which gives us functional role identifiers such as "professor," "physician," "accountant," "attorney," and "police officer." The negative connotation provides the language of prejudice and can lead to stereotyping—believing that all labeled individuals share the same undesirable traits. This gives us "egghead," "quack," "bean-counter," "ambulance chaser," and "pig."

Citizen perceptions of the police role vary from the functionally useful to the prejudiced. Sometimes these perceptions result from personal experiences with the police, but more often they result from a generalized attitude of the community. In our large, pluralistic social system, community often means subculture. "Subculture" refers to a part of the population which subscribes to and participates in the broad outlines of the social system but whose concepts, beliefs, habits, art, apparel, dwellings, or

Adapted from *The Environment of Law Enforcement: A Community Relations Guide*. Englewood Cliffs, N.J.: Prentice-Hall, Inc. 1971. pp. 67–91. Reprinted with permission of the author.

institutions exhibit characteristic patterns which distinguish it from others. A subculture has the attribute of persistence; it reproduces itself through the generations.

❖ SUBCULTURES AND LAW ENFORCEMENT ❖

In pluralistic societies, subcultures have always presented an interesting challenge to the forces of social control. In a large community, there is generally a dominant or conventional set of values, customs, and artifacts which regulate how members behave and which establish the boundaries of appropriateness. Any smaller group within the community which differs markedly in behavior invites a decision by the larger group. The decision is *whether social control will be predicated rigidly on the dominant cultural norms or on some other abstract standard*. In simplistic terms, will the different behavior be judged illegal and punishable or merely be subject to disapproval? This dilemma is inherent in most societies and particularly in a large, open society such as our own. It has consumed much time, thought, and energy since Revolutionary times—and is a basic element of the dualistic law-morality controversy. Because it is a recurring issue with endless permutations, working it out continues while we go on living and working and making difficult judgments about human conduct with the guidelines generated thus far in this continuous process.

Charged with the duty to maintain a minimum level of social order, police officers frequently confront the dilemma detailed above. They work in many different neighborhoods including those which are not socially conventional. When changing values, customs, or public behaviors antagonize the more conventionally oriented residents of the community, the police are frequently called. For some reason, even disruptive social change (loss of jobs due to technology) appears easier to accept than changing standards of behavior (lack of respect for age). Police officers are often called to mediate disputes at the boundaries of subcultures.

Large numbers of officers work primarily within subcultures. The subcultural communities served by police officers include African Americans, Hispanics, Native Americans, Chinese Americans, Japanese Americans, Hasidic Jewish Americans and many others. Although not always so classified, the wealthy constitute a subculture that can also present policing with perplexing problems.

In the urban centers of the United States, with a few notable exceptions, the community relations issue often focuses on race relations. Our analysis of relations between the police and their communities will be carried on within a framework of subcultural relations which applies to all the minority populations living in the United States. However, black and white subcultural interaction patterns have been studied most frequently. Therefore, many examples in the discussion focus on the subculture of African Americans living in the poverty zones of large cities.[1]

When considered from the perspectives of social experience, the concepts of *subcultural behavior, culture shock, and culture fatigue* can provide police officers a fresh and more accurate insight into their personal position in the total scheme of things. These concepts aid in making judgments which lead to fewer, rather than more, tensions and difficulties on the job.

❖ POLICE OFFICERS AND AFRICAN AMERICANS ❖

Relations between the police and inner-city African-American residents have become increasingly and more visibly discordant. Ironically, this has occurred during a period of growing technical competence in policing and greater police sensitivity to community reactions. But it has occurred also during a "revolution of rising expectations" among the urban poor.

Police-community relations programs have achieved popularity in recent years, but to many members of the community they seem to be "preaching to the converted" because of their limited reach. Even while African-American and police leaders meet to discuss large-scale problems, individual police officers and African-American citizens on the street find little improvement—more often a worsening—in their encounters.

These individual encounters obviously provide the medium in which the negative relationship is acted out. However, the factors which underlie these harsh confrontations were probably operating long before the officers and African-American residents came together. Unfortunately, most encounters between police and black residents are predisposed to mutual hostility before they take place. This is *not* to suggest that the outcome of every contact must be inevitably negative. It is *not* to say that all of us—police officers and citizens—are trapped in a crystallized system of behavior, a kind of human anthill, within which we act in ways that are predetermined. It is nonetheless clear to police officers and observers of police work that each police-citizen encounter begins with a lot of history behind it. Neither the officer nor the citizen enters the situation with an objective, assumption-free state of mind. Both are likely to carry into the meeting their personal quotas of "cultural baggage"—those complex networks of knowledge, attitudes, and social awareness which are indispensable to everyday living. To further complicate the equation of the encounter, there are the personalities of the officers and citizens plus the immediate conditions that brought them together.

It becomes increasingly apparent, however, that the factors of personality, individual intentions, and the conditions of meeting have less to do with the outcome of police-citizen encounters than the cultural baggage of those involved. Individual factors are overpowered by cultural forces which thrust predetermined roles on both actors in the encounter. Again, it must be emphasized that behavior in response to unconscious social forces is not inevitable. However, social perspectives operating below the level of consciousness are likely to produce spontaneous behavior unless they are brought to the surface of the mind, understood, and neutralized if undesirable. Several factors have combined to complicate the everyday experiences of police officers and city residents. They include the history of internal migration patterns which formed the nation's cities; the historical relationships between African Americans and whites; the previously mentioned revolution of rising expectations; and the patterns of behavior dominant in two distinct segments of the larger American culture. These segments can be labelled the *lower socioeconomic African-American subculture* and the *police occupational subculture*.

❖ AFRICAN-AMERICAN EXODUS FROM THE SOUTH ❖

Between 1910 and 1963 it is estimated that more than 5,000,000 African Americans migrated from the South, mostly to the large cities of the North and the West, in two distinctive patterns.[2] Between 1910 and 1940, about 1,750,000 migrants moved northward to the large cities directly in their paths ". . . from South Carolina to New York, from Georgia to Philadelphia, from Alabama to Detroit, and from Mississippi to Chicago."[3]Between 1940 and 1963 migration largely followed the second pattern. During that period most of the 3,300,000 African Americans who left the South migrated to the western as well as to the northern cities.

Frequently, the reason for moving was a desire to leave the South rather than a specific attraction of the destination. Ralph Thomlinson notes that the migrant's "knowledge of other parts of the country . . . (was) often imprecise and grossly inadequate. . . ." He found the mood of migration captured in the line from Jelly Roll Morton's song, "Mississippi water tastes like turpentine, but Michigan water tastes like sherry wine."[4] In this same vein, and typical of migrant feelings is the letter of a migrant from Texas, who stated that he ". . . would like Chicago or Philadelphia but I don't Care where so long as I Go where a man is a man."[5]

E. Franklin Frazier traced the severe cultural dislocation resulting from this migration, particularly the absence of folk relationships and lack of traditional social controls. In their flight from the South, African Americans were:

> unaware of the personal crisis they would face in the unsympathetic and impersonal environment of northern cities . . . and the absence of moral support of relatives and neighbors. . . . Primary forms of group control were dissolved and life became more secular. . . . Since tradition and sentiment no longer furnished a guide to living, migrants were forced to make their own valuations of conduct and thereby develop 'rational' attitudes toward their environment. . . . life lived according to the traditional values brings none of the rewards that the community values. Such an outlook on life easily leads to crime and other forms of antisocial behavior.[6]

❖ THE CITY AS CAULDRON ❖

Migrants who left hoping for a better life soon discovered that cities did not dispense their "goodness of life" equally. "Social vacancies" existed—largely at the bottom of the socioeconomic scale—just as they had generations previously for the Irish, German, Italian, Polish, and other immigrant populations. The large numbers of unskilled, poorly educated in-migrants from the rural South became the neighbors of settled second- and third-generation African-American residents who had done relatively well. The expectations of the newcomers were reinforced by the relative success of established black residents. The lack of opportunity was thus extremely frustrating, as the new residents fell short of their aspirations. Another result, given the nature of residential segregation in large cities, was that the long-time African-American residents bore the full impact of the flood of unskilled migrants. They were most often the victims of the crimes committed by the in-migrants. As the established black populations pushed outward, seeking adequate living space, they were confronted on the one hand by white hostility and on the other by undesirable living conditions among the undereducated, socially different newcomers. This condition appears to be similar to the "lace curtain" and "shanty" Irish division of past generations. The additional factor of dark skin blocked social assimilation, which had eventually resolved the European immigrant crises during the past 100 years.

Despite some gains by the civil rights movement in the 1960s, once again rising expectations crashed against reality. De facto segregation replaced the now illegal separation of races; job discrimination continued unabated. Some blacks became frustrated with Martin Luther King's nonviolent approach to gaining equal opportunity. Riots broke out in a number of cities including Harlem, Detroit and Los Angeles.

The urban disorders of the 1960s were followed by extensive studies of their causes. Among other things, these studies explored aspects of African-American life in cities which had been neglected until then. Separately and independently several research groups uncovered substantial support for the theory of *relative deprivation*.[7] Although the researchers rarely called this phenomenon by name, they lucidly described the condition:

> . . . people's attitudes, aspirations and grievances largely depend on the frame of reference within which they are conceived. . . . A person's satisfactions, even at the most trivial level, are conditioned by expectations. . . . It is this natural reaction which underlies the so-called "revolution of rising expectations."[8]

Daniel P. Moynihan and the members of the McCone Commission viewed the riots not as a simple consequence of poverty but, less directly, as a correlate of *perceived deprivation*. "To those who have come with high hopes and great expectations and see the success of others so close at hand, failure brings a special measure of frustration and disillusionment."[9]

Although thirty years have passed since the reports on the urban disorders, the findings are relevant to our discussion of lower socioeconomic African-American culture in large cities—and for the customary reaction of its residents to police uniforms.

❖ SUBCULTURAL IMAGES ❖

Culture has been defined by Oscar Lewis as a ". . . design for living which is passed down from generation to generation.[10] William I. Thomas believed that individuals must learn not only the social meanings of behavior, ideas and objects but also how to adjust to the demands of society.[11] Layered into the goals, values, and attitudes a culture prescribes for behavior are the particular aspects of the community or subculture to which one belongs. George C. Homans wrote that membership in a group sustains people, enabling them to maintain their equilibrium under the ordinary shocks of life.[12] Talcott Parsons discussed interaction as occurring between people "whose relation to their situations, including each other, is defined and mediated in terms of a system of culturally structured and shared symbols."[13] George Herbert Mead believed one learns a significant symbol when one shares a sign referring to a common course of experience with someone else.[14]

The idea that a "culture of poverty" exists has been with us since 1961, when Lewis used the phrase.[15] Hyman Rodman proposed the concept of a "lower-class value stretch," which permits the member of the lower socioeconomic class to scale down a set of values to an operable level without abandoning the conventional middle-class values of society.[16] Lee Rainwater explored the view that in the lower-class subculture, scaled-down values and norms constitute "legitimate cultural alternatives" to conventional norms.[17] He compared the *normative* expressions of housing project residents—"how things ought to be"—with their *existential* views— "how things are." He summarized his findings this way:

> The more impersonal socioeconomic forces and the intimate interpersonal forces of the community militate against living up to these norms and the majority of the population does not indeed live up to them.[18]

The result is that over a period of time, a set of more or less institutionalized alternatives has developed for adapting to the actual pressures under which men and women live. Robert Merton used different terms to describe the same situation; he believed social usages that were functional for some groups would be disfunctional for others. Functional deficiencies of the official structure lead to alternative unofficial structures which satisfy needs more efficiently.[19] However, the adaptations described by Merton and Rainwater may or may not satisfy those who make use of them because comparison with the larger society is inevitable— particularly with the influence of the media.

The media project a parade of images of a materialistic, affluent society flaunting the symbols of success through commercials, movies, televison programs, etc. Members of the subculture cannot escape the contrast of their environment with the idealized version. In addition, the media seize opportunities to portray worst-case scenarios in the inner city which serve both to alienate residents and to reinforce negative stereotypes of outsiders toward the subculture.

One highly publicized incident in Chicago illustrates the power of the media to create images. The story appeared across the nation in all the media. One national magazine ran a story under the headline "Calcutta, Illinois."

> The Chicago police swept into 219 North Keystone Avenue last Tuesday looking for drugs, and found children instead. There were 19 in all. Lying two deep on a pair of mattresses. Or sprawled on the apartment's cold floor amid food scraps, cigarette butts and human

excrement. Most were in dirty diapers or underwear; one boy, subsequently found to have cerebral palsy, wore bruises, belt marks and cigarette burns on his body. Two of the smallest children, reads the police report, were awake, sharing a neck bone with a dog. As the police removed the children from the residence, one pleaded to a female cop, "Will you be my mommy? I want to go home with you."[20]

Imagine the impact on officers who envision encountering such a scene themselves. Televised pictures graphically presented an indelible image. Lack of personal exposure was replaced by one abhorrent image.

Even without specific incidents, the media discuss issues on the national agenda that can create negative impressions. In the mid-1990s, President Clinton focused on reforming welfare. Illegitimacy was targeted as the underlying cause not only of poverty but crime and social disintegration in the inner cities. As one article summarized the subject:

There is a long-term price of illegitimacy as well, one that resonates at a time when the fear of crime, particularly the crimes committed by a generation of young, pitiless men and boys, has become a national obsession. When people ask where all these 16-year-old predators are coming from, one answer is chilling: from 14-year-old mothers. More than half the juvenile offenders serving prison time were raised by only one parent. If present birthrates continue over the next 10 to 15 years, the number of young people trapped in poverty and tempted by the streets will increase dramatically. Says John DiIulio, professor of politics and public affairs at Princeton University: "You have a ticking crime bomb."[21]

Elijah Anderson, a sociology professor at the University of Pennsylvania who has studied sexual norms among the urban poor was quoted as saying, "Most middle-class youths take a strong interest in their future and know what a pregnancy can do to derail it. In contrast, many inner-city youths see no future to derail."[22] The article also discussed social critics who point to the necessity of changing the patterns and assumptions that guide the behavior of young people growing up in desperate neighborhoods. "Anderson . . . argues that young black males have such trouble finding family-sustaining jobs—the traditional mark of adulthood—that they end up building their self-esteem through games that emphasize sexual prowess. Their babies become evidence of their manhood." [23] Depending on how one reads such articles, they can serve to increase compassion and understanding or to "confirm" stereotypes.

❖ THE POLICE SUBCULTURE ❖

Although efforts have been made to increase the numbers of minority and female officers, most police officers are white males who have been reared in working-class families. The generalized pattern of residential segregation makes it likely that at the time of recruitment to police service, most young white men know little more of the African-American poverty culture than they know about foreign cultures. Life in American cities normally provides few encounters with African-American communities. Relatively few white police recruits have had lasting friendships with black contemporaries. The point being stressed here is the *degree of separation* between the dominant conventional culture from which most police officers emerge and the African-American culture—particularly the poverty-level black subculture. This almost complete separation of cultures, from birth through maturity, is powerfully significant for officers' interactions with the African-American community.

In addition to childhood and adolescent socialization into the working-class culture, police recruits undergo a process of occupational socialization, through which they become identified—by themselves and their associates—as police officers. They begin to share all the perspectives relevant to the police role. Some years ago a book entitled *Boys in White* presented a model of medicine as an occupational subculture.[24] This model fits law enforcement equally as well. Much of the following section is adapted from that model.

The police subculture refers, first of all, to a set of group assumptions among police officers—assumptions about their work and their roles as officers. Secondly, there is "coherence and consistency" among the police perspectives, and those perspectives are related to the officers' role in the police organization. Responsibilities, duties, rights, and privileges are also part of the subcultural setting. "Because they all occupy the same institutional position, they tend to face the same kinds of problems, and these are the problems which arise out of the character of the position. . . . The opportunities and disabilities of the [police] role are decisive in shaping the perspectives [police officers] hold."[25] The press of new problems related to their work becomes more decisive in shaping new outlooks than prior experiences, even though backgrounds may influence individual adjustments to the new police role. We use "police subculture" then, as a kind of shorthand term for the organized sum of *police perspectives*, relevant to the *police role*.[26]

Boys in White described a number of perspectives of medical students toward medical practice and patients. A few of these perspectives are given here, followed by transformation to make them appropriate to police work.

These perspectives provide considerable insight into the dimensions and texture of the occupational subculture.

> . . . the concept of medical responsibility pictures a world in which patients may be in danger of losing their lives and identifies the true work of the physician as saving those endangered lives. Further, where the physician's work does not afford (at least in some symbolic sense) the possibility of saving a life or restoring health through skillful practice . . . the physician himself lacks some of the essence of physicianhood.[27]

Transformed for applicability to the police occupation this passage reads

> . . . the concept of police responsibility pictures a world in which the acts and intended acts of criminals threaten the lives or well-being of victims and the security of their property. The true work of the police officer is the protection of life and property by the intervention in, and solution of criminal acts. Further, where the police officer's work does not afford (at least in some symbolic sense) the possibility of protecting life or property by intervening in criminal acts, the police officer lacks some of the essence of police identity.

Those patients who can be cured are better than those who cannot. *Those cases which can be solved are better than those which cannot.* Medical practitioners worry about the dangers to their own health involved in seeing a steady stream of unscreened patients, some of whom may have dangerous communicable diseases. *Police officers are concerned about personal hazards involved in approaching a steady stream of unknown persons, some of whom are wanted criminals, some of whom may have serious behavioral problems, and some possibly having intentions of causing them injury or even death because of circumstances unknown to the police officer.*

The most interesting and applicable medical perspective—one that resounds in the police world—is the following: "Perhaps the most difficult scenes come about when patients have no respect for the doctor's authority. Physicians resent this immensely."[28] The transformation is left to the reader.

Much of the present content of the police subculture is a legacy from the move to professionalize law enforcement. Beyond concerns about eliminating political influence, professionalism focused on coolly efficient, technical competence. Police services in a pluralistic society were perceived as requiring scrupulous attention to legal and administrative objectivity. This resulted in an occupational fixation upon *process* or *technique*—to the exclusion of *function* or *goal orientation*. Police culture has rejected functions that are clearly related to community protection merely because the process or technique involved was not a traditional police method. Conversely, the police have taken on the most outlandish functions because they could be accomplished by means of traditional police procedures or because they required field forces such as the police maintain.

❖ SUBCULTURAL PERSPECTIVES OF POLICE OFFICERS ❖

Several of the police subcultural perspectives which are relevant to dealing with other subcultures are:

1. Officers are responsible for *maintaining order* in their patrol territory. There is supervisory, departmental, and general community pressure for orderliness and tranquility, although the officers may view this duty as interfering with their true mission to protect life and property by thwarting criminal acts.
2. Police officers must be *respected*.
3. In every encounter police officers must gain *control* in the sense of initiating and orienting each part of the situation and maintain that control; they must prevail; psychological and strategic advantages must be maintained.
4. Incongruous activities or conditions must be investigated to determine whether the law is being violated. *Curiosity and suspiciousness* are valued traits in the police service; they are considered indispensable to craftsmanship; they shape the appropriate frame of mind for officers as they go about their work.
5. A general sense of social *appropriateness* is as much a part of the police officer's frame of reference as is the criminal law. While officers might chafe under the pressure to maintain order, they also resent unconventional behavior. Not only does it make their job more difficult, but it conflicts with officers' expectations of what is "proper." Public displays of certain activities are to be curtailed: quarrels, drinking, loitering in large groups, loud conversation, sitting on sidewalks, and dozens of other miscellaneous activities which offend the conventional sense of propriety.
6. Police officers share a general assumption that the amount of illegal activity, the harm to human beings, and the loss of property activity far exceeds what comes to their attention. Part of their function is to seek out and deal with *elusive crime and criminals*.

There are, of course, numerous other elements in the police perspective; however, these few will serve to highlight some occupation-oriented pressures on police officers particular to their conduct in parts of the community which do not adhere to middle-class or working-class values. These areas include the neighborhoods of poor whites and African Americans and at times the habitat of the super-rich.

Whenever police officers work in a social setting greatly different from their own, they face many of the same tensions and complexities as those encountered by foreign service personnel working for the first time in another country.

❖ THE SHOCK OF CULTURE ❖

In every society, people learn the behavior that is appropriate to them and that they may expect from others in an infinite number of situations. Differing perceptions of role behavior often cause difficulties in intercultural settings because the members of each group are faced with unexpected behavior or with behavior that strikes them as inappropriate to the setting. They are also handicapped by being unsure of what is expected of them.[29]

For consideration of what happens to police officers who are assigned to a neighborhood socially different from their own, the paragraph below can set the framework. It may be tentatively stated that white, working-class police officers suffer *culture shock* during their early exposure to other subcultures. Culture shock has been defined as "an occupational disease of people who have been suddenly transplanted abroad."[30] There is a remarkable similarity between the experiences of police officers and foreign service personnel under analogous conditions.[31]

> Culture shock is set in motion by the anxiety that results from losing all one's familiar cues. These cues include the thousand and one ways in which we orient ourselves to the situations of daily life: when to shake hands and what to say when we meet people, when and how much to tip, how to make purchases, when to accept and when to refuse invitations, when to take statements seriously, and when not to. Cues to behavior (which may be words, gestures, facial expressions, or customs) are acquired in the course of growing up and are as much a part of our culture as the language we speak. All of us depend for our peace of mind and our efficiency on hundreds of cues, most of which we do not carry on a level of conscious awareness.[32]

For the police officer, personal disorientation through the loss of familiar cues is due both to problems encountered while working and to communication problems with unfamiliar "others." There is nothing quite so disruptive as a set of experiences which challenge one's working assumptions about the nature of the world and the people in it. It is useful to recognize the stages and symptoms of culture shock, for they are almost universally found among officers serving for the first time in new surroundings. "Immunity to culture shock does not come from being broadminded and full of good will. These are highly important characteristics . . . and they may aid in recovery, but they can no more prevent the illness than grim determination can prevent a cold. Individuals differ greatly in the degree to which culture shock affects them. A few people prove completely unable to make the necessary adjustments . . ."[33] But, with recognition of the problem and appropriate ameliorative measures, most people recover fully.

There are four discernible stages in the culture shock syndrome as applied to foreign cultures.[34] The first is a kind of honeymoon period, lasting anywhere from a few days to several months, depending on circumstances. During this time the newcomers are fascinated by the novelty of the strange culture. They remain polite, friendly, and perhaps a bit self-effacing. The second stage begins when they settle down to a long-run confrontation with the real conditions of life in the strange culture, and their realization of the need to function effectively there. They become hostile and aggressive toward the culture and its people. They criticize the way of life and attribute problems on the job to deliberate trouble making on the part of community members. They seek out others suffering from culture shock and, with them, endlessly belabor the customs and "shortcomings" of the local people. This is the critical period. Some never do adjust to the strange culture; they either leave the environment—voluntarily or involuntarily—or suffer debilitating emotional problems and, consequently, become ineffective in their relations with the local population. In the third stage, the newcomers are beginning to open a way into the new cultural environment. They may take a superior attitude to the local people but will joke about differences in behavior rather than bitterly criticize them. They are on their way to recovery. In the fourth stage their adjustment is about as complete as it can get. They accept the customs of the other culture as just another way of living.

Unfortunately, police officers infrequently reach the third and fourth stages. Foreign service agencies recognize, expect, and prepare for culture shock; they assume that it is a form of sociopsychological maladjustment which will respond to treatment (often informal). They expect that those affected will make the transition to satisfactory adjustment and effective cross-cultural relationships. This however, is not the experience in police departments.

A second major complex of reactions can be summed up by the term "culture fatigue." This term refers to a phenomenon different from the "culture shock" experienced immediately after encountering a new culture. Culture fatigue is the physical and emotional exhaustion that almost invariably results from the infinite series of adjustments required for long-term survival in a foreign culture. One must continually suppress automatic evaluations and judgments; must supply new interpretations to seemingly familiar behavior; must demand of oneself constant alterations in the style and content of one's authority. Whether this process is conscious or unconscious, successful or unsuccessful, it consumes an enormous amount of energy, leaving the individual decidedly fatigued.

One effect of culture fatigue is a tendency toward negative interpretations. With such a mindset, the positive aspects of close family ties in another culture are disregarded and labelled "clannishness." Personal sensitivity which might otherwise be admired becomes "sulkiness." Avoiding unpleasant subjects in some circumstances would be interpreted as tactful but with cultural fatigue, the avoidance becomes "dishonest." Just as we learned that the positive aspects of role behavior can be turned into the negativity of stereotypes, cultural fatigue can taint all perceptions and experience.

❖ SUMMARY ❖

The dissonance experienced by African Americans between the folk culture of rural southern life and the impersonal existence in urban cities to which they migrated resulted in social adaptations—sometimes called survival techniques—which rendered life at least functionally possible in urban slums. The means of reducing this dissonance is to reject the conventional cultural goals and the legitimate means of accomplishing them. Often this is done in an outburst (riots, for example) which indicates the intensity of the internal conflict. Attaching allegiance to other goals and means of achieving them brings behavior and norms into apparent alignment. The difference between these adapted norms and the conventional norms of the larger society creates attitudes both within and without the community which affect interactions between residents and the police.

Police officers are recruited predominantly from the middle and working classes. As a result of historical racial segregation patterns, recruits know almost nothing about lower socioeconomic subcultures. To compound the problem, occupational socialization produces a self-concept centered on crime fighting and life protection; police subcultural perspectives tend to reject any activities which do not match this self-concept. Yet, police assignments break down to approximately 80 percent minor regulatory functions or service calls and 20 percent serious crimes. Even that 20 percent is quickly reassigned to investigative personnel so that officers are available for additional service calls.

In addition to dissatisfaction over the nature of their actual assignments versus their occupationally generated self-image, police officers who are assigned to predominantly poor communities experience a culture shock reaction to the loss of familiar cues and symbols. They are unable to interact spontaneously with subculture residents. Neither their conventional values nor the perspectives they have been given in early training—responsibility for order, demand for respect, situational control, suspiciousness, notions of social propriety—seem to guide them into the most sensible and productive courses of action. Discovering that their twenty-one or more years of social experience and the added perspectives of their new role utterly fail them in their first few encounters, they become anxious and frustrated. After the first few unsatisfactory interactions, officers begin to anticipate unpleasant interactions. It is natural for officers to react aggressively to this frustrating experience. This becomes stage two of culture shock; they welcome any opportunity to gripe about the subculture members—their hairstyles, music, food or any aspect of inner-city life that differs from their own. As they go about their duties, officers' feelings are virtually impossible to conceal. In fact, the very nature of culture shock makes officers want to display something of what they are feeling; after all, they hold these people responsible for their new problems.

What comes across clearly to the residents of the police officers' beat is a harsh, moralistic indictment of their way of life—reflected in the words, expressions, and gestures of the officers. Community members are not insulated from the American aspiration for success, but they have found no way to climb upward from their low point in the social system. They know how they live and need nobody to tell them their standard of living falls below conventional levels; they settle for less in every way—and feel deep dissatisfaction and frustration. The police officers' visible feelings while in culture shock reactivate and intensify the residents' frustrations. The officers' reactions become an embodiment of the hostile, superior stare of middle-class society—of those who have made it, and have it made.

One of the difficulties on the police side of the relationship is the absence of measures to conquer culture shock. During its severe phase, the symptoms of culture shock are not relieved. There is no minimizing of its adverse effects on police-citizen relations during this time; nothing is done to bring about a complete recovery. In most police departments, the symptoms of culture shock in young police officers are often considered a coming of age, a first hard contact with the realities of big-city policing. Emotional support from experienced associates often comes from officers who have also experienced culture shock and have progressed into culture fatigue. This support is less likely to sensitize the new officers and guide them toward a resolution of their conflict than to toughen them to the long-run prospect of dealing with different behavior—and to crystallize this toughness. In addition, the tendency of most group members—and police officers are no exception—is that professional success depends on colleagues' evaluations. It is extraordinarily hard for new officers to reject the social perspectives of their older colleagues, on whom they depend so much.

Past experiences in both the subcultures of policing and lower socioeconomic groups become self-fulfilling prophecies. In Robert Merton's terms, false definitions of the situation evoke behavior which makes the originally false conception come true.[35] Definitions of situations depend on the expectations we have of roles—often as defined by others. In an interaction, one party can react to the other on the basis of what that person is perceived to be (the role). Thus, people who don't even know you make judgments and act accordingly—on both sides of the interaction. If this happens, the likely outcome is a pattern that endlessly reproduces itself into new generations of mutual antagonism and strife.

If, instead, the interaction is based on the actual behavior of both parties, the negative downward spiral can be halted. This requires a willingness to view other parties as individuals and to suspend automatic evaluations. Without an effort to circumvent the social shorthand that is convenient in certain circumstances, effective communication is impossible. Without effective communication, subcultures do not meet; they collide.

Notes

[1] Many of the major elements of this article were originally published in 1967 and 1971. During the intervening twenty-three years, the author's conceptualizations, as presented in this article, of the *African-American poverty subculture* and the *police subculture*, of their interaction patterns and of *culture shock* have been required reading at the FBI's National Academy.

[2] U.S. Department of Labor, *The Negroes in the United States* (Washington, DC: Government Printing Office, 1966), p. 1.

[3] Ralph Thomlinson, *Population Dynamics* (New York: Random House, Inc., 1965), pp. 219–20.

[4] Thomlinson, p. 225.

[5] E. Franklin Frazier, *The Negro Family in the United States* (Chicago: University of Chicago Press, 1966), p. 227.

[6] *Ibid.*, pp. 227–29.

[7] This term was first used in *The American Soldier: Adjustment During Army Life* by Samuel A. Stouffer et al. (Princeton: Princeton University Press, 1949).

8 W. G. Runciman, *Relative Deprivation and Social Justice* (London: Routledge & Kegan Paul Ltd., 1966), p. 6.

9 Governor's Commission on the Los Angeles Riots, *Violence in the City—An End or a Beginning?* (Los Angeles: State of California, Dec. 2, 1965), pp. 3–4.

10 Catherine S. Chilman, *Growing Up Poor* (Washington, DC: U.S. Department of Health, Education, and Welfare, 1966), p. 5.

11 Don Martindale, *The Nature and Types of Sociological Theory, 2/E* (Prospect Heights, IL: Waveland Press, 1981), p. 328.

12 *Ibid*, p. 471.

13 Talcott Parsons, *The Social System* (Glencoe, IL: The Free Press, 1951), p. 6.

14 Martindale, pp. 332–333.

15 *Ibid*.

16 Hyman Rodman, "The Lower Class Value Stretch," in *Planning for a Nation of Cities*, ed. S. B. Warner, Jr. (Cambridge: The M.I.T. Press, 1966).

17 Lee Rainwater, "The Problem of Lower Class Culture," *Pruitt-Igoe Occasional Paper No. 8*, Washington University, St. Louis, MO, 1966, p. 5.

18 Rainwater, pp. 26–31.

19 Martindale, 466.

20 David VanBiema, "Calcuta, Illinois," *Time*, February 14, 1994, p. 30.

21 Nancy Gibbs, "The Vicious Cycle," *Time*, June 20, 1994, pp. 27–28.

22 *Ibid*, p. 33.

23 *Ibid*, p. 30.

24 Howard S. Becker et al., *Boys in White* (Chicago: University of Chicago Press, 1961), p. 47.

25 *Ibid.*, pp. 46–47.

26 *Ibid.*, pp 4–7.

27 *Ibid.*, pp. 316–20.

28 *Ibid.*, pp. 320–21.

29 George M. Foster, *Traditional Cultures: and the Impact of Technological Change* (New York: Harper & Row, Publishers, 1962), p. 130.

30 Kalervo Oberg, quoted in Foster, *Traditional Cultures*, p. 187.

31 This application of the culture shock concept was first established in Victor G. Strecher, "When Subcultures Meet: Police-Negro Relations," in *Law Enforcement Science and Technology*, Ed. Sheldon Yefsky (Washington, DC: Thompson Book Co., 1967), pp. 701–7.

32 Foster, p. 188.

34 *Ibid.*, p. 189.

34 Adapted from Foster, pp. 189–92.

35 Martindale, p. 415.

14

Kinsmen in Repose
Occupational Perspectives of Patrolmen

John Van Maanen

The people on the street would miss us if we weren't there. I mean they expect us out there and we're part of the whole scene too. That's what everybody seems to miss. We've got a say in what goes on in the streets. You just can't give an honest picture of what happens in society without talking about what the cop on the street does.

A Patrolman[1]

I n the midst of derogatory epithets, laudatory salutations and apathetic silent-American acquiescence, the "man" acts out a curious societal role. To some, a policeman is a "fucking pig," a mindless brute working for a morally bankrupt institution. To others, a policeman is a courageous public servant, a defender of life and property, regulating city life along democratic lines. To most, a policeman is merely an everyday cultural stimulus, tolerated, avoided and ignored unless non-routine situational circumstances deem otherwise. Yet, virtually all persons in this society can recognize a policeman, have some conception of what it is he does, and, if asked, can share a few "cop stories" with an interested listener.

Peter K. Manning and John Van Maanen (Eds.), *Policing: A View from the Street.* (1978) pp. 115–128. Reprinted with permission of the editors. Footnotes renumbered.

Fundamentally, a police officer represents the most visible aspect of the body politic and is that aspect most likely to intervene directly in the daily lives of the citizenry. If one considers the President to be the "head" of the political system, then the patrolman on the street must be considered the "tail." The critical and symbolic nature of the police role in society is perhaps best illustrated by a number of child socialization studies indicating that it is the head **and** tail of a political system which are its most salient aspects—the features most likely to be learned first as a child develops an awareness of his surrounding environment (Hyman, 1959; Almond and Verba, 1963; Easton and Dennis, 1969, 1967).

Given this rather visible position in society, it is somewhat surprising that social scientists have, until recently, largely ignored the police. In particular, little research has been devoted to the everyday standards of police behavior. The few studies we do have tend to confirm an occupational stereotype of the police as a conservative, defiled, isolated and homogenous grouping of men bound together perceptually through a common mission (Rubenstein, 1973; Reiss, 1971; Wilson, 1968; Neiderhoffer, 1967; Skolnick, 1966). . . . Yet, what is of interest here is the recognition by the police of the implied differences between themselves and the rest of society. According to one knowledgeable observer, a former Chief of Police:

> The day the new recruit walks through the doors of the police academy he leaves society behind to enter a profession that does more than give him a job, it defines who he is. For all the years he remains, closed into the sphere of its rituals . . . he will be a cop. (Ahern, 1972:3)

Policemen generally view themselves as performing society's dirty work. Consequently, a gap is created between the police and the public. Today's patrolman feels cut off from the mainstream culture and stigmatized unfairly. In the percussive words of one young patrolman:

> I'll tell ya, as long as we're the only sonfabitches that have to handle ripe bodies that have been dead for nine days in a ninety degree room or handle skid row drunks who've been crapping in their pants for 24 hours or try to stop some prick from jump'en off the Liberty Bridge or have to grease some societal misfit who's trying to blow your goddamn head off, then we'll never be like anyone else . . . as far as I can see, no one else is ever gonna want to do that shit. But somebody's gotta do it and I guess it'll always be the police. But hell, this is the only profession where ya gotta wash your hands before you take a piss!

In short, when a policeman dons his uniform, he enters a distinct subculture governed by norms and values designed to manage the strains created by his unique role in the community. From the public point of view, a policeman is usually treated as a faceless, nameless "Rorschach-in-blue" with persons responding either favorably or unfavorably according to ideological predisposition or situational imperative. Yet, a policeman's response to the cornucopia of civilian manners and mores follows a somewhat more orderly and acquired pattern. Thus, policemen learn—in particular, patrolmen—characteristic ways of conducting themselves on the street, devices for organizing work routines about their perceived areas of responsibility, and methods of managing their own careers vis-à-vis the police department. . . .

❖ OCCUPATIONAL PERSPECTIVES ❖

Workers in all occupations develop ways and means by which they manage certain structural strains, contradictions and anomalies of their prescribed role and task. In police work, with danger, drudgery and dogma as prime occupational characteristics, these tensions are extreme. Correspondingly, the pressure on new members to bow to group standards is intense. Few, if any, pass through the socialization cycle without being persuaded— through their own experiences and the sage-like wisdom passed from generation to generation of policemen—to accept the occupational accepted frame-of-reference. This frame-of-reference includes, of course, both broad axioms related to police work in general (role) and the more specific corollaries which provide the ground rules of the workaday world (operations). In this article, the label "occupational perspectives" is affixed to the former. It is intended merely to imply that my concern is with the wider, institutional view of policing shared by patrolmen rather than explicit "how-to" work prescriptions. . . . Thus, the focus is upon the characteristic view patrolmen eventually come to hold regarding their organizational and occupational milieu—using a dramaturgic metaphor, the "backstage" views of police. Occupational perspectives represent the solution to what Schein (1961) has suggested is the critical problem of organizational socialization, namely, "coping with the emotional reality of the job." In the police world, these perspectives provide the perceptual filter through which a patrolman views his work life. In a sense, they provide him with something akin to an occupational ideology. Such an ideology—rooted in common experience and knowledge—serves to support and maintain the codes, agreements and habits existing in the work place.

Two distinct occupational perspectives are crucial for our

understanding of patrolmen. Together they form a definitive credo which shapes the personal identity of policemen and regulates the pace, style, and direction of "on-the-street" police behavior. The first perspective grows from the patrolman's unique role in the social world and concerns his "outsider" position in the community. The second perspective develops from the nature of the patrolman's task requirements and deals with the survival dictums of his occupation.

❖ THE OUTSIDER: SEPARATE AND APART ❖

A young patrolman soon learns that in uniform he is a very special sort of person. Not only does he have a low visibility vis-à-vis his superiors, but he has a monopolistic grip on the legal application of force. Amplifying this societal trust is the awesome responsibility of deciding virtually on his own and in sometimes terrible situations when to and when not to exercise this force. This feature alone places him in a solitary and somber position compared to the rest of society. Certainly there are legal and administrative guidelines set up which presumably govern his actions. Yet, in by far the majority of cases in which his right to force and violence may be utilized, the decision must be made in the emotional fever of fear or anger, the immediacy of danger, and in the flicker of an instant. In these powerful and dark moments there is not time to ponder the alternatives. Such is the ultimate responsibility of a patrolman.[2]

Of course, situations of the extreme are rare. Some officers progress through their entire career without once having to draw their weapons or physically subdue an obstinate suspect. But among those who spend their days on the street, they are few. Uncommon indeed are those officers who have not come within a hairbreadth of "squeezing-off-a-round" or who have not been through the bruising give-and-take of street battle. For most, these experiences are the defining characteristics of their occupation and it distinguishes them from other gentler ways of life.

While it would be a mistake to view police work from this danger aspect only, the symbolic importance of this feature cannot be underestimated. In large measure, these experiences (and their not infrequent retelling) set the tone for patrol work. As one young patrolman who had been on the street for several years explained:

> Most of the time this job is boring as can be. You just sit behind the
> wheel and go where they tell you. When you're not bullshitting with
> your partner, your mind kinda wanders and some nights it's a bitch
> to stay awake. . . . But somehow you never forget that the next call
> you get or car you stop might be your last. Mentally that's hard to

accept but it's real. . . . You know there's one hell of a lotta people out there who'd love to off a cop. I've gotten over that pretty much by now because you just gotta live with it. If anybody wants to kill you, there's no way you could ever stop 'em. . . . But what really gets you is that whoever it was probably wouldn't even know your name, he'd just be out to kill some cop. To the people out there we're just faceless blue suits. You sure begin to wonder what kind of crazy bastard you are for getting into this job in the first place.

The danger inherent in police work is part of the centripetal force pulling patrolmen together as well as contributing to their role as strangers to the general public. Importantly, however, the risks of policing also provide real psychological satisfaction to men who spend most of their time performing activities of the more mundane or routine variety (for example, report taking, service calls, preventive patrolling, and so on). Without danger as an omnipresent quality of the work setting, patrolmen would have little of the visceral pleasures that contribute to their evaluation of performing difficult, important, and challenging (if unappreciated) tasks.

The "outsider" perspective arises as well from the unforgettably indifferent or antagonistic manner in which he is treated by the public. The rookie painfully discovers that wherever he is to go, his presence is bound to generate anxiety. People stare at him and scrutinize his movements. While driving through his sector, he finds that a major problem is avoiding accidents caused from the almost neurotic fashion in which other drivers react to his perceptually nefarious squad car. Soon he appreciates the relatively few places where he receives a warm and friendly welcome. All-night diners, hospitals, fire stations, certain niches in the courthouse, the precinct locker room, and even a private recess where a patrolman may park his squad car unnoticed become havens from his totem-like existence, providing him an opportunity to relax (Rubenstein, 1973).

In general, there is little to link patrolmen to the private citizen in terms of establishing a socially satisfying relationship. Small businessmen have perhaps something to gain in terms of the protection a rapid response might provide. However, businessmen know that there is little likelihood that the patrolman they are friendly with today will respond to a call for help tomorrow. Similarly, patrolmen recognize accurately that few civilians are likely to return favors. For mutual concern and friendship to develop, some sort of exchange relationship must be sustained—the *quid pro quo* of Homans (1950). In the police world, patrolmen rarely see the same people twice unless the contact is of the adversary variety. And such encounters are not apt to prove rewarding to the patrolman regarding the development of friendships.[3]

Thus, it is a lonely, largely friendless world the patrolman faces. The only assistance and understanding he can expect comes solely from his brother officers who, as the police enjoy saying, have "been there." In light of his public receptivity, it should not be surprising that policemen in general have assumed many of the characteristics of other stigmatized groupings.[4]

I have suggested elsewhere that the rules and regulations of police work are so numerous and immobilizing that from the patrolman's point of view, no one could ever obey all of them (Van Maanen, 1973). This implies that police officers, to be protected from their own infractions, must protect others. While rule violations run from the trivial to the serious, no officer is free from the knowledge that in his past (and no doubt in his future) are certain acts which, if reported, could cost him his job and perhaps even his freedom. From a failure to clear with his dispatcher for lunch to perjury on the witness stand, police must live each day with the knowledge that it is the support of their brother officers that insures their continuance on the job. Thus, it is his colleagues who represent the only group to whom the patrolman can relate. As one patrol veteran suggested:

> How the fuck can I tell anyone who ain't a cop that I lie a little in court or that sometimes I won't do shit on the street 'cause I'm tired or that I made some asshole 'cause he was just all out wrong. If I told people that they'd think that I'm nothing but a turd in uniform. The only people that can understand are people who've had to pull the same shit . . . and there just ain't nobody in this department, from the Chief on down, who hasn't pulled some tricks in their time on the street.

When this officer speaks of "tricks" there are, of course, important matters of degree involved. Nevertheless, the point remains that all officers are indebted heavily to their patrol colleagues. In the last analysis, it is this two-way obligation which forms the basis of a relationship which can never be approximated with persons from the non-police world.

These features along with the more salient aspects of the occupation— the shift work, the uniform, the 24-hour nature of occupational responsibility, and so on—provide a perspective on the world which will last for as long as the patrolman remains with the department.[5] Behaviorally, all outsider groupings tend toward isolationism, secrecy, strong in-group loyalties, sacred symbols, common language, and a profound sense of estrangement from the larger society. It is these subcultural properties which underpin the common understanding among police that they are different.

The cynicism popularly attributed to police officers can, in part, be located in the unique and peculiar role police are required to play. Treated shabbily, hated, or feared by many of the contacts they have, police are asked frequently to arbitrate messy and uncertain citizen disputes. In such disputes, all concerned generally construct a particular account which exonerates them from blame. After a few years on the street, there are few accounts patrolmen have not heard. Hence, whether a claim is outrageous or plausible, police react by believing nothing and distrusting everything at the same time. Only one's colleagues can understand and appreciate such skepticism.

The hardness commonly thought to be the mask of many policemen arises to fend off the perceived curse of doing society's dirty work. To be a sponge, absorbing the misery and degradation that pass daily through a patrolman's life, is an untenable position which would soon drive one from the police midst were it accepted. Therefore the proverbial "shell" is constructed, which protects the patrolman from the effects of nasty encounters which would leave most persons visibly shaken. But in the patrol world such coldness becomes almost a legendary personal property. To wit, one inexperienced patrolman related the following story:

> Man that Sergeant Kelly is something. . . . Remember the night that David Squad nailed that shithead coming out of Mission Liquor Store? Blew him up with a couple of rifle slugs and the guy's brains were splattered all over the sidewalk. You couldn't even tell if the dude was white or black 'cause of blood he was swimming in. Anyway we're standing there waiting for the coroner to show, when Sergeant Kelly decides it's time to eat. So what does he do? He goes back to his unit, grabs his brown bag and proceeds to come back and start chowing down on an egg sandwich. Jesus! You shoulda seen the face on the kid working in the liquor store.

Only the police could understand the hardness implied in such stories. While many sordid tales are no doubt organizational fictions, they serve to denote the peculiar attributes of the police occupational code and also serve to detach patrolmen from the more polite social world of their origin.

In essence, the "outsider" perspective crystallizes the patrolman's occupational identity. It sets him off from others and provides an anchor to which he attaches his interpersonal relationships. Since the private interests and concerns of one are the interests and concerns of most others in the patrol setting (for example, avoiding injury and disciplinary action, displaying the proper amount of commitment and aggressiveness on the street, developing "pat" testimony for courtroom use, and so on), they form a common source of appeal and support. This can be summarized neatly by referring to a bond of sympathetic understanding existing among the police.[6] As one officer remarked succinctly:

To most people we seem to be inhuman, somehow separate and apart. Almost like another species. Maybe they're right but I'll tell you, I'd trust even my worst enemy in this department before I'd trust the people out there.

❖ SURVIVAL: LAY LOW AND AVOID TROUBLE ❖

Although police know that the unanticipated and nonroutine event may occur at any moment, they nonetheless have firm expectations about what work will consist of on any given shift.[7] An experienced officer establishes therefore his own tempo and style of work. Like any occupation, patrol work falls into set patterns: take a burglary report, meet complainant, interview victim, investigate open door, direct traffic, and so on. The discovery of certain organizing devices by which to categorize the myriad of work duties is a major task for young officers and—as with the perspective developed in response to their perceived déclassé social position—follows the socialization paradigm as one learns what it is like to work the streets.

Importantly, the young officer learns that there is a subtle but critical difference between "real" police work and most of what he does on patrol. "Real" police work is, in essence, his *raison d'être*. It is that part of his job that comes closest to the romantic notions of police work he possessed before attending the Police Academy. In short, "real" police work calls for a patrolman to exercise his perceived occupational expertise: to make an arrest, save a life, quell a dispute, prevent a robbery, catch a felon, stop a suspicious person, disarm a suspect, and so on. "Real" police work involves the "hot" call, the unusual "on view" felony situation, or the potentially dangerous "back-up" predicament in which an officer may have to assist a threatened colleague.[8] During such encounters all the contradictions and humiliations that accompany most of what the patrolman does evaporate as he, for example, pursues someone he believes to have committed a crime or defends his fellow-officers (and himself) in the chaos of a tavern brawl. Yet, because of this narrow definition of police work, little of his time on the street provides the opportunity to accomplish much of what he considers to be his primary function. Thus, "real" police work to the patrolman is paradoxical; a source of satisfaction and frustration.[9]

At another level, one can divide the patrolman's dispatched (radio) calls into a rush, non-rush dichotomy. Rush calls are those involving "real" police work. Statistically, however, non-rush calls are much more common.[10] The decision to rush is, of course, a learned one, developed as a patrolman learns his territory and gains knowledge of the patrol lexicon.

There is not a universal code for rush calls. They are dependent upon the dispatcher's choice of words, the time, the place, the particular unit receiving the call, and perhaps even the mood of the officer. For example, to some officers a 220 (in Union City, a so-called "dangerous mental case") represents a call demanding lightning speed; to others it is treated simply as a "normal" call and handled without undue rush or concern. Only those situations calling for "real" police work are treated seriously by all officers.

The "back-up" responsibilities of patrolmen present an interesting amendment to the limited definition of "real" police work. Back-ups are those situations—dispatched or not—in which one patrol unit will proceed to a particular sector location to assist, if necessary, the patrol unit which has been assigned to the call. Certainly, most of the time back-ups amount to simply sitting in the squad car waiting to be waived off by the other unit; yet, the symbolic importance of back-ups cannot be dismissed.

There are several classes of dispatched calls which almost automatically guarantee the presence of a back-up, providing the sector work distribution at the moment is not overloaded. For example, the "help the officer" call is treated most seriously. Almost always such calls result in the rapid appearance of all officers in the district. In another class, less critical yet nonetheless sure to receive at least one back-up, are calls such as the felony-in-progress or man-with-gun. Other calls, such as the bar disturbance or the family fight in the ghetto neighborhood, also generate *pro forma* back-up units. To a large degree these back-up situations help young officers establish their street credentials as squad members in good standing. Patrolmen note the presence (or absence) of their peers as well as the speed with which they arrived. Such behavior demonstrates to all present the mutual concern and loyalty police feel they must have for one another. It is also the measure of one's commitment and motivation to share the risks involved in working the street. In the police world, such behavior is not overlooked. One officer suggested pointedly:

> I'll put up with a hell of a lot from guys working this sector. I don't care if they're on the take, mean or just don't do anymore than they have to. . . . But if some sonfabitch isn't around on a help-the-officer call or shows up after everybody else in the city has already been there, I don't want him working around me. Those cops are dangerous.

In Union City, as in all large city departments, the work of patrolmen is difficult, if not impossible, to evaluate. There are the required annual patrolman performance ratings submitted by the sergeants, but these are essentially hollow paper exercises in which few men receive low marks. The real task of evaluating patrolmen falls on the squad sergeant, and he is most concerned with the "activity" of his men.[11] However, activity is judged differently by sergeants. The same activity that is appreciated and perhaps demanded by one sergeant is treated indifferently by another sergeant. For example, one patrolman who had worked the same sector under several sergeants noted:

> Now you take Sergeant Johnson. He was a drunk hunter. That guy wanted all the drunks off the street and you knew that if you brought in a couple of drunks in a week, you and he would get along just fine. Sergeant Moss now is a different cat. He don't give a rat's ass about drunks. What he wants are those vice pinches. Sergeant Gordon wanted tickets and he'd hound your ass for a ticket a night. So you see it all depends on who you're working for, each guy is a little different.

To patrolmen, such idiosyncratic policies, while sometimes difficult to understand, provide a margin of safety in what can be a very uncertain work environment. By satisfying the sergeant's rather unambiguous demands (tickets, drunks, vice, juveniles, field investigation reports, and so on) a man can insure a harmonious relationship with the department.[12] If he provides the activity his sergeant desires, he will be left alone to do his work. If not, he may find himself working his days off or transferred to another, less desirable sector. To the men, these activity guidelines are received with some grumbling. But, in the main, they are acknowledged as simply a fact of work life. Furthermore, they are, to some degree, valued as the lodestar of their day-to-day work activities. Patrolmen realize, of course, that these activity measures have little to do with "real" police work. Yet, when one's patrol log contains evidence of activity for the sergeant, a patrolman is provided with a certain degree of comfort as well as the gratification that follows a job completed successfully.

It is important to recognize, however, that providing one's sergeant with his required activity can be done with relative ease. Whether it is tickets, car stops, drunks, or vice, patrolmen have little trouble and spend little time accomplishing the required task. In fact, most officers in Union City would simply remark sometime during a shift something to the effect of, "well-let's-go-do-our-bit-for-the-sergeant," and proceed to casually make whatever the quota might be. One FTO explained his particular job requirement to his recruit partner in the following manner:

> Here's our little duck pond (a busy but poorly marked intersection in Union City). Just sit here for five minutes and you can write all the tickets Sergeant McCallion wants. Just bag five of those illegal left turners and you're done for the week. Keeps him off your back.

Aside from producing activity for the sergeant and the infrequent opportunities to perform "real" police work, most of the patrolman's work time is dominated by what officers call "staying-out-of-trouble." Essentially, this means that the officer will do what is assigned to him and little more. The novice patrolman soon learns that there are few incentives to work hard. He also discovers that the most satisfactory solution to the labyrinth of hierarchy, the red tape, the myriad of rules and regulations, the risks of street work, and unpleasantness which characterize the occupation is to adopt the group standard, stressing a "lay-low-and-don't-make-waves" work ethic. And the best way in which he can stay out of trouble is to minimize the amount of work he pursues.[13] [One veteran officer remarked caustically:

> The only way to survive on this job is to keep from breaking your ass . . . you just don't want to work hard on this job 'cause if ya do you're sure to get in trouble. Either some civic-minded creep is going to get outraged and you'll wind up with a complaint in your file; or the high and mighty in the department will come down on you for breaking some rules or something.

In particular, working hard implies that one will—without being cajoled either by radio or a sergeant—actively search for real police work. Thus, making street stops, checking for stolen cars, searching a neighborhood for a possible burglar, filling out a number of Field Investigations Reports, and performing cursory searches on suspicious persons and automobiles are examples of the behavioral meaning of working hard. It should be clear that working hard][14] increases the number of citizen contacts an officer may have and, therefore, represents an opportunity to make both serious and banal mistakes. Citizen contacts are always delicate when an officer is on uncertain or merely suspicious grounds. Such encounters are strained interpersonally, troublesome legally, and almost always invite disrespect. In other words, aggressive patrol tactics are bothersome. Since working hard offers few occupational rewards, the logical solution for the patrolman is to organize his activities in such a fashion as to minimize the likelihood of being sanctioned by any of his audiences. The low visibility of the patrolman's role vis-à-vis the department (that is, his sergeant) allows for such a response. Thus the pervasive adjustment is epitomized in the "hang-loose-and-lie-low" advice frequently heard in the Union City department.

Rookies were always accused of what was referred to as a "gung-ho" attitude (rushing to calls and pushing eagerly for action). They were quickly taught, however, the appropriate perspective toward their work.[15] For example, the aggressive patrolman who constantly was seeking out tasks to perform was the butt of community jokes. In fact, many police expressed the sentiment that it was wise to spend as much time off the street as possible for, as they claimed, "you-can-get-in-trouble-out-there." One experienced officer noted:

> Those goddamn rookies are dangerous. I worked with one guy who was so gung ho that every time I got in the car with him I figured I was gonna get killed. This ass used to drive like a bat outta hell just to go to lunch . . . he wanted to always be looking for stolens or stopping everybody on the street. He settled down eventually when he found out that he wasn't getting anything done except make the other cops in the squad laugh.

While staying out of trouble occupies a great deal of the patrolman's working hours, it is to be distinguished sharply from what Rubenstein (1973) calls "loafing." While one may or may not work hard on any given shift, he is always to do his share by covering his district and answering his dispatched calls. Taking a call in another man's sector is occasionally acceptable. However, to do so consistently is personally insulting and considered by all policemen to be unjust. To the squad, answering a call for another indicates that the neglectful officer no longer cares or is committed to his "team," for he will not pull his fair share of the work. Relatedly, an officer who regularly fails to appear as a back-up on a call or arrives well after the potential danger has passed is considered to be either fearful or loafing and will, if possible, be expelled from the squad. The definition of loafing is therefore quite specific. . . .

During a newcomer's first few months on the street he is self-conscious and truly in need of guidelines as to his actions. A whole folklore of tales, myths, and legends surrounding the department is communicated to the novice by his fellow-officers, conspicuously by his FTO. Through these anecdotes—dealing largely with "mistakes" or "flubs" made by policemen—the recruit begins to adopt the perspectives of his more experienced colleagues. He becomes aware that "nobody's perfect," and the only way in which one can be protected from his own mistakes is to protect others. Among members of a particular squad, this "no rat" rule has deep and meaningful roots. Violations of the rule are met with swift (albeit informal) disapproval.[16] Since all officers have at sometime in their career broken a rule or regulation, the conspiracy-like network of support remains intact. The tacit norm is to never do something which might embarrass another officer. To draw critical attention to a colleague is strictly taboo in the police world. On the other hand, it is acceptable—and often demanded—that one cover for the mistake of another. While citizen complaints are felt to be unavoidable occupational hazards, fellow officers go to great lengths to insure such complaints against one of their squad members will be ruled unfounded.[17] The sergeant plays a critical role in this regard for he screens all reports written by his men. If an account on, for example, an arrest report contains an ambiguous phrase which could possibly be interpreted negatively by the court, or the report fails to mention a detail (factual, or otherwise) which might keep an officer (and, by implication, the squad and the sergeant) out of trouble, he will have the man rewrite the report until it is flawless in his eyes. Let me quote a passage from my field notes for illustrative purposes:

> When Blazier was placed under guard in the hospital (after a rather brutal encounter in which Blazier, a black homosexual, was severely beaten in the back of a patrol wagon), we returned to the precinct station to handle the paperwork. Officer Barns filled out the many reports involved in the incident and passed them to his sergeant for approval. The sergeant carefully read each report and then returned the "paper" to Barns saying that he better claim he was kicked in the face *before* he entered the patrol wagon or Barns would get a heavy brutality complaint for sure. He also told Barns to change the charge on Blazier to felony assault from refusal-to-obey and add drunk-in-public to the disturbing-the-peace charge Barns had originally thought appropriate. According to the sergeant, the heavier charges were necessary to protect Barns from IID (Internal Investigation Division). Finally, after some discussion and two re-writes, Barns finished a report which the sergeant said "covered their asses" (February 1973).

This "cover your ass" perspective pervades all of patrol work. In a sense, it represents a sort of bureaucratic paranoia which is all but rampant in police circles. Again, the best way for patrolmen to "cover their ass" is to watch carefully the kind of activities in which they engage. It is best therefore to not take the initiative on the street but rather react primarily to departmental direction. In this way, one seldom becomes involved in those potentially explosive situations which might result in disciplinary action for the patrolman.

The "lay low" occupational perspective also develops as officers gradually discover that the external rewards of a police career are more or less fixed. The patrolman knows for example that he will be at top salary within three years after joining the department. Advancement through the hierarchical network is a realistic expectation to only a few. In Union City, almost eighty percent of the men remain at the patrolman level for the extent of their careers.

At times, patrolmen feel as if the department goes out of its way to make things uncomfortable for them. For instance, Union City patrolmen are not provided parking spaces for their private automobiles and must spend considerable time locating spots on the busy and crowded city streets. Locker room facilities are dirty, cramped, and new officers often wait a year or so before they are assigned a space. The administrative detail in checking certain records or requesting information from one of the detective bureaus is almost prohibitive. An officer must also dig into his own pockets to cover many occupational expenses, such as having his uniforms cleaned or replaced after a duty-related accident. Critically, patrolmen discover that the department answers very few of their requests; for example, assignment shifts, new equipment, car repairs, expense reimbursements, and so on. And when the organization does act, it is usually after a long delay.

In response to their situation, patrolmen assume a "don't-expect-much" stance. They begin to realize that it is the rewards of camaraderie and small favors granted to them by their sergeant that makes their daily task either pleasant or intolerable. A few extra days off, a good partner, enjoyable squad parties, an agreeable assignment, or an extra long lunch become important rewards offered by a police career. It would appear consequently that the following advice given me by an older street veteran in Union City represents a very astute analysis of the patrolman's work role. He suggested cryptically:

> . . . You gotta learn to take it easy. The department don't care about you and the public sure as hell ain't gonna cry over the fact that the patrolman always gets the shit end of the stick. The only people who do care are your brother officers. So just lay back and take it easy out here. Makes things a lot smoother for us as well as yourself.

The survival perspective is strengthened finally by the fact that patrol work prepares one for very few other occupations in this society. The knowledge and skill involved in working the street (and these are considerable) have meaning and value only in the police world. Thus, the only alternative a man has to his patrolman position is to return to the work he did before joining the department. To most this would be unthinkable, for patrol work remains, in the last analysis, far more interesting and stimulating than most occupations open to young men in the police environment. Even after an officer discovers that the work is much duller than he had imagined before his initiation into the occupation, the simple pleasures of warm fellowship and working in the heterogeneous, unpredictable world of city streets is enough to bind most men to their careers. As one officer remarked:

> If I ever quit, the only thing I guess I could do would be to go back to the market where I used to work. But the thought of stacking Del Monte tomato cans on aisle six at exactly ten o'clock every morning

would drive me nuts. This job may be slow most of the time, but
at least the routine doesn't get you down. Besides, once police work
gets into your blood, that's it! You can never really go back out there
again as a civilian.

Notes

[1] All police quotes unless otherwise stated are taken from my field study in Union City.
Following a research agreement, Union City is a pseudonym for a sprawling metropolitan
area populated by well over a million persons. The police department employs more
than 1,500 uniformed officers, has a traditional training program, and provides a salary
above the national average.

[2] One of the standing jokes among police officers is that they were taught at the academy—
from the department's point of view—that they had little discretion on the street.
According to their classroom instructors hard and fast guidelines cover all police actions.
Yet, as they discovered quickly on the street—indeed knew instinctively at the academy—
police rules and regulations offer few solutions to the intricate, dynamic, and specific
situations in which patrolmen become involved.

[3] Whyte (1943) first noted the dilemma in which street officers are caught. If the officer
takes a formal, no-discretion, duty-only position in his sector, he cuts himself off from
the personal relationships necessary to receive information or settle disputes in the area.
On the other hand, if he becomes close and involved in the personal affairs of his sector,
he must necessarily utilize much discretion and is unable to act vigorously in situations
which may demand such action. While the use of the automobile for patrol purposes
has sealed off most officers in a sort of urban spaceship (with few contacts in their sectors),
it is clear that discretion still occupies a central place in the day-to-day environment
of patrolmen and cannot be kept in the *sub rosa* position of being a simple management
control issue.

[4] See Goffman (1963) for a theoretical treatment of stigmatization.

[5] Police officers are legally bound to take action off-duty in the presence of a felony offense
and can, in fact, be fired for a failure to do so. Few patrolmen go anywhere off-duty
without first arming themselves—whether it be to the corner market, out "on-the-town,"
or to play golf. While the "off-duty" gun is more symbolic than functional, it is but
another factor isolating patrolmen from the mainstream of social life.

[6] Certainly this bond is strongest among members of a particular squad. But it exists to
some degree among all police officers. To wit, the unwritten code of never ticketing
or arresting another police officer regardless of where he may be from unless the offense
is very serious indeed.

[7] Officers soon learn that there are quiet Sundays, busy Fridays, and crazy Saturdays.
There are those days when welfare or unemployment checks are distributed and certain
sectors seem to be considerably faster than usual—drunk and disorderly calls, family
fights, muggings, and so on. Of course, there are also those ubiquitous evenings of
the full moon when, as one officer put it, "those demons wreak havoc until the sun
rises." Whether or not such perceptions are backed by statistical evidence does not matter
for most officers nonetheless have firm expectations of public conduct fixed in their

minds. And, to paraphrase W. I. Thomas's famous dictum, a man's actions are attributable to his perceptions of reality and not to reality *per se*.

[8] In most ways the popular notion of "street crime" is a misnomer. The vast majority of crime takes place inside buildings, in entranceways, in alleys, in the dark and silent public parks, in living rooms of private homes, and so on. Policemen know this and their expectations of catching a criminal "in-the-act" are consequently quite low. Thus, they wait patiently for the serendipitous "on-view" situation to arise if, in fact, it ever will.

[9] It is interesting to note that I rode with many officers who claimed—when relaxing after a busy shift answering some ten calls or so, handling several traffic stops, assisting a few citizens and driving fifty to seventy miles in and out of their respective sectors— that the night had been a "total waste" since they had not accomplished any "real" police work.

[10] See Webster (1970) and Reiss (1971).

[11] I am indebted to Rubenstein (1973) for coining the term "activity." However, in Philadelphia, where Rubenstein's work was done, activity had a specific referent in that it applied to the number of vice arrests a patrolman made. In Union City, no such departmentwide focus existed. Each sergeant was more or less free to emphasize whatever activity he individually felt important, hence, activity is used here in a much broader fashion.

[12] These demands are probably most important when a man is new to the squad. If the man responds, the sergeant will slack off, only occasionally suggesting activity to the man. Usually, a casual remark by the sergeant is enough to promote action among the newcomers. The ease or difficulty with which veteran officers respond to a sergeant's wishes is, however, another matter and considerably more complicated and problematic (to the sergeant).

[13] An example of the disdain patrolmen feel toward the "rate-buster" is provided by Whittemore's (1973) romantic account of Batman and Robin, the so-called "supercops" in New York City. These officers met their biggest problem inside, not outside, the department. Most often, this pressure came from their fellow patrolmen who actively resented their aggressive approach. At various points in their early career, both officers were told point blank to "stop making waves and just do what you're supposed to do." Another similar account is found in Maas's (1973) superior biography of Serpico, a New York officer who—aside from his violation of the police code of secrecy in front of the Knapp Commission—was distrusted by his colleagues for his "working ways."

[14] Editor's note: The material in brackets was reconstructed from John Van Maanen, "Working the Street: A Developmental View of Police Behavior." In H. Jacob (ed.) *The Potential for Reform of Criminal Justice* Volume III, Sage Criminal Justice System Annuals. Beverly Hills, California: Sage, 1974 (83–84, 87, 100–110).

[15] This "gung-ho" attitude was a real source of irritation to most veteran officers in Union City. The "gung-ho" patrolmen were thought to be overly aggressive. In police argot, they wore "big-badges." It was felt that their presence in a squad created difficult situations in which other officers would have to assume needless risk untangling. Thus, most officers did not follow a "work-hard" rule. As noted, most learned to sit back and patiently answer their calls, rarely venturing from their squad car unless otherwise directed.

¹⁶ See Westley (1951) for a more extensive account of just how deep this code runs in police circles.

¹⁷ Complaints, as well as commendations in the police world are viewed somewhat sardonically. To patrolmen, a complaint is more a sign of where an officer works than his particular policing style. For example, if an officer works a central city, black, lower-class sector, complaints are felt to be simply a taken-for-granted feature of life in the area. Reciprocally, citizen letters of commendation will be extremely rare. On the other hand, if a man works a suburban, white middle-class sector commendations will be more frequent and complaints relatively few. Patrolmen know this and therefore assign little importance to either of the two categories. Apparently, the only exception to this rule of unimportance are those extreme cases where an officer may be under investigation as a result of a serious complaint (e.g., a shooting, extreme brutality, a felony, etc.). In such cases, patrolmen, if they are allowed to remain on the street, will act discreetly until the department resolves the complaint. As patrolmen say, "they go hide because they have a big one hanging."

References

Ahern, James F. (1972). *Police in Trouble*. New York: Hawthorn Books.

Almond, Gabriel A., & Verba, S. (1963). *The Civic Culture*. Princeton: Princeton University Press.

Easton, David, & Dennis, J. (1967). The child's acquisition of regional norms: Political efficacy. *American Political Science Review*, 61:25–38.

———— (1969). *Children in the Political System: Origins of Political Legitimacy*. New York: McGraw-Hill.

Goffman, Erving (1963). *Stigma*. New York: Doubleday.

Homans, George C. (1950). *The Human Group*. New York: Harcourt, Brace and World.

Hyman, Herbert (1959). *Political Socialization*. New York: The Free Press.

Maas, Peter (1973). *Serpico*. New York: The Viking Press.

Neiderhoffer, Arthur (1967). *Behind the Shield*. Garden City, New York: Doubleday and Co.

Reiss, Albert J. (1971). *The Police and the Public*. New Haven: Yale University Press.

Rubenstein, Jonathan (1973). *City Police*. New York: Farrar, Straus and Giroux.

Schein (1961). Management development as a process of influence. *Industrial Management Review*, 2:9–77.

Skolnick, Jerome (1966). *Justice Without Trial: Law Enforcement in a Democratic Society*. New York: John Wiley & Sons.

Van Maanen, John (1973). Observations on the making of policemen. *Human Organizations*, 32:407–418.

Webster, J. A. (1970). Police task and time study. *Journal of Criminal Law, Criminology and Police Science*, 61:94–100.

Westley, William A. (1951). The Police: A Sociological Study of Law, Custom and Morality. Ph.D. Dissertation at University of Chicago.

Whittemore, L. H. (1973). *The Super Cops*. New York: Stein and Day.

Whyte, William H. (1943). *Street Corner Society*. Chicago: University of Chicago Press.

Wilson, James Q. (1968). *Varieties of Police Behavior*. Cambridge: Harvard University Press, 1968.

15

Breeding Deviant Conformity
Police Ideology and Culture

Victor E. Kappeler, Richard D. Sluder and Geoffrey P. Alpert

P olice see the world in a unique fashion. They process information about people and events in a manner that is shared by few other occupational groups. Simply put, police have a unique worldview. The concept of *worldview* is the manner in which a culture sees the world and its own role and relationship to the world (Redfield, 1953, 1952; Benedict, 1934). This means that various social groups, including the police, perceive situations differently from other social or occupational groups. For example, lawyers may view the world and its events as a source of conflict and potential litigation. Physicians may view the world as a place of disease and illness. For the physician, people may become defined by their illness rather than their social character. Likewise, the police process events with similar cognitive distortion. The police worldview has been described as a working personality. According to Jerome H. Skolnick (1966: 42), "The police as a result of combined features of their social situation, tend to develop ways of looking at the world distinctive to themselves, cognitive lenses through which to see situations and events."

The way the police view the world can be described as a "we/they" or "us/them" orientation. Police tend to see the world as being composed of insiders and outsiders—police and citizens. Persons who are not police

Forces of Deviance: The Dark Side of Policing. Prospect Heights, IL: Waveland (1994), pp. 97–121. Reprinted with permission.

officers are considered outsiders and are viewed with suspicion. This
"we/they" police worldview is created for a variety of reasons: the
techniques used to select citizens for police service; the normative orientation police bring to the profession; an exaggeration of occupational danger;
the special legal position police hold in society; and the occupational self-
perception that is internalized by people who become police officers. Before
citizens can become police officers they must pass through an elaborate
employment selection process. In order to be selected for employment,
police applicants must demonstrate that they conform to a select set of
middle-class norms and values. Police selection practices, such as the use
of physical agility tests, background investigations, polygraph examinations,
psychological tests and oral interviews, are all tools to screen-out applicants
who have not demonstrated their conformity to middle-class norms and
values. Many of the selection techniques that are used to determine the
"adequacy" of police applicants have little to do with their ability to
perform the real duties associated with police work (Gaines, Falkenberg
and Gambino, 1994; Paynes and Bernardin, 1992; Maher, 1988; Cox,
Crabtree, Joslin and Millett, 1987; Holden, 1984). Often, these tests are
designed merely to determine applicants' physical prowess, sexual
orientation, gender identification, financial stability, employment history,
and abstinence from drug and alcohol abuse. If police applicants
demonstrate conformity to a middle-class life style, they are more likely
to be considered adequate for police service. The uniform interpretation
of psychological tests, based on middle-class bias, tends to produce a
homogeneous cohort. As one researcher has noted "the usefulness of
psychological testing for police officer selection is, at best, questionable . . .
no test has been found that discriminates consistently and clearly between
individuals who will and who will not make good police officers" (Alpert,
1993: 100). . . .

A consequence of the traditional police personnel system is that it
selects officers who are unable to identify with many of the marginal groups
in society. Therefore, the police process people and events in the world
through cognitive filters that overly value conformity in ideology,
appearance, and conduct. This conformist view of the world, based on
a shared background, provides police a measuring rod by which to make
judgments concerning who is deviant and in need of state control (Matza,
1969) and what is "suspicious" (Skolnick, 1966) and in need of police
attention. The shared background of the police provides a common cognitive
framework from which police process information and respond to events.

This homogeneous group of police recruits experiences formal
socialization when it enters the police academy. The police academy refines

the cohort again by weeding out those recruits who do not conform to the demands of paramilitary training. Police recruits soon learn:

> . . . that the way to "survive" in the academy . . . is to maintain a "low profile," by being one of the group, acting like the others. Group cohesiveness and mutuality is encouraged by the instructors as well. The early roots of a separation between "the police" and "the public" is evident in many lectures and classroom discussions. In "war stories" and corridor anecdotes, it emerges as a full blown "us-them" mentality (Bahn, 1984: 392).

In fact some have argued that the paramilitary model of police training and organization is inconsistent with humanistic democratic values, demands and supports "employees who demonstrate immature personality traits," and creates dysfunctional organizations (Angell, 1977: 105; Argyris, 1957: 1–24). The encouraged traits closely resemble attributes of the authoritarian personality. In short, police are further differentiated from the public and become more homogeneous in their worldview through formal training.

As Skolnick (1966) has noted, danger is one of the most important facets in the development of a police working personality. The relationship between the "real" dangers associated with police work and the police perception of the job as hazardous is complex. While police officers perceive their work as dangerous, they realize that the chances of being injured are not as great as their preoccupation with the idea of danger. Francis T. Cullen, Bruce G. Link, Lawrence F. Travis and Terrence Lemming (1983: 460) have referred to this situation as a "paradox in policing." Their research in five police departments found that:

> . . . even though the officers surveyed did not perceive physical injury as an everyday happening, this does not mean that they were fully insulated against feelings of danger. Hence . . . it can be seen that nearly four-fifths of the sample believed that they worked at a dangerous job, and that two-thirds thought that policing was more dangerous than other kinds of employment.

The disjuncture between the potential for injury and the exaggerated sense of danger found among police officers is best explained in the remarks of David Bayley (1976: 171) who observes:

> The possibility of armed confrontation shapes training, patrol preoccupations, and operating procedures. It also shapes the relationship between citizen and policeman by generating mutual apprehension. The policeman can never forget that the individual he contacts may be armed and dangerous; the citizen can never forget that the policeman is armed and may consider the citizen dangerous.

Police vicariously experience, learn and relearn the potential for danger through "war stories" and field training after graduation from the police academy. In fact, an inordinate amount of attention and misinformation concerning the dangers of police work is provided to police recruits at police academies. Since police instructors are generally former street enforcement officers, they already have a similar cognitive framework through which their occupational experiences and view of the world have been filtered. Training instructors tend to draw on experiences and use stories to convey information to recruits. Thus, much of the material presented to new police officers serves to reinforce the existing police view of the world rather than to educate police recruits or to provide appropriate attitudes, values and beliefs (Murphy and Caplan, 1993; Cohen and Feldberg, 1991; Delattre, 1989).

Even though well intended, police instructors' ability to educate is restricted because most police training curricula overemphasize the potential for death and injury and further reinforce the danger notion by spending an inordinate amount of time on firearms skills, dangerous calls, and "officer survival." In fact, the training orientation often bears a resemblance to being prepared to be dropped behind enemy lines to begin a combat mission. This is not to dismiss the possibility of danger in police work. Certainly, police are killed and injured in the line of duty, but these figures remain relatively small in comparison to the time spent indoctrinating recruits with the notion that the world is a dangerous place— especially if you are a police officer (FBI, 1993; Kappeler, Blumberg and Potter, 1993).

. . . Police training is dominated by an attempt to develop the practical rather than the intellectual skills of recruits. Not only is a substantial amount of time spent on the skills associated with officer safety, a large block of time is spent indoctrinating police on the basic elements of criminal law and the techniques to be used to detect criminal behavior. Little time is spent on developing an understanding of constitutional law, civil rights or ethical considerations in the enforcement of the law. Police instructors evaluate student performance by weighting certain areas more heavily than others. Differential importance is given to the use of firearms, patrol procedures, and how to use force in arresting and restraining citizens. These three areas are seen as the most critical functions by instructors and are given greater emphasis in scoring the performance of recruits in the police academy.

The real and exaggerated sense of danger inherent in police work indisputably forms a great part of the police picture of the world. This allows police to see citizens as potential sources of violence or as enemies. Citizens become "symbolic assailants" to the police officer on the street

(Skolnick, 1966). The symbolic assailant is further refined in appearance by taking on the characteristics of marginal segments of society (Harris, 1973; Piliavin and Briar, 1964). The image of the symbolic assailant takes on the characteristics of the populations police are directed to control (*see for example,* Sparger and Giacopassi, 1992). To the cop in southern Texas, the young Hispanic man becomes the potential assailant; in Atlanta, the poor inner-city black man becomes a source of possible injury; and in Chinatown, the Asian becomes the criminal who may resort to violence against the police. The element of danger emphasized by the police culture does much to foster the ''we/they'' worldview; it also focuses police attention on selective behaviors of certain segments of society.

Skolnick (1966) noted that the authority vested in the police is an equally important characteristic in the development of the police working personality. The law shapes and defines interactions between people and grants social status to members of society (Black, 1976, 1970). The police, by virtue of their social role, are granted a unique position in the law. Police have a legal monopoly on the sanctioned use of violence (Reiss, 1971; Bittner, 1970; Bordua and Reiss, 1967; Westley, 1953) and coercion (Bittner, 1970; Westley, 1953) against other members of society. The legal sanctions that prevent citizens from resorting to violence are relaxed for police officers. Police often resort to violence or coercion to accomplish their organizational goals of controlling crime and enforcing the existing social order. This legal distinction between citizens and police sets officers apart from the larger culture and other occupations.

Since the primary tools used by the police are violence and coercion, it was easy for the police to develop a paramilitary model of training and organization (Bittner, 1970). In this military model, likeness of dress, action and thought is promoted; homogeneity of appearance, ideology and behavior is emphasized. This military model has done much to foster the ''we/they'' worldview of police. Such a model allows police to see themselves as a close-knit, distinct group and promotes a view of citizens as ''outsiders and enemies'' (Sherman, 1982; Westley, 1956). This feeling of separateness from the surrounding society is illustrated by the aliena-tion felt by officers who are promoted within the organization to posi-tions of management or by those who leave the profession. Such individuals often feel isolated from their reference group as their occupational membership changes. Police, who once shared the danger, fear and authority of the profession with their subcultural peers become isolated from their reference group when their organizational or occupational standing changes (Gaines, Kappeler and Vaughn, 1994).

Finally, the police worldview is jaded by the perception of policing as the most critical of social functions. As the process of socialization and culturalization continues, police begin to believe and project for the public the image that they are the "thin blue line" that stands between anarchy and order. "Brave police officers patrol mean streets" and are on the front lines of a war for social order and justice. The war for social order is seen by the police as so important that it requires sweeping authority and unlimited discretion to invoke the power of law and, if necessary, the use of force.

After all, that is what the police are trained to do—enforce the law and, when necessary, use force to gain compliance. Similarly, police believe in the goodness of maintaining order, the nobility of their occupation, and the fundamental fairness of the law and existing social order. Accordingly, the police are compelled to view disorder, lawbreaking, and lack of respect for police authority as enemies of a civilized society. "They are thus committed ('because it is right') to maintain their collective face as protectorates of the right and respectable against the wrong and the not-so-respectable. . . . Thus, the moral mandate felt by the police to be their just right at the societal level is translated and transformed into occupational and personal terms and provides both the justification and legitimation for specific acts of street justice" (Van Maanen, 1978b: 227). If law, authority and order were seen as fostering inequity or injustice, the police self-perception would be tainted and the "goodness" of the profession would be questioned by the public. Police could no longer see themselves as partners in justice, but rather partners in repression—a role most police neither sought nor would be willing to recognize. Police who begin to question the goodness of the profession, the equity of law or the criticality of maintaining the existing social order often flee or are forced out of the occupation for other careers, further solidifying the police social character of those who remain.

❖ THE SPIRIT OF POLICE SUBCULTURE ❖

The concept of *ethos* encompasses the fundamental spirit of a culture: sentiments, beliefs, customs and practices (Biesanz and Biesanz, 1964). Ethos often includes the ideas valued most by a subculture or occupational group. When this term is applied to the police subculture, three general ideas surface. First, the police value an *ethos of bravery*. Bravery is a central component of the social character of policing. As such, it is related to the perceived and actual dangers of law enforcement. The potential to become the victim of a violent encounter, the need for support by fellow officers during such encounters, and the legitimate use of violence to accomplish the police mandate all contribute to a subculture that stresses the virtue of bravery. The bravery ethos is so strong among police that two authors have remarked, "Merely talking about pain, guilt or fear has been considered taboo. If an officer has to talk about his/her personal feelings, that officer is seen as not really able to handle them . . ." To express such fears is viewed by coworkers "as not having what it takes to be a solid, dependable police officer" (Pogrebin and Poole, 1991: 398).

Also, the military trappings of policing, organizational policy such as "never back down" in the face of danger, and informal peer pressure all contribute to instilling a sense of bravery in the police subculture. It is common for training officers to wait until a new recruit has faced a dangerous situation before recommending the recruit be given full status in the organization. Peer acceptance usually does not come until new officers have proven themselves in a dangerous situation. More than anything else, training officers and others in the police subculture want to know how probationary officers will react to danger—will they show bravery?

The importance of bravery in criminal justice occupational groups was highlighted in James Marquart's participant study of the prison guard subculture. Following a confrontation that required the use of force, Marquart (1986: 20) found that:

> The fact that I had been assaulted and had defended myself in front of other officers and building tenders raised my esteem and established my reputation. The willingness to fight inmates was an important trait rewarded by ranking guards. Due to this "fortunate" event, I earned the necessary credibility to establish rapport with the prison participants and allay their previous suspicions of me. I passed the ultimate test—fighting an inmate even though in self-defense—and was now a trustworthy member of the guard subculture.

An *autonomy ethos* is also evident in the police subculture's use and concern over discretionary law enforcement. The nature of police work results in officers demanding, and normally receiving, autonomy in law enforcement and legal sanctioning. As the first line of the criminal justice process, police officers make very authoritative decisions about whom to arrest, when to arrest, and when to use force. To this extent the police are the "gatekeepers" to the criminal justice system (Alpert and Dunham, 1992). This desire for autonomy often exists despite departmental, judicial, or community standards designed to limit the discretion of street enforcement officers. The need for autonomy can contribute to a sense of personally defined justice by members of the police subculture. Depending on subcultural membership, personal interpretations of justice and personal preferences could lead to abuses of discretion. Still, police officers cling to their autonomy in the areas of law enforcement and when to use force. Any attempt to limit the autonomy of the police is viewed as an attempt to undermine the police authority to control ''real'' street crime and not as an attempt on the part of citizens to curb police abuses of authority.

A third ethos evident in police subcultures is the *ethos of secrecy*. William Westley (1953: 37), a leading scholar on policing, noted that the police ''would apply no sanction against a colleague who took the more extreme view of the right to use violence and would openly support some milder form of illegal coercion.'' Similar conclusions were reached by William J. Chambliss and Robert B. Seidman (1971) in their consideration of police discretion. The police code of secrecy is often the result of a fear of loss of autonomy and authority as external groups try to limit police discretion and decision-making ability. A second factor supporting the development of a code of secrecy is the fact that policing is fraught with the potential for mistakes. Police feel they are often called upon to make split-second decisions that can be reviewed by others not directly involved in policing. This ''split-second syndrome'' rationalization, however, has been used by the police ''to provide after-the-fact justification for unnecessary police violence'' (Fyfe, 1993: 502). The desire to protect one's coworkers from disciplinary actions and from being accused of making an improper decision can promote the development of a code of secrecy.

The police code of secrecy is also a product of the police perception of the media and their investigative function. Some researchers suggest that police officers are very concerned with the manner in which the media report their actions (Berg, Gertz and True, 1984). This, coupled with a police perception of the media as hostile, biased and unsupportive, contributes to friction in police-media relations and to increased police secrecy. However, it is sometimes mandatory for officers to refrain from making media releases, having public discussion, or commenting on current criminal investigations in order not to endanger or hinder the process. This necessity is often interpreted by the media, citizens, and others as a self-imposed censorship of information. Perceptions of this nature can promote the separation of the public and the police and create the impression of a secret police society.

❖ CULTURAL THEMES IN POLICING ❖

The concept of *themes* in a culture is related to the belief systems or ''dynamic affirmations'' (Opler, 1945) maintained by its members. Themes help to shape the quality and structure of the group's social interactions. Themes are not always readily complementary to one another; however, they do occasionally balance or interact. This fact becomes readily apparent in studying the police subculture's dominant themes of social isolation and solidarity.

Isolation is an emotional and physical condition that makes it difficult for members of one social group to have relationships and interact with members of another group. This feeling of separateness from the surrounding society is a frequently noted attribute of the American police subculture (Sherman, 1982; Harris, 1973; Manning, 1971; Westley, 1970, 1956, 1953; Reiss and Bordua, 1967; Skolnick, 1966). Social isolation, as a theme of police subculture, is a logical result of the interaction of the police "worldview" and "code of secrecy." The self-imposed social isolation of the police from the surrounding community is well documented (Swanton, 1981; Cain, 1973; Skolnick, 1966; Clark, 1965; Banton, 1964; Baldwin, 1962).

Social isolation reinforces both of the earlier discussed worldview perspectives and ethos. Persons outside the police subculture are viewed somewhat warily as potential threats to the members' physical or emotional well-being, as well as to the officer's authority and autonomy. According to James Baldwin (1962) and Jerome H. Skolnick (1966), police impose social isolation upon themselves as a means of protection against real and perceived dangers, loss of personal and professional autonomy, and social rejection. Rejection by the community stems, in part, from the resentment which sometimes arises when laws are enforced (Clark, 1965). Since no one enjoys receiving a traffic ticket or being arrested and no one enjoys being disliked, the police tend to look inward to their own members for validity and support. Therefore, the police often self-impose restrictions on personal interactions with the community.

Bruce Swanton (1981) examined the topic of police isolation. He pointed out that two primary groups of determinants promote social isolation. Swanton maintained that these determinants were either self-imposed by the police or externally imposed upon the police by the community. Self-imposed police determinants generally concerned work-related requirements of the police profession. These represent structurally induced determinants created by the organization and the police subculture. The most important of these include: administrative structures; work structures; and personality structures (Swanton, 1981: 18).

Swanton found that the traditional view of police work—enforcing the law, detecting and apprehending criminals—created a sense of suspiciousness in police officers. This suspiciousness led to a false belief that positive community interactions or kindness from citizens were designed to compromise the officer's official position. A further deterrence to the maintenance of relationships with members of the general community outside the police subculture is the ambiguity evident in the police officer's on-duty and off-duty status. Swanton (1981) noted that the long and often irregular working hours—a result of shift schedules and possible cancellation of days off or vacations—coupled with the community's perception of police work as socially unattractive contribute to the police officer's sense of isolation. Swanton's "publicly initiated determinants" of isolation include:

> . . . suspicion that police compromise their friendships with higher loyalty to their employer; resentment at police-initiated sanctions or the potential thereof; attempts at integration by those wishing to curry favor, which are resented by others; and personality of police perceived as socially unattractive, thereby reducing the motivation of non-police to form close relationships with them (1981: 18).

Using a different perspective of the police, Charles Bahn (1984: 392) summarized the problem appropriately when he stated "social isolation becomes both a consequence and a stimulus. . . . Police officers find that constraints of schedule, of secrecy, of group mystique, and of growing adaptive suspiciousness and cynicism limit their friendships and relationships in the non-police world."

The second theme evident in the police subculture is *solidarity* (Harris, 1973; Westley, 1970, 1956, 1953; Stoddard, 1968; Skolnick, 1966; Banton, 1964). Traditionally, the theme of police solidarity and loyalty was seen as the result of a need for insulation from the earlier mentioned perceived dangers and rejection of the community. Michael Brown (1981: 82) has noted the importance of loyalty and solidarity among the police. Consider his interpretation of one police officer's remarks.

> "I'm for the guys in blue! Anybody criticizes a fellow copper that's like criticizing someone in my family; we have to stick together."
> The police culture demands of a patrolman unstinting loyalty to his fellow officers, and he receives, in return, protection: a place to assuage real and imagined wrongs inflicted by a (presumably) hostile public; safety from aggressive administrators and supervisors; and the emotional support required to perform a difficult task. The most important question asked by a patrolman about a rookie is whether or not he displays the loyalty demanded by the police subculture.

Theodore N. Ferdinand (1980), however, has noted that solidarity and loyalty change in proportion to an officer's age and rank. He maintained that police cadets have the least amount of solidarity, and line officers have the greatest amount of solidarity. Ferdinand (1980) noted that until the age of forty, much of a police officer's social life is spent within the confines of the police subculture. However, solidarity declines as police move into higher ranks in the department. Members of the police administrative hierarchy are frequently seen by the line officers in much the same perspective as members of the community and other non-police characters—namely, as threatening to the welfare of the subculture.

Police solidarity, therefore, may be said to be an effect of the socialization process inherent to the subculture and police work. New members are heavily socialized to increase their solidarity with the group, and those who move away from the subculture, either through age or promotion, are gradually denied the ties of solidarity. This socialization, or cohesion, is based in part upon the "sameness" of roles, perceptions and self-imagery of the members of the police subculture.

❖ POSTULATES OF POLICE CULTURE ❖

Postulates are statements of belief held by a group which reflect its basic orientations (Opler, 1945). Postulates are the verbal links between a subculture's view of the world and their expression of that view into action. Because postulates and cultural themes may conflict, the degree to which they complement one another and are integrated is said to be indicative of the homogeneity and complexity of a culture. Postulates, then, are statements—expressions of general truth or principle that guide and direct the actions of subcultural members. Such statements enable one to understand the nuances of a subculture to a greater degree than do ethos or themes. Postulates act as oral vehicles for the transmission of culture from one generation to the next, and tend to serve as reinforcers of the subcultural worldview.

Postulates basic to an understanding of the police subculture have been collected and arranged into an informal code of police conduct. Elizabeth Reuss-Ianni (1983a), drawing from the research of many others (Manning, 1977; Rubinstein, 1973; Savitz, 1971; Stoddard, 1968; Skolnick, 1966; Westley, 1956, 1953), identified several police postulates (*also see*, Reuss-Ianni and Ianni, 1983b). Although she used these postulates to demonstrate the conflict between administrators and line officers, they can also be divided into three separate categories that reflect the culture of policing. Ruess-Ianni's work is important because it illustrates the influence that line officers have on the total organization. Her work shows that despite administrative efforts to produce organizational change, substantive change is difficult to attain without the collective efforts of group members. In the case of the police, Ruess-Ianni recognized the importance of informal work groups and the influence those groups have on structuring social relationships both in and outside of the police subculture. Hence, postulates are important in shaping not only the attitudes, values and beliefs of police officers but also a shared understanding of what are deemed to be both acceptable and unacceptable behaviors.

Postulates Shaping the Ethos of Secrecy and the Theme of Solidarity

The first group of postulates identified by Ruess-Ianni reflects the ethos of secrecy that surrounds much of police work. This secrecy has many functions, three of which seem especially important. . . . First, the public is denied knowledge of many police activities because, in the eyes of the police, they have no "need to know." While it may be prudent to restrict access to certain types of sensitive information in law enforcement, the veil of secrecy that shields police from the public has the effect of minimizing public scrutiny of police activities and behaviors. Secondly, many of the postulates identified by Ruess-Ianni are guideposts which keep officers from relaying too much information to police supervisors. For first-line police officers, these postulates are seen as necessary protections to insulate police officers from what they see as unwarranted punishment or challenges to their autonomy. Finally, these postulates may be most important in the sense that taken together, they provide first-line police officers with a sense of solidarity. Some of the postulates indicative of the ethos of secrecy and the theme of police solidarity include:

- *"Don't give up another cop"* (Ruess-Ianni, 1983: 14). As perhaps one of the most important factors contributing to a sense of solidarity and secrecy, this postulate admonishes officers to never, regardless of the seriousness or nature of a case, provide information to either superiors or non-police that would cause harm to a fellow police officer. Ruess-Ianni notes that this postulate implicitly informs a police officer that abiding by this canon and never giving up another cop means others "won't give you up."

- *"Watch out for your partner first and then the rest of the guys working that tour"* (Ruess-Ianni, 1983: 14). This postulate tells police officers they have an obligation to their partners first, and then to other officers working the same shift. "Watching out," in this context, means that an officer has a duty not only to protect fellow officers from physical harm, but also to watch out for their interests in other matters. If, for example, an officer learns that another member of his or her squad is under investigation by an internal affairs unit, the officer is obligated to inform the officer of this information. As with the postulate listed above, the implicit assumption here is that if you watch out for fellow police, they will also watch out for you.

- *"If you get caught off base, don't implicate anybody else"* (Ruess-Ianni, 1983: 14). Being caught off base can involve a number of activities, ranging from being out of one's assigned sector to being caught for engaging in prohibited activities. This postulate teaches officers that if someone discovers their involvement in proscribed activities, officers should accept the punishment and not expose fellow officers to scrutiny or possible punishment. In essence, this rule of behavior advises police officers that if caught for misbehavior, accept the punishment, but do not involve others who might also be punished. This postulate insulates other police officers from punishment and reduces the possibility that organized deviance or corruption will be uncovered.

- *"Make sure the other guys know if another cop is dangerous or 'crazy'"* (Ruess-Ianni, 1983: 14). Police are caught in a double-bind if they become aware that one of their fellow members is unstable or presents a safety hazard. In this case, the secrecy dictum prohibits a line officer from informing police supervisors of another officer's instability or unsuitability. Yet at the same time, an officer has an obligation to watch out for his or her peers. In order to deal with such a contradiction, this rule of behavior tells an officer that if he or she is aware that another officer may be dangerous or crazy, there is an obligation to let other police know of the potential safety risks, but not to take formal action against the officer. This postulate allows "problem" officers to continue to operate within the profession and reduces the chances that they will be detected by the agency administration or the public. It does, however, allow informal sanctions of exclusion to be imposed.

- *"Don't get involved in anything in another cop's sector"* (Ruess-Ianni, 1983: 14). Ruess-Ianni notes that in older, corrupt departments, this dictum advised officers not to try to hedge in on another police officer's illegal activities. In essence, this rule informed police that officers "owned" certain forms of corruption in their sector. Today, this postulate teaches officers that they are to stay out of all matters in other officers' sectors. This rule of territoriality is believed necessary because officers are responsible for activities in their respective beats. This postulate serves to limit the spread of information making it easier for officers to deny knowledge of deviance, which in turn makes deviance appear to be a mere aberration.

- *"Hold up your end of the work; don't leave work for the next tour"* (Ruess-Ianni, 1983: 14–15). These postulates teach officers that if they neglect their work responsibilities, two results are likely to occur.

First, other officers must cover for those who shirk their responsibilities. Second, malingerers call attention to everyone on a shift. Thus, there are pressures for all officers to carry their own weight. . . . If, however, an officer fails to follow this edict, other officers are expected to "cover" for the officer and to deflect attention away from the group.

- *"Don't look for favors just for yourself"* (Ruess-Ianni, 1983: 16). This dictum admonishes officers not to "suck up" to superiors. In essence, this rule tells officers that their primary responsibilities are to their peers and that attempts to curry favors with superiors will be looked down upon. This postulate prevents line officers from developing relationships with superiors that might threaten the safety of the work group.

Postulates Supporting Police Isolationism

Ruess-Ianni has identified several postulates that are reflective of the "we/they" worldview that police develop. These postulates teach new officers that non-police simply do not understand the true nature of police work. As such, these pronouncements reinforce the notion that there are vast differences between police and citizens. Further, non-police will never be able to truly understand the unique problems inherent in policing. John Van Maanen (1978a) referred to these citizens as "know nothings" because of their characterization by the police. Ultimately, this we/they worldview increases police isolation from citizens. Postulates indicative of the we/they worldview and supportive of police isolationism include:

- *"Protect your ass"* (Ruess-Ianni, 1983: 15). As perhaps one of the most important postulates leading to a sense of isolation, this rule teaches police to be wary of everyone—including citizens and superiors. At the simplest level, the rule informs police that anyone who wants to cause trouble for an officer probably can. Hence, the rule teaches police that others can not be trusted. Because of this, officers must be vigilant and take all steps necessary to protect themselves from any possible threat. While these threats might include the possibility of physical harm, they would also include the possibility of disciplinary action by superiors and the potential for citizens to complicate the lives of police by filing complaints, making allegations, or uncovering deviance.
- *"Don't trust a new guy until you have him checked out."* (Ruess-Ianni, 1983: 14). Rookie police and officers who are new to a work group are not to be automatically accorded status as a trusted group

member. Instead, outsiders are to be treated cautiously until information about them can be obtained, or until they have "proven" themselves. In some cases, rookie officers are "tested" to determine if they can be trusted. Those officers having a history with the department are checked out through the "grapevine" and are often intentionally placed in situations to see if they can be trusted.

- *"Don't talk too little or too much; don't tell anybody more than they have to know"* (Ruess-Ianni, 1983: 14–15). The themes of "don't talk too much," and "don't reveal more than necessary" inform new police officers that others—including citizens and supervisors—are not to be trusted. These dictates reinforce the notion not only that "loose lips sink ships," but also that there is no need to provide others with information beyond the minimum required. This is true because information can be distorted or used in other ways that are potentially harmful to police. At the same time, the dictate "don't talk too little" lets new police officers know that excessive silence or introversion will be seen as suspicious behavior by other officers. As Ruess-Ianni notes, the extremes of talking too much or too little are both viewed as suspicious behaviors by fellow officers. This postulate directs officers to maintain communications with the work group but to limit their exposure to administrators and citizens.

- *"Don't trust bosses to look out for your interests"* (Ruess-Ianni, 1983: 16). This maxim informs new police officers that when forced to make a choice, managers and administrators will look out for their own best interests rather than those of the officer. Whether true or not, this idea has the effect of further distancing officers from their superiors. Since line officers are taught that they can not depend on either citizens or superiors, they are forced to align themselves with the only group left for protection—fellow police.

Postulates Indicative of the Ethos of Bravery

David H. Bayley and Egon Bittner (1989) have noted that a crucial part of a police officer's job is to take charge of situations and people. Taking charge, in this sense, involves developing a "presence" to handle incidents. In essence, this means that officers must be poised to take control regardless of the situation. Yet, it is crucial not to appear too ready, since overeagerness can escalate situations. In one officer's words, "Always act . . . as if you were on vacation." At the same time, however, "One must be keyed up but not 'choke' " (Bayley and Bittner, 1989:101). A couple of Ruess-Ianni's postulates strongly suggest that above all else, new officers must always show bravery in the performance of police work. These postulates are:

- *"Show balls"* (Ruess-Ianni, 1983: 14). Police themselves characterize their work as laden with danger and fraught with hazards. Accordingly, this postulate counsels police that they are never to back down from a situation. While this is especially true for incidents that occur in view of the public, it is also important for an officer to never back down from a situation where other officers are present. This postulate is important in the eyes of the police; backing down shows the public that the police are weak. All police, therefore, are believed harmed by the cowardice of an individual officer. Thus, the idea that if an officer gets into a situation, he or she must have fortitude to control the situation. A challenge to the authority of a single officer is seen as a challenge to the authority of the entire police group. These challenges must be accepted and dealt with.

- *"Be aggressive when you have to, but don't be too eager"* (Ruess-Ianni, 1983: 14). This postulate reflects the idea that while officers should always be alert, they should not go out of their way to seek trouble. This is partly because overeagerness, or having a "chip" on one's shoulder, will only bring unneeded complications. In a sense, the maxim "If you look for trouble, it will find you," applies here. Therefore, challenges to authority must be met and dealt with, but they should not be sought out. Police are to avoid acting in ways that cause the group to undergo unnecessary scrutiny. However, this postulate teaches an officer to meet a challenge or confrontation as aggressively as necessary to handle it effectively.

Through exposure to these and other postulates, new generations of police officers combine their experiences and perceptions of the world—all of which are filtered through the unique perspective of police officers' eyes. With these "truths," officers develop a belief system which dictates acceptable and unacceptable behavior. These postulates serve as reinforcers of the police worldview and act as part of the socialization process for members of the police occupation. Through these postulates, officers are taught to keep police business "secret," the necessity for solidarity among the ranks, and the belief that police are different and isolated from larger society. Violations of these canons may lead to immediate sanctions from fellow subculture members, frequently resulting in some form of expulsion from the security of the group. It is ironic that police who violate the precepts of the subculture are doubly isolated—first from the community by nature of the occupation and later by the police subculture, for violation of its informal norms of conduct. Police officers who do not conform to the postulates of the work group become outcasts who have been stripped of the benefits of group membership.

. . . The occupational culture provides police with a unique working personality. This working personality includes the development of a worldview that teaches police to distinguish between insiders and outsiders (i.e. police/non-police)—in other words, those who are okay versus those who must be cautiously watched. This we/they perspective instills in officers a perpetual concern for the element of danger in their work. The police working personality reinforces the notion of "differentness" in three ways. First, police are taught that they are vested with the unique power to use force and violence in carrying out legal mandates. Second, the paramilitary nature of police work isolates police from others in society. Finally, police are indoctrinated with the idea that they are the "thin blue line" between anarchy and order.

Police ethos reflect the ideas valued most by the police. Some of the most important ethos transmitted by the police subculture are the ethos of bravery, the ethos of autonomy, and the ethos of secrecy.

Cultural themes are also a part of the police culturalization process. In this case, cultural themes are fairly specific rules of behavior that shape police interactions. A dominant cultural theme in policing is the idea that police are socially isolated from the rest of society. A second important cultural theme extols the need for police solidarity.

Finally, several postulates of the police culture were reviewed. Postulates are specific principles used to guide and direct the actions of subcultural members. Postulates that reinforce the need for police secrecy and solidarity include instructions to never "give up" another cop; to watch out for other police, especially one's partner; and if caught engaging in prohibited activities, never implicate other officers. Postulates that support police isolationism instruct police to "protect your ass" by being wary of everyone; not to trust new officers until they have proven themselves; and not to trust supervisors to look out for an officer's best interests. Postulates also instruct officers on the ethos of bravery: have fortitude and never back down in a situation; be aggressive but not overeager in handling situations.

References

Alpert, G. P. (1993). The role of psychological testing in law enforcement. In Dunham, R. G. and Alpert, G. P. (Eds.). *Critical Issues in Policing: Contemporary Readings* (2nd ed.) Prospect Heights, IL: Waveland Press.

Alpert, G. P., & Dunham, R. G. (1992). *Policing Urban America* (2nd ed.). Prospect Heights, IL: Waveland Press.

Angell, J. E. (1977). Toward an alternative to the classical police organizational arrangements: A democratic model. In Gaines, L. K. and Ricks, T. A. (Eds.) *Managing the Police Organization*. St. Paul, MN: West Publishing Company.

Argyris, C. (1957). The individual and organization: Some problems of mutual adjustment. *Administrative Science Quarterly*, (June): 1–24.

Bahn, C. (1984). Police socialization in the eighties: Strains in the forging of an occupational identity. *Journal of Police Science and Administration*, 12(4): 390–94.

Baldwin, J. (1962). *Nobody Knows My Name*. New York: Dell Publishing Company.

Banton, M. (1964). *The Police in the Community*. London, England: Travistock.

Bayley, D. (1976). *Forces of Order: Police Behavior in Japan and the United States*. Berkeley: University of California Press.

Bayley, D. H., & Bittner, E. (1989). Learning the skills of policing. In Dunham, R. G. and Alpert, G. P. (Eds.) *Critical Issues in Policing: Contemporary Readings*. Prospect Heights, IL: Waveland Press.

Benedict, R. (1934). *Patterns of Culture*. Boston: Houghton Mifflin Company.

Berg, B. L., Gertz, M. G., & True, E. J. (1984). Police-community relations and alienation. *Police Chief*, 51(11): 20–23.

Biesanz, J., & Biesanz, M. (1964). *Modern Society* (3rd ed.). Englewood Cliffs, NJ: Prentice-Hall.

Bittner, E. (1970). *The Functions of Police in Modern Society*. Chevy Chase, MD: National Clearinghouse for Mental Health.

Black, D. (1976). *The Behavior of Law*. New York: Academic Press.

———. (1970). Production of crime rates. *American Sociological Review*, 35: 733–48.

Brown, M. K. (1981). *Working the Street: Police Discretion and the Dilemmas of Reform*. New York: Russell Sage Foundation.

Cain, M. E. (1973). *Society and the Policeman's Role*. London, England: Routledge and Kegal Paul.

Chambliss, W. J., & Seidman, R. B. (1971). *Law, Order and Power*. Reading, MA: Addison-Wesley.

Clark, J. P. (1965). Isolation of the police: A comparison of the British and American situations. *Journal of Criminal Law, Criminology and Police Science*, 56: 307–319.

Cohen, H. S., & Feldberg, M. (1991). *Power and Restraint: The Moral Dimension of Police Work*. New York: Praeger.

Cox, T. C., Crabtree, A., Joslin, D., & Millet, A. (1987). A theoretical examination of police entry-level uncorrected visual standards. *American Journal of Criminal Justice*, 11(2): 199–208.

Cullen, F. T., Link, B. G., Travis, L. F., & Lemming, T. (1983). Paradox in policing: A note on perceptions of danger. *Journal of Police Science and Administration*, 11(4): 457–462.

Delattre, E. J. (1989). *Character and Cops: Ethics in Policing*. Washington, D.C.: American Enterprise Institute for Public Policy Research.

Federal Bureau of Investigation (1993). *Law Enforcement Officers Killed and Assaulted*. Washington, D.C.: U.S. Government Printing Office.

Ferdinand, T. H. (1980). Police attitudes and police organization: Some interdepartmental and cross-cultural comparisons. *Police Studies*, 3: 46–60.

Fyfe, J. J. (1993). The split-second syndrome and other determinates of police violence. In Dunham, R. G. and Alpert, G. P. (Eds.) *Critical Issues in Policing: Contemporary Readings* (2nd ed.). Prospect Heights, IL: Waveland Press.

Gaines, L. K., & Kappeler, V. E. (1990). The police selection process: What works. In Cordner, G. and Hale, D. (Eds.). *What Works in Policing*. Cincinnati: Anderson Publishing Company.

Gaines, L. K., Costello, P., & Crabtree, A. (1989). Police selection testing: Balancing legal requirements and employer needs. *American Journal of Police*, 8(1): 137–152.

Gaines, L. K., Falkenberg, S., & Gambino, J. A. (1994). Police physical agility testing: A historical and legal analysis. *American Journal of Police*, forthcoming.

Gaines, L. K., Kappeler, V. E., & Vaughn, J. B. (1994). *Policing in America*. Cincinnati: Anderson Publishing Company.

Harris, R. (1973). *The Police Academy: An Insider's View*. New York: John Wiley and Sons.

Holden, R. (1984). Vision standards for law enforcement: A descriptive study. *Journal of Police Science and Administration*, 12(2): 125–129.

Kappeler, V. E., Blumberg, M., & Potter, G. W. (1993). *The Mythology of Crime and Criminal Justice*. Prospect Heights, IL: Waveland Press.

Kraska, P. B., & Kappeler, V. E. (1988). Police on-duty drug use: A theoretical and descriptive examination. *American Journal of Police*, 7(1): 1–28.

Kuykendall, J., & Burns, D. (1980). The black police officer: An historical perspective. *Journal of Contemporary Criminal Justice*, 1(4): 103–113.

Maher, P. T. (1988). Police physical agility tests: Can they ever be valid. *Public Personnel Management Journal*, 17: 173–183.

Manning, P. K. (1977). *Police Work: The Social Organization of Policing*. Cambridge: The MIT Press.

———. (1971). The police: Mandate, strategies and appearances. In Gaines, L. K. and Ricks, T. A. (Eds.) *Managing The Police Organization*. St. Paul: West Publishing Company.

Marquart, J. (1986). Doing research in prison: The strengths and weaknesses of full participation as a guard. *Justice Quarterly*, 3(1): 20–32.

Matza, D. (1969). *Becoming Deviant*. Englewood Cliffs, NJ: Prentice-Hall.

Murphy, P. V., & Caplan, D. G. (1993). Fostering integrity. In Dunham, R. G. and Alpert, G. P. (Eds.). *Critical Issues in Policing: Contemporary Readings* (2nd ed.) Prospect Heights, IL: Waveland Press.

Opler, M. E. (1945). Themes as dynamic forces in culture. *The American Journal of Sociology*, 51: 198–206.

Paynes, J., & Bernardin, H. J. (1992). Entry-level police selection: The assessment center is an alternative. *Journal of Criminal Justice*, 20: 41–52.

Piliavin, I., & Briar, S. (1964). Police encounters with juveniles. *American Journal of Sociology*, 70: 206–214.

Pogrebin, M. R., & Poole, E. D. (1991). Police and tragic events: The management of emotions. *Journal of Criminal Justice*, 19: 395–403.

Reaves, B. A. (1992a). *State and local police departments, 1990*. Washington, D.C.: Bureau of Justice Statistics, U.S. Department of Justice.

_____. (1992b). *Sheriff's departments 1990*. Washington, D.C.: Bureau of Justice Statistics, U.S. Department of Justice.

_____. (1989). *Police departments in large cities, 1987*. Washington, D.C.: Bureau of Justice Statistics, U.S. Department of Justice.

Redfield, R. (1953). *The Primitive World and Its Transformations*. Ithaca, NY: Cornell University Press.

_____. (1952). The primitive worldview. *Proceedings of the American Philosophical Society*, 96: 30–36.

Reiss, A. J. (1971). *The Police and the Public*. New Haven: Yale University Press.

Reiss, A. J., & Bordua, D. J. (1967). Environment and organization: A perspective on the police. In Bordua, D. J. (Ed.) *The Police: Six Sociological Essays*. New York: John Wiley and Sons.

Reuss-Ianni, E. (1983a). *Two Cultures of Policing*. New Brunswick, NJ: Transaction Books.

Reuss-Ianni, E., & Ianni, F. A. J. (1983b). Street cops and management cops: The two cultures of policing. In Punch, M. (Ed.). *Control in the Police Organization*. Cambridge: MIT Press.

Rubinstein, J. (1973). *City Police*. New York: Farrar, Strauss and Giroux.

Savitz, L. (1971). The dimensions of police loyalty. In Hann, H. (Ed.) *Police In Urban Society*. Beverly Hills: Sage.

Sherman, L. (1982). Learning police ethics. *Criminal Justice Ethics*, 1(1):10–19.

Skolnick, J. H. (1966). *Justice Without Trial: Law Enforcement in a Democratic Society*. New York: John Wiley and Sons.

Sparger, J. R., & Giacopassi, D. J. (1992). Memphis revisited: A reexamination of police shootings after the Garner decision. *Justice Quarterly*, 9: 211–225.

Sullivan, P. S. (1989). Minority officers: Current issues. In Dunham, R. G. and Alpert, G. P. (Eds.). *Critical Issues in Policing: Contemporary Readings*. Prospect Heights, IL: Waveland Press.

Swanton, B. (1981). Social isolation of police: Structural determinants and remedies. *Police Studies*, 3: 14–21.

Van Maanen, J. (1978a). On becoming a policeman. In Manning, P. K. and Van Maanen, J. (Eds.) *Policing: A View From The Street*. Santa Monica: Goodyear.

_____. (1978b). The Asshole. In Manning, P. K. and Van Maanen, J. (Eds.) *Policing: A View From The Street*. Santa Monica: Goodyear.

Westley, W. A. (1970). *Violence and the Police: A Sociological Study of Law, Custom and Morality*. Cambridge: MIT Press.

_____. (1956). Secrecy and the police. *Social Forces*, 34(3): 254–257.

_____. (1953). Violence and the police. *American Journal of Sociology*, 59: 34–41.

Part IV

Policing Society

16

The Police on Skid-row
A Study of Peace Keeping

Egon Bittner

T he prototype of modern police organization, the Metropolitan Police of London, was created to replace an antiquated and corrupt system of law enforcement. The early planners were motivated by the mixture of hardheaded business rationality and humane sentiment that characterized liberal British thought of the first half of the nineteenth century.[1] Partly to meet the objections of a parliamentary committee, which was opposed to the establishment of the police in England, and partly because it was in line with their own thinking, the planners sought to produce an instrument that could not readily be used in the play of internal power politics but which would, instead, advance and protect conditions favorable to industry and commerce and to urban civil life in general. These intentions were not very specific and had to be reconciled with the existing structures of governing, administering justice, and keeping the peace. Consequently, the locus and mandate of the police in the modern polity were ill-defined at the outset. On the one hand, the new institution was to be a part of the executive branch of government, organized, funded, and staffed in accordance with standards that were typical for the entire system of the executive. On the other hand, the duties that were given to the police organization brought it under direct control of the judiciary in its day-to-day operation.

American Sociological Review, 32 (October 1967): 699–715. Copyright © 1967 by the American Sociological Association. Reprinted with permission.

The dual patronage of the police by the executive and the judiciary is characteristic for all democratically governed countries. Moreover, it is generally the case, or at least it is deemed desirable, that judges *rather than* executive officials have control over police use and procedure.[2] This preference is based on two considerations. First, in the tenets of the democratic creed, the possibility of direct control of the police by a government in power is repugnant.[3] Even when the specter of the police state in its more ominous forms is not a concern, close ties between those who govern and those who police are viewed as a sign of political corruption.[4] Hence, mayors, governors, and cabinet officers—although the nominal superiors of the police—tend to maintain, or to pretend, a hands-off policy. Second, it is commonly understood that the main function of the police is the control of crime. Since the concept of crime belongs wholly to the law, and its treatment is exhaustively based on considerations of legality, police procedure automatically stands under the same system of review that controls the administration of justice in general.

By nature, judicial control encompasses only those aspects of police activity that are directly related to full-dress legal prosecution of offenders. The judiciary has neither the authority nor the means to direct, supervise, and review those activities of the police that do not result in prosecution. Yet such other activities are unavoidable, frequent, and largely within the realm of public expectations. It might be assumed that in this domain of practice the police are under executive control. This is not the case, however, except in a marginal sense.[5] Not only are police departments generally free to determine what need[s to] be done and how, but aside from informal pressures they are given scant direction in these matters. Thus, there appear to exist two relatively independent domains of police activity. In one, their methods are constrained by the prospect of the future disposition of a case in the courts; in the other, they operate under some other consideration and largely with no structured and continuous outside constraint. Following the terminology suggested by Michael Banton, they may be said to function in the first instance as "law officers" and in the second instance as "peace officers."[6] It must be emphasized that the designation "peace officer" is a residual term, with only some vaguely presumptive content. The role, as Banton speaks of it, is supposed to encompass all occupational routines not directly related to making arrests, without, however, specifying what determines the limits of competence and availability of the police in such actions.

Efforts to characterize a large domain of activities of an important public agency have so far yielded only negative definitions. We know that they do not involve arrests; we also know that they do not stand under judicial control, and that they are not, in any important sense, determined by specific executive or legislative mandates. In police textbooks and manuals, these activities receive only casual attention, and the role of the "peace officer" is typically stated in terms suggesting that his work is governed mainly by the individual officer's personal wisdom, integrity, and altruism.[7] Police departments generally keep no records of procedures that do not involve making arrests. Policemen, when asked, insist that they merely use common sense when acting as "peace officers," though they tend to emphasize the elements of experience and practice in discharging the role adequately. All this ambiguity is the more remarkable for the fact that peace keeping tasks, i.e., procedures not involving the formal legal remedy of arrest, were explicitly built into the program of the modern police from the outset.[8] The early executives of the London police saw with great clarity that their organization had a dual function. While it was to be an arm of the administration of justice, in respect of which it developed certain techniques for bringing offenders to trial, it was also expected to function apart from, and at times in lieu of, the employment of full-dress legal procedure. Despite its early origin, despite a great deal of public knowledge about it, despite the fact that it is routinely done by policemen, no one can say with any clarity what it means to do a good job of keeping the peace. To be sure, there is vague consensus that when policemen direct, aid, inform, pacify, warn, discipline, roust, and do whatever else they do without making arrests, they do this with some reference to the circumstances of the occasion and, thus, somehow contribute to the maintenance of the peace and order. Peace keeping appears to be a solution to an unknown problem arrived at by unknown means.

The following is an attempt to clarify conceptually the mandate and the practice of keeping the peace. The effort will be directed not to the formulation of a comprehensive solution of the problem but to a detailed consideration of some aspects of it. Only in order to place the particular into the overall domain to which it belongs will the structural determinants of keeping the peace in general be discussed. By structural determinants are meant the typical situations that policemen perceive as *demand conditions* for action without arrest. This will be followed by a description of peace keeping in skid-row districts, with the object of identifying those aspects of it that constitute a *practical skill*.

Since the major object of this article is to elucidate peace keeping practice as a skilled performance, it is necessary to make clear how the use of the term is intended.

Practical skill will be used to refer to those methods of doing certain things, and to the information that underlies the use of the methods, that *practitioners themselves* view as proper and efficient. Skill is, therefore, a stable orientation to work tasks that is relatively independent of the personal feelings and judgments of those who employ it. Whether the exercise of this skilled performance is desirable or not, and whether it is based on correct information or not, are specifically outside the scope of interest of this presentation. The following is deliberately confined to a description of what police patrolmen consider to be the reality of their work circumstances, what they do, and what they feel they must do to do a good job. That the practice is thought to be determined by normative standards of skill minimizes but does not eliminate the factors of personal interest or inclination. Moreover, the distribution of skill varies among practitioners in the very standards they set for themselves. For example, we will show that patrolmen view a measure of rough informality as good practice vis-à-vis skid-row inhabitants. By this standard, patrolmen who are "not rough enough," or who are "too rough," or whose roughness is determined by personal feelings rather than by situational exigencies, are judged to be poor craftsmen.

The description and analysis are based on twelve months of field work with the police departments of two large cities west of the Mississippi. Eleven weeks of this time were spent in skid-row and skid-row-like districts. The observations were augmented by approximately one hundred interviews with police officers of all ranks. The formulations that will be proposed were discussed in these interviews. They were recognized by the respondents as elements of standard practice. The respondents' recognition was often accompanied by remarks indicating that they had never thought about things in this way and that they were not aware how standardized police work was.

❖ STRUCTURAL DEMAND CONDITIONS OF PEACE KEEPING ❖

There exist at least five types of relatively distinct circumstances that produce police activities that do not involve invoking the law and that are only in a trivial sense determined by those considerations of legality that determine law enforcement. This does not mean that these activities are illegal but merely that there is no legal directive that informs the acting policeman whether what he does must be done or how it is to be done. In these circumstances, policemen act as all-purpose and terminal remedial agents, and the confronted problem is solved in the field. If these practices stand under any kind of review at all, and typically they do not, it is only through internal police department control.

1. Although the executive branch of government generally refrains from exercising a controlling influence over the direction of police interest,

it manages to extract certain performances from it. Two important examples of this are the supervision of certain licensed services and premises and the regulation of traffic.[9] With respect to the first, the police tend to concentrate on what might be called the moral aspects of establishments rather than on questions relating to the technical adequacy of the service. This orientation is based on the assumption that certain types of businesses lend themselves to exploitation for undesirable and illegal purposes. Since this tendency cannot be fully controlled, it is only natural that the police will be inclined to favor licensees who are at least cooperative. This, however, transforms the task from the mere scrutiny of credentials and the passing of judgments, to the creation and maintenance of a network of connections that conveys influence, pressure, and information. The duty to inspect is the background of this network, but the resulting contacts . . . become, for patrolmen, a resource that must be continuously serviced by visits and exchanges of favors. While it is apparent that this condition lends itself to corrupt exploitation by individual officers, even the most flawlessly honest policeman must participate in this network of exchanges if he is to function adequately. Thus, engaging in such exchanges becomes an occupational task that demands attention and time.

Regulation of traffic is considerably less complex. More than anything else, traffic control symbolizes the autonomous authority of policemen. Their commands generally are met with unquestioned compliance. Even when they issue citations, which seemingly refer the case to the courts, it is common practice for the accused to view the allegation as a finding against him and to pay the fine. Police officials emphasize that it is more important to be circumspect than legalistic in traffic control. Officers are often reminded that a large segment of the public has no other contacts with the police, and that the field lends itself to public relations work by the line personnel.[10]

2. Policemen often do not arrest persons who have committed minor offenses in circumstances in which the arrest is technically possible. This practice has recently received considerable attention in legal and sociological literature. The studies were motivated by the realization that "police decisions not to invoke the criminal process determine the outer limits of law enforcement."[11] From these researches, it was learned that the police tend to impose more stringent criteria of law enforcement on certain segments of the community than on others.[12]

It was also learned that, from the perspective of the administration of justice, the decisions not to make arrests often are based on compelling reasons.[13] It is less well appreciated that policemen often not only refrain from invoking the law formally but also employ alternative sanctions. For example, it is standard practice that violators are warned not to repeat the offense. This often leads to patrolmen's "keeping an eye" on certain persons. Less frequent, though not unusual, is the practice of direct disciplining of offenders, especially when they are juveniles, which occasionally involves inducing them to repair the damage occasioned by their misconduct.[14]

The power to arrest and the freedom not to arrest can be used in cases that do not involve patent offenses. An officer can say to a person whose behavior he wishes to control, "I'll let you go this time!" without indicating to him that he could not have been arrested in any case. Nor is this always deliberate misrepresentation, for in many cases the law is sufficiently ambiguous to allow alternative interpretations. In short, not to make an arrest is rarely, if ever, merely a decision not to act; it is most often a decision to act alternatively. In the case of minor offenses, to make an arrest often is merely one of several possible proper actions.

3. There exists a public demand for police intervention in matters that contain no criminal and often no legal aspects.[15] For example, it is commonly assumed that officers will be available to arbitrate quarrels, to pacify the unruly, and to help in keeping order. They are supposed also to aid people in trouble, and there is scarcely a human predicament imaginable for which police aid has not been solicited and obtained at one time or another. Most authors writing about the police consider such activities only marginally related to the police mandate. This view fails to reckon with the fact that the availability of these performances is taken for granted and the police assign a substantial amount of their resources to such work. Although this work cannot be subsumed under the concept of legal action, it does involve the exercise of a form of authority that most people associate with the police. In fact, no matter how trivial the occasion, the device of "calling the cops" transforms any problem. It implies that a situation is, or is getting, out of hand. Police responses to public demands are always oriented to this implication, and the risk of proliferation of troubles makes every call a potentially serious matter.[16]

4. Certain mass phenomena of either a regular or a spontaneous nature require direct monitoring. Most important is the controlling of crowds in incipient stages of disorder. The specter of mob violence frequently calls for measures that involve coercion, including the use of physical force. Legal theory allows, of course, that public officials are empowered to use coercion in situations of imminent danger.[17]

Unfortunately, the doctrine is not sufficiently specific to be of much help as a rule of practice. It is based on the assumption of the adventitiousness of danger, and thus does not lend itself readily to elaborations that could direct the routines of early detection and prevention of untoward developments. It is interesting that the objective of preventing riots by informal means posed one of the central organizational problems for the police in England during the era of the Chartists.[18]

5. The police have certain special duties with respect to persons who are viewed as less than fully accountable for their actions. Examples of those eligible for special consideration are those who are under age[19] and those who are mentally ill.[20] Although it is virtually never acknowledged explicitly, those receiving special treatment include people who do not lead "normal" lives and who occupy a pariah status in society. This group includes residents of ethnic ghettos, certain types of bohemians and vagabonds, and persons of known criminal background. The special treatment of children and of sick persons is permissively sanctioned by the law, but the special treatment of others is, in principle, opposed by the leading theme of legality and the tenets of the democratic faith.[21] The important point is not that such persons are arrested more often than others, which is quite true, but that they are perceived by the police as producing a special problem that necessitates continuous attention and the use of special procedures.

The five types of demand conditions do not exclude the possibility of invoking the criminal process. Indeed, arrests do occur quite frequently in all these circumstances. But the concerns generated in these areas cause activities that usually do not terminate in an arrest. When arrests are made, there exist, at least in the ideal, certain criteria by reference to which the arrest can be judged as having been made more or less properly, and there are some persons who, in the natural course of events, actually judge the performance.[22] But for actions not resulting in arrest there are no such criteria and no such judges. How, then, can one speak of such actions as necessary and proper? Since there does not exist any official answer to this query, and since policemen act in the role of "peace officers" pretty much without external direction or constraint, the question comes down to asking how the policeman himself knows whether he has any business with a person he does not arrest, and if so, what that business might be. Furthermore, if there exists a domain of concerns and activities that is largely independent of the law enforcement mandate, it is reasonable to assume that it will exercise some degree of influence on how and to what ends the law is invoked in cases of arrests.

Skid-row presents one excellent opportunity to study these problems. The area contains a heavy concentration of persons who do not live "normal" lives in terms of prevailing standards of middle-class morality. Since the police respond to this situation by intensive patrolling, the structure of peace keeping should be readily observable. Needless to say, the findings and conclusions will not be necessarily generalizable to other types of demand conditions.

❖ THE PROBLEM OF KEEPING THE PEACE IN SKID-ROW ❖

Skid-row has always occupied a special place among the various forms of urban life. While other areas are perceived as being different in many ways, skid-row is seen as completely different. Though it is located in the heart of civilization, it is viewed as containing aspects of the primordial jungle, calling for missionary activities and offering opportunities for exotic adventure. While each inhabitant individually can be seen as tragically linked to the vicissitudes of "normal" life, allowing others to say "here but for the Grace of God go I," those who live there are believed to have repudiated the entire role-casting scheme of the majority and to live apart from normalcy. Accordingly, the traditional attitude of civic-mindedness toward skid-row has been dominated by the desire to contain it and to salvage souls from its clutches.[23] The specific task of containment has been left to the police. That this task pressed upon the police some rather special duties has never come under explicit consideration, either from the government that expects control or from the police departments that implement it. Instead, the prevailing method of carrying out the task is to assign patrolmen to the area on a fairly permanent basis and to allow them to work out their own ways of running things. External influence is confined largely to the supply of support and facilities, on the one hand, and to occasional expressions of criticism about the overall conditions, on the other. Within the limits of available resources and general expectations, patrolmen are supposed to know what to do and are free to do it.[24]

Patrolmen who are more or less permanently assigned to skid-row districts tend to develop a conception of the nature of their "domain" that is surprisingly uniform. Individual officers differ in many aspects of practice, emphasize different concerns, and maintain different contacts, but they are in fundamental agreement about the structure of skid-row life. This relatively uniform conception includes an implicit formulation of the problem of keeping the peace in skid-row.

In the view of experienced patrolmen, life on skid-row is fundamentally different from life in other parts of society. To be sure, they say, around its geographic limits the area tends to blend into the surrounding environment, and its population always encompasses some persons who are only transitionally associated with it. Basically, however, skid-row is perceived as the natural habitat of people who lack the capacities and commitments to live "normal" lives on a sustained basis. The presence of these people defines the nature of social reality in the area. In general, and especially in casual encounters, the presumption of incompetence and of the disinclination to be "normal" is the leading theme for the interpretation of all actions and relations. Not only do people approach one another in this manner, but presumably they also expect to be approached in this way, and they conduct themselves accordingly.

In practice, the restriction of interactional possibilities that is based on the patrolman's stereotyped conception of skid-row residents is always subject to revision and modification toward particular individuals. Thus, it is entirely possible, and not unusual, for patrolmen to view certain skid-row inhabitants in terms that involve non-skid-row aspects of normality. Instances of such approaches and relationships invariably involve personal acquaintance and the knowledge of a good deal of individually qualifying information. Such instances are seen, despite their relative frequency, as exceptions to the rule. The awareness of the possibility of breakdown, frustration, and betrayal is ever-present, basic wariness is never wholly dissipated, and undaunted trust can never be fully reconciled with presence on skid-row.

What patrolmen view as normal on skid-row—and what they also think is taken for granted as "life as usual" by the inhabitants—is not easily summarized. It seems to focus on the idea that the dominant consideration governing all enterprise and association is directed to the occasion of the moment. Nothing is thought of as having a background that might have led up to the present in terms of some compelling moral or practical necessity. There are some exceptions to this rule, of course: the police themselves, and those who run certain establishments, are perceived as engaged in important and necessary activities. But in order to carry them out they, too, must be geared to the overall atmosphere of fortuitousness. In this atmosphere, the range of control that persons have over one another is exceedingly narrow. Good faith, even where it is valued, is seen merely as a personal matter. Its violations are the victim's own hard luck, rather than demonstrable violations of property. There is only a private sense of irony at having been victimized. The overall air is not so much one of active distrust as it is one of irrelevance of trust; as patrolmen often emphasize, the situation does not necessarily cause all relations to be predatory, but the possibility of exploitation is not checked by the expectation that it will not happen.

Just as the past is seen by the policeman as having only the most attenuated relevance to the present, so the future implications of present situations are said to be generally devoid of prospective coherence. No venture, especially no joint venture, can be said to have a strongly predictable future in line with its initial objectives. It is a matter of adventitious circumstance whether or not matters go as anticipated. That which is not within the grasp of momentary control is outside of practical social reality.

Though patrolmen see the temporal framework of the occasion of the moment mainly as a lack of trustworthiness, they also recognize that it involves more than merely the personal motives of individuals. In addition to the fact that everybody *feels* that things matter only at the moment, irresponsibility takes an *objectified* form on skid-row. The places the residents occupy, the social relations they entertain, and the activities that engage them are not meaningfully connected over time. Thus, for example, address, occupation, marital status, etc., matter much less on skid-row than in any other part of society. The fact that present whereabouts, activities, and affiliations imply neither continuity nor direction means that life on skid-row lacks a socially structured background of accountability. Of course, everybody's life contains some sequential incongruities, but in the life of a skid-row inhabitant every moment is an accident. That a man has no "address" in the future that could be in some way inferred from where he is and what he does makes him a person of *radically reduced visibility*. If he disappears from sight and one wishes to locate him, it is virtually impossible to systematize the search. All one can know with relative certainty is that he will be somewhere on some skid-row and the only thing one can do is to trace the factual contiguities of his whereabouts.

It is commonly known that the police are expert in finding people and that they have developed an exquisite technology involving special facilities and procedures of sleuthing. It is less well appreciated that all this technology builds upon those socially structured features of everyday life that render persons findable in the first place.

Under ordinary conditions, the query as to where a person is can be addressed, from the outset, to a restricted realm of possibilities that can be further narrowed by looking into certain places and asking certain persons. The map of whereabouts that normally competent persons use whenever they wish to locate someone is constituted by the basic facts of membership in society. Insofar as membership consists of status incumbencies, each of which has an adumbrated future that substantially reduces unpredictability, it is itself a guarantee of the order within which it is quite difficult to get lost. Membership is thus visible not only now but also as its own projection into the future. It is in terms of this prospective availability that the skid-row inhabitant is a person of reduced visibility. His membership is viewed as extraordinary because its extension into the future is *not* reduced to a restricted realm of possibilities. Neither his subjective dispositions, nor his circumstances, indicate that he is oriented to any particular long-range interests. But, as he may claim every contingent opportunity, his claims are always seen as based on slight merit or right, at least to the extent that interfering with them does not constitute a substantial denial of his freedom.

This, then, constitutes the problem of keeping the peace on skid-row. Considerations of momentary expediency are seen as having unqualified priority as maxims of conduct; consequently, the controlling influences of the pursuit of sustained interests are presumed to be absent.

❖ THE PRACTICES OF KEEPING THE PEACE IN SKID-ROW ❖

From the perspective of society as a whole, skid-row inhabitants appear troublesome in a variety of ways. The uncommitted life attributed to them is perceived as inherently offensive; its very existence arouses indignation and contempt. More important, however, is the feeling that persons who have repudiated the entire role-status casting system of society, persons whose lives forever collapse into a succession of random moments, are seen as constituting a practical risk. As they have nothing to forsake, nothing is thought safe from them.[25]

The skid-row patrolman's concept of his mandate includes an awareness of this presumed risk. He is constantly attuned to the possibility of violence, and he is convinced that things to which the inhabitants have free access are as good as lost. But his concern is directed toward the continuous condition of peril *in the area* rather than *for society in general*. While he is obviously conscious of the presence of many persons who have committed crimes outside of skid-row and will arrest them when they come to his attention, this is a peripheral part of his routine activities. In general, the skid-row patrolman and his superiors take for granted that his main business is to keep the peace and enforce the laws *on skid-row*, and that he is involved only incidentally in protecting society at large. Thus, his task is formulated basically as the protection of putative predators from one another. The maintenance of peace and safety is difficult because everyday life on skid-row is viewed as an open field for reciprocal exploitation. . . . [Lacking] status incumbency, . . . self-interest does not produce order. Hence, mechanisms that control risk must work primarily from without.

External containment, to be effective, must be oriented to the realities of existence. Thus, the skid-row patrolman employs an approach that he views as appropriate to the *ad hoc* nature of skid-row life. The following are the three most prominent elements of this approach. First, the seasoned patrolman seeks to acquire a richly particularized knowledge of people and places in the area. Second, he gives the consideration of strict culpability a subordinate status among grounds for remedial sanction. Third, his use and choice of coercive interventions is determined mainly by exigencies of situations and with little regard for possible long range effects on individual persons.

The Particularization of Knowledge

The patrolman's orientation to people on skid-row is structured basically by the presupposition that if he does not know a man personally there is very little that he can assume about him. This rule determines his interaction with people who live on skid-row. Since the area also contains other types of persons, however, its applicability is not universal. To some such persons it does not apply at all, and it has a somewhat mitigated significance with certain others. For example, some persons encountered on skid-row can be recognized immediately as outsiders. Among them are workers who are employed in commercial and industrial enterprises that abut the area, persons who come for the purpose of adventurous "slumming," and some patrons of second-hand stores and pawn shops. Even with very little experience, it is relatively easy to identify these people by appearance, demeanor, and the time and place of their presence. The patrolman maintains an impersonal attitude toward them, and they are, under ordinary circumstances, not the objects of his attention.[26]

Clearly set off from these outsiders are the residents and the entire corps of personnel that services skid-row. It would be fair to say that one of the main routine activities of patrolmen is the establishment and maintenance of familiar relationships with individual members of these groups. Officers emphasize their interest in this, and they maintain that their grasp of and control over skid-row is precisely commensurate with the extent to which they "know the people." By this they do not mean having a quasi-theoretical understanding of human nature but rather the common practice of individualized and reciprocal recognition. As this group encompasses both those who render services on skid-row and those who are serviced, individualized interest is not always based on the desire to overcome uncertainty. Instead, relations with service personnel become absorbed into the network of particularized attention. Ties between patrolmen, on the one hand, and businessmen, managers, and workers, on the other hand, are often defined in terms of shared or similar interests. It bears mentioning that many persons live *and* work on skid-row. Thus, the distinction between those who service and those who are serviced is not a clearcut dichotomy but a spectrum of affiliations.

As a general rule, the skid-row patrolman possesses an immensely detailed factual knowledge of his beat. He knows, and knows a great deal about, a large number of residents. He is likely to know every person who manages or works in the local bars, hotels, shops, stores, and missions. Moreover, he probably knows every public and private place inside and out. Finally, he ordinarily remembers countless events of the past which he can recount by citing names, dates and places with remarkable precision. Though there are always some threads missing in the fabric of information, it is continuously woven and mended even as it is being used. New facts, however, are added to the texture, not in terms of structured categories but in terms of adjoining known realities. . . .

Individual patrolmen vary in the extent to which they make themselves available or actively pursue personal acquaintances. But even the most aloof are continuously greeted and engaged in conversations that indicate a background of individualistic associations. While this scarcely has the appearance of work, because of its casual character, patrolmen do not view it as an optional activity. In the course of making their rounds, patrolmen seem to have access to every place, and their entry causes no surprise or consternation. Instead, the entry tends to lead to informal exchanges of small talk. At times the rounds include entering hotels and gaining access to rooms or dormitories, often for no other purpose than asking the occupants how things are going. In all this, patrolmen address innumerable persons by name and are in turn addressed by name. The conversational style that characterizes these exchanges is casual to an extent that by non-skid-row standards might suggest intimacy. Not only does the officer himself avoid all terms of deference and respect but he does not seem to expect or demand them. For example, a patrolman said to a man radiating an alcoholic glow on the street, "You've got enough of a heat on now; I'll give you ten minutes to get your ass off the street!" Without stopping, the man answered, "Oh, why don't you go and piss in your own pot!" The officer's only response was, "All right, in ten minutes you're either in bed or on your way to the can."

This kind of expressive freedom is an intricately limited privilege. Persons of acquaintance are entitled to it and appear to exercise it mainly in routinized encounters. But strangers, too, can use it with impunity. The safe way of gaining the privilege is to respond to the patrolman in ways that do not challenge his right to ask questions and issue commands. Once the concession is made that the officer is entitled to inquire into a man's background, business, and intentions, and that he is entitled to obedience, there opens a field of colloquial license. A patrolman seems to grant expressive freedom in recognition of a person's acceptance of his access to areas of life ordinarily defined as private and subject to coercive control only under special circumstances. While patrolmen accept and seemingly even cultivate the rough *quid pro quo* of informality, and while they do not expect sincerity, candor, or obedience in their dealings with the inhabitants, they do not allow the rejection of their approach.

The explicit refusal to answer questions of a personal nature and the demand to know why the questions are asked significantly enhances a person's chances of being arrested on some minor charge. While most patrolmen tend to be personally indignant about this kind of response and use the arrest to compose their own hurt feelings, this is merely a case of affect being in line with the method. There are other officers who proceed in the same manner without taking offense, or even with feelings of regret. Such patrolmen often maintain that their colleagues' affective involvement is a corruption of an essentially valid technique. The technique is oriented to the goal of maintaining operational control. The patrolman's conception of this goal places him hierarchically above whomever he approaches, and makes him the sole judge of the propriety of the occasion. As he alone is oriented to this goal, and as he seeks to attain it by means of individualized access to persons, those who frustrate him are seen as motivated at best by the desire to "give him a hard time" and at worst by some darkly devious purpose.

Officers are quite aware that the directness of their approach and the demands they make are difficult to reconcile with the doctrines of civil liberties, but they maintain that they are in accord with the general freedom of access that persons living on skid-row normally grant one another. That is, they believe that the imposition of personalized and far-reaching control is in tune with standard expectancies. In terms of these expectancies, people are not so much denied the right to privacy as they are seen as not having any privacy. Thus, officers seek to install themselves in the center of people's lives and let the consciousness of their presence play the part of conscience.

When talking about the practical necessity of an aggressively personal approach, officers do not refer merely to the need for maintaining control. . . . They also see it as the basis for the supply of certain valued services to inhabitants of skid-row. The coerced or conceded access to persons often imposes on the patrolman tasks that are, in the main, in line with these persons' expressed or implied interest. In asserting this connection, patrolmen note that they frequently help people to obtain meals, lodging, employment, that they direct them to welfare and health services, and that they aid them in various other ways. Though patrolmen tend to describe such services mainly as the product of their own altruism, they also say that their colleagues who avoid them are simply doing a poor job of patrolling. The acceptance of the need to help people is based on the realization that the hungry, the sick, and the troubled are a potential source of problems. Moreover, that patrolmen will help people is part of the background expectancies of life on skid-row. Hotel clerks normally call policemen when someone gets so sick as to need attention; merchants expect to be taxed, in a manner of speaking, to meet the pressing needs of certain persons; and the inhabitants do not hesitate to accept, solicit, and demand every kind of aid. The domain of the patrolman's service activity is virtually limitless, and it is no exaggeration to say that the solution of every conceivable problem has at one time or another been attempted by a police officer. In one observed instance, a patrolman unceremoniously entered the room of a man he had never seen before. The man, who gave no indication that he regarded the officer's entry and questions as anything but part of life as usual, related a story of having had his dentures stolen by his wife. In the course of the subsequent rounds, the patrolman sought to locate the woman and the dentures. This did not become the evening's project but was attended to while doing other things. In the densely matted activities of the patrolman, the questioning became one more strand. . . . In all this, the officer followed the precept formulated by a somewhat more articulate patrolman: "If I want to be in control of my work and keep the street relatively peaceful, I have to know the people. To know them I must gain their trust, which means that I have to be involved in their lives. But I can't be soft like a social worker because unlike him I cannot call the cops when things go wrong. I am the cops!"[27]

The Restricted Relevance of Culpability

It is well known that policemen exercise discretionary freedom in invoking the law. It is also conceded that, in some measure, the practice is unavoidable. This being so, the outstanding problem is whether or not the decisions are in line with the intent of the law. On skid-row, patrolmen often make decisions based on reasons that the law probably does not recognize as valid. The problem can best be introduced by citing an example.

A man in a relatively mild state of intoxication (by skid-row standards) approached a patrolman to tell him that he had a room in a hotel, to which the officer responded by urging him to go to bed instead of getting drunk. As the man walked off, the officer related the following thoughts: Here is a completely lost soul. Though he probably is no more than thirty-five years old, he looks to be in his fifties. He never works and he hardly ever has a place to stay. He has been on the street for several years and is known as "Dakota." During the past few days, "Dakota" has been seen in the company of "Big Jim." The latter is an invalid living on some sort of pension with which he pays for a room in the hotel to which "Dakota" referred and for four weekly meal tickets in one of the restaurants on the street. Whatever is left he spends on wine and beer. Occasionally, "Big Jim" goes on drinking sprees in the company of someone like "Dakota." Leaving aside the consideration that there is probably a homosexual background to the association, and that it is not right that "Big Jim" should have to support the drinking habit of someone else, there is the more important risk that if "Dakota" moves in with "Big Jim" he will very likely walk off with whatever the latter keeps in his room. "Big Jim" would never dream of reporting the theft; he would just beat the hell out of "Dakota" after he sobered up. When asked what could be done to prevent the theft and the subsequent recriminations, the patrolman proposed that in this particular case he would throw "Big Jim" into jail if he found him tonight and then tell the hotel clerk to throw "Dakota" out of the room. When asked why he did not arrest "Dakota," who was, after all, drunk enough to warrant an arrest, the officer explained that this would not solve anything. While "Dakota" was in jail "Big Jim" would continue drinking and would either strike up another liaison or embrace his old buddy after he had been released. The only thing to do was to get "Big Jim" to sober up, and the only sure way of doing this was to arrest him.

As it turned out, "Big Jim" was not located that evening. But had he been located and arrested on a drunk charge, the fact that he was intoxicated would not have been the real reason for proceeding against him, but merely the pretext. The point of the example is not that it illustrates the tendency of skid-row patrolmen to arrest persons who would not be arrested under conditions of full respect for their legal rights. To be sure, this too happens. In the majority of minor arrest cases, however, the criteria the law specifies are met. But it is the rare exception that the law is invoked merely because the specifications of the law are met. That is, compliance with the law is merely the outward appearance of an intervention that is actually based on altogether different considerations. Thus, it could be said that patrolmen do not really enforce the law, even when they do invoke it, but merely use it as a resource to solve certain pressing practical problems in keeping the peace. This observation goes beyond the conclusion that many of the lesser norms of the criminal law are treated as defeasible in police work. It is patently not the case that skid-row patrolmen apply the legal norms while recognizing many exceptions to their applicability. Instead, the observation leads to the conclusion that in keeping the peace on skid-row, patrolmen encounter certain matters they attend to by means of coercive action, e.g., arrests. In doing this, they invoke legal norms that are available, and with some regard for substantive appropriateness. Hence, the problem patrolmen confront is not which drunks, beggars, or disturbers of the peace should be arrested and which can be let go as exceptions to the rule. Rather, the problem is whether, when someone "needs" to be arrested, he should be charged with drunkenness, begging, or disturbing the peace. Speculating further, one is almost compelled to infer that virtually any set of norms could be used in this manner, provided that they sanction relatively common forms of behavior.

The reduced relevance of culpability in peace keeping practice on skid-row is not readily visible. As mentioned, most arrested persons were actually found in the act, or in the state, alleged in the arrest record. It becomes partly visible when one views the treatment of persons who are not arrested even though all the legal grounds for an arrest are present. Whenever such persons are encountered and can be induced to leave, or taken to some shelter, or remanded to someone's care, then patrolmen feel, or at least maintain, that an arrest would serve no useful purpose. That is, whenever there exist means for controlling the troublesome aspects of some person's presence in some way alternative to an arrest, such means are preferentially employed, provided, of course, that the case at hand involves only a minor offense.[28]

The attenuation of the relevance of culpability is most visible when the presence of legal grounds for an arrest could be questioned, i.e., in cases that sometimes are euphemistically called "preventive arrests." In one observed instance, a man who attempted to trade a pocket knife came to the attention of a patrolman. The initial encounter was attended by a good deal of levity and the man willingly responded to the officer's inquiries about his identity and business. The man laughingly acknowledged that he needed some money to get drunk. In the course of the exchange it came to light that he had just arrived in town, traveling in his automobile. When confronted with the demand to lead the officer to the car, the man's expression became serious and he pointedly stated that he would not comply because this was none of the officer's business. After a bit more prodding, which the patrolman initially kept in the light mood, the man was arrested on a charge involving begging. In subsequent conversation the patrolman acknowledged that the charge was only speciously appropriate and mainly a pretext. Having committed himself to demanding information he could not accept defeat. When this incident was discussed with another patrolman, the second officer found fault not with the fact that the arrest was made on a pretext but with the first officer's own contribution to the creation of conditions that made it unavoidable. "You see," he continued, "there is always the risk that the man is testing you and you must let him know what is what. The best among us can usually keep the upper hand in such situations without making arrests. But when it comes down to the wire, then you can't let them get away with it."

Finally, it must be mentioned that the reduction of the significance of culpability is built into the normal order of skid-row life, as patrolmen see it. Officers almost unfailingly say, pointing to some particular person, "I know that he knows that I know that some of the things he 'owns' are stolen, and that nothing can be done about it." In saying this, they often claim to have knowledge of such a degree of certainty as would normally be sufficient for virtually any kind of action except legal proceedings. Against this background, patrolmen adopt the view that the law is not merely imperfect and difficult to implement, but that on skid-row, at least, the association between delict and sanction is distinctly occasional. Thus, to implement the law naively, i.e., to arrest someone *merely* because he committed some minor offense, is perceived as containing elements of injustice.

Moreover, patrolmen often deal with situations in which questions of culpability are profoundly ambiguous. For example, an officer was called to help in settling a violent dispute in a hotel room. The object of the quarrel was a supposedly stolen pair of trousers. As the story unfolded in the conflicting versions of the participants, it was not possible to decide who was the complainant and who was alleged to be the thief, nor did it come to light who occupied the room in which the fracas took place, or whether the trousers were taken from the room or to the room. Though the officer did ask some questions, it seemed, and was confirmed in later conversation, that he was there not to solve the puzzle of the missing trousers but to keep the situation from getting out of hand. In the end, the exhausted participants dispersed, and this was the conclusion of the case. The patrolman maintained that no one could unravel mysteries of this sort because "these people take things from each other so often that no one could tell what 'belongs' to whom." In fact, he suggested, the terms owning, stealing, and swindling, in their strict sense, do not really belong on skid-row, and all efforts to distribute guilt and innocence according to some rational formula of justice are doomed to failure.

It could be said that the term "curb-stone justice" that is sometimes applied to the procedures of patrolmen in skid-rows contains a double irony.

Not only is the procedure not legally authorized, which is the intended irony in the expression, but it does not even pretend to distribute deserts. The best among the patrolmen, according to their own standards, use the law to keep skid-row inhabitants from sinking deeper into the misery they already experience. The worst, in terms of these same standards, exploit the practice for personal aggrandizement or gain. Leaving motives aside, however, it is easy to see that if culpability is not the salient consideration leading to an arrest in cases where it is patently obvious, then the practical patrolman may not view it as being wholly out of line to make arrests lacking in formal legal justification. Conversely, he will come to view minor offense arrests made solely because legal standards are met as poor craftsmanship.

The Background of Ad Hoc Decision Making

When skid-row patrolmen are pressed to explain their reasons for minor offense arrests, they most often mention that it is done for the protection of the arrested person. This, they maintain, is the case in virtually all drunk arrests, in the majority of arrests involving begging and other nuisance offenses, and in many cases involving acts of violence. When they are asked to explain further such arrests as the one cited earlier involving the man attempting to sell the pocket knife, who was certainly not arrested for his own protection, they cite the consideration that belligerent persons constitute a much greater menace on skid-row than any place else in the city. The reasons for this are twofold. First, many of the inhabitants are old, feeble, and not too smart, all of which makes them relatively defenseless. Second, many of the inhabitants are involved in illegal activities and are known as persons of bad character, which does not make them credible victims or witnesses. Potential predators realize that the resources society has mobilized to minimize the risk of criminal victimization do not protect the predator himself. Thus, reciprocal exploitation constitutes a preferred risk. The high vulnerability of everybody on skid-row is public knowledge and causes every seemingly aggressive act to be seen as a potentially grave risk.

When, in response to all this, patrolmen are confronted with the observation that any minor offense arrests they make do not seem to involve a careful evaluation of facts before acting, they give the following explanations: First, the two reasons of protection and prevention represent a global background, and in individual cases it may sometimes not be possible to produce adequate justification on these grounds. Nor is it thought to be a problem of great moment to estimate precisely whether someone is more likely to come to grief or to cause grief when the objective is to prevent the proliferation of troubles. Second, patrolmen maintain that some of the seemingly spur-of-the-moment decisions are actually made against a background of knowledge of facts that are not readily apparent in the situations. Since experience not only contains this information but also causes it to come to mind, patrolmen claim to have developed a special sensitivity for qualities of appearances that allow an intuitive grasp of probable tendencies. In this context, little things are said to have high informational value and lead to conclusions without the intervention of explicitly reasoned chains of inferences. Third, patrolmen readily admit that they do not adhere to high standards of adequacy of justification. They do not seek to defend the adequacy of their method against some abstract criteria of merit. Instead, when questioned, they assess their methods against the background of a whole system of *ad hoc* decision making, a system that encompasses the courts, correction facilities, the welfare establishment, and medical services. In fact, policemen generally maintain that their own procedures not only measure up to the workings of this system but exceed them in the attitude of carefulness.

In addition to these recognized reasons, there are two additional background factors that play a significant part in decisions to employ coercion. One has to do with the relevance of situational factors, and the other with the evaluation of coercion as relatively insignificant in the lives of the inhabitants.

There is no doubt that the nature of the circumstances often has decisive influence on what will be done. For example, the same patrolman who arrested the man trying to sell his pocket knife was observed dealing with a young couple. Though the officer was clearly angered by what he perceived as insolence and threatened the man with arrest, he merely ordered him and his companion to leave the street. He saw them walking away in a deliberately slow manner and when he noticed them a while later, still standing only a short distance away from the place of encounter, he did not respond to their presence. The difference between the two cases was that in the first there was a crowd of amused bystanders, while the latter case was not witnessed by anyone. In another instance, the patrolman was directed to a hotel and found a father and son fighting about money. The father occupied a room in the hotel and the son occasionally shared his quarters. There were two other men present, and they made it clear that their sympathies were with the older man. The son was whisked off to jail without much study of the relative merits of the conflicting claims. In yet another case, a middle-aged woman was forcefully evacuated from a bar even after the bartender explained that her loud behavior was merely a response to goading by some foul-mouth youth.

In all such circumstances, coercive control is exercised as a means of coming to grips with situational exigencies. Force is used against particular persons but is incidental to the task. An ideal of "economy of intervention" dictates in these and similar cases that the person whose presence is most likely to perpetuate the troublesome development be removed. Moreover, the decision as to who is to be removed is arrived at very quickly. Officers feel considerable pressure to act unhesitatingly, and many give accounts of situations that got out of hand because of desires to handle cases with careful consideration. However, even when there is no apparent risk of rapid proliferation of trouble, the tactic of removing one or two persons is used to control an undesirable situation. Thus, when a patrolman ran into a group of four men sharing a bottle of wine in an alley, he emptied the remaining contents of the bottle into the gutter, arrested one man—who was no more and no less drunk than the others—and let the others disperse in various directions.

The exigential nature of control is also evident in the handling of isolated drunks. Men are arrested because of where they happen to be encountered. In this, it matters not only whether a man is found in a conspicuous place or not, but also how far away he is from his domicile. The further away he is, the less likely it is that he will make it to his room, and the more likely the arrest. Sometimes drunk arrests are made mainly because the police van is available. In one case a patrolman summoned the van to pick up an arrested man. As the van was pulling away from the curb the officer stopped the driver because he sighted another drunk stumbling across the street. The second man protested saying that he "wasn't even half drunk yet." The patrolman's response was "OK, I'll owe you half a drunk." In sum, the basic routine of keeping the peace on skid-row involves a process of matching the resources of control with situational exigencies. The overall objective is to reduce the total amount of risk in the area. In this, practicality plays a considerably more important role than legal norms. Precisely because patrolmen see legal reasons for coercive action much more widely distributed on skid-row than could ever be matched by interventions, they intervene not in the interest of law enforcement but in the interest of producing relative tranquility and order on the street.

Taking the perspective of the victim of coercive measures, one could ask why he, in particular, has to bear the cost of keeping the aggregate of troubles down while others, who are equally or perhaps even more implicated, go scot-free. Patrolmen maintain that the *ad hoc* selection of persons for attention must be viewed in the light of the following consideration: Arresting a person on skid-row on some minor charge may save him and others a lot of trouble, but it does not work any real hardships on the arrested person. It is difficult to overestimate the skid-row patrolman's feeling of certainty that his coercive and disciplinary actions toward the inhabitants have but the most passing significance in their lives. Sending a man to jail on some charge that will hold him for a couple of days is seen as a matter of such slight importance to the affected person that it could hardly give rise to scruples. Thus, every indication that a coercive measure should be taken is accompanied by the realization "I might as well, for all it matters to him." Certain realities of life on skid-row furnish the context for this belief in the attenuated relevance of coercion in the lives of the inhabitants. Foremost among them is that the use of police authority is seen as totally unremarkable by everybody on skid-row. Persons who live or work there are continuously exposed to it and take its existence for granted. Shopkeepers, hotel clerks, and bartenders call patrolmen to rid themselves of unwanted and troublesome patrons. Residents expect patrolmen to arbitrate their quarrels authoritatively. Men who receive orders, whether they obey them or not, treat them as part of life as usual. Moreover, patrolmen find that disciplinary and coercive actions apparently do not affect their friendly relations with the persons against whom these actions are taken. Those who greet and chat with them are the very same men who have been disciplined, arrested, and ordered around in the past, and who expect to be thus treated again in the future. From all this, officers gather that though the people on skid-row seek to evade police authority, they do not really object to it. Indeed, it happens quite frequently that officers encounter men who welcome being arrested and even actively ask for it. Finally, officers point out that sending someone to jail from skid-row does not upset his relatives or his family life, does not cause him to miss work or lose a job, does not lead to his being reproached by friends and associates, does not lead to failure to meet commitments or protect investments, and does not conflict with any but the most passing intentions of the arrested person. Seasoned patrolmen are not oblivious to the irony of the fact that measures intended as mechanisms for distributing deserts can be used freely because these measures are relatively impotent in their effects.

❖ SUMMARY AND CONCLUSIONS ❖

It was the purpose of this article to render an account of a domain of police practice that does not seem subject to any system of external control. Following the terminology suggested by Michael Banton, this practice was called keeping the peace. The procedures employed in keeping the peace are not determined by legal mandates but are, instead, responses to certain demand conditions. From among several demand conditions, we concentrated on the one produced by the concentration of certain types of persons in districts known as skid-row. Patrolmen maintain that the lives of the inhabitants of the area are lacking in prospective coherence. The consequent reduction in the temporal horizon of predictability constitutes the main problem of keeping the peace on skid-row.

Peace keeping procedure on skid-row consists of three elements. Patrolmen seek to acquire a rich body of concrete knowledge about people by cultivating personal acquaintance with as many residents as possible. They tend to proceed against persons mainly on the basis of perceived risk, rather than on the basis of culpability. And they are more interested in reducing the aggregate total of troubles in the area than in evaluating individual cases according to merit.

There may seem to be a discrepancy between the skid-row patrolman's objective of preventing disorder and his efforts to maintain personal acquaintance with as many persons as possible. But these efforts are principally a tactical device. By knowing someone individually the patrolman reduces ambiguity, extends trust and favors, but does not grant immunity. The informality of interaction on skid-row always contains some indications of the hierarchical superiority of the patrolman and the reality of his potential power lurks in the background of every encounter.

Though our interest was focused initially on those police procedures that did not involve invoking the law, we found that the two cannot be separated. The reason for the connection is not given in the circumstance that the roles of the ''law officer'' and of the ''peace officer'' are enacted by the same person and thus are contiguous. According to our observations, patrolmen do not act alternatively as one or the other, with certain actions being determined by the intended objective of keeping the peace and others being determined by the duty to enforce the law. Instead, we have found that *peace keeping occasionally acquires the external aspects of law enforcement.* This makes it specious to inquire whether or not police discretion in invoking the law conforms with the intention of some specific legal formula. The real reason behind an arrest is virtually always the actual state of particular social situations, or of the skid-row area in general.

We have concentrated on those procedures and considerations that skid-row patrolmen regard as necessary, proper, and efficient relative to the circumstances in which they are employed. In this way, we attempted to disclose the conception of the mandate to which the police feel summoned. It was entirely outside the scope of the presentation to review the merits of this conception and of the methods used to meet it. Only insofar as patrolmen themselves recognized instances and patterns of malpractice did we take note of them. Most of the criticism voiced by officers had to do with the use of undue harshness and with the indiscriminate use of arrest powers when these were based on personal feelings rather than the requirements of the situation. According to prevailing opinion, patrolmen guilty of such abuses make life unnecessarily difficult for themselves and for their co-workers. Despite disapproval of harshness, officers tend to be defensive about it. For example, one sergeant who was outspokenly critical of brutality, said that though in general brutal men create more problems than they solve, "they do a good job in some situations for which the better men have no stomach." Moreover, supervisory personnel exhibit a strong reluctance to direct their subordinates in the particulars of their work performance. According to our observations, control is exercised mainly through consultation with superiors, and directives take the form of requests rather than orders. In the background of all this is the belief that patrol work on skid-row requires a great deal of discretionary freedom. In the words of the same sergeant quoted above, "a good man has things worked out in his own ways on his beat and he doesn't need anybody to tell him what to do."

The virtual absence of disciplinary control and the demand for discretionary freedom are related to the idea that patrol work involves "playing by ear." For if it is true that peace keeping cannot be systematically generalized, then, of course, it cannot be organizationally constrained. What the seasoned patrolman means, however, in saying that he "plays by ear" is that he is making his decisions while being attuned to the realities of complex situations about which he has immensely detailed knowledge. This studied aspect of peace keeping generally is not made explicit, nor is the tyro or the outsider made aware of it. Quite to the contrary, the ability to discharge the duties associated with keeping the peace is viewed as a reflection of an innate talent of "getting along with people." Thus, the same demands are made of barely initiated officers as are made of experienced practitioners. Correspondingly, beginners tend to think that they can do as well as their more knowledgeable peers. As this leads to inevitable frustrations, they find themselves in a situation that is conducive to the development of a particular sense of "touchiness." Personal dispositions of individual officers are, of course, of great relevance. But the license of discretionary freedom and the expectation of success under conditions of autonomy, without any indication that the work of the successful craftsman is based on an acquired preparedness for the task, is ready-made for failure and malpractice. Moreover, it leads to slipshod practices of patrol that also infect the standards of the careful craftsman.

The uniformed patrol, and especially the foot patrol, has a low preferential value in the division of labor of police work. This is, in part, at least, due to the belief that "anyone could do it." In fact, this belief is thoroughly mistaken. At present, however, the recognition that the practice requires preparation, and the process of obtaining the preparation itself, is left entirely to the practitioner.

Notes

1 The bill for a Metropolitan Police was actually enacted under the sponsorship of Robert Peel, the Home Secretary in the Tory Government of the Duke of Wellington. There is, however, no doubt that it was one of the several reform tendencies that Peel assimilated into Tory politics in his long career. Cf. J. L. Lyman, "The Metropolitan Police Act of 1829," *Journal of Criminal Law, Criminology and Police Science*, 55 (1964), 141–154.

2 Jerome Hall, "Police and Law in a Democratic Society," *Indiana Law Journal*, 28 (1953), 133–177. Though other authors are less emphatic on this point, judicial control is generally taken for granted. The point has been made, however, that in modern times judicial control over the police has been asserted mainly because of the default of any other general controlling authority, cf. E. L. Barrett, Jr., "Police Practice and the Law," *California Law Review*, 50 (1962), 11–55.

3 A. C. German, F. D. Day and R. R. J. Gallati, *Introduction to Law Enforcement* (Springfield, IL: C. C. Thomas, 1966); "One concept, in particular, should be kept in mind. A dictatorship can never exist unless the police system of the country is under the absolute control of the dictator. There is no other way to uphold a dictatorship except by terror, and the instrument of this total terror is the secret police, whatever its name. In every country where freedom has been lost, law enforcement has been a dominant instrument in destroying it" (p. 80).

4 The point is frequently made; cf. Raymond B. Fosdick, *American Police Systems* (New York: Century Company, 1920); Bruce Smith, *Police Systems in the United States*, 2nd rev. ed. (New York: Harper, 1960).

5 The executive margin of control is set mainly in terms of budgetary determinations and the mapping of some formal aspects of the organization of departments.

6 Michael Banton, *The Policeman in the Community* (New York: Basic Books, 1964), 6–7 and 127 ff.

7 R. Bruce Holmgren, *Primary Police Functions* (New York: William C. Copp, 1962).

8 Cf. Lyman, *op. cit.*, p. 153; F. C. Mather, *Public Order in the Age of the Chartists* (Manchester: Manchester University Press, 1959), chapter IV. See also Robert H. Bremer, "Police, Penal and Parole Policies in Cleveland and Toledo," *American Journal of Economics and Sociology*, 14 (1955), 387–398, for similar recognition in the United States at about the turn of this century.

9 Smith, *op. cit.*, pp. 15 ff.

10 Orlando W. Wilson, "Police Authority in a Free Society," *Journal of Criminal Law, Criminology and Police Science*, 54 (1964), 175–177.

11 Joseph Goldstein, "Police Discretion Not to Invoke the Criminal Process," *Yale Law Journal*, 69 (1960), 543.

12 Jerome Skolnick, *Justice without Trial* (New York: Wiley, 1966).

[13] Wayne LaFave, "The Police and Nonenforcement of the Law," *Wisconsin Law Review* (1962), 104–137 and 179–239.

[14] Nathan Goldman, *The Differential Selection of Juvenile Offenders for Court Appearance*, National Research and Information Center, National Council on Crime and Delinquency (1963), 114 ff.

[15] Elaine Cumming, Ian Cumming and Laura Edell, "Policeman as Philosopher, Guide and Friend," *Social Problems*, 12 (1965), 276–286.

[16] There is little doubt that many requests for service are turned down by the police, especially when they are made over the telephone or by mail, cf. LaFave, *op. cit.*, p. 212, n. 124. The uniformed patrolman, however, finds it virtually impossible to leave the scene without becoming involved in some way or another.

[17] Hans Kelsen, *General Theory of Law and State* (New York: Russell & Russell, 1961), 278–279; H. L. A. Hart, *The Concept of Law* (Oxford: Clarendon Press, 1961), 20–21.

[18] Mather, *op. cit.*; see also, Jenifer Hart, "Reform of the Borough Police, 1835–1856," *English History Review*, 70 (1955), 411–427.

[19] Francis A. Allen, *The Borderland of Criminal Justice* (Chicago: University of Chicago Press, 1964).

[20] Egon Bittner, "Police Discretion in Emergency Apprehension of Mentally Ill Persons," *Social Problems*, 14 (1967), 278–292.

[21] It bears mentioning, however, that differential treatment is not unique with the police, but is also in many ways representative for the administration of justice in general; cf. J. E. Carlin, Jan Howard and S. L. Messinger, "Civil Justice and the Poor," *Law and Society*, 1 (1966), 9–89; Jacobus tenBroek (ed.) *The Law of the Poor* (San Francisco: Chandler Publishing Co., 1966).

[22] This is, however, true only in the ideal. It is well known that a substantial number of persons who are arrested are subsequently released without ever being charged and tried, cf. Barrett, *op. cit.*

[23] The literature on skid-row is voluminous. The classic in the field is Nels Anderson, *The Hobo* (Chicago: University of Chicago Press, 1923). Samuel E. Wallace, *Skid-Row as a Way of Life* (Totowa, New Jersey: The Bedminster Press, 1965), is a more recent descriptive account and contains a useful bibliography. Donald A. Bogue, *Skid-Row in American Cities* (Chicago: Community and Family Center, University of Chicago, 1963), contains an exhaustive quantitative survey of Chicago skid-row.

[24] One of the two cities described in this paper also employed the procedure of the "round-up" of drunks. In this, the police van toured the skid-row area twice daily, during the mid-afternoon and early evening hours, and the officers who manned it picked up drunks they sighted. A similar procedure is used in New York's Bowery and the officers who do it are called "condition men." Cf. *Bowery Project*, Bureau of Applied Social Research, Columbia University, Summary Report of a Study Undertaken under Contract Approved by the Board of Estimates, 1963, mimeo., p. 11.

[25] An illuminating parallel to the perception of skid-row can be found in the more traditional concept of vagabondage. Cf. Alexandre Vexliard, *Introduction à la Sociologie du Vagabondage* (Paris: Libraire Marcel Rivière, 1956), and "La Disparition du Vagabondage comme Fleau Social Universel," *Revue de L'Institut de Sociologie* (1963), 53–79. The classic account of English conditions up to the 19th century is C. J. Ribton-Turner, *A History of Vagrants and Vagrancy and Beggars and Begging* (London: Chapman and Hall, 1887).

26 Several patrolmen complained about the influx of "tourists" into skid-row. Since such "tourists" are perceived as seeking illicit adventure, they receive little sympathy from patrolmen when they complain about being victimized.

27 The same officer commented further, "If a man looks for something, I might help him. But I don't stay with him till he finds what he is looking for. If I did, I would never get to do anything else. In the last analysis, I really never solve any problems. The best I can hope for is to keep things from getting worse."

28 When evidence is present to indicate that a serious crime has been committed, considerations of culpability acquire a position of priority. Two such arrests were observed, both involving checkpassers. The first offender was caught *in flagrante delicto*. In the second instance, the suspect attracted the attention of the patrolman because of his sickly appearance. In the ensuing conversation the man made some remarks that led the officer to place a call with the Warrant Division of his department. According to the information that was obtained by checking records, the man was a wanted checkpasser and was immediately arrested.

17

Violence and the Police

William A. Westley

Brutality and the third degree have been identified with the municipal police of the United States since their inauguration in 1844. These aspects of police activity have been subject to exaggeration, repeated exposure, and virulent criticism. Since they are a breach of the law by the law-enforcement agents, they constitute a serious social, but intriguing sociological, problem. Yet there is little information about or understanding of the process through which such activity arises or of the purposes which it serves.

This article is concerned with the genesis and function of the illegal use of violence by the police and presents an explanation based on an interpretative understanding of the experience of the police as an occupational group.[1] It shows that (a) the police accept and morally justify their illegal use of violence; (b) such acceptance and justification arise through their occupational experience; and (c) its use is functionally related to the collective occupational, as well as to the legal, ends of the police.

The analysis which follows offers both an occupational perspective on the use of violence by the police and an explanation of policing as an occupation, from the perspective of the illegal use of violence. Thus the meaning of this use of violence is derived by relating it to the general behavior of policemen as policemen, and occupations in general are illuminated through the delineation of the manner in which a particular occupation handles one aspect of its work.

American Journal of Sociology, 59 (July 1953): 34–41. Reprinted with permission. Footnotes renumbered.

The technical demands of a man's work tend to specify the kinds of social relationships in which he will be involved and to select the groups with whom these relationships are to be maintained. The social definition of the occupation invests its members with a common prestige position. Thus, a man's occupation is a major determining factor of his conduct and social identity. This being so, it involves more than man's work, and one must go beyond the technical in the explanation of work behavior. One must discover the occupationally derived definitions of self and conduct which arise in the involvements of technical demands, social relationships between colleagues and with the public, status, and self-conception. To understand these definitions, one must track them back to the occupational problems in which they have their genesis.[2]

The policeman finds his most pressing problems in his relationships to the public. His is a service occupation but of an incongruous kind, since he must discipline those whom he serves. He is regarded as corrupt and inefficient by, and meets with hostility and criticism from, the public. He regards the public as his enemy, feels his occupation to be in conflict with the community, and regards himself to be a pariah. The experience and the feeling give rise to a collective emphasis on secrecy, an attempt to coerce respect from the public, and a belief that almost any means are legitimate in completing an important arrest. These are for the policeman basic occupational values. They arise from his experience, take precedence over his legal responsibilities, are central to an understanding of his conduct, and form the occupational contexts within which violence gains its meaning. This then is the background for our analysis.[3]

The materials which follow are drawn from a case study of a municipal police department in an industrial city of approximately one hundred and fifty thousand inhabitants. This study included participation in all types of police activities, ranging from walking the beat and cruising with policemen in a squad car to the observation of raids, interrogations, and the police school. It included intensive interviews with over half the men in the department who were representative as to rank, time in service, race, religion, and specific type of police job.

❖ DUTY AND VIOLENCE ❖

In the United States the use of violence by the police is both an occupational prerogative and a necessity. Police powers include the use of violence, for to them, within civil society, has been delegated the monopoly of the legitimate means of violence possessed by the state. Police are obliged by their duties to use violence as the only measure adequate to control and apprehension in the presence of counter-violence.

Violence in the form of the club and the gun is for the police a means of persuasion. Violence from the criminal, the drunk, the quarreling family, and the rioter arises in the course of police duty. The fighting drunk who is damaging property or assailing his fellows and who looks upon the policeman as a malicious intruder justifies for the policeman his use of force in restoring order. The armed criminal who has demonstrated a casual regard for the lives of others and a general hatred of the policeman forces the use of violence by the police in the pursuit of duty. Every policeman has some such experiences, and they proliferate in police lore. They constitute a commonsense and legal justification for the use of violence by the police and for training policemen in the skills of violence. Thus from experience in the pursuit of their legally prescribed duties, the police develop a justification for the use of violence. They come to see it as good, asuseful, and as their own. Furthermore, although legally their use of violence is limited to the requirements of the arrest and the protection of themselves and the community, the contingencies of their occupation lead them to enlarge the area in which violence may be used. Two kinds of experience—that with respect to the conviction of the felon and that with respect to the control of sexual conduct—will illustrate how and why the illegal use of violence arises.

1. **The Conviction of the Felon**. The apprehension and conviction of the felon is, for the policeman, the essence of police work. It is the source of prestige both within and outside police circles, it has career implications, and it is a major source of justification for the existence of the police before a critical and often hostile public. Out of these conditions a legitimation for the illegal use of violence is wrought.

The career and prestige implication of the "good pinch"[4] elevate it to a major end in the conduct of the policeman. It is an end which is justified both legally and through public opinion as one which should be of great concern to the police. Therefore it takes precedence over other duties and tends to justify strong means. Both trickery and violence are such means. The "third degree" has been criticized for many years, and extensive administrative controls have been devised in an effort to eliminate it. Police persistence in the face of that attitude suggests that the illegal use of violence is regarded as functional to their work. It also indicates a tendency to regard the third degree as a legitimate means for obtaining the conviction of the felon. However, to understand the strength of this legitimation, one must include other factors: the competition between patrolman and detective and the publicity value of convictions for the police department.

The patrolman has less access to cases that might result in the "good pinch" than the detective. Such cases are assigned to the detective, and for their solution he will reap the credit. Even where the patrolman first detects the crime, or actually apprehends the possible offender, the case is likely to be turned over to the detective. Therefore patrolmen are eager to obtain evidence and make the arrest before the arrival of the detectives. Intimidation and actual violence frequently come into play under these conditions. This is illustrated in the following case recounted by a young patrolman when he was questioned as to the situations in which he felt that the use of force was necessary:

> One time Joe and I found three guys in a car, and we found that they had a gun down between the seats. We wanted to find out who owned that gun before the dicks arrived so that we could make a good pinch. They told us.

Patrolmen feel that little credit is forthcoming from a clean beat (a crimeless beat), while a number of good arrests really stands out on the record. To a great extent this is actually the case, since a good arrest results in good newspaper publicity, and the policeman who has made many "good pinches" has prestige among his colleagues.

A further justification for the illegal use of violence arises from the fact that almost every police department is under continuous criticism from the community, which tends to assign its own moral responsibilities to the police. The police are therefore faced with the task of justifying themselves to the public, both as individuals and as a group. They feel that the solution of major criminal cases serves this function. This is illustrated in the following statement:

> There is a case I remember of four Negroes who held up a filling station. We got a description of them and picked them up. Then we took them down to the station and really worked them over. I guess that everybody that came into the station that night had a hand in it, and they were in pretty bad shape. Do you think that sounds cruel? Well, you know what we got out of it? We broke a big case in _____. There was a mob of twenty guys, burglars and stick-up men, and eighteen of them are in the pen now. Sometimes you have to get rough with them, see. The way I figure it is, if you can get a clue that a man is a pro and if he won't co-operate, tell you what you want to know, it is justified to rough him up a little, up to a point. You know how it is. You feel that the end justifies the means.

It is easier for the police to justify themselves to the community through the dramatic solution of big crimes than through orderly and responsible completion of their routine duties. Although they may be criticized for failures in routine areas, the criticism for the failure to solve big crimes is more intense and sets off a criticism of their work in noncriminal areas. The pressure to solve important cases therefore becomes strong. The following statement, made in reference to the use of violence in interrogations, demonstrates the point:

> If it's a big case and there is a lot of pressure on you and they tell you you can't go home until the case is finished, then naturally you are going to lose patience.

The policeman's response to this pressure is to extend the use of violence to its illegal utilization in interrogations. The apprehension of the felon or the "good pinch" thus constitutes a basis for justifying the illegal use of violence.

2. **Control of Sexual Conduct**. The police are responsible for the enforcement of laws regulating sexual conduct. This includes the suppression of sexual deviation and the protection of the public from advances and attacks of persons of deviant sexual tendencies. Here the police face a difficult task. The victims of such deviants are notoriously unwilling to cooperate, since popular curiosity and gossip about sexual crimes and the sanctions against the open discussion of sexual activities make it embarrassing for the victim to admit or describe a deviant sexual advance or attack and cause him to feel that he gains a kind of guilt by association from such admissions. Thus the police find that frequently the victims will refuse to identify or testify against the deviant.

These difficulties are intensified by the fact that, once the community becomes aware of sexual depredations, the reports of such activity multiply well beyond reasonable expectations. Since the bulk of these reports will be false, they add to the confusion of the police and consequently to the elusiveness of the offender.

The difficulties of the police are further aggravated by extreme public demand for the apprehension of the offender. The hysteria and alarm generated by reports of a peeping Tom, a rapist, or an exhibitionist result in great public pressure on the police; and, should the activities continue, the public becomes violently critical of police efficiency. The police, who feel insecure in their relationship to the public, are extremely sensitive to this criticism and feel that they must act in response to the demands made by the political and moral leaders of the community.

Thus the police find themselves caught in a dilemma. Apprehension is extremely difficult because of the confusion created by public hysteria and the scarcity of witnesses, but the police are compelled to action by extremely public demands. They dissolve this dilemma through the illegal utilization of violence.

A statement of this "misuse" of police powers is represented in the remarks of a patrolman:

> Now in my own case when I catch a guy like that I just pick him up and take him into the woods and beat him until he can't crawl. I have had seventeen cases like that in the last couple of years. I tell that guy that if I catch him doing that again I will take him out to those woods and I will shoot him. I tell him that I carry a second gun on me just in case I find guys like him and that I will plant it in his hand and say that he tried to kill and that no jury will convict me.

This statement is extreme and is not representative of policemen in general. In many instances the policeman is likely to act in a different fashion. This is illustrated in the following statement of a rookie who described what happened when he and his partner investigated a parked car which had aroused their suspicions:

> He [the partner] went up there and pretty soon he called me, and there were a couple of fellows in the car with their pants open. I couldn't understand it. I kept looking around for where the woman would be. They were both pretty plastered. One was a young kid about eighteen years old, and the other was an older man. We decided, with the kid so drunk, that bringing him in would only really ruin his reputation, and we told him to go home. Otherwise we would have pinched them. During the time we were talking to them they offered us twenty-eight dollars, and I was going to pinch them when they showed the money, but my partner said, "Never mind, let them go."

Nevertheless, most policemen would apply no sanctions against a colleague who took the more extreme view of the right to use violence and would openly support some milder form of illegal coercion. This is illustrated in the statement of another rookie:

> They feel that it's okay to rough a man up in the case of sex crimes. One of the older men advised me that if the courts didn't punish a man we should. He told me about a sex crime, the story about it, and then said that the law says the policeman has the right to use the amount of force necessary to make an arrest and that in that kind of a crime you can use just a little more force. They feel definitely, for example, in extreme cases like rape, that if a man was guilty he ought to be punished even if you could not get any evidence on him. My feeling is that all the men on the force feel that way, at least from what they have told me.

Furthermore, the police believe, and with some justification it seems, that the community supports their definition of the situation and that they are operating in terms of an implicit directive.

The point of this discussion is that the control of sexual conduct is so difficult and the demand for it so incessant that the police come to sanction the illegal use of violence in obtaining that control. This does not imply that all policemen treat all sex deviants brutally, for, as the above quotations indicate, such is not the case. Rather, it indicates that this use of violence is permitted and condoned by the police and that they come to think of it as a resource more extensive than is included in the legal definition.

❖ LEGITIMATION OF VIOLENCE ❖

The preceding discussion has indicated two ways in which the experience of the police encourages them to use violence as a general resource in the achievement of their occupational ends and thus to sanction its illegal use. The experience, thus, makes violence acceptable to the policeman as a generalized means. We now wish to indicate the particular basis on which this general resource is legitimated. In particular we wish to point out the extent to which the policeman tends to transfer violence from a legal resource to a personal resource, one which he uses to further his own ends.

Seventy-three policemen, drawn from all ranks and constituting approximately 50 percent of the patrolmen, were asked, "When do you think a policeman is justified in roughing a man up?" The intent of the question was to get them to legitimate the use of violence. Their replies are summarized in table 1.

An inspection of the types and distribution of the responses indicates (1) that violence is legitimated by illegal ends (A, C, E, F, G) in 69 percent of the cases; (2) that violence is legitimated in terms of purely personal or group ends (A) in 37 percent of the cases (this is important, since it is the largest single reason for the use of violence given); and (3) that legal ends are the bases for legitimation in 31 percent of the cases (B and D). However, this probably represents a distortion of the true feelings of some of these men, since both the police chief and the community had been severely critical of the use of violence by the men and the respondents had a tendency to be very cautious with the interviewer, whom some of them never fully trusted. Furthermore, since all the men were conscious of the chief's policy and of public criticism, it seems likely that those who did justify the use of violence for illegal and personal ends no longer

Table 1*

Bases for the Use of Force Named by 73 Policemen

Type of Response	Frequency	Percentage
(A) Disrespect for police	27	37
(B) When impossible to avoid	17	23
(C) To obtain information	14	19
(D) To make an arrest	6	8
(E) For the hardened criminal	5	7
(F) When you know man is guilty	2	3
(G) For sex criminals	2	3
Total	**73**	**100**

*Many respondents described more than one type of situation which they felt called for the use of violence. The "reason" which was either (a) given most heatedly and at greatest length and/or (b) given first was used to characterize the respondent's answer to the question. However, this table is exhaustive of the types of replies which were given.

recognized the illegality involved. They probably believed that such ends fully represented a moral legitimation for their use of violence.

The most significant finding is that at least 37 percent of the men believed that it was legitimate to use violence to coerce respect. This suggests that policemen use the resource of violence to persuade their audience (the public) to respect their occupational status. In terms of the policeman's definition of the situation, the individual who lacks respect for the police, the "wise guy" who talks back, or any individual who acts or talks in a disrespectful way, deserves brutality. This idea is epitomized in admonitions given to the rookies such as, "You gotta make them respect you" and "You gotta act tough." Examples of some of the responses to the preceding question that fall into the "disrespect for the police" category follow:

> Well, there are cases. For example, when you stop a fellow for a routine questioning, say a wise guy, and he starts talking back to you and telling you you are no good and that sort of thing. You know you can take a man in on a disorderly conduct charge, but you can practically never make it stick. So what you do in a case like that is to egg the guy on until he makes a remark where you can justifiably slap him and, then, if he fights back, you can call it resisting arrest.

Well, it varies in different cases. Most of the police use punishment if the fellow gives them any trouble. Usually you can judge a man who will give you trouble though. *If there is any slight resistance*, you can go all out on him. You shouldn't do it in the street though. Wait until you are in the squad car, because, even if you are in the right and a guy takes a poke at you, just when you are hitting back somebody's just likely to come around the corner, and what he will say is that you are beating the guy with your club.

Well, a prisoner deserves to be hit when he goes to the point where he tries to put you below him.

You gotta get rough when a man's language becomes very bad, when he is trying to make a fool of you in front of everybody else. I think most policemen try to treat people in a nice way, but usually you have to talk pretty rough. That's the only way to set a man down, to make him show a little respect.

If a fellow called a policeman a filthy name, a slap in the mouth would be a good thing, especially if it was out in the public where calling a policeman a bad name would look bad for the police.

There was the incident of a fellow I picked up. I was on the beat, and I was taking him down to the station. There were people following us. He kept saying that I wasn't in the army. Well, he kept going on like that, and I finally had to bust him one. I had to do it. The people would have thought I was afraid otherwise.

These results suggest (1) that the police believe that these private or group ends constitute a moral legitimation for violence which is equal *or superior* to the legitimation derived from the law and (2) that the monopoly of violence delegated to the police, by the state, to enforce the ends of the state has been appropriated by the police as a personal resource to be used for personal and group ends.

❖ THE USE OF VIOLENCE ❖

The sanctions for the use of violence arising from occupational experience and the fact that policemen morally justify even its illegal use may suggest that violence is employed with great frequency and little provocation. Such an impression would be erroneous, for the actual use of violence is limited by other considerations, such as individual inclinations, the threat of detection, and a sensitivity to public reactions.

Individual policemen vary of course in psychological disposition and past experience. All have been drawn from the larger community which tends to condemn the use of violence and therefore have internalized with varying degrees of intensity this other definition of violence. Their experience as policemen creates a new dimension to their self-conceptions and gives them a new perspective on the use of violence. But individual men vary in the degree to which they assimilate this new conception of self. Therefore, the amount of violence which is used and the frequency with which it is employed will vary among policemen according to their individual propensities. However, policemen cannot and do not employ sanctions against their colleagues for using violence,[5] and individual men who personally condemn the use of violence and avoid it whenever possible[6] refuse openly to condemn acts of violence by other men on the force. Thus, the collective sanction for the use of violence permits those men who are inclined to its use to employ it without fear.

All policemen, however, are conscious of the dangers of the illegal use of violence. If detected, they may be subject to a lawsuit and possibly dismissal from the force. Therefore, they limit its use to what they think they can get away with. Thus, they recognize that, if a man is guilty of a serious crime, it is easy to "cover up" for their brutality by accusing him of resisting arrest, and the extent to which they believe a man guilty tends to act as a precondition to the use of violence.[7]

The policeman, in common with members of other occupations, is sensitive to the evaluation of his occupation by the public. A man's work is an important aspect of his status, and to the extent that he is identified with his work (by himself and/or the community) he finds that his self-esteem requires the justification and social elevation of his work. Since policemen are low in the occupational prestige scale, subject to continuous criticism, and in constant contact with this criticizing and evaluating public, they are profoundly involved in justifying their work and its tactics to the public and to themselves. The way in which the police emphasize the solution of big crimes and their violent solution to the problem of the control of sexual conduct illustrate this concern. However, different portions of the public have differing definitions of conduct and are of differential importance to the policeman, and the way in which the police define different portions of the public has an effect on whether or not they will use violence.

The police believe that certain groups of persons will respond only to fear and rough treatment. In the city studied they defined both Negroes and slum dwellers in this category. The following statements, each by a different man, typify the manner in which they discriminate the public:

In the good districts you appeal to people's judgment and explain the law to them. In the South Side the only way is to appear like you are the boss.

You can't ask them a question and get an answer that is not a lie. In the South Side the only way to walk into a tavern is to walk in swaggering as if you own the place and if somebody is standing in your way give him an elbow and push him aside.

The colored people understand one thing. The policeman is the law, and he is going to treat you rough and that's the way you have to treat them. Personally, I don't think the colored are trying to help themselves one bit. If you don't treat them rough, they will sit right on top of your head.

Discriminations with respect to the public are largely based on the political power of the group, the degree to which the police believe that the group is potentially criminal, and the type of treatment which the police believe will elicit respect from it.

Variations in the administration and community setting of the police will introduce variations in their use of violence. Thus, a thoroughly corrupt police department will use violence in supporting the ends of this corruption, while a carefully administered nonpolitical department can go a long way toward reducing the illegal use of violence. However, wherever the basic conditions here described are present, it will be very difficult to eradicate the illegal use of violence.

Given these conditions, violence will be used when necessary to the pursuit of duty or when basic occupational values are threatened. Thus a threat to the respect with which the policeman believes his occupation should be regarded or the opportunity to make a "good pinch" will tend to evoke its use.

❖ CONCLUSIONS ❖

This article sets forth an explanation of the illegal use of violence by the police based on an interpretative understanding of their occupational experience. Therefore, it contains a description and analysis of *their* interpretation of *their* experience.

The policeman uses violence illegally because such usage is seen as just, acceptable, and, at times, expected by his colleague group and because it constitutes an effective means for solving problems in obtaining status and self-esteem which policemen as policemen have in common. Since the ends for which violence is illegally used are conceived to be both just and important, they function to justify, to the policeman, the illegal use of violence as a general means. Since "brutality" is strongly criticized by the larger community, the policeman must devise a defense of his brutality to himself and the community, and the defense in turn gives a deeper and more lasting justification to the "misuse of violence." This process then results in a transfer in property from the state to the colleague group. The means of violence which were originally a property of the state, in loan to its law-enforcement agent, the police, are in a psychological sense confiscated by the police, to be conceived of as a personal property to be used at their discretion. This, then, is the explanation of the illegal use of violence by the police which results from viewing it in terms of the police as an occupational group.

The explanation of the illegal use of violence by the police offers an illuminating perspective on the social nature of their occupation. The analysis of their use of brutality in dealing with sexual deviants and felons shows that it is a result of their desire to defend and improve their social status in the absence of effective legal means. This desire in turn is directly related to and makes sense in terms of the low status of the police in the community, which results in a driving need on the part of policemen to assert and improve their status. Their general legitimation of the use of violence *primarily* in terms of coercing respect and making a "good pinch" clearly points out the existence of occupational goals, which are independent of and take precedence over their legal mandate. The existence of such goals and patterns of conduct indicates that the policeman has made of his occupation a preoccupation and invested in it a large aspect of his self.

Notes

[1] Interpretative understanding is here used as defined by Max Weber (see *The Theory of Social and Economic Organization*, trans. Talcott Parsons, New York, Oxford University Press, 1947, p. 88).

[2] The ideas are not original. I am indebted for many of them to Everett C. Hughes, although he is in no way responsible for their present formulation (see E. C. Hughes, "Work and the Self" in Rohrer and Sherif, *Social Psychology at the Crossroads*, New York, Harper & Bros., 1951).

[3] The background material will be developed in subsequent papers which will analyze the occupational experience of the police and give a full description of police norms.

[4] Policemen, in the case studied, use this term to mean an arrest which (a) is politically clear and (b) likely to bring them esteem. Generally it refers to felonies, but in the case of a "real" vice drive it may include the arrest and *conviction* of an important bookie.

[5] The emphasis on secrecy among the police prevents them from using legal sanctions against their colleagues.

[6] Many men who held jobs in the police station rather than on beats indicated to the interviewer that their reason for choosing a desk job was to avoid the use of violence.

[7] In addition, the policeman is aware that the courts are highly critical of confessions obtained by violence and that, if violence is detected, it will "spoil his case."

18

The Asshole

John Van Maanen

I guess what our job really boils down to is not letting the assholes take over the city. Now I'm not talking about your regular crooks . . . they're bound to wind up in the joint anyway. What I'm talking about are those shitheads out to prove they can push everybody around. Those are the assholes we gotta deal with and take care of on patrol. . . . They're the ones that make it tough on the decent people out there. You take the majority of what we do and its nothing more than asshole control.

A veteran Patrolman[1]

❖ POLICE TYPIFICATIONS ❖

The asshole—creep, bigmouth, bastard, animal, mope, rough, jerkoff, clown, scumbag, wiseguy, phony, idiot, shithead, bum, fool, or any of a number of anatomical, oral, or incestuous terms—is a part of every policeman's world.[2] Yet the grounds upon which such a figure stands have never been examined systematically. The purpose of this article is to display the interactional origins and consequences of the label asshole as it is used by policemen, in particular, patrolmen, going about their everyday tasks. I will argue that assholes represent a distinct but familiar type of person to the police and represent, therefore, a part of their commonsense wisdom

Peter K. Manning and John Van Maanen, (Eds.), *Policing: A View from the Street*, (1978) pp. 221–38. Reprinted with permission. Footnotes renumbered.

as to the kinds of people that populate their working environment. From this standpoint, assholes are analytic types with whom the police regularly deal. More importantly, however, I will also argue that the label arises from a set of situated conditions largely unrelated to the institutional mandate of the police (i.e., to protect life and property, arrest law violators, preserve the peace, etc.) but arises in response to some occupational and personal concerns shared by virtually all policemen.

According to most knowledgeable observers, nothing characterizes policing in America more than the widespread belief on the part of the police themselves that they are primarily law enforcers—perpetually engaged in a struggle with those who would disobey, disrupt, do harm, agitate, or otherwise upset the just order of the regime. And, that as policemen, they and they alone are the most capable of sensing right from wrong; determining who is and who is not respectable; and, most critically, deciding what is to be done about it (if anything). Such heroic self-perceptions reflecting moral superiority have been noted by numerous social scientists concerned with the study of the police. Indeed, several detailed, insightful, and thoroughly accurate mappings of the police perspective exist.[3] For instance, learned discussions denote the various "outgroups" perceived by the police (e.g., Harris, 1973; Bayley and Mendelsohn, 1969); or the "symbolic assailants" which threaten the personal security of the police (e.g., Skolnick, 1966; Neiderhoffer, 1967; Rubenstein, 1973); or the "suspicious characters" recognized by the police via incongruous (nonordinary) appearances (e.g., Sacks, 1972; Black, 1968). These reports provide the background against which the pervasive police tropism to order the world into the "for us" and "against us" camps can most clearly be seen.

Yet these studies have glossed over certain unique but together commonsensical properties of the police situation with the attendant consequence of reifying the police position that the world is in fact divided into two camps. Other than noting the great disdain and disgust held by many police officers toward certain predefined segments of the population they presumably are to serve, these studies fail to fully describe and explain the range and meaning attached to the various labels used by the police themselves to affix individual responsibility for particular actions occurring within their normal workaday world. Furthermore, previous studies do not provide much analytic aid when determining how the various typifications carried by the police are recognized as relevant and hence utilized as guides for action by a police officer in a particular situation. In short, if police typifications are seen to have origins as well as consequences, the popular distinction between "suspicious" or "threatening" and the almost mythologized "normal" or "respectable" is much too simple. It ignores not only the immediate context in which street interactions take place, but it also disregards the critical signs read by the police within the interaction itself which signify to them both the moral integrity of the person with whom they are dealing and the appropriate recipe they should follow as the interaction proceeds.[4] Therefore, any distinction of the "types" of people with whom the police deal must include an explicit consideration of the ways in which the various "types" are both immediately and conditionally identified by the police. Only in this fashion is it possible to accurately depict the labels the police construct to define, explain, and take action when going about their routine and nonroutine tasks.

To begin this analysis, consider the following typology which suggests that the police tend to view their occupational world as comprised exhaustively of three types of citizens (Van Maanen, 1974). These ideal types are: (1) "suspicious persons"—those whom the police have reason to believe may have committed a serious offense; (2) "assholes"—those who do not accept the police definition of the situation; and (3) "know nothings"—those who are not either of the first two categories but are not police and therefore, according to the police, cannot know what the police are about.

This everyday typification scheme provides a clue to the expectations, thoughts, feelings, and behaviors of the police. For example, "suspicious persons" are recognized on the basis of their appearance in public surroundings. Such an appearance is seen as a furtive, nonroutine, *de trop*, or, to use Sacks's (1972) nicely turned phrase, "dramatically torturous." Crucially, such persons, when they provide the police reason to stop and interrogate them, are treated normally in a brisk, though thoroughly professional, manner. It is not their moral worth or identity which is at issue, but rather it is a possible illegal action in their immediate or not-so-immediate past which is in question. From the patrolman's point of view, he is most interested in insuring that formal procedural issues are observed. Hence the personal production of a professional police performance is called for and is presented—at least initially.[5] On the other end of the continuum reside the "know nothings," the "average" citizens, who most generally come under police scrutiny only via their request for service. The "know nothing" may be the injured or wronged party or the seeker of banal information and as such is treated with a certain amount of deference and due respect by the patrolman.

"Assholes," by way of contrast, are stigmatized by the police and treated harshly on the basis of their failure to meet police expectations arising from the *interaction situation itself*. Of course, street interaction may quickly transform suspicious persons into know nothings and know nothings into assholes, or any combination thereof. But it is the asshole category which is most imbued with moral meaning for the patrolman—establishing for him a stained or flawed identity to attribute to the citizen upon which he can justify his sometimes malevolent acts. Consequently, the asshole may well be the recipient of what the police call "street justice"—a physical attack designed to rectify what police take as personal insult. Assholes are most vulnerable to street justice, since they, as their title implies, are not granted status as worthy human beings. Their actions are viewed by the police as stupid or senseless and their feelings as incomprehensible (if they can even be said to have feelings). Indeed, as I will show, the police consistently deny an asshole a rationale or ideology to support their actions, insisting that the behavior of an asshole is understandable only as a sudden or lifelong character aberration. On the other hand, suspicious persons are less likely candidates for street justice because, in the majority of cases, their guilt may still be in question, or, if their guilt has been in fact established, their actions are likely to seem at least comprehensible and purposeful to the police (i.e., a man steals because he needs money; a man shoots his wife because she "two-timed" him; etc.). Also, there are incentives for the suspicious person to cooperate (at least nominally) when subject to police attention. The suspicious person may well be the most cooperative of all the people with whom the police deal on a face-to-face basis. This is, in part, because he is most desirous of presenting a normal appearance (unafraid, unruffled, and with nothing to hide), and, in part, because if he is in fact caught he does not want to add further difficulty to his already difficult position. Finally, know nothings are the least likely candidates for street justice since they represent the so-called client system and are therefore those persons whom the police are most interested in impressing through a polished, efficient, and courteous performance.

At this point, I should note that the above ideal types are anything but precise and absolute. One purpose of this article is to make at least one of these categories more explicit. But since I am dealing primarily with interior, subjective meanings negotiated in public with those whom the police interact, such typifications will always be subject to severe situational, temporal, and individually idiosyncratic restriction. Hence, an asshole in one context may be a know nothing in another, and vice versa. In other words, I am not arguing in this article that a general moral order is shared by all policemen as their personalized but homomorphic view of the world. Indeed, the moral order subscribed to by police is complex, multiple, and continually shifts back and forth between that which is individual and that which is collective. What I will argue, however, is that particular situational conditions (i.e., provocations) predispose most policemen toward certain perceptions of people which lead to the application of what can be shown to be rule-governed police actions. My objective, then, is simply to begin teasing out the underlying structure of police thought and to denote the features of what might be called the secondary reality of police work.

The remainder of this article is divided into four sections. The next section, "Patrol Work," describes very briefly certain understandings shared by street-level patrolmen as to what is involved in their work. In a sense, these understandings are akin to behavioral rules that can be seen to mobilize police action; hence they represent the grounds upon which the figure of the asshole is recognized. The following section, "Street Justice," deals with the characteristic processes involved in discovering, distinguishing, and treating the asshole. Some conclusions revolving around the relationship between the police and the asshole are suggested in the next section. And, finally, a few of the broad implications that flow from this analysis are outlined in the last section.

❖ PATROL WORK ❖

Policing city streets entails what Hughes (1958) refers to as a "bundle of tasks." Some of these tasks are mundane; many of them are routine; and a few of them are dangerous. Indeed, patrol work defies a general job description since it includes an almost infinite set of activities— dogcatching, first-aid, assisting elderly citizens, breaking up family fights, finding lost children, pursuing a fleeing felon, directing traffic, and so forth. Yet, as in other lines of endeavor, patrolmen develop certain insider notions about their work that may or may not reflect what outsiders believe their work to be. Such notions are of course attached firmly to the various experientially based meanings the police learn to regularly ascribe to persons, places, and things—the validity of which is established, sustained, and continually reaffirmed through everyday activity. Because these meanings are, to some degree, shared by patrolmen going about similar tasks, their collective representation can be detailed and linked to certain typical practices engaged in on the street by the police. Thus, to understand the police perspective on, and treatment of, the asshole, it is necessary also to understand the manner in which the policeman conceives of his work. Below is a very short summary of certain interrelated assumptions and beliefs that patrolmen tend to develop regarding the nature of their job.

Real Police Work

Many observers have noted the pervasive police tendency to narrowly constrict their perceived task to be primarily—and to the exclusion of other alternatives—law enforcement. As Skolnick and Woodworth (1967:129) suggest evocatively, "when a policeman can engage in real police work—act out the symbolic rites of search, chase and capture—his self-image is affirmed and morale enhanced." Yet, ironically, opportunities to enact this sequence are few and far between. In fact, estimates of the time police spend actually in real police work while on patrol vary from 0 percent (as in the case of the quiet country policeman for whom a street encounter with a bona fide "criminal" would be a spectacular exception to his daily tour of duty) to about 10 or 15 percent (as in the case of the busy urban patrolman who works a seamy cityside district in which the presence of pimps, dealers, cons, and burglars, among others, are the everyday rule). Nonetheless, most of the policeman's time is spent performing rather dry, monotonous, and relatively mundane activities of a service nature—the proverbial clerk in a patrol car routinely cruising his district and awaiting dispatched calls (see Cain, 1971; Reiss, 1971; Webster, 1970; and Cummings, Cummings and Edell, 1965, for further discussion on how the police, spend their time).

Within these boundaries, notions of real police work develop to provide at least a modicum of satisfaction to the police. To a patrolman, *real police work* involves the use of skills and special abilities he believes he possesses by virtue of his unique experience and training. Furthermore, such a perspective results in minimizing the importance of other activities he is often asked regularly to perform. In fact, an ethos of "stay-low-and-avoid-trouble-unless-real-police-work-is-called-for" permeates police organizations (Van Maanen, 1973, 1974, 1975). Only tasks involving criminal apprehension are attributed symbolic importance. For the most part, other tasks, if they cannot be avoided, are performed (barring interruption) with ceremonial dispatch and disinterest.

Territoriality

A central feature of policing at the street level is the striking autonomy maintained (and guarded jealously) by patrolmen working the beat. All patrol work is conducted by solo officers or partnerships (within a squad to whom they are linked) responsible for a given plot of territory. Over time, they come to know, in the most familiar and penetrating manner, virtually every passageway—whether alley, street, or seldom-used path—located in their sector. From such knowledge of this social stage comes the corresponding evaluations of what particular conditions are to be considered good or bad, safe or unsafe, troubled or calm, usual or unusual, and so on. Of course, these evaluations are also linked to temporal properties associated with the public use of a patrolman's area of responsibility. As Rubenstein (1973) suggests, the territorial perspective carried by patrolmen establishes the basic normative standard for the proper use of place. And those perceived by patrolmen to be beyond the pale regarding their activities in space and time are very likely to warrant police attention.

Maintaining the Edge

Charged with enforcing ambiguous generalized statutes and operating from an autonomous, largely isolated position within the city, it is not surprising that police have internalized a standard of conduct which dictates that they must control and regulate all situations in which they find themselves. At one level, police feel they have the right to initiate, terminate, or otherwise direct all encounters with members of the public. Yet such perceptions penetrate more broadly into the social scheme of things, for police feel furthermore that the public order is a product of their ability to exercise control. The absence of trouble on their beat becomes, therefore, a personalized objective providing intimate feedback as to one's worth as a patrolman. Activity which may threaten the perceived order becomes intolerable, for it signifies to the patrolman that his advantage over the conduct of others (his "edge") is in question. It is a source of embarrassment in front of a public audience, and sometimes it is considered a disgrace to the police uniform if it is viewed by one's peers or departmental superiors. Clearly, such activity cannot be allowed to persist, for it may indicate both to a patrolman's colleagues and to his superiors that the officer no longer cares for his job and has, consequently, lost the all-important respect of those he polices (endangering, it is thought, other policemen who might work the same district). Hence, to "maintain one's edge" is a key concept vis-à-vis the "how to" of police work. And, as all policemen know, to let down the facade (for they do recognize the contrived nature of the front) is to invite disrespect, chaos, and crime.

The Moral Mandate

In light of the above three features of the police frame, it should be clear that police are both representatives of the moral order and a part of it. They are thus committed ("because it is right") to maintain their collective face as protectorates of the right and respectable against the wrong and the not-so-respectable. Situations in which this face is challenged—regardless of origin—are likely to be responded to in unequivocal terms. For example, Cain (1971) writes that when the authority of an officer is questioned by a member of the nonpolice public, the officer has three broad responses available to him. He may (1) physically attack the offender; (2) swallow his pride and ignore the offender; or (3) manufacture a false excuse for the arrest of the offender. What this suggests is a highly personalized view on the part of the police as to their moral position and responsibility, one in which an attempt on the part of the citizen to disregard the wishes of a policeman may be viewed by the police as a profaning of the social and legal system itself. Such an act can also be seen to provoke moral and private indignation on the part of the officer as an individual, thus providing him with another *de rigueur* excuse to locate an appropriate remedy. Since the police personally believe that they are capable of making correct decisions regarding the culpability of an involved party, justice is likely, in the case of an offense to the moral sensibilities of a police officer, to be enacted quickly, parsimoniously, and self-righteously—whether it be the relatively trivial swift kick in the pants or the penultimate tragedy involved in the taking of a life. Thus, the moral mandate felt by the police to be their just right at the societal level is translated and transformed into occupational and personal terms and provides both the justification and legitimation for specific acts of street justice.

This truncated picture of the occupational frame involved in the doing of police work provides the rubric upon which we now can examine the making of an asshole. As one would expect, assholes are not afforded the protection of the more structured relationships police maintain with other of their categories of persons—the suspicious and the know nothings. Rather, they fall outside this fragile shelter, for their actions are seen as "senseless," so "aimless" and "irrational" that recognizable and acceptable human motives are difficult for the police to discover (i.e., from the patrolmen's perspective, there are not legitimate reasons to distrust, disagree with, make trouble for, or certainly hate the police). In this sense, it is precisely the "pointlessness" of an individual's behavior that makes him an asshole and subjects him to the police version of street justice.

❖ STREET JUSTICE ❖

Policeman to motorist stopped for speeding:
> "May I see your driver's license, please?"

Motorist:
> "Why the hell are you picking on me and not somewhere else looking for some real criminals?"

Policeman:
> "Cause you're an asshole, that's why . . . but I didn't know that
> until you opened your mouth."

The above sea story represents the peculiar reality with which patrolmen believe they must contend. The world is in part (and, to policemen, a large part) populated by individuals to whom an explanation for police behavior cannot be made, for, as the police say, "assholes don't listen to reason." The purpose of this section is to explore the commonplace and commonsense manner in which the tag asshole arises, sticks, and guides police action during a street encounter. This stigmatization process is divided into three stages which, while analytically distinct, are highly interactive and apt to occur in the real world of policing almost simultaneously. For convenience only, then, these phases are labeled *affront*, *clarification*, and *remedy*.

Throughout this discussion it should be remembered that the asshole is not necessarily a suspected law violator—although the two often overlap, thus providing double trouble, so to speak, for the labeled. Importantly, the police view of the asshole as deviant is a product of the immediate transaction between the two and not a product of an act preceding the transaction. This is not to say, however, that certain classes in society—for example, the young, the black, the militant, the homosexual—are not "fixed" by the police as a sort of permanent asshole grouping. Indeed, they are. Yet such bounded *a priori* categories can do policemen little good—except perhaps when dealing with the racial or bohemian obvious—for such stereotypes are frequently misleading and dysfunctional (e.g., the "hippie" who is a detective's prized informant; the black dressed in a purple jumpsuit who happens to be a mayor's top aide; the sign carrying protestor who is an undercover FBI agent). And, even in cases in which *a priori character* judgments are a part of the decision to stop an individual, the asshole label, if it is to play a determining role in the encounter, must arise anew. That is to say, if the asshole distinction is to have a *concrete* as opposed to *abstract* meaning, it must in some manner be tied fundamentally and irresolutely to observable social action occurring in the presence of the labeling officer.

Certainly, a policeman's past experience with an individual or with a recognizable group will influence his street behavior. For example, a rookie soon discovers (as a direct consequence of his initiation into a department) that blacks, students, Mexicans, reporters, lawyers, welfare workers, researchers, prostitutes, and gang members are not to be trusted, are unpredictable, and are usually "out-to-get-the-police." He may even sort these "outsiders" into various categories indicative of the risk he believes they present to him or the implied contrast they have with his own life-style and beliefs. Yet, without question, these categories will never be exhaustive—although the absolute size of what patrolmen call their "shit lists" may grow over the years. Consequently, to understand the police interpretation and meaning of the term "asshole" we must look directly into the field situations in which it originates.

Affront: Challenge

When a police officer approaches a civilian to issue a traffic citation or to inquire as to the whys and wherefores of one's presence or simply to pass the time of day, he directly brings the power of the state to bear on the situation and hence makes vulnerable to disgrace, embarrassment, and insult that power. Since the officer at the street level symbolizes the presence of the Leviathan in the everyday lives of the citizenry, such interactions take on dramatic properties far different from ordinary citizen-to-citizen transactions (Manning, 1974a; Silver, 1967). In a very real sense, the patrolman-to-citizen exchanges are moral contests in which the authority of the state is either confirmed, denied, or left in doubt. To the patrolman, such contests are not to be taken lightly, for the authority of the state is also his personal authority, and is, of necessity, a matter of some concern to him. To deny or raise doubt about his legitimacy is to shake the very ground upon which his self-image and corresponding views are built.

An affront, as it is used here, is a challenge to the policeman's authority, control, and definition of the immediate situation. As seen by the police, an affront is simply a response on the part of the other which indicates to them that their position and authority in the interaction are not being taken seriously. It may occur with or without intent. Whether it is the vocal student who claims to "know his rights," the stumbling drunk who says he has had "only two beers," or the lady of the evening who believes she is being questioned only because she is wearing "sexy clothes," the police will respond in particular ways to those who challenge or question their motive or right to intervene in situations that they believe demand police intervention. Clearly, overt and covert challenges to police authority will not go unnoticed. In fact, they can be seen to push the encounter to a new level wherein any further slight to an officer, however subtle, provides sufficient evidence to a patrolman that he may indeed be dealing with a certifiable asshole and that the situation is in need of rapid clarification. From this standpoint, an affront can be seen, therefore, as disrupting the smooth flow of the police performance. The argumentative motorist, the pugnacious drunk, the sometimes ludicrous behavior of com-batants in a "family beef" all interfere [with], and hence make more difficult, the police task. Of course, some officers relish such encounters. In this sense, ironically, the asshole gives status to the police rather than takes it away. However, since the label is itself a moral charge (and it need not be made salient or verbally expressed), it is open theoretically for rebuttal and evidence may or may not be forthcoming which will substantiate or contradict the charge. Such evidence is gathered in the next analytic stage.

Clarification: Confrontation

Based upon a perceived affront, the patrolman must then attempt to determine precisely the kind of person with whom he is engaged. It is no longer an idle matter to him in which his private conceptions of people can be kept private as he goes about his business. But the patrolman is now in a position wherein he may discover that his taken-for-granted authority on the street is not exactly taken for granted by another. Two commonsensical issues are critical at this point in an encounter. *First*, the officer must determine whether or not the individual under question could have, under the present circumstances, acted in an alternative fashion. To wit, did the perceived affront occur by coercion or accident through no fault of the person? Did the person even know he was dealing with a police officer? Was he acting with a gun at his head? And so on. *Second*, and equally important, given that the person could have acted differently, the officer must determine whether or not the individual was aware of the consequences that might follow his action. In other words, was the action frivolous, naive, unserious, and not meant to offend? Did the person know that his actions were likely to be interpreted offensively by the police? The answers to these two questions, provide patrolmen with material (or lack of it) to construct and sustain an asshole definition. Let us examine in some depth these questions, for they raise the very issue of personal responsibility which is at the nexus of the asshole definition.[6]

  McHugh (1969) argues persuasively that the social construction of deviant categories is a matter of elimination which proceeds logically through a series of negotiated offers and responses designed to fix responsibility for a perceived deviant act (i.e., a deviant act requires a charge before it can be said to have happened). Police follow a similar paradigm when filling, emptying, or otherwise attending to their person categories. Again, the first item to be determined in this process is the issue of whether or not the person had alternative means available to him of which he could reasonably be expected to be aware. For example, the speeding motorist who, when pulled to the side of the road, could be excused for his abusive language if it were discovered by the officer that the motorist's wife was at the same time in the back seat giving birth to a child. Similarly, juveniles "hanging out" on a public street corner at certain times of the day may be sometimes overlooked if the police feel that "those kids don't have anyplace to go." On the other hand, if it can be determined that there is no unavoidable reason behind the affronting action, the individual risks being labeled an asshole. The drunken and remorseless driver, the wife who harangues the police officer for mistreating her husband after she herself requested police service to break up a family fight, or the often-warned teenager who makes a nuisance of himself by flagrantly parading in public after curfew are all persons whom the police believe could have and should have acted differently. Their acts were not inevitable, and it could be expected that they had available to them conventional alternatives.

Given that there are no compelling deterministic accounts readily available to the patrolman to excuse a particular affront, the officer must still make a judgment about the offender's motive. In other words, as the second issue listed above suggests, the policeman must decide whether or not the person knows what he is doing. Could the person be expected to know of the consequences which follow an affront to an officer of the law? Indeed, does the person even realize that what he is doing is likely to provoke police action? Could this particular person be expected to know better? All are questions related to the establishment of a motive for action. For example, the stylized and ceremonial upright third finger when attached to the hand of a thirty-year-old man is taken by the police very differently from the same gesture attached to the hand of a four-year-old child. Loud and raucous behavior in some parts of a city may be ignored if the police feel "the people there don't know any better." Or the claim that one is Jesus Christ resurrected and is out to do battle with the wages of sin may indicate to the police that they are either in the presence of a "dope-crazed radical hippie freak" or a "soft-brained harmless mental case," depending, perhaps, on the offender's age. If the person is young, for instance, responsibility is likely to be individualized—"it is his fault"; however, if the person is old, responsibility is likely to be institutionalized—"he can't help it, he's a nut."

Summarily, the police have available to them two principles of clarification. One concerns the means available to a person guilty of an affront, and the other concerns the purposes behind the affront itself. If the affront is viewed as unavoidable or unintended, the person is unlikely to be subjected to shabby or harsh treatment at the hands of the police. The asshole, however, is one who is viewed as culpable and blameworthy for his affronting action, and, as the next section details, he will be dealt with by the police in ways they feel appropriate.

Remedy: Solution

The above portrait of the clarification principles utilized by police in labeling assholes suggests that certain typical police responses can be displayed by a simple fourfold typology. Figure 1 depicts the relationship between the police officer's assessment of responsibility for the affront and denotes, within each cell, the typical police response given the various possible assessments.

Figure 1

Does the person know what he is doing?

		Yes	No
Could the person act differently under the circumstances?	Yes	**A** Castigate	**B** Teach
	No	**C** Ignore	**D** Isolate

Cell A represents the subject case of this essay since it involves a flagrant (inexcusable) disregard for the sentiments of the police. To the police, those falling into this category are unmistakably assholes and are therefore prominent candidates to be the recipients of street justice—the aim of which is to punish or castigate the individual for a moral transgression. Persons placed in this category are also the most likely to be placed under questionable arrest. This is not so because of the original intent of the encounter (which often, by itself, is trivial) but rather because of the serious extralegal means utilized by the police to enforce their particular view of the situation upon the recalcitrant asshole—"hamming-up" or "thumping" (beating).[7] And, as Reiss (1971) suggests, the use of force is not a philosophical question to the police but rather one of who, where, when, and how much.

The use of such means requires of course that the officer manufacture post facto a legally defensible account of his action in order to, in the vernacular of the day, "cover his ass."[8] Such accounts in legalese most often take the form of "disorderly conduct," "assaulting a police officer," "the use of loud and abusive language in the presence of women and children," "disturbing the peace," or the almost legendary—due to its frequent use—"resisting arrest." The asshole from this position is subject to a police enactment of double jeopardy—justice without trial in the streets and justice, perhaps with trial, in the courts. And regardless of the outcome in the latter case, there is usually only one loser. I should emphasize, however, that I am not saying the behavior of the asshole may not be brutish, nasty, and itself thoroughly vicious. I am simply suggesting that behavior violating extralegal moral codes used by police to order their interactions— whether it be inconsiderate, barbarous, or otherwise—will be responded to in what police believe to be appropriate ways.

Cell B of Figure 1 also represents a serious affront to police integrity, and it too may be an affront which calls for an extra-legal response. An illustration provided by the remarks of a patrolman is useful in this context:

> Those goddamn kids got to learn sooner or later that we won't take a lot of shit around Cardoza (a local college campus). Next time I see one of those punks waving a Viet Cong flag I'm gonna negotiate the little bastard back into an alley and kick his rosy red ass so hard he ain't gonna carry nothing for awhile. Those kids gotta be made to see that they can't get away with this type of thing.

Whether or not such a prediction was actually carried out does not matter, for the quotation itself indicates that "teaching" occupies a particularly prominent position in the police repertoire of possible responses. Thus, the uncooperative and surly motorist finds his sobriety rudely questioned, or the smug and haughty college student discovers himself stretched over the hood of a patrol car and the target of a mortifying and brusque body search. The object of such degradation ceremonies is simply to reassert police control and demonstrate to the citizen that his behavior is considered inappropriate. Teaching techniques are numerous, with threat, ridicule, and harassment among the more widely practiced. Other examples are readily available, such as the morally-toned lectures meted out to those who would attempt to bribe, lie, or otherwise worm their way out of what a policeman sees to be a legitimate traffic citation, the traditional—but vanishing—"kick in the ass" administered to a youngster caught stealing an apple or cutting school. The intent in all these cases is clear. The person must be taught a lesson. And whether the teaching occurs in public or in the back of an alley, the person must be shown the error of his ways. He has acted perhaps out of ignorance, but nevertheless the police feel they must demonstrate that they will not casually overlook the action. However, I should note that the person in this category will remain an asshole in the eyes of the police until he has apparently learned his lesson to the satisfaction of the officers on the scene. Here a display of remorse is no doubt crucial to the police.[9]

Cell C represents the case in which the police are likely to excuse the affront due to the extenuating circumstances surrounding the affront. When it is clear to the police that there are indeed mitigating conditions, their response is to ignore the error—pretend, as it were, that such an affront never happened. For example, it is understandable to the police that the victim of a mugging may be somewhat abusive toward them when they interrogate him just after the crime (although there is a fine line to be drawn here). Similarly, if a teenage male vigorously defends the chaste and virtuous intentions of he and his girlfriend while questioned by the police in a concealed and cozy corner of a public park, it is understood by the police that the boy has few other acceptable alternative lines available. The police response is typically to adopt a somewhat bemused tolerance policy toward actions which under different circumstances may have produced the orb and scepter.

Finally, cell D in Figure 1 concerns the case of an affront which police take to lie beyond the responsibility of the actor. While such action cannot normally be allowed to continue, the moral indignation felt by police is tempered by the understanding that the person is not aware nor could be easily made aware of the rule-breaking nature of his actions. The police response is to isolate the offender, not to punish him. Thus, the ''mental case'' is shipped to the county hospital for observation and treatment; the ''foul-mouthed child'' is returned to those responsible for his behavior; the out-of-state tourist prowling an area close to his hotel but frequented by prostitutes is informed of his ''oversight'' and told in unmistakable terms to vacate the territory. It is important to note that police feel justified in using only enough force or coercive power to seal off the offender from public (and, by implication; their own) view. To use more force would be considered unreasonable.

It has been my purpose here to suggest that much of what the general public might see as capricious, random, or unnecessary behavior on the part of the police is, in fact, governed by certain rather pervasive interpretive rules which lie close enough to the surface such that they can be made visible. Certain police actions, following the model presented above, can be seen, then, to be at least logical if not legal. Furthermore, much of the power of these rules stems from their tacit or taken-for-granted basis. Indeed, were the rules to be questioned, the game could not continue. However, while these rules are applied in a like fashion by all police in a given interactional episode, the specific situated behavior of a citizen that is taken as a sign which leads to isolating, ignoring, teaching, or castigating a given individual is no doubt quite different across patrolmen. Here, the police game continues as it does because, in part, the asshole label swallows up and hides whatever individual differences exist across patrolmen. Thus, language neatly solves the problem of misunderstanding that would arise among the police were the rules to be articulated and standards sought as to how they should be a applied.

❖ SOME CONCLUSIONS ❖

It is possible, of course, to see the preceding ritualized sequence as an isolated and rarely indulged propensity of the police. However, in this section, I will argue that indeed such a sequence and the corresponding identification and treatment of the asshole is intimately related to the police production and represents an aspect of policing that is near the core of the patrolman's definition of his task. In essence, the existence of an asshole demonstrates and confirms the police view of the importance and worth of themselves both as individuals and as members of a necessary occupation. However, several other, somewhat more practical and everyday features of police work insure the ominous presence of the asshole in the police world.

First, the labeling of individuals as assholes can be seen as a technique (although invisible to most) useful to patrolmen in providing distance between themselves and their segmented audiences—to be liked by the people in the street is, in the defensive rhetoric of patrolmen, a sign of a bad cop. By profaning and degrading the actions of another, social distance can be established and maintained—a guarantee, so to speak, that the other will not come uncomfortably close. Thus, the asshole simplifies and orders the policeman's world and continually verifies his classification scheme regarding those who are "like him" and those who are "unlike him." Relatedly the labeling serves also as an immediate call to action, denoting a consensually approved, (by the police culture) means for remedying "out-of-kilter" situations.

Second, the label not only describes and prescribes but it also explains and makes meaningful the statements and actions of others. In fact, an entire set of action expectations (i.e., "they are out to make the police look bad") can be ascribed as motives to the asshole. In this sense, the police function in street interaction is not unlike that of a psychiatrist diagnosing a patient. Both explain perceived deviancy in terms of a characterological genesis. Hence, the label implies that a different, inappropriate, and strange motivational scheme is used by the "type of person" known as an asshole. In this manner, an act is made understandable by stripping away whatever meaning might be attributed to it by the actor. Thus, to make sense of the act is to assume that it does not make sense—that it is stupid, irrational, wrong, deranged, or dangerous. Any other assumption would be too threatening.

Third, the labeling process must be viewed as serving an occupational purpose. I suggested previously that the urban policeman is primarily a keeper of the peace yet he defines his job in terms of law enforcement. Furthermore, as others have noted, many patrolmen try to convert peacekeeping situations to those of law enforcement (e.g., Bittner, 1967, 1970; Wilson, 1969; Piliavin and Briar, 1964). Since real police work is seldom available, marginally legitimate arrests of assholes provide a patrolman excitement and the opportunity to engage one's valued skills. Perhaps the police cliche, "a good beat is full of deadbeats," reflects structural support for the asshole-labeling phenomena.

Fourth, the discovery and subsequent action taken when the police encounter the asshole provides an expressive outlet—almost ceremonial in its predictability—for much of the frustration policing engenders. To the patrolman, one particular asshole symbolizes all those that remain "out there" untouched, untaught, and unpunished. Such emotional outbursts provide, therefore, a reaffirmation of the moral repugnance of the asshole. Whether the officer responds by placing the handcuffs on the person's wrists such that they cut off circulation (and not incidentally cause intense, almost excruciating pain) or pushes a destitute soul through a shop window, these actions release some of the pent-up energies stored up over a period in which small but cumulative indignities are suffered by the police at the hands of the community elites, the courts, the politicians, the uncaught crooks, the press, and numerous others. The asshole stands, then, as a ready ersatz for those whom the police will never—short of a miracle—be in a position to directly encounter and confront.

Finally, the asshole can be seen as a sort of reified other, representing all those persons who would question, limit, or otherwise attempt to control the police. From this standpoint, knowing that there are assholes at large serves perhaps to rally and solidify police organizations around at least one common function. Thus, the police are, to a limited degree, unified by their disdain of those who would question their activities. Perhaps one could say that the police represent what Simmel (1950) referred to as an "invisible church" in which the faithful are fused together through their common relation to an outside phenomenon.

Consequently, assholes are not simply obscure and fanciful figments of the bedeviled imagination of the police. On the contrary, they define to a surprising degree what the police are about. And while the internal satisfactions and rewards involved in "slamming around" an asshole may seem esoteric if not loathsome to the outsider, to the patrolman who makes his living on the city streets it is not.

❖ POSTSCRIPT ❖

The foregoing description and explanation of an overlooked aspect of urban policing highlights the fact that the police officer is anything but a Weberian bureaucrat whose discretion and authority are checked rigidly. The collective myth surrounding the rulebound "policeman-as-public-servant" has no doubt never been very accurate. By virtue of their independence from superiors, their carefully guarded autonomy in the field, their deeply felt notions about real police work and those who would interfere with it, and their increasing isolation from the public they serve (as a result of mobile patrol, rotating shifts, greater specialization of the police, and the growing segmentation of the society at large with its own specialized and emerging subcultures), police-community "problems" will not disappear. And, since the police view their critics as threatening and as persons who generally should be taught or castigated, one could argue that the explosive potential of citizen-police encounters will grow.

Additionally, if the police become more sensitive to public chastisement, it could be expected that something of a self-fulfilling prophecy may well become a more important factor in the street than it is presently. That is to say, if the police increasingly view their public audience as foes—whose views are incomprehensible if not degenerate or subversive—it is likely that they will also magnify clues which will sustain the stereotype of citizen-as-enemy escalating therefore the percentage of street interactions which result in improper arrest and verbal or physical attack. Thus, the fantasy may well become the reality as stereotypes are transformed into actualities. In fact, the future may make prophetic Brendan Behan's half-jesting remark that he had never seen a situation so bad that a policeman couldn't make it worse.

To conclude, this article has implied that there is a virtual—if unintended—license in this society granted to police. In particular, when it comes to the asshole, police actions are not governed at all, given the present policies of allowing the watchers to watch themselves. It would seem that something is amiss, and, if the practical morality in urban areas is not exactly inverted, it is at least tilted. If the asshole is indeed a critical aspect of policing, then there is serious risk involved in the movement to "professionalize" the police. As other observers have remarked, successful occupational professionalization inevitably leads to increased autonomy and ultimately increased power for members of the occupation (Becker, 1962; Hughes, 1965). Professionalism may well widen the police mandate in society and therefore amplify the potential of the police to act as moral entrepreneurs. From this perspective, what is required at present is not professional police but accountable police.

Notes

[1] All police quotes are taken from field notes I compiled of conversations and observations taking place during a year of participant observation in what I have referred to anonymously in my writings as the Union City Police Department (a large, metropolitan force employing over 1,500 uniformed officers). The quotes are as accurate as my ear, memory, and notes allow. . . . I should note, also, that in this essay I use the terms "police," "police officer," patrolman," and "policemen" somewhat interchangeably. However, unless I indicate otherwise, my comments are directed solely toward the street level officer—the cop on the beat—and not toward his superiors, administrators, or colleagues in the more prestigeful detective bureaus.

[2] I chose the term "asshole" for the title of this essay simply because it is a favorite of working policemen (at least in Union City). The interested reader might check my assumption by a casual glance at what several others have to say about this linguistic matter. Most useful in this regard are the firsthand accounts police have themselves provided and can be found, for example, in Terkel (1968, 1974); Drodge, (1973); Mass (1972); Olsen (1974); Whittemore (1973); Walker (1969). I should note as well that such labeling proceeds not only because of its functional use to the police but also because it helps officers to capture perceptual distinctions (i.e., labels are "good to think"). Thus assholes are conceptually part of the ordered world of police—the statuses, the rules, the norms, and the contrasts that constitute their social system.

[3] See, for example: Rubenstein's (1973) report on the Philadelphia police; Westley's (1970) study of a midwestern police department in the late 1940s; Wilson's (1968) global accounting of the police perspective; Reiss's (1971) research into police-community interactions; LaFave's (1965) treatment of the police decision to arrest; Cain's (1973) and Banton's (1964) observations on the British police; and Berkeley's (1969) cross-cultural view of policing in democratic societies. What comes out of these excellent works is tantamount to a reaffirmation of Trotsky's famous dictum, "There is but one international and that is the police."

[4] For example, Skolnick's (1966) idea that policemen are "afraid" of certain categories of persons distorts the nature of the occupational perspective. More to the point, policemen are disgusted by certain people, envious of others, and ambivalent toward most. At times they may even vaguely admire certain criminals—those that the British police call "good villains" (Cain, 1971). Fear must of course be given its due, but the occasion of fear hangs more upon unforeseen situational contingencies (the proverbial dark alley, desolate city park, or underlife tavern) than upon certain individuals.

[5] Certainly this may not always be the case. For example, some "suspected persons," due to the nature of their alleged crime (e.g., child molestation, drug dealing, indecent exposure, political sabotage, assault [or worse] upon a police officer, etc.) are likely to provide a strong sense of moral indignation on the part of the arresting (or stopping) officers. In such cases, once identity has been established to the satisfaction of the police (and it should be noted that errors are not unknown—particularly in these volatile cases), the person suspected is transformed immediately into an asshole and is subject to a predictably harsh treatment. Thus, in effect the label arises from an offense which occurred outside the immediate presence of the officers. However, since the spoiled identity must be reestablished anew in the immediate surroundings, the properties of the "affront" correspond analytically to the more familiar case outlines in the text. And

while the distinction has theoretical value regarding the norms of the police culture (i.e., that it is not the denounced per se that is important, but rather it is the denouncer that matters—''says who?''), its practical implications are questionable because patrolmen rarely encounter such situations.

6 In most regards, the asshole is a classic case of the deviant—although not transituationally so. See Matza (1969), Becker (1963), and Cohen (1965) for a systematic elaboration of the ideas which underpin this analysis.

7 By the term ''extralegal'' I am merely implying that the formal police mandate excludes such moral considerations from actions inducing decisions made by officers on the street. The notion of professional policing makes this explicit when it is suggested that patrolmen must act impersonally without regard to individual prejudice.

8 The ''cover-your-ass'' phenomena associated with urban policing is described in more depth in Van Maanen (1974). See also Manning (1974b) for a theoretical view of the more general construct, the police lie; and Chevigny (1968) for a presentation of numerous disturbing case studies.

9 Arrests are, of course, sometimes used to teach someone a lesson. However, police believe that in many cases the asshole will arrange his release before the patrolman will have completed the paperwork necessitated by the arrest. And since the affront was moral, the legal justification to ''make the case'' in court may be lacking. Thus, the classroom more often than not is in the street. Given the opportunity to teach the asshole either by ''turning him in'' or ''doing him in,'' most police would choose the latter.

References

Banton, Michael (1964). *The Policeman in the Community*. New York: Basic Books.

Bayley, D. H., & Mendelsohn, H. (1969). *Minorities and the Police: Confrontation in America*. New York: Free Press.

Becker, Howard S. (1962). The nature of a profession. In *Education for the Professions*, 61st Yearbook of the Society for the Study of Education, Part 2. Chicago: University of Chicago Press.

_____ (1963). *Outsiders*. New York: Free Press.

Berkeley, George E. (1969). *The Democratic Policeman*. Boston: Beacon Press.

Bittner, Egon (1970). *The Functions of the Police in Modern Society*. Washington, DC: United States Government Printing Office.

_____ (1967). The police on skid row. *American Sociological Review*, 32:699–715.

Black, Donald (1968). Police Encounters and Social Organization: An Observational Study. Unpublished Ph.D. Dissertation, University of Michigan.

Cain, Maureen (1973). *Society and the Policeman's Role*. London: Kegan Paul.

_____ (1971). On the beat: Interactions and relations in rural and urban police forces. In Cohen, S. (ed.). *Images of Deviance*. Middlesex, England: Penguin Books.

Chevigny, Paul (1968). *Police Power: Police Abuses in New York*. New York: Pantheon.

Cohen, Albert K. (1965). The sociology of the deviant act. *American Sociological Review*, 30:5–14.

Cumming, E., Cumming, I., & Edell, L. (1965). The policeman as philosopher, guide and friend. *Social Problems*, 12:276–286.

Drodge, Edward F. (1973). *The Patrolman: A Cop's Story*. New York: New American Library.

Harris, Richard N. (1973). *The Police Academy: An Inside View*. New York: John Wiley & Sons.

Hughes, Everett C. (1965). Professions. In Lynn, K. S. (ed.). *Professions in America*. Boston: Beacon Press.

_____ (1958). *Men and Their Work*. Glencoe, IL: Free Press.

LaFave, W. R. (1965). *Arrest: The Decision to Take a Suspect into Custody*. Boston: Little, Brown and Company.

Manning, Peter K. (1971). The police: Mandate, strategies and appearances. In Douglas, J. (ed.). *Crime and Justice in America*. Indianapolis: Bobbs-Merrill.

_____ (1974a). Dramatic aspects of policing: Selected propositions. *Sociology and Social Research*, 59 (October).

_____ (1974b). Police lying. *Urban Life*, 3 (October).

Maas, Peter (1973). *Serpico*. New York: The Viking Press.

Matza, David (1969). *Becoming Deviant*. Englewood Cliffs, NJ: Prentice-Hall.

McHugh, Peter (1969). A common-sense perception of deviancy. In Douglas, J. (ed.). *Deviance and Respectability*. New York: Basic Books.

Neiderhoffer, Arthur (1969). *Behind the Shield*. Garden City, NY: Doubleday.

Olsen, Jack (1974). *Sweet Street*. New York: Simon and Schuster.

Piliavin, I., & Briar, S. (1964). Police encounters with juveniles. *American Journal of Sociology*, 70:206–214.

Reiss, Albert J. (1971). *The Police and the Public*. New Haven: Yale University Press.

Rubenstein, Jonathan (1973). *City Police*. New York: Farrar, Straus and Giroux.

Sacks, Harvey (1972). Notes on police assessment of moral character. In Sudnow, D. (ed.). *Studies in Social Interaction*. New York: The Free Press.

Silver, Allen (1967). The demand for order in civil society. In Bordua, D. (ed.). *The Police: Six Sociological Essays*. New York: John Wiley & Sons.

Simmel, Georg (1950). *The Sociology of Georg Simmel*. Translated, edited, and with an introduction by Kurt H. Wolff. New York: The Free Press.

Skolnick, Jerome (1966). *Justice Without Trial*. New York: John Wiley & Sons.

Skolnick, Jerome, & Woodworth, J. R. (1967). Bureaucracy, information and social control. In Bordua, D. (ed.). *The Police: Six Sociological Essays*. New York: John Wiley & Sons.

Terkel, Studs (1968). *Division Street: America*. New York: Random House.

_____ (1974). *Working*. New York: Pantheon.

Van Maanen, John (1972). Pledging the Police: A Study of Selected Aspects of Recruit Socialization in a Large Police Department. Unpublished Ph.D. Dissertation, University of California, Irvine.

_____ (1973). Observations on the making of policemen. *Human Organizations*, 32:407–418.

_____ (1974). Working the streets: A developmental view of police behavior. In Jacobs, H. (ed.). *Reality and Reform: The Criminal Justice System*. Beverly Hills: Sage Publications.

Van Maanen, John (1975). Police socialization. *Administrative Science Quarterly*, 20:207–228.

Walker, T. Mike. (1969). *Voices from the Bottom of the World: A Policeman's Journal.* New York: Grove Press.

Webster, J. A. (1970). Police task and time study. *Journal of Criminal Law, Criminology and Police Science*, 61:94–100.

Westley, William (1970). *Violence and the Police*. Cambridge: MIT Press (originally a Ph.D. Dissertation, University of Chicago, 1951).

Whittemore, L. H. (1973). *The Super Cops*. New York: Stein and Day.

Wilson, James Q. (1967). Police morale, reform and citizen respect: The Chicago case. In Bordua, D. (ed.). *The Police: Six Sociological Essays*. New York: John Wiley & Sons.

_____ (1968). *Varieties of Police Behavior*. Cambridge: Harvard University Press.

19

The Dirty Harry Problem

Carl B. Klockars

W hen and to what extent does the morally good end warrant or justify an ethically, politically, or legally dangerous means for its achievement? This is a very old question for philosophers. Although it has received extensive consideration in policelike occupations and is at the dramatic core of police fiction and detective novels, I know of not a single contribution to the criminological or sociological literature on policing which raises it explicitly and examines its implications.[1] This is the case in spite of the fact that there is considerable evidence to suggest that it is not only an ineluctable part of police work, but a moral problem with which police themselves are quite familiar. There are, I believe, a number of good reasons why social scientists have avoided or neglected what I like to call the Dirty Harry problem in policing, not the least of which is that it is insoluble. However, a great deal can be learned about police work by examining some failed solutions, three of which I consider in the following pages. First, though, it is necessary to explain what a Dirty Harry problem is and what it is about it that makes it so problematic.

❖ THE DIRTY HARRY PROBLEM ❖

The Dirty Harry problem draws its name from the 1971 Warner Brothers film *Dirty Harry* and its chief protagonist, antihero Inspector Harry "Dirty

The Annals, 452 (November 1980): 33–47. Reprinted with permission of The American Academy of Political and Social Science.

Harry'' Callahan. The film features a number of events which dramatize the Dirty Harry problem in different ways, but the one which does so most explicitly and most completely places Harry in the following situation. A 14-year-old girl has been kidnapped and is being held captive by a psychopathic killer. The killer, ''Scorpio,'' who has already struck twice, demands $200,000 ransom to release the girl, who is buried with just enough oxygen to keep her alive for a few hours. Harry gets the job of delivering the ransom and, after enormous exertion, finally meets Scorpio. At their meeting Scorpio decides to renege on his bargain, let the girl die, and kill Harry. Harry manages to stab Scorpio in the leg before he does so, but not before Scorpio seriously wounds Harry's partner, an inexperienced, idealistic, slightly ethnic, former sociology major.

Scorpio escapes, but Harry manages to track him down through the clinic where he was treated for his wounded leg. After learning that Scorpio lives on the grounds of a nearby football stadium, Harry breaks into his apartment, finds guns and other evidence of his guilt, and finally confronts Scorpio on the 50-yard line, where Harry shoots him in the leg as he is trying to escape. Standing over Scorpio, Harry demands to know where the girl is buried. Scorpio refuses to disclose her location, demanding his rights to a lawyer. As the camera draws back from the scene Harry stands on Scorpio's bullet-mangled leg to torture a confession of the girl's location from him.

As it turns out, the girl is already dead and Scorpio must be set free. Neither the gun found in the illegal search, nor the confession Harry extorted, nor any of its fruits—including the girl's body—would be admissible in court.

The preceding scene, the heart of Dirty Harry, raises a number of issues of far-reaching significance for the sociology of the police, the first of which will now be discussed.

❖ THE DIRTY HARRY PROBLEM I ❖
THE END OF INNOCENCE

As we have phrased it previously, the Dirty Harry problem asks when and to what extent does the morally good end warrant or justify an ethically, politically, or legally dangerous means to its achievement? In itself, this question assumes the possibility of a genuine moral dilemma and posits its existence in a means-ends arrangement which may be expressed schematically as follows:

MEANS

	Morally good (+)	Morally dirty (−)
Morally good (+)	**A** + +	**B** − + The Dirty Harry Problem
Morally dirty (−)	**C** + −	**D** − −

ENDS

It is important to specify clearly the terms of the Dirty Harry problem not only to show that it must involve the juxtaposition of good ends and dirty means, but also to show what must be proven to demonstrate that a Dirty Harry problem exists. If one could show, for example, that box B is always empirically empty or that in any given case the terms of the situation are better read in some other means-ends arrangement, Dirty Harry problems vanish. At this first level, however, I suspect that no one could exclude the core scene of *Dirty Harry* from the class of Dirty Harry problems. There is no question that saving the life of an innocent victim of kidnapping is a "good" thing nor that grinding the bullet-mangled leg of Scorpio to extort a confession from him is "dirty."[2]

There is, in addition, a second level of criteria of an empirical and epistemological nature that must be met before a Dirty Harry problem actually comes into being. They involve the connection between the dirty act and the good end. Principally, what must be known and, importantly, known before the dirty act is committed, is that it will result in the achievement of the good end. In any absolute sense this is, of course, impossible to know, in that no acts are ever completely certain in their consequences. Thus the question is always a matter of probabilities. But it is helpful to break those probabilities into classes which attach to various subcategories of the overall question. In the given case, this level of problem would seem to require that three questions be satisfied, though not all with the same level of certainty.

In *Dirty Harry*, the first question is, Is Scorpio able to provide the information Dirty Harry seeks? It is an epistemological question about which, in *Dirty Harry*, we are absolutely certain. Harry met Scorpio at the time of the ransom exchange. Not only did he admit the kidnapping at that time, but when he made the ransom demand, Scorpio sent one of the girl's teeth and a description of her clothing and underwear to leave no doubt about the existence of his victim.

Second, we must know there are means, dirty means and nothing other than dirty means, which are likely to achieve the good end. One can, of course, never be sure that one is aware of or has considered all possible alternatives, but in *Dirty Harry* there would appear to be no reason for Scorpio in his rational self-interest to confess to the girl's location without being coerced to do so.

The third question which must be satisfied at this empirical and epistemological level concedes that dirty means are the only method which will be effective, but asks whether or not, in the end, they will be in vain. We know in *Dirty Harry* that they were, and Harry himself, at the time of the ransom demand, admits he believes that the girl is already dead. Does not this possibility or likelihood that the girl is dead destroy the justification for Harry's dirty act? Although it surely would if Harry knew for certain that the girl was dead, I do not think it does insofar as even a small probability of her being saved exists. The reason is that the good to be achieved is so unquestionably good and so passionately felt that even a small possibility of its achievement demands that it be tried. For example, were we to ask, If it were your daughter would you want Harry to do what he did? it would be this passionate sense of unquestionable good that we are trying to dramatize. It is for this reason that in philosophical circles the Dirty Hands problem has been largely restricted to questions of national security, revolutionary terrorism, and international war. It is also why the Dirty Harry problem in detective fiction almost always involves murder.

Once we have satisfied ourselves that a Dirty Harry problem is conceptually possible and that, in fact, we can specify one set of concrete circumstances in which it exists, one might think that the most difficult question of all is, What ought to be done? I do not think it is. I suspect that there are very few people who would not want Harry to do something dirty in the situation specified. I know I would want him to do what he did, and what is more, I would want anyone who policed for me to be prepared to do so as well. Put differently, I want to have as police officers men and women of moral courage and sensitivity.

But to those who would want exactly that, the Dirty Harry problem poses its most irksome conclusion. Namely, that one cannot, at least in the specific case at hand, have a policeman who is both just and innocent. The troublesome issue in the Dirty Harry problem is not whether under some utilitarian calculus a right choice can be made, but that the choice must always be between at least two wrongs. And in choosing to do either wrong, the policeman inevitably taints or tarnishes himself.

It was this conclusion on the part of Dashiell Hammett, Raymond Chandler, Raoul Whitfield, Horace McCoy, James M. Cain, Lester Dent, and dozens of other tough-guy writers of hard-boiled detective stories that distinguished these writers from what has come to be called the "classical school" of detective fiction. What these men could not stomach about Sherlock Holmes (Conan Doyle), Inspector French (Freeman Wills Crofts), and Father Brown (Chesterton), to name a few of the best, was not that they were virtuous, but that their virtue was unsullied. Their objection was that the classical detective's occupation, how he worked, and the jobs he was called upon to do left him morally immaculate. Even the most brilliant defender of the classical detective story, W. H. Auden, was forced to confess that that conclusion gave the stories "magical function," but rendered them impossible as art.[3]

If popular conceptions of police work have relevance for its actual practice—as Egon Bittner and a host of others have argued that they do[4]—the Dirty Harry problem, found in one version or another in countless detective novels and reflected in paler imitations on countless television screens, for example, "Parental Discretion is Advised," is not an unimportant contributor to police work's "tainted" quality. But we must remember also that the revolution of the tough-guy writers, so these writers said, was not predicated on some mere artificial, aesthetic objection. With few exceptions, their claim was that their works were art. That is, at all meaningful levels, the stories were true. It is this claim I should next like to examine in the real-life context of the Dirty Harry problem.

❖ THE DIRTY HARRY PROBLEM II ❖
DIRTY MEN AND DIRTY WORK

Dirty Harry problems arise quite often. For policemen, real, everyday policemen, Dirty Harry problems are part of their job and thus considerably more than rare or artificial dramatic exceptions. To make this point, I will translate some rather familiar police practices, street stops and searches and victim and witness interrogation, into Dirty Harry problems.

Good Ends and Dirty Means

The first question our analysis of street stops and searches and victim and witness interrogation must satisfy is, For policemen, do these activities present the cognitive opportunity for the juxtaposition of good ends and dirty means to their achievement? Although the "goodness" question will be considered in some detail later, suffice it to say here that police find the prevention of crime and the punishment of wrongful or criminal behavior a good thing to achieve. Likewise, they, perhaps more than any other group in society, are intimately aware of the varieties of dirty means available for the achievement of those good ends. In the case of street stops and searches, these dirty alternatives range from falsifying probable cause for a stop, to manufacturing a false arrest to legitimate an illegal search, to simply searching without the fraudulent covering devices of either. In the case of victim or witness interrogations, dirty means range from dramaturgically "chilling" a *Miranda* warning by an edited or unemphatic reading to Harry's grinding a man's bullet-shattered leg to extort a confession from him.

While all these practices may be "dirty" enough to satisfy certain people of especially refined sensitivities, does not a special case have to be made, not for the public's perception of the "dirtiness" of certain illegal, deceptive, or sub-rosa acts, but for the police's perception of their dirtiness? Are not the police hard-boiled, less sensitive to such things than are most of us? I think there is no question that they are, and our contention about the prevalence of Dirty Harry problems in policing suggests that they are likely to be. How does this "tough-minded" attitude toward dirty means affect our argument? At least at this stage it seems to strengthen it. That is, the failure of police to regard dirty means with the same hesitation that most citizens do seems to suggest that they juxtapose them to the achievement of good ends more quickly and more readily than most of us.

The Dirty Means Must Work

In phrasing the second standard for the Dirty Harry problem as "The dirty means must work," we gloss over a whole range of qualifying conditions, some of which we have already considered. The most critical, implied in *Dirty Harry*, is that the person on whom dirty means are to be used must be guilty. It should be pointed out, however, that this standard is far higher than any student of the Dirty Hands problem in politics has ever been willing to admit. In fact, the moral dilemma of Dirty Hands is often dramatized by the fact that dirty means must be visited on quite innocent victims. It is the blood of such innocents, for example, whom the Communist leader Hoerderer in Sartre's *Dirty Hands* refers to when he says, "I have dirty hands. Right up to the elbows. I've plunged them in filth and blood. But what do you hope? Do you think you can govern innocently?"[5]

But even if cases in which innocent victims suffer dirty means commonly qualify as Dirty Harry problems, and by extension innocent victims would be allowable in Dirty Harry problems, there are a number of factors in the nature and context of policing which suggest that police themselves are inclined toward the higher "guilty victim" standard. Although there may be others, the following are probably the most salient.

1 *The Operative Assumption of Guilt.* In street stops and searches as well as interrogations, it is in the nature of the police task that guilt is assumed as a working premise. That is, in order for a policeman to do his job, he must, unless he clearly knows otherwise, assume that the person he sees is guilty and the behavior he is witnessing is evidence of some concealed or hidden offense. If a driver looks at him "too long" or not at all or if a witness or suspect talks too little or too much, it is only his operative assumption of guilt that makes those actions meaningful. Moreover, the policeman is often not in a position to suspend his working assumption until he has taken action, sometimes dirty action, to disconfirm it.

2 *The Worst of all Possible Guilt.* The matter of the operative assumption of guilt is complicated further because the policeman is obliged to make a still higher-order assumption of guilt, namely, that the person is not only guilty, but dangerously so. In the case of street stops and searches, for instance, although the probability of coming upon a dangerous felon is extremely low, policemen quite reasonably take the possibility of doing so as a working assumption on the understandable premise that once is enough. Likewise the premise that the one who has the most to hide will try hardest to hide it is a reasonable assumption for interrogation.

3 *The Great Guilty Place Assumption.* The frequency with which policemen confront the worst of people, places, and occasions creates an epistemological problem of serious psychological proportions. As a consequence of his job, the policeman is constantly exposed to highly selective samples of his environment. That he comes to read a clump of bushes as a place to hide, a roadside rest as a homosexual "tearoom," a sweet old lady as a robbery looking for a place to happen, or a poor young black as someone willing to oblige her is not a question of a perverse, pessimistic, or racist personality, but of a person whose job requires that he strive to see race, age, sex, and even nature in an ecology of guilt, which can include him if he fails to see it so.[6]

4 *The Not Guilty (This Time) Assumption.* With considerable sociological research and conventional wisdom to support him, the policeman knows that most people in the great guilty place in which he works

have committed numerous crimes for which they have never been caught. Thus when a stop proves unwarranted, a search comes up "dry," or an interrogation fails, despite the dirty means, the policeman is not at all obliged to conclude that the person victimized by them is innocent, only that, and even this need not always be conceded, he is innocent this time.

Dirty Means as Ends in Themselves

How do these features of police work, all of which seem to incline police to accept a standard of a guilty victim for their dirty means, bear upon the Dirty Harry problem from which they derive? The most dangerous reading suggests that if police are inclined, and often quite rightly inclined, to believe they are dealing with factually, if not legally, guilty subjects, they become likely to see their dirty acts, not as means to the achievement of good ends, but as ends in themselves—as punishment of guilty people whom the police believe deserve to be punished.

If this line of argument is true, it has the effect, in terms of police perceptions, of moving Dirty Harry problems completely outside of the fourfold table of means-ends combinations created in order to define it. Importantly as well, in terms of our perceptions, Dirty Harry problems of this type can no longer be read as cases of dirty means employed to the achievement of good ends. For unless we are willing to admit in a democratic society a police which arrogates to itself the task of punishing those who they think are guilty, we are forced to conclude that Dirty Harry problems represent cases of employing dirty means to dirty ends, in which case, nobody, not the police and certainly not us, is left with any kind of moral dilemma.

The possibility is quite real and quite fearsome, but it is mediated by certain features of police work, some of which inhere in the nature of the work itself and others, imposed from outside, which have a quite explicit impact on it. The most important of the "naturalistic" features of policing which belie the preceding argument is that the assumption of guilt and all the configurations in the policeman's world which serve to support it often turn out wrong. It is precisely because the operative assumption of guilt can be forced on everything and everyone that the policeman who must use it constantly comes to find it leads him astray more often than it confirms his suspicions.

Similarly, a great many of the things policemen do, some of which we have already conceded appear to police as less dirty than they appear to us—faked probable cause for a street stop, manipulated *Miranda* warnings, and so forth—are simply impossible to read as punishments.

This is so particularly if we grant a hard-boiled character to our cops.

Of course, neither of these naturalistic restrictions on the obliteration of the means-ends schema is or should be terribly comforting. To the extent that the first is helpful at all assumes a certain skill and capacity of mind that we may not wish to award to all policemen. The willingness to engage in the constant refutation of one's working worldview presumes a certain intellectual integrity which can certainly go awry. Likewise, the second merely admits that on occasion policemen do some things which reveal they appreciate that the state's capacity to punish is sometimes greater than theirs.

To both these "natural" restrictions on the obliteration of the means-ends character of Dirty Harry problems, we can add the exclusionary rule. Although the exclusionary rule is the manifest target of *Dirty Harry*, it, more than anything else, makes Dirty Harry problems a reality in everyday policing. It is the great virtue of exclusionary rules—applying in various forms to stops, searches, seizures, and interrogations—that they hit directly upon the intolerable, though often, I think, moral desire of police to punish. These rules make the very simple point to police that the more they wish to see a felon punished, the more they are advised to be scrupulous in their treatment of him. Put differently, the best thing Harry could have done *for* Scorpio was to step on his leg, extort his confession, and break into his apartment.

If certain natural features of policing and particularly exclusionary rules combine to maintain the possibility of Dirty Harry problems in a context in which a real danger appears to be their disappearance, it does not follow that police cannot or do not collapse the dirty means-good ends division on some occasions and become punishers. I only hold that on many other occasions, collapse does not occur and Dirty Harry problems, as defined, are still widely possible. What must be remembered next, on the way to making their possibility real, is that policemen know, or think they know, before they employ a dirty means that a dirty means and only a dirty means will work.

Only a Dirty Means Will Work

The moral standard that a policeman know in advance of resorting to a dirty means that a dirty means and only a dirty means will work, rests heavily on two technical dimensions: (1) the professional competence of the policeman and (2) the range of legitimate working options available to him. Both are intimately connected, though the distinction to be preserved between them is that the first is a matter of the policeman's individual competence and the second of the competence of the institutions for which (his department) and with which (the law) the policeman works.

In any concrete case, the relations between these moral and technical dimensions of the Dirty Harry problem are extremely complicated. But a priori it follows that the more competent a policeman is at the use of legal means, the less he will be obliged to resort to dirty alternatives. Likewise, the department that trains its policemen well and supplies them with the resources—knowledge and material—to do their work will find that the policemen who work for them will not resort to dirty means "unnecessarily," meaning only those occasions when an acceptable means will work as well as a dirty one.

While these two premises flow a priori from raising the Dirty Harry problem, questions involving the moral and technical roles of laws governing police means invite a very dangerous type of a priori reasoning:

> Combating distrust [of the police] requires getting across the rather complicated message that granting the police specific forms of new authority may be the most effective means for reducing abuse of authority which is now theirs; that it is the absence of properly proscribed forms of authority that often impels the police to engage in questionable or outright illegal conduct. Before state legislatures enacted statutes giving limited authority to the police to stop and question persons suspected of criminal involvement, police nevertheless stopped and questioned people. It is inconceivable how any police agency could be expected to operate without doing so. But since the basis for their actions was unclear, the police—if they thought a challenge likely—would use the guise of arresting the individual on a minor charge (often without clear evidence) to provide a semblance of legality. Enactment of stopping and questioning statutes eliminated the need for this sham.[7]

Herman Goldstein's preceding argument and observations are undoubtedly true, but the danger in them is that they can be extended to apply to any dirty means, not only illegal arrests to legitimate necessary street stops, but dirty means to accomplish subsequent searches and seizures all the way to beating confessions out of suspects when no other means will work. But, of course, Goldstein does not intend his argument to be extended in these ways.

Nevertheless, his a priori argument, dangerous though it may be, points to the fact that Dirty Harry problems can arise wherever restrictions are placed on police methods and are particularly likely to do so when police themselves perceive that those restrictions are undesirable, unreasonable, or unfair. His argument succeeds in doing what police who face Dirty Harry problems constantly do: rendering the law problematic.

But while Goldstein, one of the most distinguished legal scholars in America, can follow his finding with books, articles, and lectures which urge change, it is left to the policeman to take upon himself the moral responsibility of subverting it with dirty and hidden means.

Compelling and Unquestionable Ends

If Dirty Harry problems can be shown to exist in their technical dimensions—as genuine means-ends problems where only dirty means will work—the question of the magnitude and urgency of the ends that the dirty means may be employed to achieve must still be confronted. Specifically, it must be shown that the ends of dirty means are so desirable that the failure to achieve them would cast the person who is in a position to do so in moral disrepute.

The two most widely acknowledged ends of policing are peace keeping and law enforcement. It would follow, of course, that if both these ends were held to be unworthy, Dirty Harry problems would disappear. There are arguments challenging both ends. For instance, certain radical critiques of policing attempt to reduce the peace-keeping and law-enforcing functions of the police in the United States to nothing more than acts of capitalist oppression. From such a position flows not only the denial of the legitimacy of any talk of Dirty Harry problems, but also the denial of the legitimacy of the entire police function.[8]

Regardless of the merits of such critiques, it will suffice for the purpose of this analysis to maintain that there is a large "clientele," to use Albert Reiss's term, for both types of police function.[9] And it should come as no surprise to anyone that the police themselves accept the legitimacy of their own peace-keeping and law-enforcing ends. Some comment is needed, though, on how large that clientele for those functions is and how compelling and unquestionable the ends of peace keeping and law enforcement are for them.

There is no more popular, compelling, urgent, nor more broadly appealing idea than peace. In international relations, it is potent enough to legitimate the stockpiling of enough nuclear weapons to exterminate every living thing on earth a dozen times over. In domestic affairs, it gives legitimacy to the idea of the state, and the aspirations to it have succeeded in granting to the state an absolute monopoly on the right to legitimate the use of force and a near monopoly on its actual, legitimate use: the police. That peace has managed to legitimate these highly dangerous means to its achievement in virtually every advanced nation in the world is adequate testimony to the fact that it qualifies, if any end does, as a good end so unquestionable and so compelling that it can legitimate risking the most dangerous and dirtiest of means.

The fact is, though, that most American policemen prefer to define their work as law enforcement rather than peace keeping, even though they may, in fact, do more of the latter. It is a distinction that should not be allowed to slip away in assuming, for instance, that the policeman's purpose in enforcing the law is to keep the peace. Likewise, though it is a possibility, it will not do to assume that police simply enforce the law as an end in itself, without meaning and without purpose or end. The widely discretionary behavior of working policemen and the enormous under-enforcement of the law which characterizes most police agencies simply belie that possibility.

An interpretation of law enforcement which is compatible with empirical studies of police behavior—as peace keeping is—and police talk in America—which peace keeping generally is not—is an understanding of the ends of law enforcement as punishment. There are, of course, many theories of punishment, but the police seem inclined toward the simplest: the belief that certain people who have committed certain acts deserve to be punished for them. What can one say of the compelling and unquestionable character of this retributive ambition as an end of policing and policemen?

Both historically and sociologically there is ample evidence that punishment is almost as unquestionable and compelling an end as peace. Historically, we have a long and painful history of punishment, a history longer in fact than the history of the end of peace. Sociologically, the application of what may well be the only culturally universal norm, the norm of reciprocity, implies the direct and natural relations between wrongful acts and their punishments.[10] Possibly the best evidence for the strength and urgency of the desire to punish in modern society is the extraordinary complex of rules and procedures democratic states have assembled which prevents legitimate punishment from being administered wrongfully or frivolously.

If we can conclude that peace and punishment are ends unquestionable and compelling enough to satisfy the demands of Dirty Harry problems, we are led to one final question on which we may draw from some sociological theories of the police for assistance. If the Dirty Harry problem is at the core of the police role, or at least near to it, how is it that police can or do come to reconcile their use of—or their failure to use—dirty means to achieve unquestionably good and compelling ends?

❖ PUBLIC POLICY AND POLICE MORALITY ❖
THREE DEFECTIVE RESOLUTIONS OF THE DIRTY HARRY PROBLEM

The contemporary literature on policing appears to contain three quite different types of solution or resolution. But because the Dirty Harry problem is a genuine moral dilemma, that is, a situation which will admit no real solution or resolution, each is necessarily defective. Also, understandably, each solution or resolution presents itself as an answer to a somewhat different problem. In matters of public policy, such concealments are often necessary and probably wise, although they have a way of coming around to haunt their architects sooner or later. In discovering that each is flawed and in disclosing the concealments which allow the appearance of resolution, we do not urge that it be held against sociologists that they are not philosophers nor do we argue that they should succeed where philosophers before them have failed. Rather, we only wish to make clear what is risked by each concealment and to face candidly the inevitably unfortunate ramifications which must proceed from it.

Snappy Bureaucrats

In the works of August Vollmer, Bruce Smith, O. W. Wilson, and those progressive police administrators who still follow their lead, a vision of the perfect police agency and the perfect policeman has gained considerable ground. Labeled "the professional model" in police circles—though entirely different from any classical sense of profession or professional—it envisions a highly trained, technologically sophisticated police department operating free from political interference with a corps of well-educated police responding obediently to the policies, orders, and directives of a central administrative command. It is a vision of police officers, to use Bittner's phrasing, as "snappy bureaucrats,"[11] cogs in a quasi-military machine who do what they are told out of a mix of fear, loyalty, routine, and detailed specification of duties.

The professional model, unlike other solutions to be considered, is based on the assumption that the policeman's motives for working can be made to locate within his department. He will, if told, work vice or traffic, juvenile or homicide, patrol passively or aggressively, and produce one, two, four, or six arrests, pedestrian stops, or reports per hour, day, or week as his department sees fit. In this way the assumption and vision of the professional model in policing is little different from that of any bureaucracy which seeks by specifying tasks and setting expectations for levels of production—work quotas—to coordinate a regular, predictable, and efficient service for its clientele.

The problem with this vision of *sine ira et studio* service by obedient operatives is that when the product to be delivered is some form of human service—education, welfare, health, and police bureaucracies are similar in this way—the vision seems always to fall short of expectations. On the one hand the would-be bureaucratic operatives—teachers, social workers, nurses, and policemen—resent being treated as mere bureaucrats and resist the translation of their work into quotas, directives, rules, regulations, or other abstract specifications. On the other hand, to the extent that the vision of an efficient and obedient human service bureaucracy is realized, the clientele of such institutions typically come away with the impression that no one in the institution truly *cares* about their problems. And, of course, in that the aim of bureaucratization is to locate employees' motives for work within the bureaucracy, they are absolutely correct in their feelings.

To the extent that the professional model succeeds in making the ends of policing locate within the agency as opposed to moral demands of the tasks which policemen are asked by their clients to do, it appears to solve the Dirty Harry problem. When it succeeds, it does so by replacing the morally compelling ends of punishment and peace with the less human, though by no means uncompelling, ends of bureaucratic performance. However, this resolution certainly does not imply that dirty means will disappear, only that the motives for their use will be career advancement and promotion. Likewise, on those occasions when a morally sensitive policeman would be compelled by the demands of the situational exigencies before him to use a dirty means, the bureaucratic operative envisioned by the professional model will merely do his job. Ambitious bureaucrats and obedient timeservers fail at being the type of morally sensitive souls we want to be policemen. The professional model's bureaucratic resolution of the Dirty Harry problem fails in policing for the same reason it fails in every other human service agency: it is quite simply an impossibility to create a bureaucrat who cares for anything but his bureaucracy.

The idealized image of the professional model, which has been responded to with an ideal critique, is probably unrealizable. Reality intervenes as the ideal type is approached. The bureaucracy seems to take on weight as it approaches the pole, is slowed, and may even collapse in approaching.

Bittner's Peace

A second effort in the literature of contemporary policing also attempts to address the Dirty Harry problem by substituting an alternative to the presently prevailing police ends of punishment. Where the professional model sought to substitute bureaucratic rewards and sanctions for the moral end of punishment, the elegant polemics by Egon Bittner in *The Functions of Police in Modern Society* and "Florence Nightingale in Pursuit of Willie Sutton: A Theory of the Police" seek to substitute the end of peace. In beautifully chosen words, examples, and phrasing, Bittner leads his readers to conclude that peace is historically, empirically, intellectually, and morally the most compelling, unquestionable, and humane end of policing. Bittner is, I fear, absolutely right.

It is the end of peace which legitimates the extension of police responsibilities into a wide variety of civil matters—neighborhood disputes, loud parties, corner lounging, lovers' quarrels, political rallies, disobedient children, bicycle registration, pet control, and a hundred other types of tasks which a modern "service" style police department regularly is called upon to perform. With these responsibilities, which most "good" police agencies now accept willingly and officially, also comes the need for an extension of police powers. Arrest is, after all, too crude a tool to be used in all the various situations in which our peace-keeping policemen are routinely asked to be of help. "Why should," asks Herman Goldstein, in a manner in which Bittner would approve, "a police officer arrest and charge a disorderly tavern patron if ordering him to leave the tavern will suffice? Must he arrest and charge one of the parties in a lovers' quarrel if assistance in forcing a separation is all that is desired?"[12] There is no question that both those situations could be handled more peacefully if police were granted new powers which would allow them to handle those situations in the way Goldstein rhetorically asks if they should. That such extensions of police powers will be asked for by our most enlightened police departments in the interests of keeping the peace is absolutely certain. If the success of the decriminalization of police arrests for public intoxication, vagrancy, mental illness, and the virtually unrestricted two-hour right of detention made possible by the Uniform Law of Arrest are any indication of the likelihood of extensions being received favorably, the end of peace and its superiority over punishment in legitimating the extension of police powers seem exceedingly likely to prevail further.

The problem with peace is that it is not the only end of policing so compelling, unquestionable, and in the end, humane. Amid the good work toward the end of peace that we increasingly want our police to do, it is certain that individuals or groups will arise who the police, in all their peace-keeping benevolence, will conclude, on moral if not political or institutional grounds, have "got it coming." And all the once dirty means which were bleached in the brilliant light of peace will return to their true colors.

Skolnick's Craftsman

The third and final attempt to resolve the Dirty Harry problem is offered by Jerome Skolnick, who in *Justice Without Trial* comes extremely close to stating the Dirty Harry problem openly when he writes:

> . . . He (the policeman) sees himself as a craftsman, at his best, a master of his trade . . . [he] draws a moral distinction between criminal law and criminal procedure. The distinction is drawn somewhat as follows: The substantive law of crimes is intended to control the behavior of people who wilfully injure persons or property, or who engage in behaviors having such a consequence, such as the use of narcotics. Criminal procedure, by contrast, is intended to control authorities, not criminals. As such, it does not fall into the same *moral* class of constraint as substantive criminal law. If a policeman were himself to use narcotics, or to steal, or to assault, *outside the line of duty*, much the same standards would be applied to him by other policemen as to the ordinary citizen. When, however, the issue concerns the policeman's freedom to carry out his *duties*, another moral realm is entered.[13]

What is more, Skolnick's craftsman finds support from his peers, department, his community, and the law for the moral rightness of his calling. He cares about his work and finds it just.

What troubles Skolnick about his craftsman is his craft. The craftsman refuses to see, as Skolnick thinks he ought to, that the dirty means he sometimes uses to achieve his good ends stand in the same moral class of wrongs as those he is employed to fight. Skolnick's craftsman reaches this conclusion by understanding that his unquestionably good and compelling ends, on certain occasions, justify his employment of dirty means to their achievement. Skolnick's craftsman, as Skolnick understands him, resolves the Dirty Harry problem by denying the dirtiness of his means.

Skolnick's craftsman's resolution is, speaking precisely, Machiavellian. It should come as no surprise to find the representative of one of the classic attempts to resolve the problem of Dirty Hands to be a front runner in response to Dirty Harry. What is worrisome about such a resolution? What does it conceal that makes our genuine dilemma disappear? The problem is not that the craftsman will sometimes choose to use dirty means. If he is morally sensitive to its demands, every policeman's work will sometimes require as much. What is worrisome about Skolnick's craftsman is that he does not regard his means as dirty and, as Skolnick tells us, does not suffer from their use. The craftsman, if Skolnick's portrait of him is correct, will resort to dirty means too readily and too easily. He lacks the restraint that can come only from struggling to justify them and from taking seriously the hazards involved.

In 1966, when *Justice Without Trial* first appeared, Skolnick regarded the prospects of creating a more morally sensitive craftsman exceedingly dim. He could not imagine that the craftsman's community, employer, peers, or the courts could come to reward him more for his legal compliance than for the achievement of the ends of his craft. However, in phrasing the prospects in terms of a Dirty Harry problem, one can not only agree with Skolnick that denying the goodness of unquestionably good ends is a practical and political impossibility, but can also uncover another alternative, one which Skolnick does not pursue.

The alternative the Dirty Harry problem leads us to is ensuring that the craftsman regards his dirty means as dirty by applying the same retributive principles of punishment to his wrongful acts that he is quite willing to apply to others'. It is, in fact, only when his wrongful acts are punished that he will come to see them as wrongful and will appreciate the genuine moral—rather than technical or occupational—choice he makes in resorting to them. The prospects for punishment of such acts are by no means dim, and considerable strides in this area have been made. It requires far fewer resources to punish than to reward. Secondly, the likelihood that juries in civil suits will find dirty means dirtier than police do is confirmed by police claims that outsiders cannot appreciate the same moral and technical distinctions that they do. Finally, severe financial losses to police agencies as well as to their officers eventually communicate to both that vigorously policing themselves is cheaper and more pleasing than having to pay so heavily if they do not. If under such conditions our craftsman police officer is still willing to risk the employment of dirty means to achieve what he understands to be unquestionably good ends, he will not only know that he has behaved justly, but that in doing so he must run the risk of becoming genuinely guilty as well.

❖ A FINAL NOTE ❖

In urging the punishment of policemen who resort to dirty means to achieve some unquestionably good and morally compelling end, we recognize that we create a Dirty Harry problem for ourselves and for those we urge to effect such punishments. It is a fitting end, one which teaches once again that the danger in Dirty Harry problems is never in their resolution, but in thinking that one has found a resolution with which one can truly live in peace.

Notes

¹ In the contemporary philosophical literature, particularly when raised for the vocation of politics, the question is commonly referred to as the Dirty Hands problem after J. P. Sartre's treatment of it in *Dirty Hands*, (*Les Maines Sales*, 1948) and in *No Exit and Three Other Plays* (New York: Modern Library, 1950). Despite its modern name, the problem is very old and has been taken up by Machiavelli in *The Prince* (1513) and *The Discourses* (1519) (New York: Modern Library, 1950); by Max Weber, "Politics as a Vocation," (1919) in *Max Weber: Essays in Sociology*, eds. and trans. H. Gerth and C. W. Wills (New York: Oxford University Press, 1946); and by Albert Camus, "The Just Assassins" (1949) in *Caligula and Three Other Plays* (New York: Alfred A. Knopf, 1958). *See* Michael Walzer's brilliant critique of these contributions, "Political Action: The Problem of Dirty Hands," *Philosophy and Public Affairs*, 2(2) (Winter 1972). Likewise the Dirty Hands/Dirty Harry problem is implicitly or explicitly raised in virtually every work of Raymond Chandler, Dashiell Hammett, James Cain, and other *Tough Guy Writers of the Thirties*, ed. David Madden (Carbondale: Southern Illinois University Press, 1968), as they are in all of the best work of Joseph Wambaugh, particularly *The Blue Knight*, *The New Centurions*, and *The Choirboys*.

² "Dirty" here means both "repugnant" in that it offends widely shared standards of human decency and dignity and "dangerous" in that it breaks commonly shared and supported norms, rules, or laws for conduct. To "dirty" acts there must be both a deontologically based face validity of immorality and a consequentialist threat to the prevailing rules for social order.

³ W. H. Auden, "The Guilty Vicarage," in *The Dyer's Hand and Other Essays* (New York: Alfred A. Knopf, 1956), 146–58.

⁴ Egon Bittner, *The Functions of Police in Modern Society* (New York: Jason Aronson, 1975) and "Florence Nightingale in Pursuit of Willie Sutton," in *The Potential for Reform of the Criminal Justice System*, vol. 3, ed. H. Jacob (Beverly Hills: Sage Publications, 1974), 11–44.

⁵ Sartre, *Dirty Hands*, p. 224.

⁶ One of Wambaugh's characters in *The Choirboys* makes this final point most dramatically when he fails to notice that a young boy's buttocks are flatter than they should be and reads the child's large stomach as a sign of adequate nutrition. When the child dies through his mother's neglect and abuse, the officer rightly includes himself in his ecology of guilt.

⁷ Herman Goldstein, *Policing a Free Society* (Cambridge, MA: Ballinger Publishing, 1977), 72.

⁸ *See*, for example, John F. Galliher, "Explanations of Police Behavior: A Critical Review and Analysis," *The Sociological Quarterly*, 12 (Summer 1971), 308–18; Richard Quinney, *Class, State, and Crime* (New York: David McKay, 1977).

⁹ Albert J. Reiss, Jr., *The Police and the Public* (New Haven: Yale University Press, 1971), 122.

¹⁰ These two assertions are drawn from Graeme Newman's *The Punishment Response* (Philadelphia: J. B. Lippincott Co., 1978).

¹¹ Bittner, p. 53.

¹² Ibid., p. 72.

¹³ Jerome Skolnick, *Justice Without Trial*, 2nd ed. (New York: John Wiley & Sons, 1975), 182.

Part V

The Police in Post-Modern Society

20

The Legacy of Conservative Ideology and Police

Carl B. Klockars

$\mathbf{T}$he topic of the legacy of conservative ideology and police must be approached with the greatest caution. The fact is that both "conservatism" and "police" have meant, do mean, and can mean so many different things to so many different people that it is scarcely possible to speak of either of them without being seriously misunderstood. To avoid this problem I will adopt the pedantic academic custom of defining my terms in some detail. Please bear with me. The great problem in debate over any variety of politics is not in eliciting opinion about where anybody stands. Just ask them and they will tell you. It is rather to pose the questions of politics in a sufficiently provocative enough manner to make discussion of where one stands and why one does so a topic worthy of discussion.

❖ POLICE ❖

By "police" I have in mind the domestic institution and individuals in the direct and full-time employ of the state to whom the state gives the general right to use coercive force. It is their general right to use coercive force which defines police and distinguishes them from all other citizens.

Police Forum, 3 (1) (1993): 1–6. Reprinted with permission of the Academy of Criminal Justice Sciences.

It is the special competence of police and what police and no one else make available to us in modern society.

Understanding "police" in this way has at least one immediate political virtue. It permits us to dispose of a major issue that is often understood and discussed in ideological terms, when it is an ineluctable property of the role of police, a role that is largely immune to change in any free society. This problem I would like [to] attempt to jettison at the outset is the charge that the focus of police effort is disproportionately on the activities of the poor and ignores for the most part the crimes and delicts of corporate and white collar criminals. The charge is absolutely true, the evidence for it is empirically overwhelming, and anyone with even passing familiarity with the routine activities of a patrol officer or detective in any contemporary American city would be obliged to agree with it. Largely the work of the police consists of superintending the activities of poor people.

The question, though, is whether this predominant focus of police activity is a reflection of discrimination and class bias and ought to be interpreted and understood in ideological terms. I do not believe it should for the same reason that I find no political message in the discovery that · the clients of the welfare system are largely poor people, that those of stock brokers are mostly well to do, or that those of hospitals are predominantly the sick. The police, like other vendors of services, offer a service that tends to be of use to certain categories of persons on certain types of occasions. The service that police make available is, to use Egon Bittner's phrase, the "distribution of non-negotiably coercive force." And we should not be surprised that certain people should have need for this service more frequently than others. One reason that the cops attend predominantly to the lives of poor people is that poor people require and request their services far more frequently than anyone else. That police attend predominantly to the lives and activities of poor people largely upon request of poor people is, though, only half the story. The other half is that crimes poor people are likely to commit and the circumstances under which they are likely to commit them are radically different from those of corporate or white collar offenders. Three features of the crimes of the poor are of particular relevance to the police. First, the type of crimes that poor people tend to commit are more likely to involve interpersonal violence than those of white collar or corporate offenders. White collar and corporate offenders steal with paper, pens, contracts, and computers, poor people by breaking, entering, and threatening. Second, poor people are far more likely to resist their apprehension by forceful means. White collar and corporate offenders employ lawyers and accountants to offer resistance. And, third, poor people are more likely to flee to avoid arrest and prosecution than the white collar offender with a stable, valuable place of residence or a corporate address.

Each of these differences is critical because of the different demand it makes on the special competence of the police, the right to use coercive force, to deal with it. Consider an example: a NYPD officer is sitting in his patrol car on a Manhattan street. An agitated pedestrian approaches the vehicle and explains to the officer that he is convinced that insider trading is afoot on Wall Street. The officer, aware that such activity is a crime and that millions may be involved, tells the complainant to hop in his patrol car. He slips the Crown Vic into gear, flips on his Twin Sonics and speeds to Wall Street. Upon arrival he leaves his car, one hand on his new 9mm the other fingering his PR-24. Tall, broad shouldered, with an air of confidence he strides onto the floor of the stock exchange, the epiphany of New York's finest. He is, of course, received there as some kind of nut.

What makes this imaginary officer's behavior preposterous is that he has no competence for the task he has undertaken because all the tools of the police trade are inappropriate and virtually useless in the environment he has entered. It is not because the officer himself is not outraged by insider trading. He may find it to be a more serious type of offense than he has ever been called upon to deal with, considering that the welfare of his pension fund, life insurance, and personal investments all depend on a fair market, not to mention the general economy.

But despite his feelings, neither he nor any other NYPD officer will deal with a complaint of such a crime. They will advise the complainant to contact a regulatory agency with the special competence necessary to deal with this problem, probably the Securities and Exchange Commission. My point can now be stated very simply. What is often spoken of as the ideological bias of police, their unwillingness to focus on crimes of the rich and their disproportionate attention to the behavior of the poor is largely without a political dimension. Such behavior on the part of the police does not stem from ideology but from the special and defining competence of police. We should find no more political nor ideological information in the discovery that policing is disproportionately focused on poor people than the discovery that grammar school teachers focus their attentions primarily upon the behavior of young children. It is simply what they are competent to do.

Having said that much about the definition of police and having attempted to show that it permits us to dismiss as wrong headed what is often advanced as a major ideological critique of police practice, I would like now to turn to the problem of defining a concept of conservatism that will be helpful in adumbrating its legacy. There are at least three active strains of conservative ideology that bear directly on police and have shaped not only the institution but its practitioners and our societal response to them. I will refer to these three varieties of conservatism as libertarianism, traditionalism, and populism. Each is far more complex than I will be able to consider here and, within each, one can find advocates of rather different stripes. I thus confess that I will treat each of them crudely but, I trust, respectfully for their respective ideological contributions.

❖ TRADITIONALISM ❖

First, *traditionalism*. Conservatism as a historical political philosophy is probably best understood as a reaction to both a philosophy and a historical event. The philosophy was that of the Enlightenment, probably best represented by Rousseau, and the event the French Revolution. Both reflected an abhorrence for all received institutions and a confidence in the capacity of enlightened individual reason to solve all human problems.

In contrast to this faith, conservatives held that society and social order were the product of an infinitely rich and complex historical evolution, one that was not reducible to a set of political principles or formulae, one whose ecology was, on the whole, so intricate that the best minds could not comprehend it. For the conservatives tradition was the guide and when it ran afoul of some set of abstract principles, rational argument, or political theory that challenged it, the inclination of conservatives, from Edmund Burke to William Buckley, is to doubt the wisdom of the principle, the argument, or the theory and to side with tradition.

Police and Traditionalism

Because police are the agents of the government in power, because the law often changes slowly and in response to challenge, criticism, or complaint, much of the work of police is in defense of the *status quo*. This is particularly so under conditions in which efforts to change law take the form of protest, defiance, and civil disobedience. It does not matter whether the issue is the right of the Ku Klux Klan to march through a black neighborhood; an anti-abortion group to block the entrance to a clinic; a union to block scabs from crossing a picket line, or; students shutting down a university to protest a tuition increase or an immoral war. In each of these cases police find themselves defenders of the *status quo* and bound by law to use their coercive capacities against those who would disturb it.

Structurally, as an institution, police are committed to such a position irrespective of their personal preferences. We should not be surprised, however, to find that those whose work calls upon them so often to defend the *status quo* should develop occupational ideologies that reconcile them to it. Although attempts to establish the "authoritarian personality" of police have not survived methodological scrutiny, attitudes of police are probably more traditional than those in the general population, not only because the work they are called upon to do inclines them to adopt a personal political philosophy that comports with it, but because those who are attracted to police work are reasonably likely to begin with a traditional political orientation. Police are, in this sense, traditionalist conservatives. It is a political position they are structurally obliged to assume and whose ideology they are occupationally inclined to embrace.

❖ POPULISM ❖

The second strain of conservatism I should like to consider is populism. In identifying it as a strain of conservative thinking I do so in the knowledge that many conservatives intentionally distance themselves from it and find its terms offensive. It is the conservatism of Archie Bunker, David Duke, and Morton Downey, Jr. not that of George Will, Irving Kristol, or Norman Podhoretz, who regard it not as a strain but as a perversion of conservatism. While traditionalist conservatives find suspect abstractions that purport to challenge it, populists convert these sentiments to anti-intellectualism and crude intolerance of difference. Populism celebrates the ignorance and prejudices of the common man.

Populism is an occupational hazard of police work and one to which an unknown but probably substantial number of officers succumb. The best analysis I know of this problem is offered by William Ker Muir, Jr. in his extraordinary book, *Police: Streetcorner Politicians*. To understand Muir's analysis one must begin by accepting the fact that policing is a profoundly *moral occupation*. By "moral occupation" I mean an occupation in which its practitioners must come to a personal moral and intellectual reconciliation with the requirements of their job. What makes policing a moral occupation is the police officer's obligation to coerce, to threaten to hurt, and on occasion, to actually do so. To be a competent police officer one must become both morally and intellectually comfortable with doing so. One way to do so is to come to embrace a whole set of popular prejudices and crude characterizations that reduce the people on whom coercive means may have to be employed to something less than human beings—assholes, scumbags, skells, scrotes, shads, and groids—the litany is endless, replete with local variations, and need not be repeated here.

We should expect that police, as a product of dealing routinely in crises, will develop a certain hardness and insensitivity to suffering. However, it is important to understand exactly why a populist resolution to the moral obligation to coerce and hurt is unacceptable. It is not that such terms are offensive in polite society. Rather, it is that in effecting such a reconciliation with the obligation to coerce and hurt, the police officer so distorts the reality in which he works that it compromises his ability to work there competently. A world divided into good and evil, black and white, scrotes and honest folks is a cartoon world. It is a view of the world which makes Archie Bunker a buffoon, and any policeman who tries to work in such a world incompetent.

It is probably the case that public figures like David Duke and other crude populists tend to give support to such defective resolutions of the policeman's moral mandate. It is the obvious obligation of police leaders to stand against such sentiments and inexcusable, as in the case of Darryl Gates, when they fail to do so.

❖ LIBERTARIANISM ❖

The third strain of modern conservatism I should like to consider is *libertarianism*. Like populism it is a strain of conservatism over which there is, among conservatives, sharp division. Historically, the mark of both liberals and radicals of the left has been a faith that the state, through central planning, social engineering, and enlightened regulation of both social and economic life would produce the good society. Conservatives, by contrast, have stood for the minimization of the role of the state and resisted the expansion of the role of the state, distrusting profoundly its professed beneficence.

The irony in the liberal and radical positions on the one hand and in the conservative on the other is that both appear to reverse themselves on the issue of police. Typically critics of police, both liberals and radicals, by pressing for extensions of the state role, enlarge the police role at the same moment they despise the police. Conservatives, by contrast, typically resist and distrust the extension of the state in virtually every area of social and economic life, but generally support efforts that expand the police role and tend to resist those that limit or restrain it. In short, liberals and radicals ought to love the police and conservatives ought to find them suspect, but at least historically neither has behaved in this way.

They have not, I suspect, because both traditionalist and populist sympathies for police have overwhelmed the libertarian sentiments that ought to incline against them. The extent to which this domination will continue would seem to depend upon the degree to which police continue to appear to serve traditionalist and populist interests. They may well continue to do so. But if there is a single lesson to be learned from contemporary politics, it is how quickly yesterday's enemies can become friends—and vice versa.

21

Violence and Symbolic Violence

Peter K. Manning

T his brief comment on Carl Klockars' essay contains two main points. I find his basic conception of the police mandate and its relationship to violence quite convincing. Certainly, violence is an ineluctable aspect of policing in Western Democratic societies, and perhaps in all developed societies. Furthermore, the police in Anglo-American societies are granted an almost exclusive legitimate right or mandate to use coercive force. Having made this point, Klockars overlooks the changing meaning and definition of "violence" and police adaptation to such changes. I believe he misconstrues the causes for the "poor-focus" of the police and the portent for policing that this carries for the future. To delineate the present police preoccupations does not serve to envision the contours and demands of policing in the next century.

❖ VIOLENCE AND THE POLICE ❖

What follows is a sketch of my own conception of modern policing. Policing as an institution is ubiquitous in developed societies. Yet, it takes many forms, performs a wide range of functions, has diverse political and historical origins, and possesses various levels of legitimacy (Bayley, 1985). Although policing is in part "law enforcement," in practice, the common law in Anglo-American policing plays a symbolic role and acts as a resource

Police Forum, 3 (1) (1993): 1–6. Reprinted with permission of the Academy of Criminal Justice Sciences.

when other control strategies fail. The law provides little guidance as to where, when, and in what quantity it should be applied. In the nation-state context, policing serves the state, but the state's interests are rarely directly served. The police, as the behavior of Chief Daryl Gates and the LAPD illustrates, also serve frequently their own political and moral interests in a rather complex fashion. (This subtle concatenation of activities is something of a quandary for police scholars such as David Bayley who have sought a functional theory to account for patterns of police tasks, imagery and structure.)

As Bittner and Kelsen (1961) have argued, the police mandate is constrained by two matters: the right to apply violence and the grounding norm of state authority. The police are an archaic occupation. The core role expectation is the situational application of force. They moderate strength and restraint. The police are linked symbolically with the Medieval Christian tradition of knighthood, honor and duty. They serve the state's higher espoused principles and stated mottos. Their attachment to force and honor places them outside the sectarian stream of everyday events. They are watchers, standing above the moral fray until and unless they define their proximal role as once again plunging into the secular world to: right a balance (as they read it); seek the just (as they see it); and produce a good (as they define it). Police violence blends subtle avoidance of frequent application and an appreciation of its aberrant origins and quotidian character. For a patrol officer, the key to effectiveness is judgment and restraint, not applied violence.

Klockars' conception, also drawing on Bittner, is both sound and insightful. It avoids a functionalist argument that police must carry out particular named functions (Cf. the ABA listing circa 1972), and a class-repression model of police actions. In practice, Klockars claims, the police focus on the control of the poor. The police deliver "services" to the poor. The poor need corrective violence, or at least close supervision, he asserts, because they commit more violent crimes than other groups, resist apprehension by violent means, and more often flee to avoid prosecution.

This formulation rests on a slight misreading of the history of Anglo-American policing and restricts the definition of violence to concretely applied force. It thus ignores the importance of symbolic violence, violations of the social space of a person or group in the name of the state. Ironically, while policing has focused previously on control of the poor, it is now expanding into the management of symbolic violence.

❖ A WATCHFUL, QUESTIONING POSE ❖

To claim that contemporary Anglo-American police employ violence against the poor because the poor behave in ways that demand such overlooks the historic use of the criminal law as a tool, or means of ordering and regulating often large and contentious marginal populations. Policing has attended primarily to the political control of the poor and the disorderly as these matters have been defined by the dominant societal coalition and the government of the nation state. Historically, it is not true that intrinsically the poor require ordering. Rather, the criminal law, with other legal sanctions and regulatory actions, is used by the police to restrict the movements and activities of the poor and marginal and to protect property. It has been used to control rising groups as in the case of the English Factories Act (Carson, 1970). Sometimes ironically, since it involves controlling population segments from similar class and ethnic origins, the police are actively engaged in dramatic marking and arranging of the vertical and horizontal order and in defending, in a variety of ways, the status quo.

This drama of policing, maintaining the vertical order and the symbolic hierarchy of worth, has been played out in several ways in Anglo-American societies.

1. As activities either slip away from popularity, or drift downward to the lower classes, they are defined as criminal and subject to arrest and prosecution. This can be seen in a close analysis of changes in the English sports of hunting, and bull and bear baiting, various forms of gambling, drug use and sex.

2. Certain "deviant" life-styles are stigmatized and defined as "criminal." Activities publicly associated with lower class, native people's, or immigrant pastimes and life-styles, such as cock-fighting, dog fights, and peyote use, are subject to criminal sanction.

3. Space is regulated to maintain control of symbolically valued property and places. Changes in the uses and control of space marginalize certain powerless groups and place them at risk from public and private policing.

4. Shared activities are differentially sanctioned. When leisure patterns are shared by middle and lower middle classes, such as sport gambling, the middle class form is legalized while the lower class form(s) are made subject to the criminal sanction and police-initiated control.

5. As newly respectable activities gain respectability they are de-criminalized and are diffused widely e.g., marijuana and alcohol use.

6. Life-style conflicts or "cultural wars" between cultural segments such as the fundamentalist Catholics and Protestants and more liberal or agnostic groups, e.g. alcohol use and legal abortion, may lead to a movement to redefine some behavior or life-styles as criminal. The targets of control shift from providers to those demanding the goods

or services. In effect, a market is controlled with the aim of eradication rather than symbolic regulation.

7. Dissent such as flag burning, public demonstrations and draft evasion, when carried out by members of the dominant coalition, is treated sub rosa, and with discretion within the criminal justice system, while marginal groups are given the full benefit and force of the law.

Change arises from the dialectic between class interests and control processes. Suffice it to note that the content of the "threat" and "disorder" shifts while the form (criminal sanctioning) and direction of governmental social control (down) remains. The background aim is class control and political ordering. Only definitions of phenomena in need of control change. Both rising groups and the powerless are potential targets for control and regulation. Since adherence to a rule, any rule, is itself the source of rewards and status, the indirect value of compliance is that one does not lose symbolic capital. Those on the political edges of society are denied not only access to the material resources of the society, but the symbolic resources as well. By constant changes in control strategies, misrecognition of the powerless of their interests and the interests of the police remains.

Having noted this about the relationships between "poor" and violence historically, the "service" notion used by Klockars is problematic. The implicit idea in "service" is that it is requested. While this is true for some police activities, some of the "service" applied to the poor is unwanted, deserved or not. The application of coercive force, stop and frisk and street sweeps, serving search warrants, especially in poor areas for drug violations, are police-initiated activities, not reactive. The residents of Central Los Angeles did not request a war on the Afro-American poor (Davis, 1992). It is misleading to attribute essential qualities to groups when these are typically a product of historic developments and patterns of social domination.

❖ NEW FORMS OF VIOLENCE AND CONTROL ❖

The Klockars essay does not address the growing significance of new forms of violence. Some violence is perpetrated by the police against middle class citizens under various ideological covers. By "symbolic violence," I mean the ideological acceptance of directly deleterious costs and social patterns by those experiencing them even as they support the dominant order (Bourdieu, 1977: 190–197). The concrete notion of violence used colors and limits the scope of Klockars' essay.

Anglo-American democratic societies are in many ways less violent than they were one hundred and certainly two hundred years ago, but the public preoccupation with violence remains. The "new violence" is symbolic, and it at least in part derives from actions of the state's agents against its citizens. This is not a novel idea, but the capacity of the agents to carry out their fantasies of control has vastly increased in the last ten years. To say this is not to minimize the high incidence and prevalence of violence in American society. Contemporary violence arises from the violation of public trust, the rending asunder of civil ties and moral obligations, especially of those in positions of trust in government and amongst what C. Wright Mills called the "Higher Circles of Power," as well as against and amongst the poor.

❖ A NEW FOCAL CONCERN ❖

The focus of control of the police is changing. They are sensitive to and part of creating new forms of symbolic violence. The focus of symbolic control for Anglo-American urban police is changing from the visible street disorder and crimes that shaped the mandate, strategy and style of the 19th century police. An emerging police focus is "risk prevention" through "proactive," "community," "problem-solving," and window-sensitive (Wilson and Kelling, 1982) policing and new forms of technologically-assisted surveillance. The police are almost unintentionally becoming "information workers" (Ericson, 1992), becoming experts in gathering, storing and retrieving information from an assemblage of strategic data bases. The focal interest of the police is shifting from "crime" in the sense of street crime, to control of matters that involve trust violations, risk prevention and management. They are actively devising and commodifying new modes of "security." As the legally granted permission for police monitoring and synthesizing gathered information increases, their ability to do so surreptitiously, and even illegally, has escalated.

A number of trends suggest the growth in patterns of use of symbolic violence by the police against citizens. Some are subtle expansions in the police mandate, while others are technologically-driven.

1. Police variously penetrate private relations using quasi-legal powers. They sometimes employ the vehicle of high politics and national security, such as a declining public order, a needed "War on Drugs" and new threats of foreign espionage of industrial secrets, to justify their security measures.

2. Increased penetration of the family and private relations, the result of increased police powers, reduced legal controls on police

interventions in private relations, and the punishment of domestic violence by arrest.

3. Police, with the cooperation of AT&T, have developed new forms of surveillance that allow sophisticated tracking of vehicles and invisible monitoring of telephone calls (especially of cellular phones), e-mail, and faxes.

4. Police use forensic-genetic evidence to eliminate or include suspects in criminal cases.

5. Police encourage and use on themselves random drug testing. It is used also in government, many critical occupations, and schools without permission. Information so gathered can be used by the police as a basis for further investigation.

6. The police in many cities mobilize DARE programs that place uniformed officers in third and fifth grade classrooms. They preach often incorrect information about drugs and urge total abstinence without differentiating critically amongst the costs and benefits of currently legal and illegal drugs.

7. Policing is characterized by a growing integration of public and private policing, mutual cooperation and data-sharing.

8. Police, as they move away from a sanctioning mode to a restitutive and preventive mode, seek to control the conditions or circumstances under which crime occurs. They refine "preventive" and "risk management" strategies.

These trends appear to increase the potential for policing to evolve beyond current preoccupations into more subtle forms of control and security assurance.

❖ COMMENT ❖

The police are not the servants of the government of the day, the poor, or the rich. They apply violence, and as the definition of violence changes, they can be counted upon to apply it to classes marginal to the dominant order. The work of policing is changing and entails new forms of state-created monitoring and surveillance. In this sense, they may well use their authority in innovative ways, including policing violations of trust by other information workers. These issues are neither liberal nor conservative in character.

References

Bayley, D. (1985). *Patterns of Policing*. Rutgers: Rutgers University Press.

Bourdieu, P. (1977). *Outline of a Theory of Practice*. Cambridge: Cambridge University Press.

Carson, W. G. O. (1970). White collar crime and the enforcement of factory legislation. *British Journal of Criminology*, 10:383–398.

Davis, M. (1992). *City of Quartz*. New York: Random House.

Ericson, R. (1992). The division of labour and the concept of security. Unpublished paper, University of Toronto, Centre of Criminology, Fall, 1992.

Kelsen, H. (1961). *A General Theory of Law and the State*. New York: Russell and Russell.

Wilson, J. Q., & Kelling, G. (1982). The police and neighborhood safety: Broken windows. *Atlantic*, 127 (March): 29–38.

22

Making the Police Proactive
An Impossible Task for Improbable Reasons

Frank P. Williams, III and Carl P. Wagoner

T
he standard position today, heard from both the public and the police, is that our crime problem is getting out of hand. Begging the question of whether we actually have a crime wave or a media-based crime-reporting wave (Fishman, 1977), we propose to discuss the issue of what society can do about crime in the context of police reform and police services. With some ideological exceptions, those who study crime and the police are fairly well agreed that police can be expected to have very little direct effect on crime and criminality and that, further, preventing crime is not really the function of the police.

Unfortunately, neither the public nor their quasi-elected officials share this opinion regarding the function of the police. Their position is grounded in a conservative ideology which stresses deterrence and "taking the handcuffs off police," in addition to advocating the adding of more police and more technological innovation, in order to increase the apprehension of offenders. However, there is abundant evidence to the effect that crime is not reduced nor apprehension increased by adding police or, for example, by eliminating the exclusionary rule (Walker, 1989).

This resistance to evidence that police, by themselves, can do little about crime is itself an interesting situation. As noted above, we suspect

Police Forum, 2 (2) (1992): 1–5. Reprinted with permission of the Academy of Criminal Justice Sciences.

that it is based in the current conservative mentality and movement, the political utility of crime in providing a "mantle of law and order" and, ironically, the police themselves. This latter source is intriguing because both the rise and fall of crime rates have long been used as a political ploy by law enforcement to gain access to greater resources (Weis and Milakovich, 1974). The latent function of such a ploy, however, is that police departments then invite the public to hold them accountable for crime itself.

The connection between "doing something" about crime and recent calls for proactive policing has created an expectation that police should, indeed, engage in proactive crime prevention. Historically, there is some merit to this expectation. The origins of modern policing lie in the private forces created by the Bow Street merchants of London and the Thames River police of the West Indies Merchants Association. These forces were clearly proactive in their approach to "crime." Yet, as police forces became public entities, they became more reactive in approach and lost their direct connection to citizens. This is further illustrated by the changing nature of the police role in the movement from mechanical to organic solidarity, and the corresponding changes in the nature of criminals and the increasing rates of crime (Lundman, 1980).

In short, police forces evolved concurrently with the state's emergence under the social contract in the dual role of victim and enforcer of restitution. This process resulted in a police role as chief enforcer of the social contract and, in modern times, placed the police directly as a servant of the government, not as a servant of the people. The point here is that modern police are reactive in nature and respond directly to government rather than to the citizenry. Indirectly, of course, police do respond to the people through the representatives of government.

This is not to suggest that the police are completely devoid of an ability to be proactive. It is the case that both in law enforcement situations and in order maintenance situations police can take the initiative. However, when they do so it is usually in response to internal pressure from top administration, which is often acting in response to external pressure.

When a call is issued to "do something about crime," government (local or otherwise) instructs its law enforcement agent to respond, either with action or with explanations. Unfortunately, the police are not for the most part, designed as proactive agents. This is illustrated in the limited success community crime prevention programs ("neighborhood watch," "operation identification," and home security surveys) have had (Currie, 1985; Turk and Grimes, 1992). Even more problematic from our viewpoint is that the type of response which is demanded from law enforcement, and the form of response generated, varies by the type of "public" making the demand.

A common observation is that power (or potential power) defines the type of public and the form of response. Thus, demands that the police respond to crime take various forms and precipitate commensurate demands for change in police philosophy and structure.

The primary intent of this article is to critique proactive policing and calls for police change. To do this, we will explore the relationship between crime, proactive policies, and three "ideal types" of public, which we will refer to as citizens, interest groups, and elites. A secondary intent is to stimulate discussion on the issue of police change in a proactive direction. As a result, we have chosen to eschew an objective and carefully documented approach in favor of a more subjective and controversial one.

❖ PUBLIC POWER AND PROACTIVE POLICING ❖

Our first concern is to determine the type of response that would be required in order to generate proactive policing under our three types of publics. A demand from citizens requires a more diffuse and broader response(s) than from the other types of publics. In fact, for such a demand to be made is itself an extraordinary event, since the "public" is not often united or does not often see the world through the same colored glasses, particularly in a heterogeneous, urban/industrial society. In keeping with the nature of the demand, the police response will likely result in substantial resource expenditure (if this is possible in an era of steady state or decreasing resources), perhaps even requiring major structural and philosophical changes. The likelihood of such changes is minimal since, as we will note later, law enforcement organizations are particularly resistant to change.

Demands from interest groups, on the other hand, are commonplace and often require little adaptation on the part of the police, other than the shifting of focus and resources from one area of concern to another. Our form of government is well-adapted to interest groups and, thus, one might even argue that police structure and philosophy are currently products designed to meet this form of public demand. The chief characteristic we expect here is that the demands are individualistic and specific.

The elite demand requires a non-specific response by the police. In fact, the nature of the response is unlikely to be directly generated by the police themselves. Instead, the response is likely to be in the form of police reaction to new laws or political philosophies. Such responses can be profound and far-reaching, but will tend to produce new enforcement strategies and/or directions of activity aimed at particular segments of society rather than changes in police philosophy or organizational structure. In short, we see citizen demands as resulting in a return to a more mechanical style of policing (as opposed to a contemporary organic style), interest group responses as service-oriented, and elite demands as selective repression.

❖ CHANGE ❖

Because of the changing nature of society, as well as the changing nature and increased amount of crime, many have argued that change of the police is both desirable and/or eminent (Currie, 1985; Germann, 1985; Wilson, 1985; Goldstein, 1979). If so, our second concern is to describe the form that changes might take under our three types of publics. Under the citizen type of demand, we believe that any police change would be toward development into a more citizen-responsive force and oriented to a closer relationship with the community. Such a change, if real rather than superficial, would require a substantial increase in new resources and recommitment of current resources, significant changes in philosophy, and potentially massive restructuring of police organizations.

The term interest group as used here refers to associations and coalitions of persons with a common concern which binds them together. Their effectiveness is determined by the degree of pressure they can bring to the police directly or indirectly through other governmental agencies. It needs to be noted that many such interest groups are transitory in nature, and are often issue specific. Interest-group demands would produce change oriented toward specific services such as peace-keeping and enclave protection. Further, because the nature of interest groups is both pluralistic and individualistic, change to meet their demands would entail a certain amount of decentralization in order to quickly respond to shifting priorities and allegiances. Critical variables influencing the extent of change are the degree of resources dispersed among the interest groups, the form of those resources, and the temporal nature of those resources.

Elite demands would result in selective repression of those who constitute a threat to the existing social order. Thus, change in policing requires a reordering of priorities and, potentially, some degree of new organizational structure. Because some older parts of the structure can be dispensed with, structural changes may merely mean a reshuffling of resources and reorganization. Centralized authority and the chain of command would remain important due to the necessity of ensuring the transmission of the new priorities and the preparation for, and the development of, new attitudes on the part of the rank and file in regard to the "new" threat. Critical variables here include the extent of police agreement with the values to be defended, perceptions police have of the newly criminalized community, and the relative threat to the existing social order.

Given these potential avenues of change, the question is not what police organizations will become but in what directions have the police already responded? A few brief examples will serve to demonstrate an irony that the triad of publics does indeed affect the nature of policing and, at the same time, produces conflict that results in little actual change.

Citizen-based Change

The clearest example of reaction to this power source is the development of community policing. Although by 1990 more than 300 police departments in the United States had reported some form of community policing, there remains today a relative lack of understanding as to what constitutes community policing (Strecher, 1991). At times it has been substituted for what is still a community-relations approach, at times it has been synonymous with "problem-oriented policing," and at times foot patrol has been equated with community policing (Trojanowicz and Bucqueroux, 1990).

Instead, community policing requires a substantial change in both structure and form, including attitudinal, organizational, and subcultural change. It represents a "new" philosophy of policing whereby police officers and the community work together to solve community problems of crime and related social ills. This means giving citizens of the community a direct say in the solutions and activities that regulate crime. Community policing also requires an organizational structure which is flattened, with horizontal as well as vertical communication. Centralized authority is minimized, with area captains becoming "mini-chiefs" with full decision-making authority, and with individual community-policing officers sharing decision making, particularly on their own beat. Police officers are given authority not only to create their own solutions to problems but also to contact and request assistance from other governmental agencies and private entities. In short, police officers become citizens of their own neighborhoods and combine with residents to produce a healthy neighborhood.

Thus the problems here are that real community policing requires a radical restructuring of police organizations and a new sense of function. All we know of organizational theory tells us that such change will be resisted. A project manager of one of the five sites for the national community policing experiment aptly described the adaptations required of police officers and the organization as "traumatic" (McPherson, 1992). Further, as Van Horn and Van Meter (1977), among others, have noted, the predisposition of the people in the agency to support the implementation of new policy is a crucial variable in determining the success of the policy.

Other governmental agencies also play a key role in the success of this transformation. If they have different agendas, or see the "citizen mandate" as conflicting, responses to the requests of individual community police officers will be problematic. These agencies can defeat community policing philosophies either by failing to participate or simply by dragging their feet on requests. The probability of all affected government agencies buying into the same citizen-oriented philosophy is exceedingly low.

Similarly, because police officers will come and go in neighborhoods (and of course there will be several shifts involved), officers themselves cannot be responsible for community policing—the community itself must be. Getting a community to realize this in today's specialized world is no small feat, in and of itself. In effect, the ultimate feasibility and success of community policing is beyond the control of the police. The five-site national experiment has demonstrated the way in which these difficulties have combined to effectively disassemble the citizen-oriented approach. Only one of the sites (San Diego) remains committed to community policing and that site had an existing heritage of a community orientation. The other four have not only fallen by the wayside, but in one case the experiment caused the downfall of the [Tulsa] chief of police (McPherson, 1992).

Interest Group-based Change

Reactions to this power source require the ability to make swift responses to potentially immediate concerns of changing interest groups. We suggest this can result in the creation of decentralized teams to police and protect the various interest groups. In operation such decentralized teams (such as an anti-gang task force with the responsibility of quickly moving into an area, conducting a sweep for possible law violators and then moving out) may be responding to interest groups such as the "public at large" or to the organized interests of a particular neighborhood. Further, such interest groups may demand or require other than purely law enforcement activities on the part of police. Wilson (1968) has written at length on the "interests" of particular communities centering around service functions.

While this service orientation may share appearances, and even some techniques, with community based-policing, or with problem-oriented policing, the reality is that the police organization is merely responding to various pressures brought about by various special-interest groups. Therefore, the result is policy based on short-term decisions and assignments, with ever-increasing resources devoted to immediate problems. Such a situation leads to relative chaos and the inability of police to respond to changing conditions in the community at large.

With squandered resources and a lack of organized policy and planning, a reasonable expectation is that geographic enclaves derived from the more powerful and long-term interest groups will develop. We refer to these as "enclaves" because the concept of enclaved and walled communities, whether based on cultural factors or on environmental design, is an excellent exemplar. Residents identify with the area and non-residents are seen as intruders and potential criminals. Emergent police responses to the enclave movement are concerned with maintaining the enclave community at the expense of the larger community. Examples of the form of policing required here include stopping of blacks who are in an enclave where they "do not ordinarily belong" (e.g., Jamal Wilkes, former Los Angeles Lakers basketball star being detained "on suspicion" while driving his Rolls Royce in the "Wilshire Corridor" in Los Angeles; an episode of LA Law where a black attorney jogging in an upper-class neighborhood was accosted and arrested by police).

Neighborhood watch programs exemplify the response of police organizations to this source of governmental power. In a real sense, these programs are not oriented toward protecting citizens of the general community, but rather are a method of focusing service on selective areas. Those who have been in police departments operating neighborhood watch programs tell us that, when a "neighborhood" is advised of a possible displacement effect on crime, the invariable response from residents is that they don't care, they just want their neighborhood safe from crime. This is analogous to the NIMBY (Not In My Back Yard) phenomenon which routinely occurs in prison site selection.

The irony here is that as services are continually focused on the interest group enclaves, the proactive nature of police crime prevention can serve to displace crime into the larger non-enclaved community, thus creating a "battle-ground" and greater demands of protection from the enclaves. The cycle of demand for protection and focus of resources has the potential to render impotent the police organization and to destroy the enclaves themselves.

Elite-based Change

Changes in police derived from this power base require selective enforcement of laws, proliferation of special-interest laws, and order maintenance exerted on the masses. All are based on a re-emphasis of basic (elite) values in society and the emergence of a strident conservatism. A number of current modifications of police structure are predicated on the drug war and are, in some sense, a reorientation of the earlier war on crime of the 1970s. For example, resource allocations from the federal government, designed to encourage and reward police departments for their crime-fighting efforts, were moved into drunken-driving campaigns and now have been moved into the drug war. Police departments, as a result, have eliminated some older crime-fighting units and substituted drug enforcement programs.

This most recent phase, the war on drugs, has once again succeeded in connecting drug use with crime, thus providing a rationale for police to adopt the ideology of the new drug war. In addition, the war has succeeded in criminalizing (and thus delegitimizing) a major portion of those who might threaten the elite value system. In part because drug use has been associated with the liberal values of the 1960s, elite conservative values have been able to dominate the present era. Moreover, both an emphasis on the repression of drug-users and the advent of work place drug-testing have been used to resolve elite concerns about societal productivity.

It is likely that in a democratic society there will ultimately be a reaction, and there will be attempts to shift power (at least momentarily) in efforts to liberalize the laws concerning drug possession and use. Thus, it could be argued that repression contains the seeds of its own overthrow and may ultimately result in image problems for the police, as well as distrust and greater regulation of police activity. The police themselves have been placed in a quandary of having to eliminate a large number of otherwise desirable recruits because of a history of drug use. A recent recruiting solution has been to ask about the kind of drugs and make selective decisions while ignoring the presumptive illegality of all drug use.

❖ CONCLUSIONS ❖

While some change is undoubtedly taking place among police and in police organizations, the current situation leads us to believe that nothing substantial is taking place except, perhaps, in idiosyncratic circumstances and isolated instances. Further, our separation of the public into three types is misleading in the sense that each appears to be acting independently. Actually, all three types act in concert, with the more powerful having the greatest potential effect. Each one, however, tends to offset the others and dissipates the entire effect of change. The most probable approach to police change is that there will be a mixture of all these variations, in response to the mixture of the public types. This means that none of the potential approaches above will become commonplace, none will be logically and systematically approached, and in the end police will not become proactive. We predict that the police will maintain their current para-military form and bureaucratic structure. In the face of conflicting masters and differential demands, informal organizational goals serving survival will yield resistance to change and no viable new alternatives will emerge. We do not, however, rule out incremental change, particularly that change associated with larger societal concerns.

The most likely scenario is that crime will decrease by the turn of the century, largely due to demographic changes. The decrease in crime will, in turn, take pressure off the police to "do something about it." Thus, through the end of this decade, there will be minor modifications in policing, all of which will be strongly resisted, or modified to such an extent that the consequences will be minimal or nonexistent.

This, however, belies the function of the police and takes as granted the fact that police can affect crime. We believe there is sufficient evidence to support the assertion that any reduction of crime must come from outside the police. Therefore, the real question is not whether the police can prevent and control crime but, instead, whether and how efficiently and effectively the police can react to crime. Our constructed scenarios for proactive police roles are all unlikely, or else undesirable, in our present society. We would do well, then, to focus on the police as a reactive force and, if enhancement of this function is desirable, find methods of stripping proactive pretense from police organizations. If we must have a specific proactive force to control and prevent crime, a far better choice is to create an agency specifically responsible for that function and empower it to respond to crime on a far larger scope. Such an agency would presumably engage in the improvement of education, health, recreation, community renovation, and the myriad of other factors associated with the emergence of crime in our society. The police, however, should simply be assigned the task of reacting to crime as, or after, it is committed.

References

Currie, E. (1985). *Confronting Crime: An American Challenge*. New York: Pantheon Books.

Fishman, M. (1977). Crime waves as ideology. *Social Problems*, 25:531–543.

Germann, A. C. (1985). Law enforcement: A look into the future. In Blumberg, Abraham, and Neiderhoffer, Elaine (eds.). *The Ambivalent Force: Perspectives on the Police*, 3rd ed. New York: Holt, Rinehart and Winston.

Goldstein, A. (1979). Improving the police: A problem-oriented approach. *Crime and Delinquency*, 25:236–258.

Inciardi, J. (1992). *The War on Drugs II*. Mountain View, CA: Mayfield Publishing Company.

McPherson, N. (1992). Problem oriented policing in San Diego. Comments made during panel presentation at the annual meeting of the Western Society of Criminology, San Diego, CA.

Strecher, V. G. (1991). Histories and futures of policing: Readings and misreadings of a pivotal present. *Police Forum*, 1(1): 1–9.

Trojanowicz, R., & Bucqueroux, B. (1990). *Community Policing: A Contemporary Perspective*. Cincinnati: Anderson Publishing Company.

Turk, A. T., & Grimes, R. (1992). Neighborhood watch committees: Participation and impact. Paper delivered at the annual meeting of the Western Society of Criminology, San Diego, CA.

Van Horn, C. E., & Van Meter, D. S. (1977). The implementation of intergovernmental policy. In Nagel, S. S. (ed.). *Policy Studies Review Annual*, Vol. 1. Beverly Hills: Sage.

Walker, S. (1989). *Sense and Nonsense About Crime: A Policy Guide*. 2nd ed. Pacific Grove, CA: Brooks-Cole Publishing Company.

Weis, K., & Milikovich, M. E. (1974). Political misuses of crime rates. *Transaction*, 11(5): 27–33.

Wilson, J. Q. (1968). *Varieties of Police Behavior*. Cambridge: Harvard University Press.

_____ (1985). *Thinking About Crime*. Rev. ed. New York: Vintage Press.

23

Economic Rhetoric and Policing Reform

Peter K. Manning

Important changes have occurred in American urban policing since 1970. These changes include alterations in police budgets, in the pattern of public support for police, in police involvement with the media, and in the links between reform groups and some police command officers. Other changes include increases in the educational level of police, as well as changes in the sexual and ethnic composition of urban forces, in the extent of legal constraint on police practice, and in the presence of news information technologies.[1] The police are losing their monopoly on legitimate violence, and now compete with self-help groups, private security firms, and the media for dominance in social control. Perhaps because the police have lost this monopoly and are now competing with other groups, the language of economics and management has been used to reconceptualize the police mandate. Increasingly this language has penetrated the police literature and is shaping police training. I discuss these changes here and examine some of the consequences.

The first noteworthy changes are economic. The infrastructure of cities has deteriorated, even as city budgets have grown massively. The escalating costs of governance now exceed taxpayers' willingness to meet them. This economic distress is passed on to police budgets. Budgets have shrunk. In urban areas, there were fewer officers per citizen in 1991 than

Criminal Justice Research Bulletin, 7(4): 1–8, 1992. Reprinted with permission.

15 years ago.[2] It is not clear whether monetary support for policing, when contrasted with other agencies funded by municipal budgets, has increased proportionately in this century (Bordua and Haurek, 1971). Many police forces continue to face serious budget cuts, layoffs, and cycles of hiring blitzes and freezes. These oscillations surely affect morale and the degree of officers' loyalty to command personnel, and may well increase turnover.

A more difficult matter is gauging variations in the degree of public support for police and policing. Public support for policing in urban areas, as measured by public opinion polls, has declined, while fear of violent crime and drug-related crimes has increased.

In spite of research demonstrating that the police provide a variety of functions and that there is virtually no systematic statistical relationship between police strength and official crime statistics, the police continue to claim that they are primarily, if not exclusively, "crime fighters." Some academic writers also argue that the core mission of the police is to control crime (Moore, Trojanowicz, and Kelling, 1988). Many people dispute this flat statement, however, and it begs the question of the extent to which this mission is practical or even possible, in view of the other factors that determine and alter crime rates and the commission of crimes.[3]

In this dynamic relationship between crime, fear of crime, and public support, the media are playing a more prominent role than in the past (Altheide, 1992). The media, with police cooperation, play on crime news and amplify public fear (Ericson, 1989, 1991). In addition, the media have elevated the quality of police leadership and the nature of police practices, especially the use of violence, into national issues.[4] The police, in turn, have developed sophisticated media skills, which enable them to influence public perceptions of crime. The police and the media form the *media reality* of crime. Television produces crime simulation shows, which combine news films of events, reenactments, voice over narration by actors and actresses, and grainy video filming with hand-held cameras intended to simulate "reality." In addition, shows such as "Cops" screen well-shot and engaging films of actual stops and raids. For the modern citizen in a large city, media reality is intertwined with personal experience, simulations of events, feature films, the news, and on-the-spot videos such as those of the Rodney King beating in March 1991 in Los Angeles and the Joanne Was beating in Detroit in August 1991. A new social construction of the meaning of crime and social control is emerging.[5]

A new police reform movement has arisen and flourished since the Police Foundation was funded by the Ford Foundation in the late 1960s. The police reform movement now features police leaders and researchers in organizations such as the Police Executive Research Forum, the Police Foundation, the National Institutes of Justice, the International Association of Chiefs of Police, and the National Council of Mayors. The foci of police reform are numerous, but the most visible vehicle is a programmatic approach called "community policing." Community policing has had a wide, if not deep, impact on the rhetoric of policing in virtually every town in America (Mastrofski, 1988).

The educational level of officers has risen, in part as a reflection of the increase in education in the society as a whole, and in part as a result of the massive financial support for officers' higher education furnished by the Law Enforcement Assistance Administration in the 1970s (Mastrofski, 1990; Sherman and National Advisory Commission, 1978). It is not clear what this change in educational level signifies for police practice or for the quality of life in large American cities, but it has altered union-management negotiations about pay and conditions of work. In due course it may change other practices such as recruitment, promotion, evaluation, and supervision.

The composition of urban forces also has changed. Once a white male occupation, policing now has diversified. In 1972 women made up 4.2 percent of police officers serving in urban departments in areas with populations of more than 50,000. By late 1988 this figure had increased to 8.8 percent (Martin, 1990). The percentages of African-Americans and members of other minorities in departments of the same size are difficult to determine but probably are increasing, especially in very large cities (Mastrofski, 1990:20). Civilianization has increased rapidly; the proportion of civilians rose from 16.5 to 20.4 percent of police department personnel between 1976 and 1986 (Mastrofski, 1990:21).

Criminal and civil law have grown in importance as constraints on police practice. Policing continues to be shaped by the *Miranda*, *Escobedo*, and *Mapp v. Ohio* decisions and by recent Supreme Court cases that open up the admissibility of coerced confessions and evidence seized in illegal searches; these cases bear on procedural aspects of criminal law. Police formerly were protected from civil suits, but now are liable. Negotiated out-of-court settlements now are a major source of expenditures in large cities (Mastrofski, 1990). Civil liability may be influencing policing by increasing the perceived costs of violence to the department and the officers involved.

New information technology promises to erode the traditional authority of police command and to alter significantly the role structure of police departments (Manning, 1992). A very powerful potential resides in the information technologies now being adopted in large city departments. These include centralized call collection using a three-digit number such as 911; enhanced 911, which enables call tracing and display of the caller's address; computer-assisted dispatching (CAD); and associated techniques such as management information systems and computerized record systems. Networking, creating interfaces with other systems, is possible with a computer-based information system. Networking permits police departments to exchange information among themselves and [to] access the FBI's National Crime Information Center (NCIC) (Stevens, 1989; Tien and Colton, 1979).

As I will discuss in the remainder of the article, the police now are viewed by some observers as businesses rather than as public service agencies. One indication of this trend is the popularity of business management jargon to describe policing. Police chiefs are seen as analogous to CEOs, managing businesses and taking risks in a market context. Institutions offer accreditation and continuing education seminars such as "Advanced Management for Law Enforcement Executives" (Southwestern Law Enforcement Institute, Richardson, Texas) and "Law Enforcement Management" (Southwestern Law Enforcement Institute and Sam Houston State University). Researchers urge increased efficiency and effectiveness in policing (Clarke and Hough, 1980; Heaphy and Wolfe, 1975). The currently fashionable language of economics and management used by command personnel to describe police functions, command obligations, and planning creates a picture of policing as a business. Innovations such as computer-assisted dispatching are advocated on the grounds that they will increase efficiency or reduce costs (Hough, 1980a, 1980b; Tien and Colton, 1979). Police programs (community policing, for example) are claimed to be a cost-effective means of delivering "service" to "customers" while remaining sensitive to community needs. Advocates of community policing argue that it enhances crime fighting while reestablishing the territorial or neighborhood basis for police accountability (Moore and Trojanowicz, 1988).

The growth of a management focus in policing is not unrelated to trends that show a deterioration in the police monopoly of force (Bittner, 1990). The public police are no longer a monopoly but compete with private security firms, community action groups, and the media for the right to provide legitimate application of social control.

Consequences

These changes have had several important consequences. The traditional bases of the police mandate—commitment to maintaining the collective good, serving with honor and loyalty, and observing tradition—are being modified (Bordua and Reiss, 1966). These traditions conflict with pragmatic concerns such as avoiding legal liabilities and civil suits. They also conflict with businesslike accounting procedures and tight budgetary constraints.

Policing, as shown in economic discourse, is being incorporated into the political economy of capitalism. Its traditional quasi-sacred status as a "calling," an occupation insulated from the demands and exigencies of the market, is quickly being eroded. It is less now than in the past "an occupationally organized community that sets itself apart" (Bordua and Reiss, 1966:68). Now the distinctive mode of organizing policing bureaucratically to reduce the claims of other loyalties, such as the market, ethnic communities, and family, is challenged by a market orientation to policing (Bordua and Reiss, 1966:68). The degree of competition with other forms of social control, namely self-help (Black, 1980) and private security, is increasing.

A more pragmatic, businesslike form of policing, competing to win a market share, risks the loss of the legally granted police monopoly on force. The effects of market competition, like those of deregulation, have yet to be envisioned fully. These developments possess a historical background worthy of a brief review.

❖ HISTORICAL BACKGROUND ❖

English Sources of Policing

Anglo-American policing as a social institution originated in England in the mid-eighteenth century (Hart, 1951). Jonathan Wilde developed a scheme of "thief-taking" that enabled private citizens to recover stolen goods by paying a fee. The fact that Wilde and his associates initially may have stolen the items merely reduced the search time. In conspiracy with a judge who had bought his office, Wilde was an effective and efficient officer of the court (Howson, 1970). His use of force and extortion was legitimate under the legal system but was a form of private justice, inequitable and unaccountable.

In the 1750s the Fielding brothers, Joseph and Henry, opposed corruption. They developed an independent set of officers of the courts, "The Bow Street Runners," who served warrants and pursued criminals. Again, personal corruption and venality destroyed the virtue of the idea. Patrick Colquhoun's creation, the Thames River Police, was a compromise between private and public policing; his ideas of prevention and restraint in action were adopted later by Robert Peel for publicly funded policing in London.

As Sir Leon Radzinowicz (1962–1968) shows in his history of English law, various forms of volunteer and private policing were the rule in London until the "bobbies" appeared in 1829. The evils of private justice and fee-for-service policing were well known. In addition to the element of revenge that animated policing and informants, "blood money" was paid for information and led to false accusations designed to even scores by using police authority. Other excesses of quasi-private policing in the late eighteenth century would now be called "corruption." "Justice," including judicial office and freedom from arrest and charge, could be bought and sold; force was used to extract confessions; riots and demonstrations against the Crown were frequent reactions to unfair and brutal justice; and large criminal areas were left without policing.

Peel's innovation (with the assistance of Charles Rowan and Richard Mayne, the first commissioners of the Metropolitan Police) was to substitute bureaucratic authority for personalized, local, and violent private forms of policing. The aim of policing reform in the early part of the nineteenth century was to create a formal, paid, trained, and neutral third-party force that would act on behalf of the citizen in the name of the state, and in doing so would reduce inequities and riot, lessen the fear of crime, and make the police accountable (in this case, to the Home Secretary; Silver, 1966). Because of the centralization of the British police, the accepted and legitimate authority of the Crown, a homogeneous population (with no significant ethnic minorities), and a strong cultural consensus, a public system of policing was in place in England by 1856 (Hart, 1956).

American Policing and Reform

The elements that allowed policing to be established in England were and are lacking in American society; the decentralized patchwork of local forces in this country reflects this situation. Control of police hiring (a patronage question), police command and tactics, the ethnic composition of the police, and modes of control through law or municipal authority all remain salient issues in American cities. Because of the lack of consensus, the frontier-based violence, and themes of individualism and pragmatism, American police were armed as early as 1836.

Tensions between public and private authority remain in American society. They are illustrated by the current emphasis on "market controls" and by periodic attempts to reform the American police.

In the mid-twentieth century, reform meant political reform. American police reformers of the 1920s and 1930s, such as Raymond Fosdick, August Vollmer, and Bruce Smith, were trained as lawyers and public administrators (Stead, 1977). The goals of police reform in that era appear to have been the following. First, these reformers aimed to isolate and protect policing from the corrupting forces of urban, ethnically based machine politics. Second, they sought to ensure that departments recruited, trained, and supervised officers with a commitment to the organization above and beyond ethnic, religious, and political (often territorially based) loyalties (Bordua, 1966). Third, they hoped to develop a version of "scientific policing" based on applied technology, the crime lab, the radio, and the automobile. Vollmer in particular sought to understand the causes of crime and the modes of prevention and control, and connected the police mandate with the idea of active, effective crime control. Fourth, they were eager to reform the education of police command personnel to reflect developments in modern public administration. Fifth, the overall purpose of this wave of reform was to enhance the prestige, political power, and authority of police organizations.[6]

These coherent themes constituted the basis for policing reform; the reformers sought to develop a new police mandate. It is clear, however, that the political processes and traditions of American cities influenced this movement and gave it local color and texture (Reppetto, 1978). The mandate, or the underlying rationale for police authority, was to be based on a strong and centralized command and rational legal authority (Bordua and Reiss, 1966). Guided by bureaucratic rules and applied science, professional policing would be legitimated in American cities (Wilson, 1963).

A number of developments have shaped police reform since this period. Police administration became concerned with command and control of officers rather than with crime control or political efficacy. Because a scientific mandate required command, control, and direction of officers, attention shifted subtly, in the work and writings of O. W. Wilson, to questions of internal control, "efficiency," and applying the wisdom of public administration to governance of police departments. Policing in effect was to become "police administration" (Carte and Carte, 1977).

Police research became an aspect of police reform in the late 1960s. The idea that research would guide and transform policing had great credence in academic circles after the publication of the Report of the President's Crime Commission in 1967. William Westley's (1970) work posed the paradigmatic questions about the sources and role of secrecy, prejudice, and violence in policing. Westley noted the police dislike of homosexuals and blacks and described the roots of their hatred and the rationalizations for violence directed toward those groups. He pointed out the contradiction between police violence toward minorities and their commitment to fair law enforcement. Jerome Skolnick (1966) argued that the themes of discipline, uniformity, and control fit uneasily with protection of the freedoms of a democratic society. Street justice, "justice without trial," was in conflict with the rule of law. Skolnick appeared to place confidence in legal reforms and constraints. The work of James Q. Wilson bridged the reformers' interests and those of social researchers. In his now classic *Varieties of Police Behavior* (1968), he insightfully noted that styles of policing were somehow formed by the local "political culture." He argued, however, that police administrators had turned inward, seeking to avoid mistakes, public embarrassment, and scandal. They made little effort to develop long-term plans.

With the possible exception of Wilson's work, police research did not examine "management" or command. In 1966 Bordua and Reiss observed, in a still-valid statement, "To our knowledge, there is no detailed empirical description of command processes in a police department" (p. 68). Brown (1981) studied the impact of different policies and administrative styles on the street, but he provided no context within which such polices were interpreted or understood. How such policies were implemented remains unclear.

The language of productivity or efficiency was not employed until the early 1970s, when it was used in an attempt to reform felony arrest processing (Forst, Lucianovic and Cox, 1977), detective work (Eck, 1983), and police communications (Hough 1980a, 1980b; Manning, 1988).

Modern police administrators are well aware of these works and this history. Often well-educated, and with degrees in sociology, criminal justice, psychology, and political science, they now hear themselves talking to themselves. They have read the works of Egon Bittner, Jerome Skolnick, O. W. Wilson, J. Q. Wilson, A. J. Reiss Jr., and Jonathan Rubinstein of the first generation of reformers, and the fictions and semifictions of Joseph Wambaugh, Mark Baker, and others. Some have taught or are teaching in criminal justice programs. Police now participate in the dialogue of post-industrial society using the language of the policy sciences and economics to describe policing. They are subject to and aware of their own reflexive actions and discourse (Giddens, 1990). The current rhetoric of choice is not that of public administration, but that of managerial economics.

These changes in policing, especially the metaphoric tendency whereby policing is conceived as an economic institution, are part of the overall movement toward privatization of control, reduction of government supervision in favor of the market and private governments, and the use of the media and the market to substitute symbolic imagery for direct, forceful authority. The present appeal to market forces for reform, analogous to deregulation, is a retrograde step with regard to civic control over police command and police accountability.

❖ THE "CORPORATE STRATEGY" OF POLICING ❖

In 1988 Mark Moore, an economist, and Robert Trojanowicz, a professor of criminal justice, published an article titled "Corporate Strategies for Policing." Widely distributed by the U.S. Department of Justice and at the Kennedy School, Harvard University, it explicitly applies the corporate metaphor and management language to policing.

Moore and Trojanowicz discuss policing as an expensive "service" (costing the taxpayers some $20 billion a year). These monetary resources are "redeployed" with authority based on a "corporate strategy," a term borrowed from the private sector. This strategy refers to:

> the principal financial and social goals the organization will pursue, and the principal products, technologies and production processes on which it will rely to achieve its goals. It also defines how the organization will relate to its employees and to its other constituencies such as shareholders, creditors, suppliers and customers. In short, a corporate strategy seeks to define for the organization how the organization will pursue values and the sort of an organization it will be (1988:2).

The authors analyze current policing by using the concept of corporate strategy. They view policing, like other service industries, as occupying a market niche and competing through strategic means to maintain it (1988). The corporate strategy of the American police in the past 50 years, according to Moore and Trojanowicz, has been "professional crime fighting." This approach is based on centralization of command, control, and communications, sharpened focus on crime control, and on substantial investment in modern technology and training. This strategy, the authors believe, is now exhausted and outmoded. They suggest a new corporate strategy and discuss new facets or modes such as "problem solving policing," "strategic (or proactive) policing," and "community policing." In addition, they argue for expanding the mission of the police with a combination of problem solving as a technique, a focus on dangerous offenders, and fear reduction programs. Moore and Trojanowicz also note a tension between what they advocate—decentralized problem solving, a geographic definition of problems, and close interactions with the community—and the previously emphasized administrative centralization, specialization, and independence from communities. They recommend a corporate shift to "professional, strategic, community problem-solving policing" (p. 14).

These remarks are important not only because they outline a new strategy for policing, but also because of the connotations of the choice of rhetoric. It implies competition for resources that subsequently are redeployed, mobilization of those resources in a competitive market, and a concern for demonstrating successful market strategies to the relevant (but unnamed) constituencies. Earlier strategies will be (or should be) replaced because they failed in the marketplace. The police mission should be justified by maintaining a market niche and ensuring social profitability.

This view contrasts not only with previous visions of police reform, but also with traditional institutional economic views of policing. Rather than regarding policing as an inherent "collective good" (Samuelson, 1954), the new approach sees it as a competitive, service-producing activity that must show a social profit and must produce, advertise, package, market, and distribute its "services" to "customers" or "clients."

Applying economic metaphors to policing has both individual and group consequences. Consider first the *individual* effects. Market participation and individual choice of services are valued; individually focused notions about how and to whom services will be rendered are consistent with deploying resources on the basis of social "profit." Citizens are defined as "customers" or "clients." Aggregated ordering of individual problems constitutes a police service area. Contracts and exchange relations are elevated at the expense of collective goods and noncontractual aspects of contracts (MacCauley, 1965). Shopping for "social control services" and distrust of the sources of control increase. Stable and trusting relationships are established with the individual service provider (the officer) rather than with the state or the organization as a whole. Money "talks" or is the "bottom line" in considering whether a practice will continue.

If the economic metaphor is applied at the *group* level, other consequences ensue. The corporate strategy emphasizes competition, market shares, and the rise and fall of corporate profits. Strategy and tactics are used to deploy resources and are the basis for calculating the rate of return on investment. Gains in corporate profits are scrutinized on the basis of the surplus labor value that can be extracted from the human resources (employees). Income and earnings, the "bottom line," effectiveness, and productivity become watch words disconnected from precise measures of what these terms might mean operationally. A police product or "service" is produced, distributed, promoted, and sold. The value of the services rendered is calculated in economic terms; money differentiates the audiences served, the quality of the service received, and the soundness of a long-term investment strategy.

In this context, the use of force against the lower classes is seen as a service to the respectable classes. The irony perhaps is that a substantial minority of policing is not requested (it is not direct service to an individual), and in fact is coercive force and constraint applied in the name of the state.

Advertising the use of the correct media and public relations that leads to finding the right "spin" on any "fact" takes on new importance (Jackall, 1988, ch. 6). Packaging and promotion, such as the billboard ads and television publicity campaigns urging people to call 911 ("Watch out, there's a thief about") are intended to increase "demand" for police "services." The result of increasing demand, given a labor-intensive industry, is that policing is privately controlled and rationed by bureaucratic means of filtering, screening, and denying requests or by withholding a promised level of response (Lipsky, 1980).

❖ SOME IMPLICATIONS OF THE ECONOMIC RHETORIC FOR POLICING ❖

Let us now review some of the implications of the economic metaphor as applied to policing. The idea that policing, like defense, education, and sewer and water treatment, is not profitable but is required to maintain the quality of life in industrialized societies, is being supplanted by the notion that policing can be made profitable and competitive. It is merely one of several modes of social control. If policing is viewed as a service and is evaluated in monetary terms as a "commodity" and in competition with other forms of social control, then a number of important consequences can be anticipated.

The emphasis on "market competition" suggests that private and industrial security suppliers and government organizations will view their already somewhat ad hoc relationships explicitly as competitive and zero-sum. Perhaps police organizations will focus their competition on manageable dimensions of performance. For example, one could imagine private organizations emphasizing speed of response, frequency of patrols, sensitivity to private demands, and quality of service to differentiate themselves from the public police.

Competition also may heighten invidious comparisons between groups (class, ethnic, or neighborhood) concerning level and quality of police service. Policing has been shown to be remarkably democratic with respect to the distribution of response to requests for service by patrol units.[7] If one cannot afford private police and if very little public policing is available, then the fact of absent service is combined with the expressive symbolism that is attached to receiving little or no service. This process suggests even further differentiation of groups along class and racial lines.

If conceptions of service are privatized, this situation may encourage some clients who can pay for and contract for better service, in part by "double coverage," to feel that they are better served and to be less willing to pay city and county taxes to underwrite policing costs.

In general, one would expect competition to increase the present inequities in policing. At the present, service is rendered to middle-class consumers (and victims) and businesses, while force and violence are used against the lower classes. Thus providing "crime control services" means something quite different to those *to* whom they are delivered and to those *for* whom they are delivered.

Privatization will exaggerate the already well-established tendency for police to segregate their audiences and to play out different scenarios for the "respectable classes" and for the others. Competition and privatization forces should lead to security "shopping" and to an increase in legitimate market competition between public police organizations and between these organizations and private police.

The role of citizens also will change. Citizens have an active role in the economic metaphor of policing. They are to provide the police with guidance to their demands to indicate what they will "buy" and pay for, and to state the extent to which they will take responsibility for social problems. The responsibility for order thus is shifted from the police to the public, who must "buy" in good faith, provide tax dollars, and participate in informal social control. The community will also be expected to exchange information, rewards, and support for the services received. *Caveat emptor* will reign. The economic view of policing, when combined with a community policing program, is expected to offer solutions in the form of integrated crime-fighting tactics as well as maintaining community well-being, insofar as the community demands and is willing to pay for these amenities.

The role of the officer will change as well. The officer's role, as envisioned by economic rhetoric, is to serve as a *demand manager*: often stationed nominally in a neighborhood school, storefront, or mini-station when not earnestly serving the public on foot patrol, the officer represents or symbolizes an active form of generalized or dedifferentiated social control. Officers are to act as community members and are expected to serve as active moralists-in-residence. They are symbols for and of the community, and stand in contrast to the stereotypic crime-focused specialist. Yet they also must apply force when, in their judgment, it is required.

Economic rhetoric has increased internal effects as well. The potential for salary competition between legal and illegal sources arises. Organized crime and legitimate police forces compete, in effect, for the loyalty of officers as well as for "customers" and the "quality of service." Corruption can result. Further use of legal standards and procedures to govern private relations also will affect policing, in part because the growth of markets and contracts is fundamental to the political economy of capitalism.

In this model, the organization is intended to serve general community needs. It is focused on diverse disorder, on building markets for service, and on an increased buying power and an enhanced quality of life. This metaphor of policing contains an implicit basis for internal authority. The authority of the officer in the economic model will arise from his or her capacity to create, sustain, and satisfy public demand.

The monetary metric for evaluation of performance, raises, and so on is joined with legal standards for performance and competence, and links performance and service to money. Lurking in the background is the fee-for-service model, which is the theoretic basis for market transactions.

Crime statistics, the most frequently used performance measures of policing, have serious flaws. Their validity is dubious, and they tend to equate the quality of the performance with crime control. This method excludes concern with "peacekeeping," maintaining public order, and providing citizens with reassurance, support, education, and succor.

Budgeting and management will be seen increasingly as abstract, rational activities carried out by functionaries who have little or no appreciation for the substance and process of police work. Can a Harvard MBA with no police experience command the police department in Lansing, Cambridge, or Sioux Falls? Is efficiency the primary criterion by which to evaluate policing? What other highly regarded American values, such as the protection of individual rights and ambivalence about the application of governmental authority, might conflict with "police efficiency" or maintaining a proper "market share"?

If central bureaucratic controls are weakened and if service to local neighborhood groups is valued in community policing, the old dilemma of loyalty to command reappears. Officers will have two sets of significant others: their peers and the residents of the neighborhood where they serve. The more complex the social environment in which they work, the more likely that they will be oriented to their police peers rather than to members of the communities they police (Cain, 1973).

Policing already is threatened by the rise of self-help groups and vigilantes in urban areas, and economic pressures are likely to be translated by the police into reduced service. Reasonable responses for declining organizations are either to decrease service or to increase productivity. We have no evidence for the presence of a consensus about what the police produce; therefore, there is certainly no known means of increasing "productivity." Evaluating policing as a profit-making or at least as not a profit-losing institution suggests that decreasing the services is a more likely option. Politically weak and expensive areas of a city, unable to buy alternative service, would be vulnerable to budget reductions.

Command officers also might consider establishing or tolerating longer average response times, reducing the number of units on patrol, and creating differential response schemes. Costs also might be decreased by "call suppression" programs, such as those instituted in Minneapolis and Boston; these programs are designed to minimize calls defined by the police as unnecessary or nonemergency. Thus, shrinking budgets and economic rhetoric provide a rationale for reducing service differentially. Crime attack strategies are also advocated and advanced as more efficient than mobile patrol, regardless of the possible implications for civil liberties, community relations, or trust in the police (Sherman, 1986).

Finally, the question of the precise utility and impact of new information technologies remains unanswered. These technologies can be used to increase the quality and equality of police service and the humanity of policing, or they can be used to control officers, suppress and filter calls to reduce the workload, and distance the police further from the public.

❖ COMMENT ❖

The primary purpose of this article is to highlight the power of the economic metaphor and to discuss the consequences of defining policing and police reform in economic terms. The long-term consequences of further privatizing control and personalizing authority in this fashion should be the subject of future research. Some general points may bear restating.

The economic metaphor for policing and police reform has emerged in the last ten years and is consistent with the economic philosophy of the Reagan-Bush administrations. It urges one to think of policing in terms of supply and demand, and in market-competitive terms. From this perspective policing is viewed as a "service," a distributional activity that serves to reallocate collective goods. Yet "police services" are not indefinitely expansive, and citizens' demand, although elastic, is not permitted to expand beyond the limits set privately by police. The police continue to pattern the rationing of service as always, and to dramatize the efficacy of their own actions.

Ironically, as long as police exercise authority and force in the name of the state, they will be feared and loathed by some segments of the community. They will represent this potential for violence to all segments of the community. Police exercise force and will be periodically unpopular, will be the target of protest, and will be viewed ambivalently. Thus the economic or market metaphor, which emphasizes "choice" and "demand," is inadequate to explain those "services" which are not chosen by an individual but which serve the interests of the state. These include the power to regulate, to arrest, to fine, to incarcerate, and to use deadly force. The economic conception emphasizes the service, choice, and demand management aspects of policing, but denies the central fact of policing: its use of force in the interests of the state (Bittner, 1990).

Notes

[1] On the general issue of the role of technology in policing, see Manning (1992, forthcoming).

[2] The ratio of officers to citizens in urban areas has increased (Mastrofski, 1990).

[3] Although it is claimed by Moore, Trojanowicz and Kelling that no one disputes this statement, studies of police practice and workload studies suggest that the primary mission of the police is not crime control as measured in stops, arrests, clearances, and the like, but diverse service (for a summary, see Goldstein, 1990).

[4] See the recent media events, such as an interview with Daryl Gates in *Playboy*, (July, 1991), a long feature story about Gates in the August 1991 *Vanity Fair* and a two-part series on the LAPD in the NYRB (Donne, 1991). Chief (now ex-Chief) Elizabeth Watson of Houston was the subject of a long C-SPAN interview, 1990, reshown during the summer of 1991. A 1990 PBS television feature, "Police Chiefs," profiled Chief Daryl Gates of Los Angeles; Anthony Bouza, former police chief in Minneapolis; and Lee Brown, Commissioner of Police in New York City.

[5] See Ericson (1989, 1991); Surette (1991).

[6] See histories of police reform written by Bittner (1990), Caiden (1977), Fogelson (1979), Lane (1967), and Reppetto (1978).

[7] Studies of the distribution of police service suggest that on the whole, police do not discriminate in reactive services as measured by response time or time spent in response to calls. As Black (1980) shows, however, the character of these activities varies by class. Middle-class people are more likely to be victims, witnesses to crimes, or complainants, whereas lower-class people are more likely to be suspects.

References

Altheide, D. (1992). Gonzo justice. *Symbolic Interaction*, 15(1): 69–86.

Bittner, E. (1990). *Aspects of Police Work*. Boston: Northeastern University Press.

Black, D. (1980). *Manners and Customs of the Police*. New York: Academic Press.

Bordua, D. (1966). The police. In *International Encyclopedia of Social Sciences*. New York: The Free Press.

Bordua, D., & Haurek, E. (1971). The policeman's lot. In Hahn (Ed.) *Urban Policing*. Los Angeles: Sage.

Bordua, D., & Reiss, A. J., Jr. (July 1966). Command, control and charisma: Reflections on police bureaucracy. *AJS*, 72:68–76.

Brown, M. (1981). *Working the Street*. New York: Russell Sage.

Caiden, G. (1977). *Police Revitalization*. Lexington, MA: D.C. Heath.

Cain, M. (1973). *Society and the Policeman's Role*. London: RKP.

Carte, Gene E., & Carte, Elaine (1977). O. W. Wilson, in Stead, J. (Ed.) *Pioneers in Policing*, pp. 207-223. Montclair, NJ: Patterson Smith.

Clarke, R., & Hough, M. (Eds.) (1980). *The Effectiveness of the Police*. Aldershot: Gower.

Donne, John Gregory (1991). Law and disorder in Los Angeles. *New York Review of Books*, Oct. 10:23-29; Oct. 24:62-70.

Eck, J. (1983). *Solving Crimes*. Washington, DC: The Police Foundation.

Ericson, R. V. (1989). Patrolling the facts: Secrecy and publicity in policework. *British Journal of Sociology,* 40:205-226

―――― (1991). Mass media, crime, law, and justice. *The British Journal of Criminology,* 31:219-249.

Fogelson, R. M. (1978). *Big City Police*. Cambridge: Harvard University Press.

Forst, B., Lucianovic, J., & Cox, S. J. (1977). *What Happens after Arrest*. Washington, DC: Institute for Law and Social Research.

Giddens, A. (1990). *The Consequences of Modernity*. Palo Alto: Stanford University Press.

Goldstein, H. (1990). *Problem-Oriented Policing*. New York: McGraw-Hill.

Hart, J. W. (1951). *The British Police*. London: Allen and Unwin.

―――― (1956). The reform of borough police: 1835-1856. *English Historical Review*, 70:411-427.

Hough, J. M. (1980a). Managing with less technology. *British Journal of Criminology*, 20:344-357.

―――― (1980b). *Uniformed Police Work and Management Technology*. Home Office. Research and Planning Unit Paper 1. London: HM Stationery Office.

Howson, G. (1970). *The Thief-Taker*. London: Hutchinson.

Jackall, Robert (1988). *Moral Mazes*. New York: Oxford University Press.

Lane, Robert (1967). *Policing the City*. Cambridge: Harvard University Press.

Lipsky, M. (1980). *Street-Level Bureaucracies*. New York: Russell Sage.

MacCauley, S. (1965). Non-contractual relations in business. *ASR,* 28:55-67.

Manning, P. K. (1988). *Symbolic Communication*. Cambridge: MIT Press.

―――― (Forthcoming). Technological dramas and the police. Unpublished seminar paper presented to the University of Michigan Organizational Studies Seminar to be published in *Criminology,* 30 (August).

―――― (1992). The police and information technologies. In Morris, N., and Tonry, M. (Eds.) *Modern Policing*. Vol. 13, *Crime and Justice Annuals*. Chicago: University of Chicago Press.

Martin, S. (1990). *Progress in Policing*. Washington: Police Foundation.

Mastrofski, S. (1988). Community policing as reform. In Greene, J., and Mastrofski, S. (Eds.) *Community Policing*. New York: Praeger.

―――― (1990). The prospects of change in police patrol: A decade in review. *American Journal of Police,* 9(3):1-79.

Moore, Mark, & Trojanowicz, R. (1988). Corporate strategies for policing. *Perspectives on Policing,* 4. Washington, DC: U.S. Department of Justice, National Institute of Justice.

Moore, Mark, Trojanowicz, R., & Kelling, G. (1988). Crime and policing. *Perspectives on Policing*, 3. Washington, DC: U.S. Department of Justice, National Institute of Justitice.

Radzinowicz, L. (1962-1966). *A History of English Criminal Law*. 4 vols. London: Stevens.

Reppetto, T. (1978). *The Blue Parade*. New York: Macmillan.

Samuelson, P. (1954). The pure theory of public expenditure. *Review of Economics and Statistics*, 36 (November): 387-390.

Sherman, L. W., & the National Advisory Commission on Higher Education for Police Officers (1978). *The Quality of Police Education*. San Francisco: Josey-Bass.

Sherman, L. W. (1986). Policing communities: What really works? In Reiss, A. J., Jr., and Tonry, M. (Eds.) *Crime and the Community*. Vol. 20, *Crime and Justice Annuals*. Chicago: University of Chicago Press.

Silver, A. (1966). The demand for order in civil society. In Bordua, D. (Ed.) *The Police: Six Sociological Essays*. New York: John Wiley.

Skolnick, J. (1966). *Justice Without Trial*. New York: John Wiley.

Stead, J. (Ed.) (1977). *Pioneers in Policing*. Montclair, NJ: Patterson Smith.

Stevens, J. (1989). Computer technology. In Bailey, William G. (Ed.) *Encyclopedia of Police Science*. New York and London: Garland.

Surette, R. (1991). *Media, Crime, and Criminal Justice*. Monterey, CA: Brooks Cole.

Tien, James, & Colton, K. (1979). Police command, control, and communications. In *What Works*? LEAA. Washington, DC: United States Government Printing Office.

Westley, W. (1970). *Violence and the Police*. Cambridge: MIT Press.

Wilson, James Q. (1963). The police and their problems. *Public Policy*, 12:189-216.

_____ (1968). *Varieties of Police Behavior*. Cambridge: Harvard University Press.

Wolfe, Joan L., & Heaphy, J. (Eds.) (1979). Readings in productivity. In *Policing*. Washington, DC: Police Foundation.

Index